MODERN CATHOLIC SOCIAL TEACHING

MODERN CATHOLIC SOCIAL TEACHING

The Popes Confront the Industrial Age
1740–1958

Joe Holland

PAULIST PRESS
New York/Mahwah, N.J.

Selections from the encyclicals *Mirari vos* of Pope Gregory XVI and *Nostis et nobiscum* of Pope Pius IX, translated by Claudia Carlen, I.H.M., are reprinted by permission from *The Papal Encyclicals 1740–1878*, published by The Pierian Press. Selections from *Quanta curia* of Pope Pius IX are reprinted by permission of the American Catholic Historical Society. Selections from *Rerum novarum* of Pope Leo XIII are taken from the text appreaing in *The Church Speaks to the Modern World: The Social Teachings of Leo XIII*, edited by Étienne Gilson, published by Doubleday. Selections from *Il fermo proposito* of Pope Pius X are taken from *All Things in Christ: Encyclicals and Selected Documents of Saint Pius X*, edited by Vincent A. Yzermans, published by Newman Press. Selections from the encyclical *Quadragesimo anno* of Pope Pius IX are taken from *On Reconstructing the Social Order*, edited by Francis J. Haas and Martin R.P. McGuire, published by the National Catholic Welfare Conference (USCC). Selections from *Pascendi dominici gregis* of Pope Pius X are reprinted by permission of *The Tablet*.

Published in cooperation with Pax Romana
Catholic Movement for Intellectual and Cultural Affairs
www.PaxRomana.org

Book design by Lynn Else
Cover design by Tim McKeen

Library of Congress Cataloging-in-Publication Data

Holland, Joe.
    Modern Catholic social teaching : the popes confront the industrial age, 1740–1958 / Joe Holland.
        p.   cm.
    Includes bibliographical references and index.
    ISBN 0-8091-4225-2 (alk. paper)
    1. Sociology, Christian (Catholic)—History of doctrines.   2. Capitalism—Religious aspects—Catholic Church.   3. Papacy—History.   4. Church and social problems—Catholic Church—History.   5. Christianity and politics—History.   6. Catholic Church—Doctrines—History.   7. Encyclicals, Papal.   I. Title.
BX1753 .H614 2004
261.8′088′282—dc22

                                                                        2003015826

Published by Paulist Press
997 Macarthur Boulevard
Mahwah, New Jersey 07430

www.paulistpress.com

Printed and bound in the
United States of America

Contents

Acknowledgments

Some thirty years have passed since I originally began this project of analyzing the tradition of Catholic social teaching. Along the way, countless individuals have influenced its outcome—some in obvious ways, others in ways more subtle. Deep thanks are due to all of them, only some of whom I can name.

I thank first the members of *Para* in Santiago, Chile, who became close friends while I was on a Fulbright there. I shared with them the first sketch of this study and received wise feedback. From that group, I am especially grateful to Charlie Curry, Pat and Trish Ahern, Marge Schuler, and Joe Eldridge. Thanks also to other supportive friends from Chile days, particularly Gonzalo Arroyo, Sergio Torres, and the Moreno family.

From the Divinity School of the University of Chicago, I thank my two revered friends and teachers, Gibson Winter and Al Pitcher, both now deceased. I also thank other teachers and friends at Chicago, particularly Don Browning, David Tracy, William Schweiker, Franklin Gamwell, and Richard Rosengarten.

Again from those days in Chicago, I thank special friends with whom my wife, Paquita, and I shared community in Mir House. They watched, listened, and offered ideas and criticism as the model of this study awkwardly unfolded. I think especially of Marsha and Lee Cormie, Trish and Mike Poole, and Ruth and Dale Fast in the community, as well as Robert Burns, John Donahue, Eileen Dooley, and Pat and Charlaine McAnnany, who were all good friends of our community. From that same period, I also thank and sadly remember my dear friend, the deceased Guatemalan Jesuit César Jerez, who constantly encouraged me to continue this project.

Deep thanks are due also to warm friends from earlier years who indirectly stimulated my interest in Catholic social teaching. I think first of all of Paulo Freire, who generously worked with a group of us in South Norwalk, Connecticut, to develop an alternative school for high-school dropouts, and whose ideas pointed me toward this study. Thanks as well to warm friends and community leaders in Norwalk, particularly George Heron, Marina Rivera, Daniel Maldonado, Jaime Aguayo, Hank Yordan, Jeanette Blatz, and the late Bishop Walter Curtis.

I also thank the staff of the Center of Concern where I spent fifteen years. Center members often patiently listened to my exploration of the model and then offered their own rich thoughts. My gratitude goes particularly to the center's founder and dear friend, Bill Ryan, who pushed me into a long but helpful detour by suggesting that I develop an analysis of the stage-evolution of industrial capitalism to correlate with the ecclesial stage-evolution already undertaken. Thanks also to others who served at the Center of Concern during those years, including Pete Henriot, Bill Callahan, Dolly Pomerleau, Mary Burke, Eileen Olsen, Mary Ann Mason, Mike Petty, Jane Blewett, the late Phil Land, Maria Riley, Maurice Monette, Jeanine Maynard, David Simmons, and Jim Hug. Thanks also to John Coleman and Tom Clarke, who were most helpful in a seminar on this project organized by the Center of Concern in cooperation with the Woodstock Center for Theological Studies.

So many more need to be mentioned. I thank friends from my work in Appalachia, particularly Les Schmidt, Pat Speer, Evelyn Mattern, Walter Sullivan, Evelyn Dettling, Mary Priniski, Todd Garland, and Carol Whelan, who all helped me to see the connection of the model with that region. I thank too Harry Boyte and Arthur Waskow, who, in the years we worked with the late Michael Harrington, helped me explore political and religious insights that went beyond the logic of modern culture. I also thank Alan Kissler, Jack Dunne, Gerry Shea, Jackie Ruff, and Mike Nash, who helped me to learn about and work with the American labor movement. In addition, thanks to Jack Clancey of Hong Kong and Rob Lambert of South Africa, who taught me so much about the international relationship of religion and labor; to Mike Gilgannon and Joan Mury, who enabled me to learn from the Aymara and Quechua peoples of the South Andes; to Mary Litell, who has proved such a life-giving visionary; and to Dick Snyder, who has always been there and seen the vision.

Then too I wish to thank for encouragement and support the countless members and friends of Pax Romana, a more than eighty-year-old international movement of Catholic intellectuals and professionals, particularly the Kirchner family with Ed, Louisa, and Joe, plus Anselmo Lee, Mark Wolff, Manu Alphonse, Patricio Rodé, Xavier Iguiñez, Teresa Mourad, Kevin Ahern, Paul Snatchko, Geza Ziegler, Sarah Potts, Peter Ruggere, Roma Hayda, DeAnne Connolly, Sixto Garcia, Diane Maguire, Jim Donovan, Maria Sharpe, and Grazyna Kolondra.

Perhaps most of all, I thank the literally thousands of grass-roots Christian pastoral workers, activists, and scholars all around the world who, during my many years as an itinerant speaker, offered important feedback and profound insight during countless lectures, seminars, and workshops. In particular, I warmly remember and thank friends made in Ireland from these programs, especially Evelyn Murphy, Kevin O'Rourke, John Sweeney, Peter McVerry, and Frank Sammon.

Special thanks also to those fine people with whom I was privileged to work in the attempt to develop a fresh lay movement in the world church. Here I remember especially the staffs, boards, and friends of the American Catholic Lay Network, of the Pallottine Institute for Lay Leadership and Apostolate Research, and of the Leadership Council of Catholic Laity. A special word of thanks to Betty and Fred Leone, Lou Fischer, Mary Leopold, Emily Schwartz, Peter and Deirdre Carter, Bob Maxwell, Lisa Sosa, Leonard Anguiano, Mary Anne and Margaret Mary Moore, Cora Dubitsky, Harriet Heaney, Pat Pressler, Ann Barsanti, Celie Mercadante, Jim and Lynn Cummings, Sam Swansen, the late Ralph Firneno, David Abalos with his whole family, Gerry O'Connell, Peter Coughlin, MayLee Johnson, and Ray and Beth Ann Rufo.

Thanks also to the members of the Christian Family Movement community in Blessed Sacrament Parish in Washington, D.C., particularly Betty and Jack O'Connor and Steve Paddack and the late Marie Maloney. Deep gratitude as well to the lay leaders of the National Office of Black Catholics and the National Black Catholic Lay Caucus, especially Walter Hubbard, the late Jimmy McConduit, and Elizabeth Thomas, with extra thanks to Walter for devoted friendship and personal support. Abundant thanks also to my good friend Don Conroy of the International Consortium on Religion and Ecology. Don watched this study grow over many years and has himself contributed countless insights.

Also I wish to thank the many friends at St. Thomas University and in Miami, Florida, who provided personal and scholarly support for my research and writing. In particular, thanks to Marene Clarke, Norma Goonen, Richard Greene, Elizabeth Ferrero, Olga Huchingson, Joe and Mercedes Iannone, the late Ray Apicella, Ray Rufo, Mark Wolff, Margaret Elliston, James Conley, Gary Feinberg, Helen Rosenthal, Ken and Dottie Stibbler, Franklyn Casale, Mark Rogers, Maria Duarte, Cristobal Serrán-Pagan, Jacquelyn Derby, Ishtar Govia, Nathan Connolly, Thomas Jackson, Selwyn Spanner, and Marlene Lauritzen. I especially wish to thank St. Thomas's Frank Sicius, who generously read most of the text both as a proof-reader and a stimulating intellectual colleague and dear friend, as well as his lovely wife, Isabel Valenzuela, and their beautiful children, all of whom offered themselves as my surrogate family during the many years when I was commuting to Miami from Washington, D.C.

In addition, I wish to thank my immediate family—my beloved wife, Paquita Biascoechea-Martinez Holland, our children, Daniel and Natanya, my parents, Ed and Peg Holland, my sister Maureen, my brother Dave and his wife, Anne, and my sister Sue and her husband, Gene, all of whom provided ongoing encouragement and for whom this long project was often the subject of loving family humor. I especially thank my father who, though in his late eighties and losing his eyesight through macular degeneration, insisted on using a very large magnifying glass to proof read several chapters with his still sharp lawyer's eye. I also owe a very special debt of gratitude to my sister Maureen who, with the fine skills of her long years in publishing and with her wonderful mastery of the English language, carefully and insightfully went over an earlier version of the entire manuscript.

I have also learned endlessly from the many scholars on whose work I humbly draw here, and who often know so much more about the subject than this author. I have learned from all of them and owe them all a great debt. Of course, any errors or inadequacies in this study belong not to them but only to me.

Finally, because after more than thirty years the first of two books in my review of the development of Catholic social teaching is now done, I gratefully acknowledge the ultimate source of human creativity with a quiet *Deo gratias!*

In memory of
Gibson Winter
Priest, Scholar, Teacher, Friend, and Mentor

1

Introduction

The Papal Encyclicals, Industrial Capitalism, and Modern Liberal Culture

---

This book is a study of the modern phase of contemporary Catholic social teaching, including its premodern background, as officially codified in the papal encyclicals from 1740 to 1958. A future book will explore the postmodern phase of contemporary Catholic social teaching from 1958 to 2000. So *contemporary* here means the full range of the papal-encyclical tradition that began in 1740 (a few decades before the Industrial Revolution) and continues to develop in our own times. The term *modern* requires more explanation.

In 1740, Benedict XIV, a scholarly and pastoral pope continuing the reforms of the Council of Trent, initiated the contemporary encyclical genre. He did so mainly in response to the modern European Enlightenment with its new philosophy of liberalism. Out of that philosophical movement, liberal democracy and industrial capitalism later emerged, and still later the more radical developments of industrial socialism and communism. All these socio-historical movements, along with the liberal philosophy that stood beneath them, constituted the historical-strategic challenges that called forth the contemporary tradition of Catholic social teaching. The tradition continues today and as of the year 2000 had spanned two hundred and sixty years.

Within this framework of two hundred and sixty years, we may discern within the corpus of the papal encyclicals three distinct historical periods of papal strategy.[1]

- *The Anti-modern Papal Strategy: 1740 to 1878.* This might also be called the premodern strategy of Catholic social teaching, since the popes of this time frame largely rejected the modern liberal philosophy of the European Enlightenment with its derivative movements of liberal democracy and industrial capitalism. This period ran from the election of Benedict XIV in 1740 to the death of Pius IX in 1878. Though generally cast in an anti-modern cultural style, this first strategic period needs to be seen in relation to the subsequent modern period of Catholic social teaching, first because it was actually addressing the early modern liberal context, and second because it established an abiding Catholic foundational philosophical and theological critique of the modern liberal philosophy.

- *The Modern Papal Strategy: 1878 to 1958.* The ecclesial period, which runs from Leo XIII (elected in 1878) to Pius XII (deceased in 1958), may properly be called modern. Whereas the popes of the prior strategic period had largely rejected the modern world of liberalism, democracy, and industrialism in order to defend the aristocratic ancien régime, the popes of this second period, following the new strategy defined by Leo, devoted themselves to a Catholic reform of liberalism, democracy, and industrialism, all in the name of a modernized bourgeois version of Eurocentric Christian civilization. Yet this new strategy, though shifting from a posture of rejection to one of reform, still insisted on the foundational philosophical and theological critique of liberalism from the prior period. The key figure in this phase was, of course, Leo XIII, whose landmark 1891 document *Rerum novarum* has often been called the Magna Charta of modern Catholic social teaching. (Many analysts, who study only the second strategic period and not also the prior strategy, fail to appreciate that the earlier critique of liberalism still grounded this second strategy and also the third, which will now be described.)

- *The Postmodern Papal Strategy: 1958–.* John XXIII (elected in 1958) defined yet a third strategy for Catholic social teaching, this time rejecting the vision of a modernized Eurocentric Christian civilization and seeking instead to point the newly emerging "world church" toward global ecumenism, interfaith cooperation, cross-ideological dialogue, and a prophetic path of justice and peace, all in service of a new humanistic civilization on a planetary scale. This third strategy may best be described as postmodern, since both the historical challenge and the strategic response move beyond the philosophical and geo-cultural framework of Eurocentric modernity. It breaks both with the first strategy of anti-modern traditionalist restoration and with the second strategy of modern adaptive reform, and moves beyond the logic of all modern culture and modern ideologies.

Again, this book examines the development of modern Catholic social teaching, including both the background of first or premodern papal strategy and the foreground of the second or modern papal strategy. Both strategies either explicitly or implicitly had to deal with the modern experience of the European Enlightenment, liberal democracy, and industrial capitalism. As noted, the first Catholic strategy largely rejected them all in defense of aristocratic Christian civilization, while the second Catholic strategy sought to reform them in the name of a bourgeois Christian civilization, and both clung to a Eurocentric vision. In the next book, soon to be completed, I will examine the third or postmodern strategy of contemporary Catholic social teaching.

The Papal Encyclicals and Catholic Social Teaching

We need to analyze the development of Catholic social teaching in the papal encyclicals both in their literal texts and in their historical contexts. While living energy for Catholic social teaching has always come and continues to come from the grass roots, these documents consolidate the achievements of past generations, and provide a platform for new achievements by future generations. In this study, I only point to the deeper and creative source of this tradition in the courageous and visionary work of grass-roots leaders and popular movements. Fortunately other scholars have undertaken inspiring and detailed studies of these still-living roots.[2]

Following Pope Leo XIII's 1891 encyclical *Rerum novarum*, certain encyclicals have been designated as specifically "social" documents. These texts carefully articulate the principles of contemporary Catholic social teaching across its long development. But these specifically social texts need to be placed within the context of the entire corpus of papal encyclicals. For only this full range of texts, including others besides specifically designated social documents and including the full range of papal encyclicals back to 1740, gives us a complete view of the foundational and developing interpretation of church and society by the Catholic popes. Thus, as already noted, looking at this larger corpus of papal documents requires examining the papacy's initial strategic response to the philosophy of the modern European Enlightenment and to the modern liberal movements of cultural, political, and economic emancipation that arose from it.

Throughout its entire history from 1740 forward, the development of contemporary Catholic social teaching has been consistently a turbulent process. The popes who articulated these teachings had to contend with the breakdown of premodern European aristocratic Christian civilization, with the triumph of a modern anti-Catholic European bourgeois civilization, and now with emergence of a postmodern planetary civilization. They also faced the threatening ideologies of mechanistic capitalism, secular socialism, atheistic communism, and pagan fascism, as well as dramatic historical transformations in Catholic consciousness itself.

The strategic responses of these popes, though now neatly recorded in somber library tomes, came out of the terrifying experiences of exploitation, oppression, war, insurrection, revolution, and persecution. G. W. F. Hegel once called history a slaughter-bench. The long waves of social transformation to which these popes were responding fit well Hegel's brutal description.

In addressing such turbulence these popes were hardly Olympian figures who stood above the battle. Their responses were often dramatic and varied profoundly. Some grew reactionary and vindictive. Others became confused and remained ignorant and naive. Some made painful mistakes. Yet for the most part they were devoted and sincere leaders who honestly searched for a viable path for church and society and eventually found one for at least the social-welfare period of the center countries of industrial capitalism. Now, however, as the North-Atlantic social-welfare synthesis of revisionist liberalism is breaking down, and as a new capitalist globalization is maturing, the search continues for a fresh and adequate Catholic strategy commensurate with the challenges of the new postmodern planetary civilization.

These contemporary papal encyclicals constitute privileged institutional expressions of what today is called practical theology or alternately praxis theology or even strategic theology.[3] The documents contain the official statement of Catholic teaching for the social world and as such offer philosophical and theological guidance for the business enterprise, workers' organizations, the state, the media, education, the family, human sexuality, and countless other expressions of humanity's social creativity, as well as for the internal life of the Christian community itself.

While representing on one side a creative venture in practical theology, Catholic social teaching may be also described nonconfessionally as a social philosophy, or alternately as a philosophical social ethics. While influenced in a constitutive way by Catholic theology and in turn carrying powerful biblical roots, this teaching, at least since the time of Pope Leo XIII, has also been strongly grounded time in philosophy and largely in a neo-Thomist appropriation of the organic Aristotelian tradition. Catholic social teaching has very consciously drawn on the neo-Thomist interpretation of Aristotle to critique certain mechanistic assumptions of the modern liberal philosophy. Yet over time, Catholic social teaching has been itself reshaped by the modern liberal tradition, has appropriated some of liberalism's and even of socialism's richest gifts (democracy, human rights, the priority of labor, and so forth), and has sought to provide deeper philosophical and theological grounding for these very gifts.

Dialogue with the philosophy of Catholic social teaching is proposed as open to all humanity, and so is seen as not requiring a Catholic theological commitment. Thus, in the Catholic perspective that sees reason and faith as complementary, this social teaching represents not simply a contribution to Christian social evangelization, though it certainly represents that too, but also a contribution to the new multicultural philosophical conversation about a new global ethics.[4]

Amid their often imperfect and searching human efforts, the popes of contemporary Catholic social teaching have left a lasting legacy for the future of Catholic Christianity, and hopefully for the entire human family. Like the older corpus of medieval Christian Aristotelianism, and like the still older corpus of classical Greco-Roman Christian neo-Platonism, the corpus of contemporary Catholic social teaching has already become a vibrant tree in the rich and diverse garden of the Catholic tradition.

Recent Studies of Catholic Social Teaching

Research on Catholic social teaching has become a growing field of inquiry. This indicates how central social teaching is now becoming to Catholic-Christian identity, mission, and ministry, and to Catholic Christianity's contribution to a public social philosophy.

It may be useful, therefore, to set this particular study of Catholic social teaching within the context of some major contributions to this field. I limit my summary here to Europe and the Americas, because so far the teaching has been largely Western. I also humbly acknowledge that these are the only areas I know well and express my desire to learn more from creative developments in Africa and Asia, which are now major sources of new grass-roots developments in Catholic social teaching. No doubt in the future these regions will themselves be the source of rich scholarship from writers more broadly informed than myself.

European Studies

Among older European studies of Christian social teaching in general, *The Social Teachings of the Christian Churches* by Ernst Troeltsh remains the classic text.[5] But this study ended with the eighteenth century and so did not significantly address most of the corpus of the contemporary papal encyclicals. Nonetheless, it provides an important ecumenical backdrop to later research.

European Catholic studies on the papal encyclicals have adopted a variety of perspectives. One well-known European school, seen in the work of the French scholars Jean-Yves Calvez and Jacques Perrin, has offered helpful commentaries on texts, with particular emphasis on political and economic analyses in relation to Catholic social action.[6] Another, seen in the recent work of British

Roger Charles, has approached these teachings as magisterial articulations of natural law, and hence as a subdivision of moral theology for the social realm.[7] In yet another perspective, the late Italian political thinker Amintore Fanfani interpreted the papal encyclicals as part of a profound cultural clash between Catholicism and industrial capitalism.[8]

An initial European move toward correlation of Catholic social teaching with an economic stage-analysis arose with the German scholar Heinrich Pesch (and his disciple Franz Mueller), whose work in turn has profoundly influenced Pope John Paul II.[9] Analyzing the shift from local to national capitalism and working in the early and middle years of this century, this school could not foresee the third or global stage of industrial capitalism now emerging.

Recently the Irish scholar Donal Dorr has approached the tradition from the fresh and creative perspective pioneered by the Latin American church, namely the "option for the poor."[10] Another Irish scholar, Sean McDonagh, has called for a centering of Catholic social thought in ecology.[11] Ian Linden, of the Catholic Institute for International Relations in London, has written a challenging overview of the tradition, with an emphasis on lay leadership.[12] The French theologian Marie-Dominique Chenu criticized the entire tradition of papal encyclicals as "ideology."[13]

Latin American Studies

The school of thought with the closest affinity to the approach sketched here is Latin American liberation theology, and I am deeply in debt to implicit mentoring from this school. Founded especially by Peruvian Gustavo Gutiérrez and with its method perhaps best articulated by Brazilian Clodovis Boff, liberation theology has developed a significant theological awareness of the new global scale of industrial capitalism and thus has provided pioneering insights that have already strongly influenced new developments in Catholic social teaching.[14]

Of particular help to me from this school, at least on the ecclesial side, was Gutiérrez's own three-stage analysis of Catholic strategy, revised slightly from Brazilian Paulo Freire's discussion of "three churches" (actually meaning three strategies), as well as Chilean Arturo Gaete's analysis of three stages of papal response to socialism.[15]

Countless other figures within the Latin American tradition have contributed to recent research on Catholic social teaching. To mention only a few, Ricardo Antoncich of Colombia has offered a Latin American hermeneutic of Catholic social teaching from the perspective of liberation,[16] while Pablo Richard of Chile (long-time resident in Costa Rica) and Leonardo Boff of Brazil have both called for an ecological or biocentric perspective that would link Earth and the poor.[17] Diego Irrarázaval of Chile, living now more than twenty years in Peru among the Aymara people of the high plains of the Andes, has given powerful voice to the wisdom of the continent's living indigenous legacy.[18] Ivone Gebara, a Brazilian nun who critiques the Greek philosophical bases of Western theology, has written powerfully from an eco-feminist perspective.[19] Important Protestant voices have also contributed to liberation theology, for example, Elsa Tamez, who has also added a feminist perspective.[20]

North American Studies

North America has also recently shown itself fertile ground for a range of scholarly work in what was once a largely European arena. The late Philip Land, whose adult life was lived at the heart of Catholic social teaching, provided a rich personal reflection on the challenges that confronted the tradition in the second half of the twentieth century.[21] The neo-conservative theologian Michael Novak has placed the Anglo-American variant of liberalism (neither anticlerical nor rationalistically authoritarian like its continental European cousin) in a dialogue with the evolving corpus of Catholic social teaching.[22] The progressive theologian David Hollenback has approached papal social teaching through the modern tradition of human rights and in the process has attempted to broaden the American secular rights tradition (which has tended to favor political rights but to ignore social rights).[23]

Other important North American contemporary scholars on the papal encyclical tradition include historian David O'Brien, sociologists John Coleman and Andrew Greeley, and theologians Brian Hehir, Charles Curran, Gregory Baum, Mary Hobgood, Christine Gudorf, Michael and Kenneth Himes, and Michael Schuck. O'Brien has detailed the progressive historical evolution of Catholic social teaching, with a special emphasis on the opening to liberalism.[24] Coleman has reflected on its major internal shifts as well as on key sources of the tradition.[25] Greeley has highlighted the principle of subsidiarity.[26] Hehir has emphasized church-state issues and particularly just-war theory.[27] Curran has fruitfully researched American figures in the tradition.[28] Baum has highlighted the tradition's dialogue with Marxism.[29] Hobgood has pointed out the contradictory use of economic models in social-analysis and policy-recommendations.[30] Gudorf has analyzed the uneven impact of the liberation perspective on race, class, and gender.[31] The Himes brothers have begun to build an important bridge between social teaching and systematic theology.[32] And Schuck has developed a comprehensive overview of the rooted communitarian orientation of the encyclicals throughout the eighteenth, nineteenth, and twentieth centuries.[33]

In terms of correlating the development of industrial capitalism with strategic responses by papal social teaching, a masterful contribution can be found in the historical studies of another North American, Paul Misner. His first volume, *Social Catholicism in Europe* (in a projected two-volume set), links the development of the modern Catholic social movement, out of which papal social teaching grew, with the history of European industrialization from its origins to the period between World War I and World War II. The projected second volume promises to continue the correlation up to the 1960s.[34]

Recently within the United States there seems to be a renaissance of publishing on Catholic social teaching. In particular, two scholars have provided important studies on the heroic grass-root leaders and popular movements that actually stand behind the papacy's articulation of the teaching. Marvin L. Krier Mich roots the teaching in the prophetic movements from which it arose.[35] Thomas Bokenkotter tells the powerful story of the movements' heroic leaders.[36] In addition, Peter Henriot, Edward DeBerri, and Michael Schultheis have published a fine summary of Catholic social teaching in the papal encyclicals.[37] Maria Riley and Nancy Sylvester have creatively raised the feminist challenge.[38] Fred Kramer has offered a rich primer.[39] *The New Dictionary of Catholic Social Thought* is a valuable resource.[40] Walter Burghardt has given insights on integrating the tradition into preaching.[41] Building on Schuck's important work, David Boileau has edited a collection of largely European essays on the principles at the root of the tradition.[42] Perry Roets has created a "Catechism" of the tradition.[43] J. Brian Benestad has analyzed policy statements of the US Catholic bishops.[44] Thomas Masaro has written a fine action-oriented introduction to the tradition.[45] Brennan R. Hill has explored the emergence of an ecological perspective within the tradition (and in Protestant social teaching as well).[46] Most recently Charles Curran has published an historical and systematic study of the tradition beginning with 1891 from the perspective of a liberal interpretation of Catholic moral theology.[47]

Beginning with 1740

Most analysts of the social encyclicals, with the exception of Schuck and Misner, have addressed contemporary papal social teaching as beginning with Pope Leo XIII. Yet as already noted, and as the five-volume set of English translations of the contemporary papal encyclicals edited by Claudia Carlin makes clear, the papal encyclical tradition in the modern era actually began in 1740, albeit with a premodern perspective.[48] Schuck has emphatically pointed this out, and Coleman has subsequently acknowledged the earlier beginning.[49]

Including the older documents, Schuck has insightfully articulated a three-stage model of papal social teaching that supports the pattern proposed here for the ecclesial side.[50] Indeed, I have sometimes gratefully used Schuck's "pre-Leonine, Leonine, and post-Leonine" for the three papal strategies identified in this study, though overall I prefer "premodern, modern, and postmodern," and also refer to the post-Leonine stage as "Johannine" (meaning grounded in the vision of John XXIII). On the societal side, Schuck's rich study leaves us with hints of the external correlation with industrial capitalism, but he does not develop the correlation. Further, he does speak of three "industrial revolutions" but draws on an earlier periodization originally chronicled by Werner Sombart, in which all stages are complete in the time of the Leonine teaching.[51]

Further, in his analysis of post-Leonine (or Johannine) documents, Schuck notes briefly some of the new economic and technological phenomena that correspond to what is described here as a third stage of industrial capitalism. But he no longer uses the metaphor of stages for the economic structure, nor does he develop his brief allusions.[52] Although he constantly refers to the societal context, Schuck's real interest is the internal coherence and continuity of the papal teaching, which, as mentioned, he sees as representing a rooted communitarian social ethic.[53] In my view Schuck's study is the finest comprehensive internal analysis of the entire contemporary corpus of papal social teaching.

This present study builds on the above-mentioned wealth of scholarship and modestly seeks to add to that wealth by charting the proposed three-stage correlation of strategic ecclesial responses to shifting structural challenges from industrial capitalism. Hopefully this model will prove a helpful resource for the tasks of social analysis, evangelical reflection, and strategic planning in the new planetary stage of social and religious history.

Catholic Social Teaching and Industrial Capitalism

Overall, these papal documents of contemporary Catholic social teaching constitute key ecclesial-societal guides for Catholic Christianity's strategic response to the unfolding of industrial capitalism, as well as to industrial socialism and industrial communism, and to the whole underlying dynamic of modern bourgeois liberal culture.

Modern bourgeois liberal culture had early roots in the merchant classes of the medieval European Crusades and of the early modern European Renaissance. While its philosophical ground can be traced back to medieval Nominalism, it achieved cultural power only with the print revolution, the Protestant Reformation, and the scientific revolution. Finally it emerged in mature philosophical expression with the modern European Enlightenment—establishing the liberal philosophy as the foundation of modern democracy and industrial capitalism.

As industrial capitalism unfolded, it revealed its own internal polarization between the normative voluntarist free-market version and the heretically hyper-rationalist version of state capitalism (with both moderate socialist and extreme communist forms). "Scientific" socialism and communism, despite their anti-bourgeois rhetoric, always remained intellectual projects of the radically rationalist wing of the modern bourgeois liberal intelligentsia and thus need to be seen as part of the broad sweep of the modern liberal project.

Though emerging first in response to philosophical and political challenges of liberalism, contemporary Catholic social teaching soon emphasized the economic challenge of industrial capitalist penetration rapidly overwhelming Europe's premodern peasant-aristocratic world and the subsequent threat from socialism and communism, particularly their atheistic strands. Catholic social teaching then followed the evolution of modern capitalism through its local, national, and now global stages, with the postmodern strategy today responding to the birth of a new planetary era precipitated by the electronic revolution.

Three Stages of Industrial Capitalism

To understand fully contemporary Catholic social teaching, we need to correlate the evolving contextual challenges from modern industrial capitalism with innovative strategic Catholic responses. In this challenge-response model, the historical-structural stage of capitalism presents a contextual societal challenge for a strategic ecclesial response.[54] The responding church strategy is then seen as reshaping the consciousness, policies, and structure of the church in service of its contexualized mission. Thus any new Catholic strategy would embody the leadership's judgment on how best to pursue both evangelization and social transformation in the new historical context.[55]

The challenge-response model proposed here grew out of my study several decades earlier of strategic shifts in papal Catholic social thought and practice.[56] I noted then clear and distinct shifts within Catholic social teaching, first in the late nineteenth century with Pope Leo XIII (1878–1903) and again in the mid-twentieth century with Pope John XXIII (1958–63).[57]

Such shifts need not mean that Catholic social teaching is historically relativistic. On the contrary, I affirm Michael Schuck's claim that this papal corpus has a relatively consistent and coherent core, centered in a rooted communitarian and rooted ethos. Yet, as Schuck has himself acknowledged, this core has remained open—however slowly and awkwardly—to unfolding developments, particularly regarding historical consciousness and the historical transformation of social structures.[58]

Originally my inclination was to deal with these strategic shifts from a "cultural-lag" perspective—seeing the Catholic Church as slowly catching up first with liberal, then with socialist expressions of the modern world.[59] The closer I looked, however, the more it seemed that industrial capitalism and its foundational culture of modern liberalism were also shifting in parallel with the Catholic shifts.[60]

This perception of shifting Catholic strategies, precipitated by structural shifts of industrial capitalism, led me to sketch an ideal-type model of three Catholic strategies for evangelization, functioning as distinct strategic responses to three distinct contextual stages of industrial capitalism.[61] I subsequently supplemented this construct with a secondary probe of parallel shifts in modern industrial socialism, which I came to see as a radical variant of modern industrial capitalism.[62] The three stages of this ideal-type model will be developed at greater length in the next book. Again, this book will address Catholic social teaching within the first two stages, while the next book will address its role in the third stage. The whole model may be summarized briefly as follows.

The Pre-Leonine Papacy and Local Capitalism

In the first technological wave of the Industrial Revolution, industrial capitalism was in its early or local phase, grounded in the factory revolution with relatively little machinery and guided by the young laissez-faire expression of the modern liberal philosophy. It may be called the local phase because industrial production was still confined to small regions and largely organized into the localized business system of the family firm. Britain was, of course, the site where the Industrial Revolution first emerged in this local stage, roughly around 1760.

The new industrial ideology then spread to continental Europe but met fierce resistance in the Catholic Latin territories where the resisting aristocracy was still quite strong (the aristocracy in Protestant lands having been weakened by the Reformation). Thus the Catholic papacy first met industrial capitalism not directly in economic form but more as preindustrial attacks of cultural and political revolution challenging the entrenched ancien régime of the Catholic aristocracy (including the aristocratic pope and aristocratic bishops). Despite the rhetoric of the liberal philosophy about democracy, however, liberalism in the Catholic Latin world (in marked contrast to the English-speaking world) carried a sharply anticlerical and at times a harshly authoritarian character.

After the French Revolution, when this first stage of modern industrial capitalism truly exploded upon the Catholic continental European world, the Catholic papacy reeled in strategic shock. The classical aristocratic paradigm, which for a millennium and a half had provided the societal foundation for the identity, mission, and ministry of European Catholic leadership, was suddenly doomed. In reaction, for most of the nineteenth century the popes clung to a premodern strategy of vehemently condemning the emerging bourgeois liberal movement, then in its laissez-faire form, as a destroyer of aristocratic Christian civilization.

In their largely premodern strategic response through most of the nineteenth century, the popes of this pre-Leonine period remained tragically enmeshed in dying aristocratic assumptions about society and religion, assumptions that would not survive industrial modernization. Yet they also prophetically warned about profound spiritual-cultural dangers within the modern bourgeois path, dangers that in the twentieth century would indeed lead modern culture into profound spiritual, societal, and ecological crises.

The Leonine Papacy and National Capitalism

The new stage of industrial capitalism was grounded in the second technological wave of the Industrial Revolution, that is, the onset of heavy machinery, in turn creating a larger scale economy that was national in structure. The year 1880 may be assigned somewhat arbitrarily as a point when the transition to the new stage was clear. Key technologies of the new stage were the railroad and telegraph, which provided the technological infrastructure for the emergence of new national corporations that organized finance, production, and marketing on a maturely national scale. Now, for the first time, the majority of the laboring force of the industrialized nations began to be uprooted from the land and drawn into the new industrial system. Thanks to the railroad, the agricultural system was directly integrated into the industrial system and a new mechanized factory form of farming began to develop. This national industrial economic structure in turn became the economic foundation for a new external nationalism marked by great industrial wars and by a new industrial colonialism, now made feasible by the machine revolution. The steamship, the railroad, and the machine gun as well gave European and European-American national governments the power to invade and conquer all of the Third World. And the machine gun, the tank, and the aircraft would enable the great industrial powers to turn their destructive energies against one another.

By the close of the nineteenth century, when industrial capitalism was beginning to move into this middle or national stage, Pope Leo XIII (1878–1903) opened an adaptive modern strategic path for Catholic Christianity. He promoted a reforming Catholic engagement with moderate liberalism in order to counter what he saw as the more serious threat of secular socialism. The working class was growing so large that the popes could no longer ignore it, nor could they ignore the attractiveness of socialism to the working class. In this turn, Anglo-American Catholicism eventually became a valuable strategic resource. (Again, in contrast to Europe's Latin Catholicism, English-speaking Catholics had been more comfortable with liberalism, since the Anglo-American strain had not been militantly anticlerical and had been more democratic.) In the resulting modern papal-liberal alliance, industrial capitalism's original ideology of classical laissez-faire liberalism was revised into the reforming ideology of social-welfare liberalism. In this social-welfare context, what Michael Schuck has called "the Leonine strategy" held as remarkably strong and stable for the next four popes through to Pius XII (1939–58).[63]

In this modern adaptive and reforming strategy, beginning in 1878 and continuing throughout the first half of the twentieth century, the Leonine popes played a more proactive role than their reactive pre-Leonine predecessors and made important contributions to social reform. Their social teaching supported workers' unions, a moderate social-welfare state, and an organic-hierarchical understanding of society, and through the principle of subsidiarity offered resistance to totalitarian governments. In addition, even more than their predecessors, they defended the family as society's foundational cell. Even so, they seemed largely unaware of the deep realities of racism, sexism, and ecological erosion.

The Johannine Papacy and Global Capitalism

In the second half of the twentieth century yet a third stage of modern industrial capitalism burst forth, this time from the electronic revolution. Under the slogan of "globalization," this new stage is presently revolutionizing the entire planet and in turn opening culturally on a postmodern planetary civilization. Perhaps the dramatic year of 1968 may be chosen as the turning point, although the transition occurred slowly over decades. The electronic revolution, the third technological wave of innovation emerging from the Industrial Revolution, has made feasible intense and rapid networks of communication and transportation on a global scale. This in turn has made possible the emergence of gargantuan transnational enterprises, or multinational corporations, which are absorbing so much of the planetary economy and becoming the most powerful forces on Earth, not only economically but also culturally through their control of global media. With this new stage the mechanistic vision of the liberal philosophy is now colonizing the entire planet, but with growing signs of profound spiritual, societal, and ecological crisis for the whole human family.

At the beginning of this new stage, Pope John XXIII (1958–63) prophetically began yet another strategic shift for Catholic Christianity. He undertook a transforming dialogue with all ideologies, embraced Christians of all traditions, called for internal church renewal, and linked the gospel of Jesus with a global humanist mission of justice and peace. Yet, with a shifting reminiscent of the nineteenth-century popes, his successors have not found a stable center for the strategy. The early postmodern period of Catholicism has unfortunately become divided by bitter polarization between competing so-called progressive and conservative interpretations of the Johannine legacy. Again, the next book will explore in detail this search for a Catholic strategy adequate to the new global realities.

Chart 1 gives a summary overview of this three-stage correlation of the evolution of industrial capitalism and of the development of Catholic social teaching, alternately described here as Catholic strategy. This correlation is the model informing both this and the next book.

Chart 1.
Correlation of Societal-Ecclesial Development

	Industrial Capitalism	Catholic Social Teaching
Stage 1	Local Capitalism Modern Laissez-Faire Liberalism 1760–1880 *(Factory Revolution)*	Anti-Modern Catholic Strategy Pre-Leonine Conservative Defense 1740–1878 *(Aristocratic Eurocentric Christian Civilization)*
Stage 2	National Capitalism Modern Social-Welfare Liberalism 1880–1960 *(Machine Revolution)*	Modern Catholic Strategy Leonine Adaptive Reform 1878–1958 *(Bourgeois Eurocentric Christian Civilization)*
Stage 3	Global Capitalism Postmodern Crisis of Liberalism 1960– *(Electronic Revolution)*	Postmodern Catholic Strategy Johannine Radical Regeneration 1958– *(Global Humanistic Spiritual Civilization)*

Across these three stages the papacy's social teaching needs to be interpreted within distinct historical-structural contexts. This requires examining the distinct technological-economic revolutions grounding the three stages of industrial capitalism, as well as the distinct political form of liberalism for each stage. It also requires examining the profound spiritual-cultural changes arising within each of these stages, though that is more a matter for a future study.

Similarly, we need to examine how the above technological-economic and cultural-spiritual changes reshape the mediating arenas of politics and law. In these three dimensions of humanity's organizational life (the embodied technological-economic dimension, the symbolic cultural-spiritual dimension, and their mediating political-legal dimension), church and society share a single world. These three dimensions holistically shape the changing societal contexts and strategic challenges for Catholic Christianity's mission and ministry.

In the next book, again on the postmodern stage of Catholic social teaching as found in the Johannine encyclicals from John XXIII through to John Paul II, I will provide a fuller introductory analysis of these three stages of industrial capitalism. Yet a more detailed analysis of industrial capitalism is available in my separate study, *The Evolution of Modern Industrial Capitalist Society and the Birth of the Postmodern Electronic-Ecological Era*.[64]

Capitalism and Modern Racism

It is not sufficient ultimately to examine only the internal development of capitalism within the industrial countries of the First World. Modern capitalism, first in mercantile and later in industrial form, has been partly grounded economically in the Western racist plunder of non-European peoples and their lands, particularly in what is today called the Third World. This plunder included:

- under mercantile capitalism, the early modern European and European-American imperialist exploitation and devastation of the native peoples and lands of the Americas;

- also under mercantile capitalism, the early modern European and European-American imperialist-colonialist exploitation of countless generations of Africans and their descendants by the Atlantic slave trade and by the Atlantic slave system; and

- later under industrial capitalism, the modern European and European-American imperialist plunder of the vast territories, resources, and peoples of Africa and Asia, as well as of Latin America.

Such plunder was foundational to the rise of modern industrial capitalism, as was the brutal harshness of the early British factory system that copied the "efficiency" of the slave system of the Americas. The modern "scientific" articulations of racism, though recently shown to be anything but scientific, arose to justify this brutal exploitation and plunder.[65]

Unfortunately until the second half of the twentieth century, with a few notable exceptions, Catholic social teaching largely ignored the great racist sins of the genocidal attack on the native peoples and lands of the Americas, the Atlantic slave system, and the Western colonialist plunder of Africa, Asia, and the Americas. Even in recent times the teaching has only begun to address adequately the past and present realities of those terrible social sins. Until the Second Vatican Council (1962–65), Catholic social teaching spoke almost exclusively to the industrial class experience of the First World.

Postmodern Challenges of Feminism and Ecology

Further, only recently has Catholic social teaching begun to address two other powerful dimensions of structural sin, namely, the societal oppression of women and the ecological oppression of the Earth. The two powerful movements arising today from these oppressions, namely, the feminist movement and the ecological movement, constitute, along with the multicultural movements of non-European peoples, the strongest new cultural-spiritual energies of challenge across the planet. These movements cannot be considered in isolation from the abiding importance of the class dimension, which has been central to Catholic social teaching, but they cannot be adequately understood only through the eyes of either the capitalist or socialist variants of the modern liberal philosophy.

Thus only in the second half of the twentieth century, that is, in the early postmodern period, did Catholic social teaching begin to move beyond its deeply entrenched Eurocentrism. In turn, only in the second half of the twentieth century did the tradition begin to develop a truly global consciousness and begin to reflect on the foundational dimensions of race, gender, and ecology and to link them to its formerly central emphasis on the class dimension. All of these themes will be the subject of the follow-up book on postmodern Catholic social teaching.

This recent wider opening of the tradition of Catholic social teaching seems particularly important, since the Western industrial capitalist system, and indeed the entire modern Western cultural system, now appears to be falling deeper and deeper into a postmodern spiritual, societal, and ecological crisis precipitated by the new electronically grounded capitalist "globalization." In this book, however, I will not examine the dynamics of this profound crisis within postmodern capitalist globalization but only its earlier roots in local and national capitalism.

The deep roots of the postmodern Western crisis are at once political-economic and cultural-spiritual, and these two dimensions are intimately interwoven. This book on the modern phase of Catholic social teaching, and the subsequent book on the postmodern phase, predominately address the political-economic dimension, seen here in the correlative evolution of industrial capitalism and of the strategic response of Catholic social teaching. In a third book, yet to be written, I plan to address in a deeper way the cultural-spiritual breakdown of the modern Western bourgeois project in both its capitalist and socialist expressions.

Defining Some Terms

Before concluding, it may be helpful to define some of the terms used here to describe the three stages of industrial capitalism. Let us begin with the three distinct, though interrelated, functional regions of society, namely, economics, politics, and culture.

- *Economics* is addressed here in terms of two levels. The *deep* economic level refers to the primary or foundational structure of human workers and their technological tools in the production and reproduction of material life. The *surface* economic level refers to secondary or derivative phenomena like wages, working conditions, purchasing power, and so forth.

- *Politics* refers here to the institutional ordering of economic society. While the actual political order of a particular society is not necessarily determined by its economic form (in Marxist terms, its "mode of production"), the political order must nonetheless seek a creative way of ordering the society's actual economic processes. Thus, for example, political orders have been quite different for nomadic hunter-gather societies, sedentary agricultural societies, and industrial societies. So, although not determined by economics, politics is clearly related to it, as early theorists of liberalism acknowledged when they spoke holistically of the liberal "political economy."

- *Culture* refers here to the symbolic-mythic-ritualistic system of meaning, which functions especially through cultural institutions like the arts, sports, religion, education, and media. Cultural symbols, myths, and rituals can initiate, sustain, resist, undermine, or transform the legitimacy of a given historical form of the political economy.[66] The *deep* cultural level grounds the cosmological root metaphor or foundational cultural paradigm out of which the political economy operates (for example, for the modern print era a mechanistic-emotive root metaphor, and for the postmodern electronic era an ecological-artistic root metaphor). The *surface* cultural level is produced by the political economy (for example, the culture of consumerism). At both levels, I propose, spirituality (or a pseudo-spirituality) is the heart of culture.

Again, though cultural experience is addressed here predominately from within its surface structure, this does not represent the orthodox Marxist doctrine of the economic "infrastructure" determining the cultural "superstructure." That is the case only *within* industrial capitalism, and only at the surface, secondary, or derivative level of culture. The fundamental cultural assumptions that have grounded the birth and unfolding of industrial capitalism (again, for example, the mechanistic-emotive root metaphor) represent the deep, primary, or generative level of culture. At this deep level the liberal culture and its mechanistic-emotive paradigm are seen as the real ground. Nonetheless, my focus here will be on the political economy constructed out of this cultural ground, while, as noted, I hope to address the deeper spiritual dynamics of the liberal culture in a future study.

It may also be helpful to define how various historical-ideological terms are used here in reference to the modern experience.

- *Industrial capitalism* means here that form of society which, having emerged from the Industrial Revolution, was based on the assumption that strategic guidance for political-economic organization of nature, human labor, and technology is best left to the free-market process of capital accumulation. The purpose of this market orientation is that the modern Enlightenment's mechanistic-emotive paradigm of freedom and progress may develop most rapidly. The guiding social principle of industrial capitalism may thus be described as the *priority of the market*. The market, in turn, is seen philosophically as driven by economic self-interest, or more narrowly for the business enterprise by the pursuit of profit.[67]

- *Industrial socialism* means here "scientific" socialism with Marxist roots, as expressed in both dictatorial communist and democratic socialist forms, and with both seen as state-centered and radically rationalistic variants of industrial capitalism. While the normative form of industrial capitalism is based on the priority of the market, this variant is based on the *priority of the state*. It assigns guidance for the political-economic organization of nature, labor, and technology to the intelligentsia of the socialist or communist political party, and through them to the "scientific" state. The state and party are seen ideologically as pursuing the collective interest of the working class, although the actual driving force is the interest of the bourgeois bureaucratic class. As with industrial capitalism, the motive here is also that the modern Enlightenment's mechanistic-emotive paradigm of freedom and progress develop most rapidly, although the path of this development is seen in more rationalist than voluntarist terms.[68]

- *Liberalism* refers here *narrowly* to the foundational ideology of industrial capitalism, including both its political-economic and its cultural-spiritual philosophy.[69] There is a *broader meaning* of liberalism, however, namely the philosophical foundation of all modern culture (with its grounding cosmology of a mechanistic-emotive root metaphor as the basis for understanding freedom and progress). In this sense modern socialism becomes a political radicalization of modern liberalism's deepest assumptions about the mechanization of economic life, in contrast to normative capitalism's economic radicalization of those same mechanistic assumptions.[70] This wider reach of the liberal culture, including its socialist ideologies, is captured by the term *progressive.* From a regenerative postmodern perspective, both normative industrial capitalism's economic priority of the market and the socialist variant's political priority of the state may be seen as competing embodiments of the overarching modern mechanistic principle of the *priority of capital.* In the dominant or normative form the priority of capital is mediated through the market, while in the socialist variant, it is mediated through the state.

In his prophetic encyclical on human work *Laborem exercens*, Pope John Paul II articulated an alternative postmodern principle, namely, the *priority of labor*, to which both the market and the state need to be accountable.[71] From a deeper social perspective one might highlight as even more fundamental the *priority of family*, that is, the priority of organic relationships over the detached individuals of a "free" labor market. (I refer not to the problematic late-modern nuclear family but to the richer notion of extended family and wider kinship system, including deceased ancestors.) From a deeper ecological perspective, one might even speak of the *priority of nature* within which humanity arises, while from the deepest religious perspective we need to speak of the *priority of the Mystery* from which all creation emerges.[72]

Concluding Reflections

Before concluding this Introduction, it may be helpful to say a few words about the status, structure, and limits of this study.

Status

This study constitutes the first of two books that together offer a cognitive map linking wide ranges of religious, societal, and ecological phenomena. Clarifying and correlating the three stages of Catholic strategy with the contextual stages of industrial capitalism represents the project's central task. As such, it both addresses the philosophical dimensions of Catholic social teaching, especially regarding economic and political philosophy, and also serves as a constructive contribution to contemporary praxis theology, increasingly described as practical theology.

Within the project, definition of each Catholic strategy is largely taken from its articulation by the papacy, as seen through its medium of the encyclical tradition, though occasional reference will also be made to other magisterial sources of this teaching. The analysis of the papal documents is based on two sources: (1) primary materials, namely, each period's major encyclicals that bear on interpretation of the societal context; and (2) secondary materials, namely, standard general works of social and ecclesial history for the period, including those addressing papal social teaching.

This whole exercise may be viewed as a *tertiary* level of scholarship, drawing on the existing bodies of primary and secondary literature and organizing many of their insights into a synthetic, though always tentative whole so necessary for the strategic analysis of a broadly reaching practical theology.[73] Such a strategic approach requires preceding primary and secondary scholarship, but primary and secondary work in turn require a tertiary framework for strategic interpretation.[74]

My apologies in advance for what we now know as non-inclusive gender language in the citations from encyclicals, for example, the non-inclusive use of "man" for "humanity." Since these are citations from other sources, I am not at liberty to change them.

Structure

The project as a whole, encompassing the two books, is divided into three parts, namely:

- *The Pre-Leonine Strategy*—the social teaching of the pre-Leonine popes in strategic response to the societal challenges of industrial capitalism in its local stage;

- *The Leonine Strategy*—the social teaching of the Leonine popes in strategic response to the societal challenges of industrial capitalism in its national stage; and

- *The Johannine Strategy*—the social teaching of the Johannine popes in strategic response to the societal challenges of industrial capitalism in its global stage.

As noted, this first book addresses the first two periods, while the second book will address the third period. For each period there is a similar series of two-step investigations:

- *Contexts*—historical review of church and society for the period, particularly in light of the stage of capitalist development (local, national, and global); and

- *Texts*—examination of the encyclicals for the period, as they are structured into a wider and semi-coherent strategy (pre-Leonine, Leonine, and Johannine).

Finally, the conclusions of the first and second books will each offer interpretive summaries of the legacy of Catholic social teaching. The conclusion of the second book will also offer a constructive proposal for the future of Catholic social teaching in the new postmodern, planetary, multicultural, and ecological period of history that we have already entered.

Limitations

Lastly, a few caveats may be in order about the limitations of this whole project. All these caveats indicate that it represents only a partial perspective and thus remains incomplete without enrichment from additional perspectives.

- *Class Perspective.* First, the project addresses primarily the class axis of the social division of labor. It would look quite different if the focus of its analysis were the racial-ethnic, gender, generational, center/periphery, or ecological axis, though these all will figure prominently in the concluding futurist projections of the second study. Such alternative perspectives are as important as, and sometimes more important than, the class perspective offered here. But the importance of a class analysis remains, even while it needs to be integrated with these other analyses.

- *Urban Perspective.* Second, the project assumes the viewpoint of the urban industrial system. It would be equally interesting, and in the light of the ecological crisis perhaps more important, to study the rural agricultural impact of industrial capitalism, especially in the system's periphery. Yet, despite the foundational importance of the rural experience, the need for an analysis of the urban industrial centers remains important in its own right.

- *US Perspective.* Third, this is a study done from within the first-world capitalist experience of the North Atlantic countries, and within those from the now sole superpower of the United States. As such, it certainly needs to be complemented by critical and creative contributions from the Third World and the Second World as well as from other locations in the First World. Nonetheless, it is to be hoped that an analysis of the first-world experience, even from the perspective of the United States, will still be of use to analysts who address other geographic and geo-political dimensions.

- *Strategic Perspective.* Fourth, this is a study of the institutional life of the Catholic Church. It is not a study of popular Catholicism, that is, of the actual experience of local Catholic communities. Institutional strategy and popular religion are presumably linked, but one cannot be reduced to the other.

- *Catholic Perspective.* Finally, because of its Catholic focus, the study does not take into account the full ecumenical range of Christian response to industrial capitalism, or more broadly, to modern culture—something that would be indispensable for a full Christian interpretation.[75]

When beginning this research project many decades ago, I tended to view the class factor as only one in a growing holistic conversation with factors of gender, race, ecology, and so on—with none of these factors granted primacy. Since then, I have come to see the ecological dimension as foundational, with the various human dimensions of race/ethnicity, sex/gender, class, and so on, as still highly important and interwoven, but with all centered in ecology. Nonetheless, any interpretation of the ecological dimension is always filtered through the strengths and weaknesses of particular experiences of gender, race, class, and so forth, which in turn are filtered through one another. Thus, none of these dimensions stands alone as an autonomous perception. Rather each perspective always needs to be integrated into some kind of holistic, albeit incomplete, gestalt.

Further and most certainly, as Immanuel Wallerstein and others have made clear, at any stage of modern capitalism the experience of the center countries is not truly comprehensible apart from the linked experience of the periphery and semi-periphery. Nonetheless, as already mentioned, there is still a need to understand the internal dynamics of the center countries, including the United States, without claiming that their internal life provides a comprehensive analysis.

In summary, this study reviews the correlative and evolutionary interaction of industrial capitalism and Catholic social teaching as seen through the papal encyclicals, predominately from within the First World and especially from class, urban, US, and Catholic perspectives. It proposes that the emergence of a third stage of global industrial capitalism opens the door to the transition to a fresh postmodern, multicultural, ecological, and planetary society, which may eventually prove to be post-capitalist and post-socialist.[76] Further, it proposes that this transition carries the cultural and technological capacity to inflict horrendous damage upon the creative communion of ecological, societal, and spiritual life or to midwife co-creative postmodern energies for the regeneration of this creative communion.

How all Christians, and perhaps especially the enormous global family of Catholic Christians, respond to this deep cultural transition from a modern Western mechanistic culture to a postmodern global ecological culture may determine whether death-dealing or life-giving energies flow strongest. Whatever the limits of this study, I hope that it will in some small way assist Catholic Christian communities, and Christian communities from other traditions as well, to chart a regenerative path for the still young postmodern planetary journey.

Part I.

Anti-Modern Background

The Pre-Leonine Encyclicals
and Local Capitalism
1740–1878

Anti-Modern Papal Condemnation
of the European Enlightenment
and Laissez-Faire Liberalism in Defense
of the Dying Aristocratic Christian Civilization

2

The Pre-Leonine Papal Strategy of Rejecting Local Capitalism

Modern Liberal Defeat of Premodern Aristocratic Christian Civilization

During most of the early or local phase of modern industrial capitalism (Stage 1), Western European Catholicism did not yet feel the full economic impact of the Industrial Revolution. Instead, it suffered the fierce cultural and political attacks of an anticlerical continental liberal movement attempting to destroy the aristocratic political power of the premodern Catholic elites, often by authoritarian means. So strong was the political power of the continental European Catholic aristocracy that industrial capitalist modernization could not penetrate most of the Catholic areas of continental Europe without first breaking the power of the aristocratic Catholic hierarchy, both clerical and lay.

Especially in Latin Catholic lands, the traditional aristocracy had been stronger and more socially isolated than in Protestant or mixed countries, where industrialism had developed with less violent political revolution. This was because in Latin countries traditional Catholicism continued to hold a religious monopoly, with church elites constituting an important sector of the ruling aristocracy. By contrast, in Protestant and mixed territories, the Reformation had weakened aristocratic control over society and had opened the door to bourgeois pluralism and secularization.[1]

31

Such weakening of religious control in Protestant lands made it easier for the intellectual revolution of the Enlightenment to prepare the soil for democratic political and industrial economic transformation. But the opposite situation prevailed in the Latin Catholic lands. Thus, as Michael Novak has repeatedly pointed out, liberalism in the continental Catholic world had to mount an anticlerical movement, something quite different from the more tolerant variant of liberalism found in the Anglo-American Protestant world.[2]

The liberal challenge to Latin Catholicism in Europe took the form of an intense political conflict between church and state. Liberal forces attempted to use the state to secularize society, particularly by ending the Catholic Church's control over marriage and the education of youth. Liberal forces also strove to take from the Catholic leadership massive amounts of property, a process called secularization, which had begun earlier in the Reformation.

More profoundly, however, the confrontation was cultural. In the name of the Enlightenment's bourgeois mechanistic-emotive paradigm of freedom and progress, continental liberals mounted a powerful intellectual attack upon the Catholic Church's aristocratic organic-hierarchical paradigm of tradition and order. In response, aristocratic Catholic elites defended the ancien régime as reflecting the cosmological order and behind that the divine order. They perceived the liberal attacks as threatening an historical devastation of Christian civilization itself.[3]

The popes of this pre-Leonine strategic period scarcely addressed the Industrial Revolution, nor did they speak to the new social question of the industrial proletariat. Instead, they responded to the liberal attacks on the same cultural and political terrains. Eventually the new bourgeois offensive became a life-threatening political issue for a papacy still functioning as an aristocratic kingship and still ruling over vast feudal estates in the central area of Italy.

The great political offensive of the liberal attack came in 1789 with the French Revolution. It then expanded across Europe with Napoleon's conquests. In reaction, papal policy passed through three historical phases.

- *The Attack.* Immediately after the French Revolution, the initial papal response was largely to wait—hoping that the political storm was a local French problem that would eventually blow over.

- *The Counterattack.* When it became clear that the liberal revolution had spread across Western Europe and even beyond, the papacy supported the Congress of Vienna's (1814–15) reactionary counterattack by means of a continental coalition attempting to restore the Old Regime.

- *The Defeat.* Following the European revolutions of 1848, when the aristocratic counterattack failed and the definitive triumph of modern liberalism loomed on the horizon, and even more after 1870 when the Papal States were lost forever, the papacy retreated to the spiritual ghetto of a religious counter-culture. Yet this retreat found support in populist lay sympathy and was accompanied by vigorous missionary expansion across the industrial colonies of the Third World.[4]

The Attack:
The French Revolution and Napoleon's Empire

Viewing history from a nineteenth-century aristocratic viewpoint, the popes of the pre-Leonine period saw the modern world as having launched three historical assaults against the classical aristocratic Catholic European paradigm of evangelization: (1) the Protestant Reformation; (2) the modern secular Enlightenment; and (3) the French Revolution. In particular, the "zealot" *(zealoti)* wing of the papal bureaucracy interpreted the modern threat as beginning with Christian heresy in the Reformation, next as developing into a secular philosophy with the Enlightenment, and finally as mobilizing a revolt of the masses in the French Revolution and in its subsequent ideological expansion throughout Western Europe.[5]

Three Modern Assaults

The Reformation. According to the pre-Leonine papal analysis, the Protestant Reformation marked the first strategic assault. At the foundation of the modern era, the printing press, so closely connected to the Reformation, provided the new information technology that made elite religious leadership feasible for urban bourgeois professionals employing popular use of the vernacular Bible.[6] Both the Reformation and the printing press were in turn closely tied to the supporting educational vehicle of the free university, independent of papal control.[7] With the Reformation came the Catholic loss of many feudal privileges and properties of the Catholic leadership, the end of Christendom as a relatively united imperial system, and a violent wave of religious and military battles between Catholic and Protestant powers.

In the wake of the Reformation's assault, despite major Catholic losses in Northern Europe, the Catholic hierarchy was able to preserve for the remaining Catholic lands its classical aristocratic paradigm of evangelization. In 1648, after approximately a hundred years of bloody war between Protestants and Catholics, the Peace of Westphalia established for the first time in history the modern system of sovereign nation-states, symbolized by its famous declaration of "cuius regio, eius religio." Protestantism was thus geographically contained, the remaining Catholic territories were politically secured, and a pattern of relatively peaceful coexistence began.[8]

But all was not the same. The demise of the Holy Roman Empire meant the decline of the papacy's international authority. The new post-Christendom political model of nationalism was emerging even in the Catholic territories. With modern nationalism came not simply Protestant national churches, but also attempts by absolutist Catholic monarchs to gain greater political control over the Catholic Church within their own territories. As a result, the popes of this period faced strategic political battles with strong movements of even Catholic religious nationalism, known as Gallicanism, Josephism, and Febronianism.[9]

In addition, the Catholic Counter-Reformation brought to the classical Catholic strategy for evangelization a number of modern bourgeois innovations. These included a modern seminary-trained literate clergy, a modern apostolic model of religious life, and a modern spirituality of psychological interiority. (This spirituality grew out of the late medieval bourgeois *devotio moderna* and began to neglect the divine presence in the natural and social worlds.) Further, there emerged a modern parish-based professional pastoral model, uprooted from the kinship system that since apostolic times had been the primary carrier of evangelization. But dramatic as these Catholic bourgeois changes were, none of them challenged the deeply aristocratic paradigm of the episcopacy and papacy.[10]

The Enlightenment. The second assault, the European secular Enlightenment, attacked classical aristocratic Catholicism with the modern paradigm of science. Challenging ideologically the organic and hierarchical root metaphors grounding classical culture, the bourgeois Enlightenment promoted the mechanistic and emotive root metaphors that would prove foundational for all of modern culture. It also heightened the anticlericalism of many bourgeois intellectuals and expanded their mechanistic view of the physical world to project a deist or even a purely materialistic cosmology.

Nonetheless, the broad Catholic laity, as well as most of the Catholic clergy and religious, for a long time continued to live in social enclaves relatively immune from infection by the small subculture of the liberal bourgeois intelligentsia. This was particularly so in the case of the still vast Catholic peasantry. Further, within Catholicism, even when liberal infection did threaten, ecclesial censorship and burning of printed books, backed up by repressive Catholic state power, held the Enlightenment in check for a long time.[11]

In response to the Enlightenment, the Catholic Church did make further modern bourgeois innovations. For one thing, the new wave of apostolic religious orders, increasingly made up of educated women, began to create a modern Catholic educational system. This innovation met the intellectual aspirations of the developing Catholic middle class but kept those aspirations within a controlled Catholic framework safe from contamination by dangerous Protestant or liberal ideas. These Catholic schools also supported the *devotio moderna*, again a bourgeois model of spirituality detached from ecological and societal consciousness, but now placed at the service of apostolic mission. Yet even with these changes, the aristocratic paradigm for evangelization still held for the episcopacy and papacy.[12]

The French Revolution. With the French Revolution, the classical aristocratic Catholic paradigm was finally threatened with strategic devastation.[13] For the first time in modern history, secularizing bourgeois forces gained state power, and this in the land called the "eldest daughter" of the Catholic Church. During the Revolution and its extension across Europe, as the wider aristocracy came under attack, Catholic ecclesial elites often became the special object of political persecution. The end result would be the death of the European aristocratic society, the social world on which the classical Catholic strategy for evangelization had been based for more than a thousand years.

Impact of the Revolution

Reflecting its bourgeois leadership, the French Revolution and its continental expansion by Napoleon began to clear France and much of Western Europe of old mercantile and feudal restraints on free trade. This clearing opened the door to economic penetration by industrial capitalism and consequently began to undermine the Catholic aristocratic monopoly of religious-cultural control.

The blow was so much greater as the revolution spread far beyond France and eventually shook the entire Western world. In the words of Roger Aubert, the revolution constituted "the epicenter of an earthquake which within a few years caused the fall of the antiquated structures of the Catholic Church in a large part of Europe, and profoundly transformed the position of the Catholic Church."[14]

Undermining Aristocratic Control. Prior to the French Revolution, aristocratic France had been the key strategic base of Western Catholic Christianity. Since the time of Charlemagne, a Franco-papal alliance had provided the Catholic popes with crucial military, political, economic, intellectual, and spiritual support. For example, French troops had regularly defended the papacy from enemies. Against this background, the revolution's creation of an anti-Catholic and even antireligious bourgeois French state was a shocking blow. [15]

With this revolutionary breach in Catholic aristocratic power, it would become difficult to maintain rigid confessional walls between Protestant and Catholic territories or to contain the threatening liberal or rationalist intelligentsia of the Enlightenment within a censored subculture. For along with the increasing exchange of commercial goods would come the growing penetration of Protestant and liberal ideas and the spread of

Freemasonry, which promoted liberalism. Like the evangelical ideas of the Reformation, the liberal ideas of the Enlightenment were spread by the modern medium of print, especially through the urban guilds, with industrial printing exploding the number of books, pamphlets, and newspapers.

Revolutionary Anticlericalism. Though initially receiving broad clerical support, particularly from the lower clergy, the French Revolution ultimately turned against the Catholic Church. The moderate bourgeoisie, who early on led the uprising, had been intent only on liberalizing France's economic and political life and so had limited their changes to a series of political-economic transformations. These included enclosure of common lands for property-seeking rural entrepreneurs, banning of trade unions among the working class, and abolition of the feudal guilds and corporations of artisan monopolies. Many of the lower clergy supported these changes.[16]

A serious problem arose, however, with the Civil Constitution of the Clergy, which represented an extreme version of nationalist Gallicanism. The constitution would have turned the French Catholic Church into a department of the French government. As a battle developed between church and state, many Catholics found themselves turning, in perhaps the first expression of modern Catholic ultramontanism, to alliance with the pope.[17]

As anti-Gallican French Catholics also sought alliance with the royalist opposition, Roman Catholicism became the religion of counterrevolution. This development was strengthened by Pope Pius VI's condemnation of the Declaration of the Rights of Man, of the principles of the French Revolution, and of the Civil Constitution of the Clergy, as well as by the pope's initial moral support for a foreign counterrevolutionary invasion. In the subsequent Jacobin terror that arose to fight against the counterrevolution, thousands of priests and religious were executed, thousands more imprisoned, and still thousands more fled abroad.[18]

Spreading outward through Napoleon's military defeat of counterrevolutionary armies, the revolution soon reached Italy. Napoleon invaded the Papal States, occupied Rome, and established a Roman Republic. In a radical attempt to eradicate religion in Rome, French Jacobins and their local supporters seized and desecrated church possessions. Pius VI was sent in exile to the south of France, where he died in 1799. Persecution of the church prevented Italian-Catholic compromise with the revolution. In reaction, there arose Catholic counterrevolutionary guerrilla warfare, often with priests as commanders.[19]

The Return to "Order"

When Napoleon became ruler over France, he understood the need for stabilizing religious life in order to consolidate the gains of the bourgeois revolution. So in 1801 he signed the French concordat with Pius VII. In this agreement Roman Catholicism was recognized as "the religion of the great majority of the French people." The concordat marked the end of revolutionary cults, provided salaries for Catholic clergy, and gave the pope the right to remove bishops—something that would never have been acceptable to aristocratic clerical and lay elites of the Old Regime. (On his own, however, Napoleon added to the concordat the Organic Articles, which restated contentious Gallican claims.) The resulting expanded authority of the pope in naming local bishops, as well as the state-salaried clergy's desire for an outside ally, contributed further to the developing movement of ultramontanism.[20]

The French concordat was negotiated for Pius VII by his cardinal secretary of state, Ercole Consalvi. Both Pius and Consalvi were clearly conservatives but not rigid ones. Consalvi, from a noble Roman family, might be considered the architect of the modern Catholic Church's overall strategy for negotiation by concordats with modern liberal nation-states. But he would never compromise in essentials, and Napoleon came to despise him. Pius VII, also a noble by birth, and by training a lawyer and so accustomed to negotiation, had earlier revealed his own compromising spirit. In a famous 1897 sermon preached while he was still Bishop of Imola, he tentatively supported democracy and even cited favorably the teachings of Rousseau.[21]

Toward the Modern Papacy

The French-papal concordat became a model for church-state relations in the new liberal society, and such concordats soon constituted a strategic plank in the modern papal paradigm. This model placed the pope rather than local bishops as the main church negotiator with national governments. It also gave a central role for ecclesial policy to the expanding papal diplomatic corps and to the expanding papal bureaucracy. Before the revolution, the main role of the papal bureaucracy had been administration of the Papal States.

Implicitly, this new model treated the papacy as itself a negotiating nation-state, in contrast to the medieval understanding of the papacy as a supra-imperial authority. Hence, even while reacting to the rise of modern liberalism, the papacy was at the same time imitating the modern states' style of sovereign nationalism and centralizing bureaucracy.

When proclaimed emperor in 1804, Napoleon invited the pope to crown him, though he then upstaged the pope by crowning himself. (During the long journey from Rome to France, the pope received huge outpourings of popular warmth—a phenomenon the ultramontanists carefully noted.) The title of emperor, however, no longer referred to the ancient Holy Roman Empire, but rather to modern imperialism. In 1806, two years later, Francis II, emperor of Austria, formally declared the end of Christendom. Long since dead, it was finally given a public funeral.[22]

In 1806, because Pius VII refused to become in effect an agent of the French emperor, Napoleon again occupied Rome and made the Papal States part of the French Empire. The pope retaliated by excommunicating the emperor, and pro-papal ultramontanist popular sentiments grew stronger. The pope was then taken to France for five years of imprisonment.

Finally Napoleon was defeated, first when Paris was occupied in 1814 and then for the last time in 1815 at Waterloo.[23] The revolutionary phase had ended, and the attempt at restoration was about to begin.

The Restoration:
The Congress of Vienna and Counterrevolution

After the defeat of Napoleon, Austria became the dominant European power. Gathering the other major European powers at the

Congress of Vienna, Austria's Prince Metternich forcibly began the restoration of the ancien régime by establishing the Bourbon monarchy in France. Metternich also supported the Russian czar's Holy Alliance of Austria, Prussia, and Russia, but his real instrument of restoration was the Quadruple Alliance, including Great Britain. For more than a decade he presided firmly over a continent-wide restoration of political absolutism, suppression of liberal nationalism, and preservation of the status quo. Central to his work was the creation of a vast network of spies and police agents.[24]

The Revolutions of 1830

Around 1830 a wave of liberal revolutions challenged the restoration of the ancien régime. In France, the *grande bourgeoisie* financed a revolt against the ultra-reactionary Bourbon king, Charles X, who then fled. The new king, Louis Philippe, established a bourgeois constitutional monarchy. In 1831 Belgian Catholics allied with liberals to revolt from the Dutch and declared their independence. In 1829 Catholics in Ireland secured political emancipation. In 1832 Britain's Reform Act represented an accomplishment similar to the French July Revolution of 1830. Also, civil war broke out between liberals and clericalists in Portugal and Spain. Even in the United States, Jacksonian democracy defeated propertied oligarchs. There were also revolts against the pope in his own Papal States, and against the Hapsburgs in Parma and Modena, though Metternich successfully crushed all these. Similarly, a Polish revolt was put down by the czar.[25] Writing especially of Britain, France, and Belgium, Eric Hobsbawm noted:

> The revolutionary wave of 1830…marks the definitive defeat of aristocratic by bourgeois power in Western Europe. The ruling class of the next fifty years was to be the "grande bourgeoisie" of bankers, big industrialists, and sometimes top civil servants, accepted by an aristocracy which effaced itself or agreed to promote primarily bourgeois policies, unchallenged as yet by universal suffrage.[26]

But Metternich's restoration still held in the Austrian Empire and in the Papal States. Again, Hobsbawm noted:

> The revolutions split Europe into two major regions. West of the Rhine they broke the hold of the united reactionary powers for good. Moderate liberalism triumphed in France, Britain, and Belgium...The Holy Alliance could no longer intervene in these regions, as it still did elsewhere east of the Rhine...East of the Rhine the situation remained superficially as before 1830, for all the revolutions were suppressed.[27]

In the wake of this wave of revolt, a split also began to grow between moderate liberals, who represented the expanding middle classes, and proletarian-oriented socialists. These two groups had previously formed a common front against the aristocratic power of the Old Regime. In the new bourgeois context, however, the socialist movement began to threaten the new liberal powers. But the full impact of that split would not be felt until the revolutions of 1848.[28]

Debate over Papal Strategy

During the restoration Pope Pius VII officially had claimed neutrality before both the Congress of Vienna and the Holy Alliance, but his reappointed secretary of state, Cardinal Consalvi, had been an active participant in the congress. At the congress, as noted, Consalvi had negotiated a new series of national concordats that furthered the modern relationship between the papacy and nation-states, and in turn strengthened the papacy's control over local episcopacies. Consalvi had also begun there his successful campaign for the restoration of papal rule over the Papal States.[29]

Apart from the Papal States, the economic gains of Catholic elites from the restoration remained limited. In France, most feudal ecclesial privileges were gone forever, and most secularized church property was never returned. But the Catholic Church had been restored to a position of public religious authority, and this made possible the beginning of an official "re-Christianization" of French society.[30]

Amid all this upheaval, the papal bureaucracy was divided over the best tactics for restoration. On the center-left side were the "politicians" like Pius VII and Consalvi, who preferred to seek restoration through diplomatic compromise with the reigning powers. Those of this group were also sometimes called liberals. They kept an open mind toward many aspects of modernity, provided these did not threaten Catholic faith.

On the center-right side were the "zealots" (*zealoti*), who constituted the majority of the cardinals and opposed all compromise with modernity. Initially the zealots favored absolute authority, the uncontested establishment of Catholicism as the official religion, and total independence of the church's mission from any government influence. They wished to rely more on force than persuasion. Their top priority was cultural-pastoral, that is, to protect the Catholic people from contamination by modern liberal principles. They saw modern liberalism with its religious tolerance as part of a slippery slope that began with the Reformation and would lead to atheism. Rather than looking to the concordats of papal diplomacy, they turned to the religious orders with their modern psychological devotionalism and modern professional missions.[31]

Though continuing its opposition to liberalism and ecclesial compromise, the *zealoti* split in two, with the younger wing adopting certain modern tactics. Aubert summarizes this new orientation:

> The adherents of the second position, involved as they were with the beginnings of the new ultramontane movement, did not hesitate to recommend the employment of some modern methods for the realization of their ideal. Disappointed by the insistent jurisdictionalism of the courts, and out of their knowledge of the support the masses had given the Church in its struggle against Napoleon, they favored an active Christian policy for regaining lost ground. Their plan would include a popular base and would make more use of the press and of lay organizations than of the powers of the police in addressing consciences directly and inculcating true principles as a foundation for the restoration of a society in the Christian spirit.[32]

Apart from this twofold tendency within the zealot party, the wider debate in the Western European church was between nationalists on one side and ultramontanists on the other side. The former sought to maintain traditional limits on papal control over the local churches and supported significant concessions for national state control over the local church. The latter rallied around the papacy against national state power encroaching on the church. As liberal nationalism became increasingly anti-Catholic, the ultramontanists gained the upper hand over papal strategy.[33]

Three Strains of Ultramontanism

Ultramontanism was not a static or monolithic movement. Rather, it evolved into three divergent tendencies.

The Conservative Traditionalist Strain. The first strain, described as traditionalist and typified by the writings of the French Count Joseph de Maistre, was firmly allied with the aristocratic counterrevolution. Regarding the French Revolution as a Satanic work, de Maistre in his famous 1819 work, *The Pope*, portrayed the papacy as the supreme guardian of civilization.

All political authority in Europe, de Maistre claimed, as well as the European vitality of the arts and sciences, and even of authentic liberty, depended on the supreme authority of the pope. De Maistre challenged schismatic Christians who broke with the pope by arguing that they would quickly fall into Protestantism and from there into philosophical indifferentism. He differed from other traditionalist French Catholics like Louis Gabriel Ambroise and Viscomte Louis de Bonald, who tended to be Gallican and to resist papal encroachment on the local episcopal authorities of the Old Regime. But like de Bonald and other traditionalists, he fought to restore the Bourbons and the alliance of throne and altar. Though Roman theologians eventually condemned de Maistre's position, it was attractive to the older wing of the Roman bureaucracy's zealot party.[34]

The Progressive Liberal Strain. The second ultramontanist tendency represented the first European expression of liberal Catholicism and came to be epitomized in the voice of the popular French diocesan priest Hugo Félicité Robert Lamennais.[35] A militant ultramontanist, Lamennais at first espoused the traditionalist version of ultramontanism and stressed the conservative theme that religion was essential for the stability and vitality of society. Emphasizing Catholicism's Roman center, he insisted that Catholicism was the true religion and hence the true guardian of society. He further accused Gallicanism of introducing democratic principles into the church. Like de Maistre, he argued that the Reformation had prepared the way for deism, which in turn had prepared the way for religious indifferentism, atheism, and for a fundamental attack on human nature. This early Lamennais gained a broad following among the younger clergy in their tensions with the largely Gallican older clergy, including much of the episcopacy.

But, as the attempt of the French government to take over the church intensified, Lamennais shifted his perspective and became the leading exponent for a new liberal or democratic form of ultramontanism. Influenced this time by the American experience, he began to argue fervently for separation of church and state and for constitutional liberties for all religions. Originally a monarchist, Lamennais now switched sides to equate monarchies with tyranny and oppression. Realizing that the fall of the Bourbons was inevitable, he then sought to replace the traditionalist alliance of throne and altar with a progressive liberal alliance of church and democracy. As he predicted, the Bourbon monarchy fell in the revolution of 1830.

Together with the Dominican priest Jean-Baptiste Henri Lacordaire and the layman Comte Charles de Montalembert, Lamennais promoted liberal ultramontanist ideas in the journal L'Avenir, a liberal Catholic alternative to the traditionalist publication L'Ami de la Religion et du Roi. In this new alliance Lamennais saw a major role for the pope as a vital transnational voice above the anarchy of nations. Naively he hoped that the pope would become a supranational champion of democracy. In reality, the pope was one of the last Western European aristocratic kings and was desperately attempting to suppress democratic insurrections in his own Papal States.

After a visit to Rome and a direct appeal to the pope, Lamennais found his ideas condemned by Pope Gregory XVI in the 1832 encyclical Mirari vos. Though the condemnation was to be expected and did not mention him by name, Lamennais was shocked and began to drift away from Catholicism. His subsequent confessional book, *Paroles d'un croyant* (drawing on the work of the revolutionary Polish poet Mickiewicz), was condemned by Gregory in yet another encyclical, this time one explicitly referring to Lamennais and to his book. Soon thereafter he moved still further leftward to the newly emerging socialist camp. Sadly, this visionary pioneer of liberal and Social Catholicism never found a real home with the secular left. Instead, he became a tragic and lost figure.[36]

The Bureaucratic Institutional Strain. The third version of ultramontanism, and the one that came to dominate, was neither traditionalist nor liberal but institutional. Promoted especially by the younger wing of the zealot party in the papal bureaucracy, it sought to build a strong populist base for pastoral support of the pope and to strengthen the control of the papacy over the rest of the church. In the long run this institutional variant would control the new stance of papal strategy.[37]

Other Strategic Currents

Liberal Catholicism. At the same time that ultramontanism was taking shape, liberal Catholicism became a notable current of Catholic thought, though with its own diverging streams and by no means all ultramontanist.[38] Perhaps the most significant expression was the non-ultramontanist Americanist variant in the young church once led by John Carroll, democratically elected by his priests as America's first Catholic bishop. Americanist Catholics unquestionably accepted liberal democracy and separation of church and state. Lamennais, influenced by the distant American experience, had led the French parallel.

Strong liberal Catholic movements, calling for both independence and democracy, also arose in Poland and Ireland, as well as in Belgium. These movements emerged in countries where the non-Catholic component was a foreign oppressor: English for Ireland, Russian for Poland, and Dutch for Belgium. In these three cases, revolutionary liberal ideas served popular Catholic interests. In the Irish and Polish cases, however, the papacy condemned the Catholic movements for independence. In the Belgian case, perhaps because of the diplomatic skill of the Belgian bishops, that did not happen.

Thus a beachhead for liberal Catholicism was first established in Belgium, particularly with the foundation of the Catholic University of Louvain.[39]

Social Catholicism. A third strategic strain, distinct from both ultramontanism and liberal Catholicism, was Social Catholicism, although Lamennais was also a pioneer of this movement.[40] This was the seminal Catholic expression of concern with the social question of the new industrial working class. (Social Catholicism will be discussed more extensively in the next chapter, particularly its German version.)

In the first half of the nineteenth century the growth of Social Catholicism was limited, since industrial penetration of the core Catholic countries was itself limited. Aubert comments about the Europe of 1815:

> Of the 100 million Catholics, more than 60 percent lived in three countries relatively untouched by the Industrial Revolution and in which the clergy, in spite of the increasing importance of urbanization, continued to reflect mainly the values of their agrarian congregations.[41]

Catholic Romanticism. A final stream in the background of all these currents was Catholic Romanticism. Reacting to the mechanistic and utilitarian biases of liberal rationalism, this alternative vision stressed aesthetics and an organic sense of ecological and social community. For romantics, religion played a key role. Traditionalist Catholicism, liberal Catholicism, and Social Catholicism were all in varying degrees influenced by the anti-mechanistic protest of Romanticism.[42]

Summary of the Period

To summarize, in this period papal policy came to support ultramontanism and eventually only its institutional strain, but not liberal Catholicism nor Social Catholicism. As the old aristocratic order faded and the new bourgeois order emerged, Catholic ecclesial elites gradually lost their powerful public role in society, though the popes still clung to the Papal States until well into the second half of the century. But already a new model of the papacy was beginning to appear, a modern model created by both the "politician" and "zealot" wings of the papal bureaucracy and stressing Roman centralization, Vatican diplomatic negotiation with nation-states, modern devotionalism, and carefully controlled lay mobilization.

From the center-left papal "politicians" party, which stressed the ecclesial institution's instrumental power, there came the externally oriented diplomatic policy of concordats, giving the Catholic Church a new legal status in increasingly liberalized societies.[43] In these concordats, Rome rather than local bishops represented the church to local governments.

From the second generation of center-right "zealots" party, which stressed the ecclesial institution's expressive power, there came the new internally oriented pastoral wave of populist spiritual renewal, emphasizing the person of the pope and allied with countless new religious congregations directed to apostolic and missionary works.[44] In turn, both the politicians and the zealots supported the modernization and expansion of the papal bureaucracy.

The Defeat:
Revolutions of 1848 and Loss of the Papal States

In 1846 the cardinals elected as pope Giovanni Maria Mastai-Ferretti, a compromise between the zealots' and politicians' candidates. He took the name Pius IX in memory of the earlier Pius who had been imprisoned by Napoleon, yet who also as Bishop of Imola had preached a 1797 sermon in favor of the compatibility of democracy and Christianity. During his student days in Rome, Mastai-Ferretti had become a friend of Pius VII, and like him became the Bishop of Imola. While a bishop, he had criticized the harsh clerical administration of the Papal States and was known to be a fervent reader of liberal publications.[45]

A Liberal Pope?

Upon the election of Pio Nono (his Italian name, which became popular with English commentators), there was a strong feeling that a liberal had become pope. The early lay leader and

Christian democrat Frédérick Ozanam believed that the new pope was "truly sent by God to accomplish the main business of the nineteenth century—the alliance of religion and liberty."[46] Reportedly, the pope even sent a message to the alienated Lamennais that he waited to embrace him. In reality, however, Pio Nono was not a liberal but an enlightened and compassionate conservative.[47]

Right after his election, it seemed that Pio Nono was about to lead a nationalistic movement of Italian unification and constitutional democracy, and even to become king of Italy. The pope released by amnesty thousands of prisoners from papal jails. He also welcomed home hundreds of banned exiles. In addition, he supported technological and political reforms for the backward Papal States. He established a commission for railroads, planned gas lighting, and placed laymen in the papal government. Further, he set up a consultative assembly for governance of the Papal States and enacted a customs union with Tuscany and Piedmont. He even forced Metternich to withdraw Austrian troops from the northern section of the Papal States. The pope immediately became an Italian hero.[48]

But Pio Nono was caught in a double contradiction. First, though sympathetic to the movement of Italian nationalism, he could not allow himself to become king of Italy; he would then inevitably be placed in military conflict with other Catholic powers of Europe. That would undermine his universal spiritual power as pope and perhaps also drive his enemies into the Protestant fold.[49] Second, though wishing to bless the democratic reforms sweeping the Western European world, he also thought it indispensable for his papal spiritual leadership to maintain his own temporal power as king of the Papal States.[50]

Perceiving these contradictions, the shrewd Metternich described this pope as "warm of heart and weak of intellect." He predicted that Pio Nono would soon be forced out of Rome.[51] With the revolutions of 1848, Metternich's prophecy came true.

After Metternich himself was forced to flee from Vienna, Italian nationalists rallied to drive the Austrians out of Italy. But Pio Nono refused to turn his troops against the Austrians, since they were fellow Catholics. Instead, he repudiated the Italian *Risorgimento*.

The pope's popularity immediately vanished, and "the Roman Question" came quickly to the fore.[52]

The Roman Question referred to the fact that, if the pope continued to cling to his sovereign power over the middle belt of Italy, there could be no unified Italian nation. (France and Austria well understood this reality and so supported the Papal States to prevent the emergence of a unified Italian nation.) In the words of Derek Holmes, "If the Pope's role as an Italian secular ruler was incompatible with his spiritual office, should he not be expected to surrender his temporal power since this was harming the Italian nation as a whole?"[53]

After defeat by Austria, the Italian nationalists gathered in Rome against the pope. The pope's lay prime minister, Count Alessandro Rossi, was assassinated. Revolution broke out, and the papal cabinet resigned. In disguise, Pio Nono fled south to exile in Gaeta within the Kingdom of Naples. With the pope overthrown, anticlerical republicans from all over Italy set up another Roman Republic.[54] Similar revolutions erupted across Europe.

Following Pius IX's flight to Gaeta, an "international brigade" of radicals merged in Rome. These included the initial group of Italian nationalists led by Mazzini, some of Garibaldi's followers from the south, and even a legion of Polish revolutionaries. But their model of liberty was hardly democratic. Mazzini, seeing himself as a Rousseau-like expression of "the people," became an even more autocratic ruler than the pope he had driven out. Neither did Mazzini's model of liberty support separation of church and state. Rather, he ridiculed this "English concept" and instead proclaimed a new civic religion of "God and the people," with God understood as Condorcet's "Progress and Humanity."[55]

From Gaeta, Pio Nono issued a statement condemning the idea that the church would benefit from the loss of its temporal power. He also repudiated the revolution and all ideas of liberalizing his regime.

In 1849, with Austrian troops reestablishing papal authority in the north, French troops occupied the city of Rome for the pope. The following year Pio Nono took up again his temporal power as king of the Papal States. He now supported antidemocratic ultramontanists like Louis Veuillot in France. He also made the new journal *Civiltà*

Cattolica, founded by the Neapolitan Jesuit Carlo Curci, into an important ultramontanist vehicle. Further, in 1860 Pio Nono encouraged the founding of a special newspaper within the papal bureaucracy, *Osservatore Romano*, in order to connect the pope personally with Catholics all over the world. From this point, according to Aubert, the pope came under the strong influence of the Jesuits, with their "systematic plan" for an ultramontanist strategy.[56]

The Threat of Socialism

Yet in France, in surprising contrast to the Italian experience, a Christian socialist coalition suddenly appeared, as many radicals became enthusiastically pro-Christian.[57] The European socialist movement was becoming a major carrier of the call for economic reform and for expansion of democracy to the workers. Lamennais's "social Christianity," as well as the writings of socialist convert to Catholicism Philippe Buchez, had apparently influenced a whole generation of formerly anticlerical workers and radicals. In 1849 a group of French socialist priests even held a banquet in Paris to celebrate Jesus as "the father of socialism." Their socialism was, of course, pre-Marxian and vague in its practical meaning.[58]

The French Catholic enthusiasm for socialism was shattered when a violent proletarian revolution broke out in Paris. Attempting to mediate between the opposing sides, the Archbishop of Paris was shot—though apparently not by the workers, whose cause he had taken up, for they sincerely mourned his loss. The surviving French bishops denounced the uprising as the work of socialist agitators. Quickly a conservative bourgeois coup d'etat was organized, Louis Napoleon became the head of the Second Empire, and the threatened social classes of the bourgeoisie (even its anticlerical wing), the property-owning peasantry, and the nobility all rallied to the church in the name of order.[59]

For the first time European Catholic ecclesial elites clearly distinguished the modern socialist movement from the wider liberal movement within which it had formerly lived. The monthly review of the Italian Jesuits, *Civiltà Cattolica*, founded in 1850 under Pius IX's patronage, gave a great deal of attention to this new phenomenon of socialism. As early as the 1850s, it was writing about Saint-Simon, Fourier, Babeuf, and Prouhon.[60]

Although some in the small French social-Catholic movement continued to embrace socialism, the French church at large became militantly anti-socialist. In the same vein, the bourgeois struggle, formerly focused on overthrowing the old aristocracy, found a new and different enemy in the new socialists. The earlier bourgeois battle against the reactionary aristocracy defending the Old Regime yielded to a bourgeois battle against radical socialists organizing proletarian workers.

In reaction to the acute socialist threat, the Catholic Church and the bourgeoisie in France formed a strong alliance. Soon the church was given a major hand in French education (attractive to the expanding middle classes), and state financing of the church increased. The pope congratulated Napoleon for his suppression of dissent, and the numbers of French priests and religious grew dramatically.

In addition, over time a new kind of bishop became the norm—no longer born of the aristocracy but rather from the expanding middle classes or the property-owning peasantry.

Also, the small movement of liberal Catholicism became divided. While some liberal Catholics like Frédérick Ozanam continued to insist on the social question of the workers, others like Montalembert, and even to some degree the Dominican Lacordaire, insulated their political liberalism from calls for economic justice.[61]

Under Pius IX the papacy became acutely aware of the threats of socialism and communism. But in Italy this awareness did not yet translate into a strategic papal alliance with the bourgeoisie against the socialists, as had happened in France. For the Italian bourgeoisie, centered in Piedmont in the north, had yet to destroy the political power of the Italian clerical aristocracy in the Papal States. Thus in Italy proponents of laissez-faire capitalism and radical socialists still joined hands as fellow anticlericalists. As a result, at least for the papacy, the revolutionary mix of liberals and socialists continued to appear as a single threatening stew, with the emergence of the socialists only heightening the overall sense of liberal danger.

The Papacy in Retreat

When Count Camillo Benso Cavour came to political power in Piedmont (the center of early Italian industrialization and the controlling center in the drive for the national unification of Italy), he mounted a relentless attack against contemplative Catholic religious orders and against Catholic holy days, all in the name of industrial efficiency. Like Mazzini, Cavour identified modern progress with anti-Catholicism, but now with clearly capitalist economic motives. The Catholic contemplative orders controlled large capital pools and vast agricultural landholdings, all jealously eyed by the rising bourgeois class. (By contrast, the more modern apostolic religious orders, whose mission focused on professional social ministries of health and education and which often possessed little wealth, were usually not challenged.) Further, spiritual contemplation, so irritating to industrial capitalism's utilitarian efficiency, seemed like a terrible cultural obstacle to economic modernization. And last, heir to a decidedly non-utilitarian spirit, the Catholic Church had established a vast system of work-free holy days, plus wide-ranging economic support for the poor, thus undermining industrial capitalism's free market of labor.[62]

The situation was further compounded by conflicting military ambitions among the Catholic powers of France, Austria, and Piedmont. By the end of 1860 the pope had lost control over his northern lands in Umbria, the Marches, and the Legations. To defend the remaining papal territories, he encouraged the formation of a papal army made up of volunteers from all over Catholic Europe. But by now Cavour was extending the liberal revolution and anticlerical legislation to all of Italy. Before long the pope was isolated in Rome, protected only by a small French garrison. In this difficult context, close to the end of the Papal States, the papacy became an island fortress of clerical aristocracy threatened by a rising sea of modern secularizing bourgeois liberalism, followed by an even more frightening socialist wave.[63]

With nowhere to turn, Pio Nono led the reactive Catholic conservative strategy into a psychological withdrawal from the modern liberal European world. From this withdrawal, modern liberal society was perceived only in negative terms. In no way could it become the foundation for evangelization. Just the opposite. In the pope's analysis, the defense of the church vitally depended on resisting liberalism to the last. Holmes's words summarize well this strategic retreat.

> The Pope and the Ultramontanists...came to believe that there was an absolute dichotomy between Catholicism and the contemporary world, and they actually encouraged a Catholic withdrawal from modern society as well as modern thought. In 1850 the Roman clergy were ordered to wear the cassock instead of breeches and frock coat in order to distinguish the clergy more clearly from the "men of the age, infected with liberal principles." Donoso Cortes, one of the leading Spanish Ultramontanists, identified Catholicism with absolute good and modern civilization with absolute evil, while the pope himself, as Wilfred Ward remarked, "took up the position that Christendom had apostatized. The appropriate action of Catholics was intense loyalty to the central power, unity among themselves, and separation from the outside world."[64]

The Ultramontanist Triumph

As anti-worldly ultramontanism became the all-embracing papal strategy, the Western Catholic Church was pressured by Vatican officials to become ever more Roman.[65] Just as the Vatican bureaucracy had gained control over the episcopacy, so now it sought a standardized Roman model for all of Western Catholicism. The papal bureaucracy promoted a standardized Roman liturgy in the name of liturgical reform and the training of future bishops in Roman seminaries. It also promoted Roman devotions like Forty Hours, Roman clerical dress, expansion of Roman colleges for foreign seminarians, and extensive granting among priests of the Roman clerical title *monsignor* (an honorary aristocratic appellation meaning "my lord," a title normally used at the time for aristocrats, including aristocratic bishops).

During his pontificate Pius IX appointed more *monsignori* than all the popes of the prior two centuries. More important, because of the unusual length of his term, he personally appointed practically every Catholic bishop in the world. This allowed him to tailor the international episcopacy according to ultramontanist criteria, increasingly including seminary formation in a Roman college. In addition, he revived on a global scale the ancient local practice of periodic personal *ad limina* visits by bishops to the pope. At the same time, the papal bureaucracy became less a place for political administrators of the papal territories, and more the home of theologians and church lawyers administering the international church. In addition, he reduced the role of the cardinalate, expanded the role of diplomatic nuncios, and generally supported religious priests in fights with local bishops.[66]

The institutional ultramontanist strategy also supported modern devotions and dramatic canonization of saints. Reflecting a still strong antidemocratic spirit within ultramontanism, it promoted a cult of the Sacred Heart as both a monarchist and pro-Roman symbol. In 1854 the pope defined the dogma of the Immaculate Conception. The papacy also supported popular devotions centered on reported Marian apparitions to Catherine Labouré in 1830, to children at LaSalette in 1846, and to Bernadette Soubirous at Lourdes in 1858. By contrast, liberal Catholic congresses held in 1863 at Malines and Munich received only negative reaction from the pope, including a formal condemnation of Montalembert.[67]

Finally, in 1864 came the most dramatic event of Pio Nono's intriguing papacy, the publishing of the Syllabus of Errors appended to his encyclical *Quanta cura*.[68] The Syllabus condemned all the "errors of the modern age" and set the pope officially against liberalism, progress, and modern civilization.

Many have argued that the papal condemnations need to be read in the light of the virulently anticlerical and even anti-Catholic peculiarities of the Italian liberalism of the time. But since the encyclical was addressed to the bishops of the whole world, the opposite seemed the case. Following a line of policy laid out for him by the Jesuits of *Civiltà Cattolica*, the pope had read the world-historical movement of liberalism through the narrow lenses of his provincial Italian experience. Seeing the old Roman world crumbling under his feet, facing Bismarck's *Kulturkampf* against the German Catholic Church, and shocked by the 1871 Paris

Commune, it must have seemed to him that Catholicism was truly under siege by the entire modern world.[69]

To respond to the new situation, in 1869, on the feast of the Immaculate Conception, Pio Nono formally convened Vatican Council I, the first ecumenical council held since the Council of Trent.[70] Signaling the new de facto separation of church and state, heads of Catholic governments were not invited to attend—for the first time since the ancient Constantinean marriage of church and empire.

For Vatican Council I the strategic threat was no longer the Protestant theologians of the Reformation, but rather the rationalists, pantheists, and deists of the modern Enlightenment. Thus, whereas the Council of Trent had attempted to defend the Catholic interpretation of Christian truths against the Reformer's heretical but still Christian interpretations, this council was defending the very foundations of Christianity itself. For this reason the council's schema *Dei Filius* sought to uphold the supernatural character of the Christian faith, and its schema *de Ecclesia* attempted to defend the hierarchical structure of the church and its relationship to society.

While the Franco-Prussian war prevented the council from getting to the issue of the papacy's "temporal power" (the Papal States), the bishops dramatically approved the doctrine of papal infallibility. Overall, the First Vatican Council brought to fulfillment all the efforts of the ultramontanists to create a viable defensive papal strategy in response to the modern continental liberal attack.

During this same time, since France (preoccupied over war with Prussia) could no longer spare troops to defend Rome, Pio Nono suddenly found himself at the mercy of the Piedmontese, and all the more so following France's defeat. In 1870, on September 20, after only a token resistance by papal forces, Pio Nono ordered a white flag raised, and Victor Emmanuel's military occupied Rome. The thousand-year-old temporal power of the papacy came to a mute end. In an act symbolic of the new strategic phase, the pope refused to flee and instead retreated within to become the voluntary "prisoner of the Vatican."

According to David Kertzer, a factor undermining Pius IX's appeal to popular support for the Papal States was the case of his abducting a six-year-old Jewish boy, Edgardo Mortara, from his parents in Bologna's Jewish ghetto. Reportedly without his parents' permission or knowledge, the boy had been baptized by an illiterate Catholic maid when he was gravely ill. The pope insisted that, under the laws of the Papal States, the boy had to be raised a Catholic. He had papal guards take him by force from his parents, brought to Rome to be raised a Catholic, and even legally adopted him as his own son. The case became infamous across Europe. The boy later became a Catholic priest.[71] Ironically, during his initial openness after becoming pope, Pius IX had ordered the walls of the Jewish ghettos in the Papal States torn down. After the revolutions of 1848, however, he had them rebuilt. Still worse, according to David Kertzer, who wrote the scholarly study of the kidnapping of the Jewish boy, Pius IX and his antiliberal Catholic allies instituted many strongly anti-Semitic measures that would later become part of Hitler's anti-Semitic reign of terror.[72]

In November the new Italian government passed its Laws of Guarantees to regulate Italy's relations with the papacy. These would continue until the 1929 Lateran Treaty. But the pope refused to participate in negotiating these laws. Paradoxically, he had established his own defiant separation of church and state. In a similar vein he forbade Italian Catholics to participate in Italian politics, either as voters or as candidates. A few years later, in 1878, Pius IX died.[73]

An Appraisal of Pius IX

In Hales's appraisal, Pio Nono was a tragic but prophetic leader. Though caught in a dying aristocratic vision, he defended the Catholic Church against the ambitious nationalism of the continental liberal state, which had sought to destroy Catholicism or else to reduce it to a government department, and against the corrosive rationalism and individualism of the modern Enlightenment. While today his condemnations of modern civilization seem clearly reactionary, and indeed they were, paradoxically they were also visionary. As Hales points out:

> Few thoughtful men, in 1900, thought he had been right. It was necessary to find excuses for the Syllabus—better, even, to forget it. But we, today, who have met the

children and grandchildren of European Liberalism and
the Revolution, who have seen Mazzini turn into
Mussolini, Herder into Hitler, and the idealistic socialists
into the intransigent communists, are able from a new
vantage ground to consider once more whether Pio
Nono, or the optimistic believers in an infallible
progress...will have, in the eyes of eternity, the better of
the argument.[74]

Despite his often vitriolic rhetoric, Pio Nono in person reportedly never lost his disarming and charming sense of humor and
compassion. For example, in a surprising expression of love for the
anticlerical Italian revolutionary Garibaldi, the pope once
remarked, "If you see Garibaldi, tell him that I know he curses me
daily; but that I always bless him." And once he so won over
Garibaldi's troops imprisoned in his own jails that they wept and
kissed his hands.[75]

Also, the more Pio Nono retreated before his enemies on his
premodern aristocratic political ground, the stronger he grew on
modern populist spiritual ground. Supported by his leadership,
Catholic devotional inwardness and missionary outreach expanded
throughout the world, and with them a powerful spiritual renewal
spread across Catholic Christianity.

But tragically this modern Catholic spirituality of psychological
interiority, and the wider modern ultramontanist strategy of which it
was part, isolated itself from awareness of the societal and ecological
dimensions of God's creative presence in history. In particular, as
Catholicism compensated for its decline in Western Europe by vast
missionary outreach, particularly to Africa, there was little prophetic
awareness that the Catholic Church was working in an oppressive
alliance with the incredible social and ecological exploitation of
modern industrial-capitalist colonialism.

Further, the pope and his ultramontanist supporters remained
silent on the economic sufferings of the European industrial proletariat. As a bishop, Mastai-Ferretti had read widely on the labor question and had showed himself sympathetic to the plight of industrial
workers. But as pope he had seen only socialist agitation. Perhaps for
this reason, the ultramontanist strategy did not have much success

among the males of new working classes of Latin Europe, and the secular socialist movement quickly filled the void.

The ultramontanist strategy did work, however, among workers in the English-speaking industrial world. There the Catholic Church was almost exclusively working class and its bishops, drawn themselves largely from the working class, consistently supported Catholic industrial workers in the face of exploitation by largely Protestant employers. Further, across the English-speaking world, Pius IX fostered a new Irish missionary model (repeating the ancient Irish missions from the "dark ages') to the expanding immigrant populations of English-speaking industrial capitalism, namely, the British Isles, North America, Australia, and New Zealand. The Irish hierarchy, the British government, and the papal bureaucracy had all worked together to promote this new model of industrial evangelization and to mute the revolutionary spirit back in Ireland.[76]

Again, the Irish tactic worked because the Irish Catholic Church, from which these missionaries came, had not been marked by any strong class divisions (most everyone was poor and oppressed by the British)—so markedly different from the bitter class struggle that surrounded the Catholic continental churches of Western Europe. In Ireland the oppressive aristocracy was largely foreign and Protestant, while the oppressed peasantry was almost totally Catholic.[77]

Would history have been different in Latin Europe had Pio Nono spoken out early against the social injustices of industrial capitalism? In France, when Lamennais and Buchez had linked the Gospel of Jesus with the cause of poor and exploited labor, French workers had responded enthusiastically. But Lamennais and Buchez were condemned, and the young movement of Social Catholicism received no papal support.

So Pio Nono, despite his spiritual triumph, must also carry the burden of what has been called "the loss of the working class," at least of males in major sectors of the Latin countries of continental Europe. Hales, though sympathetic to Pius IX, judged that this pope "cannot be acquitted of some responsibility for what was the greatest tragedy of his pontificate; namely the failure of the Church, as a whole, to win the affection and respect of the new proletariat in the rapidly growing towns."[78]

With the death of Pius IX, the classical aristocratic strategy for Catholic evangelization came to its end, and a new strategy, germinating within the ultramontanist movement, was waiting to be born through positive engagement with the modern liberal world. The reactive tactics of both the zealots' and politicians' parties had paradoxically brought Catholicism into the modern world, and the transition to a truly modern model of the papacy was ready to be completed. The new modern papal strategy would blossom only with the next pope, Leo XIII.

But before exploring the Leonine strategy, let us first examine the encyclical letters of the pre-Leonine strategy.

3

The Pre-Leonine Encyclicals from Benedict XIV to Pius IX

From Defense of the Ancien Régime to the Triumph of Ultramontanism

---

In the language of Michael Schuck, the premodern encyclicals of industrial capitalism's local stage may be described as pre-Leonine, that is, as prior to the adaptive strategy set by Leo XIII (1878–1903). Issued partly in reaction to continental liberal attacks on the political and cultural terrain, these documents fall mainly into the three main phases analyzed in the preceding chapter, although there is also a small set of encyclicals that offer a pre-revolutionary response to the modern European Enlightenment. Following the pre-revolutionary documents, the three main sets of texts may be described as follows.

- *Encyclicals of the Revolution.* These encyclicals addressed the initial shock of the French Revolution. They were marked by a wait-and-see attitude—hoping the Revolution was a local French storm soon to blow over.

- *Encyclicals of the Counterrevolution.* The next set largely supported the attempted restoration of the monarchies and aristocracy, that is, the antirevolutionary coalition of continental-wide forces attempting to reverse the revolution and to restore the ancien régime.

- *Encyclicals of Retreat.* Following the breakdown of the restoration, the last set of encyclicals signaled defeat of the papacy in its monarchical-aristocratic claims and the papacy's retreat to a countercultural religious ghetto, but they also planted the seeds for a modern spiritual model of the papacy.

The popes issuing encyclicals during this strategic period were, for the pre-revolutionary phase, Benedict XIV, Clement XIII, and Clement VIV; for the revolutionary phase, Pius VI and Pius VII; for the restoration phase, Leo XII, Pius VIII, and Gregory XVI; and for the retreat phase, Pius IX. Overall, their documents reflected a reactionary defense of premodern aristocratic Christian civilization, but they also planted seeds for foundational assumptions of modern Catholic social teaching.

Before examining the three main sets of documents, let us first review briefly the pre-revolutionary documents at the start of the genre of contemporary papal encyclicals.

Pre-revolutionary Encyclicals

Reflecting philosophical and theological responses to the Enlightenment on its own media terrain of print, these encyclicals showed no real evidence of strategic breakdown in either church or society. The texts largely encouraged implementation of the internal ecclesial reforms decreed at the Council of Trent, warned of serious but not acute dangers from the society, and addressed particular local problems of internal church life. They contained both positive and negative attitudes toward the print medium and showed growing concern about the surrounding culture.

Though not of great interest for contemporary Catholic social teaching, these documents are nonetheless historically important because they launch the contemporary papal encyclical tradition.

Encyclicals of Benedict XIV

Shortly before the Industrial Revolution the modern tradition of papal encyclicals began with a 1740 inaugural document of Benedict XIV (1740–58), formerly Prospero Lambertini.[1] During the nineteen years of his pontificate, this pope issued thirteen encyclicals.

Claudia Carlin notes that Benedict, whom she describes as a scholarly and pastoral figure, began the contemporary encyclical tradition on a positive note.

> Not satisfied with the mere condemnation of error, he began in the first years of his pontificate to issue encyclical letters in order to apply the doctrine of the Church to the problems of his age, fully aware of the need to integrate the divergent cultures of scientific and religious thought.[2]

Benedict's 1740 inaugural document, *Ubi primum*, issued to all the Catholic bishops of the world, repeated the calls for clerical reform from the Council of Trent, but also in the language of the new secular Enlightenment culture it called for the clergy themselves to be "enlightened."[3] It employed the pastoral metaphors of "lambs and sheep" and warned of dangers from "wolves," as well as of the need to "pluck…thorn bushes, prickles, and weeds" from "the Lord's field." But it did not specify what these dangers or bad growths actually were.[4]

Benedict's next encyclical, *Quanta curam*, issued in 1741 to all the bishops, was a brief document condemning selling religious masses for profit and warning clerics against avarice.[5]

Next *Nimiam licentiam* (1743), to the bishops of Poland, decried dissolution of marriages in Poland's church courts, condemned "hidden marriages," and required the presence at Catholic marriages of the pastor as witness as well as the pre-publication of nuptial banns.[6]

Two years later *Vix pervenit* (1745), to the bishops and clergy of Italy, addressed the themes of interest and usury by condemning any interest on loans given to help another in need but allowing interest on funds invested for business purposes or retirement.[7]

Magnae nobis (1748), again to the bishops of Poland, once more took up the theme of Christian marriage, this time complaining that the Polish bishops were granting dispensations reserved to the pope. It condemned Catholics marrying "heretics," except in cases of dispensations granted "for a reasonable cause" in "regions in which Catholics live together with heretics."[8]

Perigrinantes (1749), addressed to all the faithful, proclaimed a holy year for 1750 and invited "those who have left the church" to "return to the Unity of the Catholic faith." For the first time, in an apparent reference to the new cultural and economic liberalism, it also called for "a new kind of war" against "the license of thinking and acting," as well as against "cupidity for gain." Nonetheless, reflecting a positive attitude toward the modern communications revolution, this pope proudly concluded his document by noting that he had requested that the letter be "printed," so that it "may more easily reach all of the faithful." He assured readers that such printing would carry "the same authority which the present letter would have if shown and displayed."[9]

In the same year *Apostolica constitutio*, a rather long document addressed to all the bishops, called for pilgrimages to Rome and defended such pilgrimages against the criticism of "heretics." It also appealed to the Jubilee letters of the famous Trentine reforming bishop of Milan, Charles Borromeo. Further, it defended indulgences granted at the time of the Jubilee and pointed to the benefits of confession, including its defense by Cardinal Bellarmine.[10]

Of sadly negative note was one strongly anti-Semitic encyclical, *A quo primum* (1751), written by Benedict XIV to the bishops of Poland (interestingly, his third to the Polish episcopacy).[11] While condemning the killing of Jews by Polish Catholics, he nonetheless decried the increase of Jews within Poland. He also criticized Christians working in the service of Jews and argued that the reverse should be the case. He described Jews as destroying "the wealth and inheritance of Christians," forbade that Jews should live in the same cities with Christians, and called upon Christians not to do business with Jews. Apparently referring to Christian commerce with Jews, he ominously called upon the Polish bishops to "remove this stain from Poland."[12]

Of Benedict's five remaining encyclicals, the first, *Cum religiosi* (1754), promoted catechesis, while the second, *Quod provinciale* (1754), condemned the use of Islamic names by Christians in Albania.

The third, *Allatae sunt* (1755), addressed to missionaries in the "Orient," gave lengthy instructions on the Greek, Armenian, Syriac, and Coptic rites of the Catholic Church. But it imperialistically insisted that "the Latin rite should be preferred to all other rites." It also condemned the practice of women acting as altar servers.[13] The fourth, *Ex quo primum* (1756), also of great length and related to the preceding text, was addressed to Greek Rite Catholics.[14]

The last encyclical of Benedict XIV, *Ex Omnibus* (1756), to the bishops of France, dealt with the 1713 papal bull against Jansenism, *Unigenitus Dei Filius*. Calling for support of the political power of King Louis of France, it insisted that *viaticum* be denied to those who rejected the 1713 bull.[15]

Encyclicals of Clement XIII

Formerly Carlo della Torre Rezzonico, Clement XIII (1758–69), whom Claudia Carlin describes as a gentle pastoral figure who was deeply committed to the poor, served as pope during the time of the French Encyclopedists. He issued six encyclicals.

Clement XIII's inaugural document, *A quo die* (1758), to all the Catholic bishops of the world, warned of the gathering of an enemy waging war not simply against the church but against the "human race." His own strategic battle plan of response was to preserve the unity of church by removing "from the hearts of the faithful seeds of any kind of dissention." This was to be done by the bishops seeking peace, rejecting the desire for glory, and caring for the poor. He also stressed the importance of the Eucharist, catechesis, worthy priests, and the canons of the Council of Trent.[16] His next encyclical, *Cum primum* (1759), again addressed to all the bishops, condemned the desire for wealth among many clerics and even among some monks.[17]

The following document, *Appetente sacro* (1759), also to all the bishops, commended fasting, as well as prayer and almsgiving.[18] Then, with *In dominico agro* (1761), Clement positively stressed the importance of catechesis and the Roman Catechism (published according to a decree of the Council of Trent). He also negatively wrote of using "the sword of anathema" to cut "the poisonous bud of growing error."[19]

Another pre-revolutionary document, *Christianae reipublicae*, which Clement XIII issued in 1766, warned of the "contagious plague of books" that, drawing on "a detestable and insane freedom of thought," "pollute the pure waters of belief, and destroy the foundations of religion."[20] Noting the invasive power of the new medium, the document cried out:

> What desolation the plague of their books can cause! Well and cunningly written these books are always with us and forever within our reach. They travel with us, stay at home with us, and enter bedrooms which would be shut to their evil and deception.[21]

Faithful to the classical aristocratic strategy, Clement still assumed that Catholic princes would guard the church against this threat. Thus he wrote to the bishops concerning the princes: "Since they do not carry the sword without cause, urge them with the united authority of state and of priesthood, to vigorously rout those accursed men who fight against the armies of Israel."[22] Using the metaphor of a wall, Clement then summoned the bishops to defense of the traditional church: "It is principally your duty to stand as a wall so that no foundation can be laid other than the one that is already laid. Watch over the most holy deposit of faith."[23]

Clement XIII's final and brief encyclical, *Summa quae* (1768), supported the Polish bishops against what the pope described as "storms which sought to undermine religion." In this document he again portrayed the church's defense with the metaphor of a wall.[24]

Encyclicals of Clement XIV

Elected, according to Claudia Carlin, with the support of the Bourbons in order to suppress the Jesuits, Clement XIV (1769–74), formerly Giovanni Vincenzo Antonio Ganganelli, issued only four encyclicals. Once a consultor to the Holy Office (the successor to the Roman Inquisition), he reportedly led his pontificate into a nest of secrecy and ended his papal role psychologically isolated in fear and depression.[25]

Clement's first encyclical, *Decet quam maxime* (1769), addressed to all the bishops of Sardinia, appealed to the reforms of the Council of Trent to condemn clerical abuses in taxes and benefices.

His next, *Inscrutabili divinae sapientiae* (1769), addressed to all the faithful, proclaimed a Jubilee, with plenary indulgences granted to those who would visit specific churches designated by local bishops, along with fasting, confession, communion, and almsgiving. In this document, the Jubilee was not explicitly linked to any concrete challenge to the church.

This pope's third document, *Cum summi* (1769), addressed to the bishops, explained the social challenge that prompted the Jubilee. Clement wrote of the "bark of Peter" being "shaken by great floods and all but submerged by the force of the tempest." He lashed out at "ideas aimed at weakening religion," and "men enticed by novelty and led on by an eagerness for alien knowledge." He called on the bishops to use their authority "to repel this audacity and insanity which stalks even divine and most holy matters." The bishops, he wrote, needed to "contain the attacks of enemies and blunt their weapons" through their preaching.[26]

Also in this document Clement warned that "there is a strong bond between divine and human rights," and that only rulers who protected divine rights would themselves be protected in the social order. He urged the bishops to "instill in people obedience and deference to rulers," and said that rulers "carry the sword as vindicators" of God's wrath. Seven years before the American Revolution and twenty years before the French Revolution, the new Enlightenment ideas were beginning to be perceived as a strategy threat.[27]

Clement's final encyclical, *Salutis nostrae* (1774), addressed to all the faithful, proclaimed another Jubilee or Holy Year for 1775 in the city of Rome. He granted a plenary indulgence to all who would confess and receive communion, visit the city's three basilicas, and "pray to God for the exaltation of Holy Church, the destruction of heresies, peace among Catholic rulers, and the safety and quiet of the Christian people." Still later in the text he invited the bishops to "join Us in prayer for the safety of the Catholic faith, for the return of all peoples who have strayed from its unity, for the peace of the Church, and for the happiness of all Christian princes."[28]

Very soon in Western Europe, however, the safety of the Catholic faith, the peace of the church, and the happiness of Christian princes would be shattered by the French Revolution.

Revolution:
The Encyclicals of Pius VI and Pius VII
(1775–1823)

Encyclicals of Pius VI

Giovanni Angelo Bracchi, or Pius VI (1775–99), was the pope who faced the terrible shock of the French Revolution. This was the single most powerful eighteenth-century event forcing the classical aristocratic Catholic paradigm for evangelization into a strategic defensive. This pope produced only two encyclicals.

Inscrutabile. In his first but brief encyclical, *Inscrutabile*, issued well before the French Revolution on Christmas Day 1775 as an inaugural message to the Catholic bishops of the world, Pius VI sounded a note of impending crisis.[29] He saw church, society, and humanity as all under intellectual attack from the Enlightenment's *philosophes*. He defined the mission of his pontificate as combating these threats. On the religious front the pope charged these philosophers with denying God's existence (atheism) or with defining God as remote and impersonal (deism) and with claiming that religion itself was a product of inexperienced, fear-ridden minds. On the societal front he accused these same philosophers of undermining the unity of the people with their rulers:

> They keep proclaiming that man is born free and subject to no one, that society accordingly is a crowd of foolish men who stupidly yield to priests who deceive them and to kings who oppress them, so that the harmony of priest and ruler is only a monstrous conspiracy against the innate liberty of man.[30]

Pius VI further warned that the teachings of these philosophers were spreading like a cancer into educational institutions, into the houses of the aristocracy and royalty, and even among the clergy.

Inscrutabile's strategic response began on the religious front with an appeal to the bishops to pray for counsel and courage. It also urged the bishops to be careful in their selection of those admitted into the clergy, to train candidates in separate seminaries, and to create seminaries where they did not exist. Supporting the Counter-Reformation's stress on the institutionally visible church, he urged the bishops to beautify their churches and not to place the furnishing of their own houses above the furnishing of the house of God. On the societal side, however, he offered no concrete strategy. The document concluded with a call for a renewal like the ancient Deuteronomic reform of Israel of old.

Perhaps the encyclical said little on the societal side because the Enlightenment had already penetrated so extensively among the aristocracy—in the pope's words, forcing its way "into the houses of the great, into the palaces of kings." Nonetheless, he warned that this matter deeply concerned "the peace of the empire and the safety of nations." His reference to the empire indicated that he still accepted the classical paradigm of Christendom, though his failure to articulate a societal strategy suggested that the papacy was no longer playing an overarching role within it.

This document's defining biblical metaphors were first the shepherd gathering and protecting his flock, and second the warrior-ruler who presides from his throne and guards the people with his military power. Its style was clearly one of Christic or Davidic kingship. Pius VI even compared his own ascent to the papal throne with God's raising young David "to rule His people on a glorious throne, and make them acceptable to God by means of the rod of guidance." As kingly spiritual warriors, the bishops themselves were to "arise and gird on [the] sword, which is the word of God, to expel this foul contagion." While both metaphors were strongly hierarchical, they also were simultaneously organic. The church was seen as one community, one in the love of the Lord, with "one faith, one baptism, and one spirit." The hierarchical element was seen as conserving the organic unity.[31]

Charitas. Pius VI's second encyclical, *Charitas,* issued in 1791 and addressed to the French church during the full heat of the revolution, was a direct response to the French Revolution's Civil Constitution of the Clergy.[32] This text saw the constitution as part of a "war against the Catholic religion which has been started by the revolutionary thinkers who as a group formed a majority in the National Assembly of France." Behind this war was the "philosophy of the present age." The pope defined the Civil Constitution of the

Clergy as the start of a national "schism." Yet his appeal was primarily to the king, reflecting his assumption that the monarchy would continue as the legitimate and accepted authority in the French nation.[33]

Pius VI's primary objection to the Civil Constitution of the Clergy was that it turned the selection of church authorities into a local civic function, attempting to reduce the church to a department of government:

> Lawful pastors and ministers were driven out, by force if necessary, [and] the municipal districts could set about electing new bishops and parish priests. Upon election these men were to disregard the metropolitans and senior bishops who had refused the oath, and to go to the Assembly Executive which would appoint some bishops to ordain them.[34]

Further, he complained, the election of these clerical leaders lost its ecclesial character, because the new bishops "were elected in the municipal districts by laity, heretics, unbelievers, and Jews as the published decrees commanded." He lamented that the church was being relinquished "into the hands of laymen," and spoke of a "low mob of the laity."[35]

Apparently unaware that the original church had been a strongly egalitarian and distinctly lay movement and that Jesus had presented himself as a lay teacher,[36] Pius interpreted this attempted reduction of church authority to a department of government as a loss of clerical power to the laity. The church-state issue was thus mistakenly perceived as a clerical-lay issue. The pope firmly rejected the idea that the Assembly's democratic model is "a better form of Church order...closer to the purity of the early centuries." Of course, the proposed revolutionary alternative of a state-controlled church with bishops elected by all citizens regardless of their faith was quite different from the original nonclerical model of the early church, and necessarily unacceptable. Rightly did Pius describe it as schismatic and even heretical.

In response to the government's assuming power over the election of bishops, Pius insisted that "the right of ordaining bishops belongs only to the Apostolic See, as the Council of Trent declares," and cannot be assumed by any bishop or metropolitan without papal assent. Pius's purpose for insisting on papal authority over the ordination of bishops was his concern for the unity of the church. Toward the end of the document, he urged all Catholics of France to "stay close to Us...For no one can be in the Church of Christ without being in unity with its visible head and founded on the See of Peter."[37]

Shaping the pope's concern for unity was the patriarchal metaphor of the *paterfamilias* (father as head of the family). As we will see throughout the encyclicals of this period, the pope was portrayed symbolically as father, the bishops as brothers to the pope, priests as his sons, and laity as his children, with all external to the church, which was described as the mother.[38]

Encyclicals of Pope Pius VII

Diu satis. The next pope, Barnaba Chiarmonti or Pius VII (1800–1823) issued only one encyclical, *Diu satis*, promulgated in 1800, the first year of his pontificate.[39] The document lamented "attempts to overthrow the House of God" and "a wicked war with the See of Peter." Like earlier encyclicals, it traced these attacks to the "defiling plague of false philosophy," namely the Enlightenment.[40] In response, it appealed to Jesus' prayer for unity, as narrated in the gospel of John.

> May Christ's prayer to His Father never leave our minds: "Holy Father, keep them in your name that they may be one as We...not for these only (i.e., the Apostles) do I pray, but also for those who through their word will believe in me that they may be one as you, Father, in me and I in you, that they also may be one in us."[41]

Pius VII seemed to believe that by premodern means the tide of error could be turned back and the old ways restored. He stressed vigilance concerning those admitted to the clergy; protection of the minds of the young in seminaries, colleges, and secondary schools; the burning of books that "oppose the teaching of Christ"; general repression of the "great license of thinking, speaking, writing, and reading"; defense of the Church's laws, which are "like foundations laid down to bear the weight of faith"; and return of church property that had been stolen.[42]

In this last matter of property he appealed to the two great political patrons of the classical Catholic strategy, Constantine and Charlemagne:

> Constantine the Great and Charlemagne were like these kings, and their noble generosity and justice were chiefly directed to the Church. The former asserted that he had known many kingdoms whose kings had perished because they had despoiled the Church. Because of this he commanded and urged his children and their successors at the head of the state: "...let them be helpers and defenders of the churches and of the service of God in so far as they can."[43]

Michael Schuck has suggested that the first modern papal reference to socialism, albeit an indirect one, occurred in this document when Pius VII referred to "the enemies of private property and states who are trying to confound all laws, divine and human."[44] But there was as yet no explicit mention of socialism.

Restoration:
The Encyclicals of Leo XII, Pius VIII, and Gregory XVI
(1823–46)

As noted, in addition to Pius VII during his closing year, three popes presided over the restoration phase: Leo XII, Pius VIII, and Gregory XVI. Leo and Gregory represented the intransigent zealot party within the Vatican, while Pius VIII represented the compromising politician party. Leo produced three encyclicals in seven years, Pius VIII only one in a short reign spanning two years, and Gregory nine encyclicals in a long reign of sixteen years.

Encyclicals of Pope Leo XII

Elected by conservative zealots opposed to the accomodation-ist strategy of political concordats, Annibale Sermattei della Genga or Leo XII (1823–29) was an austere religious rigorist. He closed Roman wine shops, banned the waltz at Roman carnivals, and said that anyone vaccinated against smallpox was no longer a child of God. (He believed that smallpox should be accepted as God's judgment.) This pope also supported anti-independence forces in Latin America and brutally strengthened police repression in the Papal States.[45]

Surprisingly, for a brief time Leo XII later swung over to sympathy with Consalvi and his accomodationist tactics, maintained a dialogue with Lamennais, and came under the influence of the younger and populist wing of the zealot ultramontanism, particularly the Theatine priest Ventura. But his opening to these modern currents quickly led to fear of rebellion. By the eve of the revolutions of 1830, he had already swung back to the repressive model of Metternich. Leo XII died in 1829 — despised by the Roman people and widely viewed by European liberals as a cruel tyrant.[46]

Ubi primum. Leo XII's inaugural document, *Ubi primum*, issued in 1824, ended the twenty-four-year silence of the encyclical tradition following the French Revolution. Addressed to the Catholic bishops of the world, it opened with an appeal to words of Pope Leo I, known as Leo the Great.[47] Following the past pattern, the framing biblical metaphors of Leo XII's first encyclical were again the shepherd-ruler and the holy warrior. In the first half of the document he referred to internal ecclesial concerns, namely, the reforms of the Council of Trent, particularly careful scrutiny of clerical candidates, the importance of seminaries, and the need for bishops to reside in their dioceses and to conduct regular pastoral visits. The bulk of the document, however, addressed external societal threats, which were described in diabolical and apocalyptic language. No doubt reflecting his own emotional pain, Leo wrote: "Who can reflect without weeping on the fierce and mighty conflicts which have raged in Our times and continue to rage almost daily against the Catholic religion?"[48]

In diagnosing the first external strategic threat to the Catholic Church, Leo followed the reading of his immediate predecessors by blaming the philosophers of the European Enlightenment for the contemporary suffering. The main problems arising from their teaching of individual freedom, private judgment, and unbridled license were, he asserted, religious tolerance and religious indifferentism, which then undermined the religious monopoly of Catholicism and replaced it with deism and naturalism. In challenging this teaching he appealed to patristic sources, to Augustine, to rational argument, and to the teaching "that there is no salvation outside the Church." Those who promoted these false teachings were labeled "madmen" and carriers of a "perverted mind corresponding to the symbol of iniquity which was written on the forehead of the wicked woman of the Apocalypse." The threatening medium of this teaching was "the flood of evil books."[49]

The second strategic threat, religious rather than philosophical, also arose, he argued, from the growing power of print, namely, the Bible societies spreading vernacular translations of the scriptures. Leo noted that the Bible itself was being used against the Catholic Church. Warning that these often "mistranslated" editions would produce "a gospel of the devil," he decried them as harmful to faith and morals and urged bishops to keep them from their flocks, particularly by strictly observing the rules of the Congregation of the Index.[50]

The root problem for Leo was not simply the libertarian ideas of the Enlightenment philosophers or the vernacular translations of the Bible societies, but rather an underlying and pervasive contempt for the authority of the church, particularly for the "See of Peter." It was Peter, he claimed, who maintained the pastors in guarding the flocks; it was Peter upon whom Christ conferred the gift of constancy; and it was Peter who in turn conferred authority on the successors of the apostles. With historical foresight he warned that, if the secular princes were wise, they would support the church's authority, for without it their own authority would certainly fall.[51]

Quod hoc ineunte. Reflecting his temporary turn to the populist wing of zealot ultramontanism, Leo's second encyclical, *Quod hoc ineunte*, issued in 1824 and directed to all the Christian faithful, renewed the tradition of Jubilee pilgrimages to Rome as the seat of Peter.[52] (No Jubilee pilgrimage had been held since the French Revolution.) The pope hoped this spiritual event would "renew all

things in Christ by a salutary purification of the entire Christian people." He linked the authority of the princes with what he described
as the more powerful authority of the church. He also made an
appeal to those "who are still removed from the true Church and the
road to salvation" to use the Jubilee pilgrimage as a path to reconciliation "with the mother Church, outside of whose teaching there is
no salvation."[53]

Charitate Christi. Leo's third and final encyclical, *Charitate
Christi*, issued the following year in 1825 and again in populist
fashion addressed to the "Whole Catholic Flock," extended the
plenary indulgence of the 1924 Jubilee to all the regions of the
world.[54] The document, like many others, revealed the still deep-
seated Roman legacy of the ancient pagan cult of the *magna mater*
goddess, for it described the church as a compassionate "mother"
distinct from its members: "Let the faithful consider how the Church
pities the weakness of her children."[55] Again, in this metaphor the
laity were children of the church, not those who made up the
church itself.

Also, no doubt judging the recent attacks on ecclesial elites to
be the product of sin, Leo discoursed at length about the importance
of the sacrament of penance. He noted the danger of civil marriage
(initiated by the French Revolution), as well as the fact that the "iniquitous convention between Catholics and heretics has grown to such
an extent that" children are often not being raised Catholic. He
placed special emphasis on Catholic education, reflecting the
growth of new educational congregations. And there was another bitter warning against dangerous books:

> Especially, however, see that they [youth] are on their
> guard against seduction, so that they may shutter at the
> evil opinions propagated by these miserable times and at
> the books inimical to religion, morals, and public peace,
> from which this foul crop of wickedness has grown. May
> it be kept as a pest, far from the faithful people. Remind
> them again and again how popes and princes of the past
> attacked such books; in this matter do not consider your
> vigilance too great.[56]

After another traditional appeal to the Council of Trent, with its emphasis on supervision of clerical candidates in separate seminaries, there appeared the first mention in a papal encyclical since the French Revolution of the social category of the poor. But as yet there was no reference to industrialism. Rather, the danger to the poor was seen as coming from usury. Against usury, Leo supported "banks of commodities and money-lending," devised by pious people, "approved by popes, and spreading all over the world." In Leo's view the poor were special because it was they "for whom Christ confessed that he was sent by the Father and in whose favor he gave such renowned and singular arguments of good will." The excess wealth of the church was to be given to them, he argued, and Christians should seek the aid of the wealthy on their behalf, as well as defending them from the injustice of unscrupulous moneylenders.[57]

Encyclicals of Pope Pius VIII

The next pope, Francesco Saverio Castiglioni or Pius VIII (1829–30), a figure of ill health who survived only twenty months, proved more sympathetic to the pro-compromise politician party and softened repression in the Papal States. In France, despite the anti-clerical tone of the July Revolution and against the protests of the zealots, he recognized the bourgeois monarchy of Louis Philippe rather than insisting on the reactionary aristocrat Charles X as the legitimate claimant to the throne.[58]

Traditi humiliati. Pius VIII's inaugural encyclical and his only one, *Traditi humiliati*, was issued in 1829 and addressed to the Catholic bishops of the world.[59] It began immediately with the pastoral metaphor of shepherd and flock by directing the bishops "not only to feed, rule, and direct the lambs, namely the Christian people, but also the sheep, that is, the clergy."

Then he moved to the "revolt against religion" promoted by Enlightenment philosophers in the name of natural reason.[60] On the ecclesial front this pope saw this "revolt" as first attempting to attack the Roman See and to destroy the unity of the church. He challenged the argument of religious indifferentism on logical grounds, claiming that if one religion is true, the others must be false. Against Protestantism, he decried vernacular translations of the Bible promoted by the Bible societies, given "free even to the uneducated," and he appealed against them to the Index of Forbidden Books published by the Council of Trent.[61] On the societal front Pius warned of the danger of secret societies (presumably referring to groups like the Italian Carbonari[62]) and connected the attack on the church with the attack on society:

> Eradicate those secret societies of factitious men who, completely opposed to God and to the princes, are wholly dedicated to bringing about the fall of the Church, the destruction of kingdoms, and disorder in the whole world. Having cast off the restraints of true religion, they prepare the way for shameful crimes.[63]

Jumping back to church concerns as his response, this pope repeated the Council of Trent's emphasis on good pastors, condemned the fact that "heretics have disseminated pestilential books everywhere," and insisted that marriage be under the control of the church. In addressing Christian marriage he made the unusual theological claim that the purpose of marriage was the education of children for God and religion.[64]

Finally, this pope concluded with the theme of "restoration" — referring to the restoration of Israel after its penitence. He appealed again to the "princes" to defend the church and noted that the encyclical was issued on "the anniversary of Our predecessor, Pius VII's restoration to the city of Rome after he had suffered so many adversities." Yet in the following year, at least west of the Rhine, the aristocratic restoration came to a crashing end.[65]

Encyclicals of Pope Gregory XVI

Derek Holmes notes that in 1799, fresh on the heels of the French Revolution, an Italian Camoldolese friar of noble birth, Bartolomeo Alberto Cappellari, had published a prophetic work, *Il Trionfo della Santa Sede*.[66] At a time when Pius VI was dying as a prisoner of the French, Cappellari's writing foresaw the future definition of papal infallibility and the triumph of the papacy over nationalist and Gallican churches. Amid revolutionary upheavals, this friar became the next pope, Gregory XVI (1831–46).

Clearly a member of the zealot party, Cappellari took the name of the ancient monk-pope Gregory I, also known as Gregory the Great.[67] Recalling his predecessor's style, the new Gregory encouraged a revival of monasticism, as well as the creation of new religious congregations and devotions oriented to Rome. Most important, as a former prefect of Propaganda (the Roman office charged with supervising the church's missionary work), he made missionary outreach a principal concern and placed it under clear papal control.

On the progressive side, in an 1839 document Gregory condemned the opposition of many Christians to the emancipation of slaves.[68] Also, against Spain he supported the independence of the Latin American republics. In his own Papal States, however, he had no hesitation in suppressing rebellion and appealed to Austria to crush the uprisings of 1831.

Gregory condemned naturalistic philosophy and political liberalism, as well as separation of church and state, and firmly supported monarchical regimes. (Presumably the term *naturalism* referred to the critique of religion by the skeptical philosopher of the Scottish Enlightenment, David Hume, whose 1755 work, *The Natural History of Religion*, rejected entirely the supernatural dimension.) Gregory also opposed the construction of railroads in the Papal States, for fear that they would bring in dangerous ideas.

Initial Encyclicals. Gregory's first encyclical, *Summo jugiter studio*, issued in 1832, addressed the problem of mixed marriages in Bavaria.[69] He appealed to "the canons forbidding the marriages of Catholics with heretics" and denied that "heretics may attain eternal life." Repeating the guiding metaphor of the shepherd guarding the flock, he enjoined the king of Bavaria to enforce these canons "so that our most holy religion may be restored and protected throughout Bavaria." His reason for insisting on these canons was the "necessity of maintaining Catholic unity." He also defended the indissolubility of Christian marriage and noted "how strong by divine law is the bond of marriage," which "cannot be broken by human authority."[70]

Gregory's second encyclical, *Cum primum*, issued in 1832 and addressed to the bishops of Poland, condemned a recent revolt in that land.[71] Appealing again to the metaphor of shepherd, he ascribed the revolt to fraudulent teachers, insisted on the legitimate authority of the princes, and demanded absolute obedience to them, since their authority was established by God. In support of his insistence, he cited Paul in Romans 12:1, 2, 5 and 1 Peter 2:13, and recounted how the first Christians had served the emperor so well, even defending the state in battle when others had deserted.[72]

Gregory is best known for his two dramatic condemnations of liberalism, *Mirari vos* (a forerunner of the 1864 Syllabus of Errors of Pius IX) and his later *Singulari nos*. The former was precipitated by an appeal of Lamennais on behalf of Christian Democracy, and the latter explicitly condemned Lamennais's book *Paroles d'un croyant*. Apart from the well-known person of Lamennais against whom these documents were targeted, their teachings were not remarkably different from the wider corpus of the time. Their significance lay in the fact that, by repudiating Lamennais, they clearly rejected the path of Christian Democracy, and implicitly of Christian Socialism or Social Catholicism (the two phrases tended to be used interchangeably), for Lamennais was a founding voice in both movements.

Mirari vos. Published on the feast of the Assumption in 1832 and directed to all the bishops of the Catholic world, *Mirari vos* began by recounting the civil rebellion that the pope himself had recently faced in the Papal States. It continued to tell how in reaction the pope had to use his "God-given authority to restrain the great obstinacy of these men with the rod."[73] It portrayed the fundamental problem as a spiritual revolt in the name of freedom against legitimate authority, both societal and ecclesial, and ultimately against God.

While perceiving this revolt as rooted immediately in the Enlightenment, Gregory now claimed that its deeper roots were found in the precursors of the Protestant Reformation: "Waldensians, the Beghards, the Wycliffites, and other such sons of Belial," as well as in Luther himself.[74] Of these older movements, he wrote:

> Indeed this great mass of calamities had its inception in the heretical societies and sects in which all that is sacrilegious, infamous, and blasphemous has gathered as bilge water in a ship's hold, a congealed mass of filth.[75]

He then attacked the contemporary "shameless lovers of liberty." "For no other reason do experienced deceivers devote their efforts, except so that they, along with Luther, might joyfully deem themselves 'free of all.'"[76] According to Gregory, freedom's revolt included:

- questioning church discipline, and even an "abominable conspiracy against celibacy…promoted by profligate philosophers, some even from the clerical order";

- a rejection of the indissolubility of the sacrament of marriage;

- the "perverse opinion" of religious indifferentism "spread on all sides by the fraud of the wicked who claim that it is possible to obtain the eternal salvation of the soul by the profession of any kind of religion, as long as morality is maintained";

- the "absurd and erroneous proposition which claims that *liberty of conscience* must be maintained for everyone;

- the "harmful and never sufficiently denounced freedom to publish any writings whatever"; and

- the lighting of "torches of treason" that "attack the trust and submission due to princes."[77]

Theologically Gregory appealed to the teaching of Paul that "there is no authority except from God."[78] Regarding the church, he rejected any claim that it could be subject to reform:

It is obviously absurd and injurious to propose a certain "restoration and regeneration" for her as though necessary for her safety and growth, as if she could be considered subject to defect or obscuration or other misfortune.[79]

Regarding the state, he warned that when "all restraints (on freedom) are removed," then society is propelled "to ruin":

Experience shows, even from earliest times, that cities renowned for wealth, dominion, and glory perished as a result of this single evil, namely immoderate freedom of opinion, license of free speech, and desire for novelty.[80]

On the positive side Gregory held up the classical model of church and empire working in harmony, and argued that "subjection to the princes necessarily proceeded from the most holy precepts of the Christian religion." Like his predecessor, he further cited the example of the early Christians who, he claimed, unhesitatingly served in the military of even a pagan emperor.[81]

> And it is for this reason that the early Christians, lest they should be stained by such great infamy, deserved well of the emperors and of the safety of the state even while persecution raged. This they proved splendidly by their fidelity in performing perfectly and promptly whatever they were commanded which was not opposed to their religion, and even more by their constancy and the shedding of their blood in battle.[82]

The dominant biblical metaphors were again pastoral (shepherd and flock) and military (battle with enemies). The paradigm of evangelization was again kingly, although in his view these "men… have broken the everlasting covenant."[83]

Gregory encouraged the bishops to defend the authority of the church, particularly the papacy, as the guarantor of sound teaching and of the bond of unity in both church and society. Similarly, he insisted on the authority of the princes, in partnership with the bishops, and proposed that both work together to censor and repress the threat of liberty in faith, in thought, and in politics. The control of printed books, begun at the Council of Trent with the Index, was also central to this strategy. He concluded by urging the bishops to "take up the shield of faith and fight the battles of the Lord vigorously," and by urging the princes to use their God-given authority "not only for the government of the world, but especially for the defense of the Church." His final appeal was to the "most holy Virgin Mary, who alone crushes all heresies."[84]

Singulari nos. Two years later, in 1834, Gregory issued *Singulari nos*, which referred back to *Mirari vos* and this time explicitly attacked

Lamennais and his booklet *Parole d'un croyant*. The document lamented "the harsh wound inflicted to Our heart by the error of Our son." (Lamennais had failed to obey the teachings of *Mirari vos*.[85]) The catalogue of perceived errors was once more listed: failure to submit to authority; religious indifferentism; license of thought and speech; freedom of conscience; and the various conspiracies against church and state. Seeing Lamennais's *Parole* as attempting to give Christian legitimization to what Gregory saw as these destructive errors, the encyclical harshly condemned the work, again re-emphasized the condemnation, and then connected its reputed errors with pre-Reformation Christian dissidents.

> By Our apostolic power, we condemn the book: furthermore, We decree that it be perpetually condemned. It corrupts the people by a wicked abuse of the word of God, to dissolve the bonds of all public order and to weaken all authority. It arouses, fosters, and strengthens seditions, riots, and rebellions in the empires. We condemn the book because it contains false, calumnious, and rash propositions which lead to anarchy; which are contrary to the word of God; which are impious, scandalous, and erroneous; and which the Church already condemned, especially in regard to the Waldensians, Wycliffites, Hussites, and other heretics of this kind.[86]

Lamennais's appeal to wed ultramontanism and democracy was decisively rejected. In a personal letter to Lamennais, Gregory even demanded unqualified acceptance of legitimist absolutism and a total rejection of democratic principles. The condemnation of Lamennais was especially harsh, perhaps because the Austrian chancellor Prince Metternich viewed him as a serious threat to the aristocratic social order.[87]

In the next period of papal strategy Leo XIII would abandon Gregory's harsh condemnation of Lamennais's program of Christian Democracy and Social Catholicism. But this would happen only after large sectors of the European working classes had already been alienated from Christianity, and only after the socialist movement, which in France had been briefly drawn in a Christian direction, turned militantly antireligious.

Quo graviora. Issued by Gregory in 1833 (between *Mirari vos* and *Singulari nos*) and addressed to the bishops of the Upper Rhineland, *Quo graviora* was the first serious acknowledgment that the outer societal crisis was institutionally affecting the internal life of the church in a way beyond the personal threat of Lamennais.[88] In this encyclical the pope spoke of priests who promoted a "deluded (as they call it) regeneration," described these calls as "this very evil sedition of the reformers," and decried that they were attempting to effect "a revolution in the church" and were pretending "to renew the church."[89]

Previous encyclicals had noted that false teachings sometimes infected inner church life, but they always gave the impression of minor or individual dangers. With this encyclical, however, there was a more heightened sense of internal threat. In response, the document completely rejected any claim that the discipline of the Catholic Church was in need of "reform" in relation to its foundational roots or of "updating" in light of the needs of the age. ("Updating" is the very term that much later Pope John XXIII would use, perhaps consciously as a devoted historian, to describe the mission of Vatican Council II.)

Then, as with *Mirari vos,* there came a catalogue of false teachings regarding internal church discipline. These included:

- the "vile plot" against clerical celibacy;

- the desire to limit indulgences to the lifting of public canonical sanctions;

- the desire to reform the sacrament of penance;

- the call for abolition of Mass stipends and for reduction of the number of Masses for the dead; and

- the creation of a new ritual in the vernacular language.

All these represented for this pope threatening anti-Catholic innovations.[90]

Gregory concluded with a summary statement of the new strategic situation. He described the church as "pillaged by the attack of internal and external enemies and by evils which oppress it and reduce it to this disgraceful captivity." Zion was now a captive in an internal Babylon, and enemies were found both outside and inside the church. Yet, undaunted by these enemies, the pope proclaimed, "We shall not retreat until the Catholic Church is restored to the original freedom which totally belongs to its divine constitution and until the mouth of the slanderers is blocked up."[91]

Commissum divinitus. Issued by Gregory in 1835 to the bishops and priests of Switzerland, *Commissum divinitus* showed again how the classical paradigm confused the broad sector of "laity" with the narrow sector of secularizing political elites.[92] Like his predecessors apparently ignorant of the lay origins of the early Christian movement, Leo insisted that the church had been established "not in accordance with lay authority, but in spite of it." To support this, he cited the words of Basil: "What more can I say to you about lay people? I have nothing else to say except that it is not permitted for you to speak concerning ecclesiastical matters."[93]

Probe nostis. Yet despite this negative interpretation of the laity, Gregory's next encyclical, *Probe nostis*, issued in 1840 to all the bishops on missionary work and particularly the new organization known as the Propagation of the Faith, marked the first official recognition and encouragement of a new lay movement. Elsewhere this movement was beginning to be called Catholic Action, a phrase apparently first coined by Lamennais.[94]

In response to decades of attacks against the Catholic Church, small groups of middle-class lay activists had begun to organize in defense of the church and in support of its mission.[95] Gregory was now eager to enlist the support of such lay groups in a united front against heretical and unbelieving enemies. "This is surely the time 'when the Christian battle line should smash the devil as he rages all over the world'; it is indeed the time for the faithful to join in this holy union with the priests."[96]

The term that Gregory used for lay members of all such Catholic groups was not *laity* but *faithful*. Such a term, used in earlier encyclicals, enabled him to avoid the problematic clergy-lay language of the classical theocratic paradigm, particularly since in its contemporary usage the term *lay* was now frequently used to describe enemies of the church.[97] Thus even while the old aristocratic clergy-over-laity paradigm was being rigorously defended, the seed of a new bourgeois laity-helping-clergy paradigm was being planted.

Note that it was a pope of the more conservative zealots' party who gave the Catholic lay movement its first official recognition. The explanation lies in the fact that for the zealots the main concern was not instrumental, that is, not diplomatic defense of the church's legal place in society achieved through elite concordats. Rather, the zealot party's concern was expressive, that is, pastoral defense of the church's evangelization of symbolic consciousness. The younger zealots sought to realize this goal by mobilizing bourgeois lay movements. This populist variant of the ultramontanist strategy required middle-class lay action.[98]

The alliance with ecclesial lay groups would eventually draw the papacy into the modern social question of the industrial proletariat. Fighting against what Gregory called "heretics and unbelievers," particularly "in the large cities," these laity were eventually confronted with the suffering of the new industrial working class.[99] As one of leading lay apostolic figures of the time, Frédérick Ozanam, wrote in 1836, "The question which agitates the world today is not a question of *political forms*, but a *social* question." Twelve years later, on the eve of the revolutions of 1848, Ozanam would again write, "It is a social question; do away with misery, Christianize the people, and you will make an end of revolutions."[100]

In *Quas vestro*, issued in 1841, Gregory again addressed the problem of mixed marriages, this time in Hungary.[101]

Inter praecipuas. His final encyclical, *Inter praecipuas*, issued in 1844 (the same year in which Karl Marx produced his youthful economic and philosophical manuscripts) and sent to all the bishops, addressed once more the problem of Bible societies. The pope traced the immediate origin of the Bible societies to England, and specifically warned of a new society called The Christian League, founded only a year earlier in New York and directed especially at Italian immigrants. The possibility of Italian immigrants becoming Protestants seemed especially shocking to him. The pope complained that vernacular translations encouraged private interpretation and implicitly rejected the authority and tradition of the church [102]

This 1844 document also explicitly connected the rise of political and economic liberalism with the danger of religious freedom, and in turn connected religious freedom with the Reformation and printing.[103] Gregory recalled that Innocent III had "issued warnings concerning the secret gatherings of laymen and women, under the pretext of piety, for the reading of Scripture," and he cited Saint Jerome about a group in his own day.

> They make the art of understanding the Scriptures without a teacher "common to babbling old women and crazy old men and verbose sophists," and to anyone who can read, no matter what his status.[104]

While the pope's concern about church authority and tradition represented important Catholic principles, those principles appeared to him to be mediated exclusively through a clerical aristocracy, as his complaint "no matter what his status" suggests.[105]

Gregory also recalled that over the centuries secret lay groups had regularly tried to use unauthorized vernacular translations of the Bible but noted that the threat had expanded when Lutherans and Calvinists "were aided in multiplying copies and quickly spreading them by the newly invented art of printing." He reported that the response of the Council of Trent was to place these translations on the Index of forbidden books.[106]

Never did there appear any suggestion that Catholic strategy could compete with the Bible societies or liberalism generally by disseminating Catholic vernacular translations of the Bible or of Catholic philosophical works.

In perhaps the first clear mention of economic liberalism in a papal encyclical, Gregory linked the promotion of vernacular Bibles with religious indifference and then linked both with the promotion of political liberty and the promise of economic prosperity, all of which he condemned as erroneous.

> Therefore they are determined to give everyone the gift of liberty of conscience, or rather of error; they liken it to a fountain from which political liberty and increased public prosperity may spring forth.[107]

With Gregory XVI the restoration phase of the reactive conservative strategy experienced its last vibrant moment. During the long term of the next pope, Pius IX, the attempted restoration of the ancien régime would completely break down, even in the Papal States. Yet out of the ashes would emerge the foundation for a modern and more spiritual model of the papacy.

Retreat:
The Encyclicals of Pius IX
(1846–78)

In an unusually long pontificate spanning thirty-four years Giovanni Mastai-Ferretti or Pius IX (1846–78), affectionately called even in English Pio Nono, issued thirty-eight encyclicals. Since the number was so great, it is feasible here to address in detail only key documents that bear explicitly on the articulation of papal strategy.

Inaugural Encyclical of 1846

Though there was a popular impression that the new pope was a liberal, Pius IX's inaugural encyclical, *Qui pluribus*, issued in 1846 to all the Catholic bishops, provided no evidence for that claim.[108] On the contrary, it boldly restated the defensively conservative analysis and strategy of his predecessor.

Opening with the two traditional pastoral and military metaphors, the document urged the bishops of the world to keep up their "night-watches over the flock," to raise "a protecting wall," and to battle "like good soldiers of Christ against the hateful enemy." The strategic context was "a bitter and fearsome war against the whole Catholic commonwealth," and the war was being "stirred up by men bound together in a lawless alliance." Their goal was to "overthrow the Catholic religion and civil society." The leaders of this war were still those who claimed the name "philosophers," meaning the spokespersons of the modern European Enlightenment. According to the pope, their main errors were to set reason against faith and to attempt to import the "doctrine of human progress" into the Catholic faith, so as to make religion the evolving work of men rather than a gift of God.[109]

As Michael Schuck has perceptively noted, "*Qui pluribus* added to the received social analysis an extended reflection on the mutuality and compatibility of faith and reason."[110] Further, Schuck has pointed out how throughout this period the papal pastoral metaphor of the world as "a pasture" (shepherd guarding flock amid this "dangerous" pasture) contrasted sharply with the Enlightenment's mechanistic metaphor of the world as a "machine."[111] Far in the future, regenerative postmodern ecologists and feminists would offer a similar organic alternative to modernity's mechanistic vision.[112]

If the replacement of faith by reason alone was the first error of these "philosophers," and the reduction of religion to an expression of evolutionary human "progress" was their second error, their third error, according to *Qui pluribus*, was the rejection of ecclesial "authority." This applied especially to papal authority, with the consequent attempt to "explain and interpret the words of God by their own judgment." In a pre-statement of Vatican Council I, Pio Nono responded to this third error by insisting that the Holy See was the infallible authority. The carriers of all these errors were again "secret sects" (presumably Masonic societies and Jacobin clubs), as well as "crafty Bible societies," both of which, the pope charged, promoted the theory of religious indifference.[113]

In the first explicit modern papal reference to communism, Pio Nono warned that there was also arising the "unspeakable doctrine of Communism." He argued that this new doctrine was "most opposed to the very natural law" and that "if this doctrine were accepted, the complete destruction of everyone's laws, government, property, and even of human society itself would follow." Writing on the eve of the 1847 publication of Marx and Engels's *Communist Manifesto* and also shortly before the socialist revolts of 1848, Pius IX would certainly have been informed by Metternich's spies of the development of this new movement. In addition, foreign ambassadors in Rome and his own nuncios and bishops would have reported to him on the growth of the communist movement. Curiously the pope included his warning against communism in the same paragraph with an attack on those who questioned the discipline of clerical celibacy. He saw both "errors" as the fruit of "a method which deceives and corrupts incautious youth in a wretched manner and gives it as drink the poison of the serpent in the goblet of Babylon."[114]

The utopian socialist ideas and experiments of Charles Fourier, Robert Owen, and Claude Henri de Saint-Simon had emerged earlier in the century. By the 1830s socialist intellectuals had begun allying with the downwardly mobile artisans of the new industrial working class, with a notable rebellion in 1834 by silk weavers in Lyon. Also in the 1830s London and Birmingham saw street demonstrations of over ten thousand workers. By 1837 August Blanqui had organized his conspiratorial Society of Seasons. And by 1843 Karl Marx had moved to Paris, the home of the great socialists of the age, after the newspaper that he had edited in Germany, the *Rheinische Zeitung*, had been suppressed. In Paris, Marx had teamed up with Frederick Engels.[115]

But, while Pius clearly noted the presence of a communist movement and would continue to warn bitterly of its dangers, he did not isolate communism from the other "errors of the age." Though perceived as an especially pernicious doctrine, communism was for him still but a part and consequence of the larger contemporary liberal war on church and society.

Repeating again the social analysis of his predecessors, Pio Nono continued to decry the print medium as the instrument of all these dangers. Thus he complained of

> the widespread disgusting infection from books and pamphlets, which teach the lessons of sinning. These works, well-written and filled with deceit and cunning, are scattered at immense cost through every region for the destruction of the Christian people. They spread pestilential doctrines everywhere and deprave the minds especially of the imprudent, occasioning great losses for religion.[116]

Pio Nono's proposed strategic response was similar to that of prior encyclicals. On the societal front, rulers of governments were due complete obedience, since their authority was from God. These rulers in turn were to use their authority to protect both the society and the church from dangerous groups and publications. On the ecclesial front, the appeal was again to the reforms of the Council of Trent. Clerics were to be carefully selected and trained in special seminaries. Church buildings were to beautified, and bishops were to do battle in defense of their flocks.[117]

But other themes suggested a new psychological withdrawal of the church from the modern world. Now priests were to avoid contamination of "the world," to pray the breviary, to practice "spiritual exercises," and to make retreats "to wipe away stains caused by the dust of the world." Heightening this sense of avoiding contamination, the pope concluded with a dramatic appeal to "the most holy Virgin Mary, Immaculate Mother of God."[118]

Selected Encyclicals from 1847 to 1864

Ubi primum. In the wake of the revolutions of 1848 Pius IX issued *Ubi primum* (1849), addressed to the bishops of the world. This was the papal encyclical proclaiming the solemn definition of the dogma of the Immaculate Conception, that is, the doctrine that Mary, the Mother of God, was "conceived without stain of original sin."[119] The appeal to Mary was hardly sentimental, since she signified for this pope the ancient militant symbol of the virgin warrior queen:

> Her foot has crushed the head of Satan. Set up between Christ and His Church, Mary, ever lovable and full of grace, has always delivered the Christian people from their greatest calamities and from the snares and assaults of all their enemies, ever rescuing them from ruin.[120]

Nostis et nobiscum. Next followed an 1849 encyclical on the Papal States, *Nostis et nobiscum*, addressed to the bishops of Italy. It was issued from Naples, where Pio Nono was still in exile, though the city of Rome and the northern provinces of the Papal States had already been restored to his authority by French and Austrian troops.[121] Clearly shaken by his overthrow, Pius nonetheless did not focus on the "temporal power" but rather on what he perceived as religious and ideological threats to the Italian people, namely, "Protestantism" and "Socialism and Communism." Of the first threat he wrote:

> These enemies of the Church...shamelessly affirm and cry it abroad that the Catholic religion is opposed to the glory, greatness and prosperity of the Italian nation. So

they say that Protestantism should be brought in, set up, and increased to replace Catholicism. Then Italy could once more acquire its former splendor of ancient, that is, pagan times.[122]

The reference to the promise of "prosperity" no doubt referred to the argument commonly made in the north of Italy that the Catholic religious monopoly, tied to vast aristocratic landholdings by the higher clergy and the contemplative religious orders, was an obstacle to capitalist industrial development. In a response that implicitly rejected the new industrial capitalist economy, Pio Nono cited the preindustrial glory of classical Italy under the Catholic religion.[123]

Pius's rejection of laissez-faire economics may not have been simply rhetorical. In a distinctly non–laissez-faire style, Pio Nono's closest aide, Cardinal Giacomo Antonelli, and the cardinal's two brothers (one he had appointed governor of the Banco di Roma and the other was granted a monopoly of Roman corn-grain import) conspired to fix the price of corn in Rome. They amassed a huge fortune. The pope was in turn dependent on Cardinal Antonelli for his own generation of revenues, so crucial at a time when his most important sources of papal income, the northern provinces of the Papal States, were constantly threatened.[124]

Regarding the second threat, the pope, extending the zealots' claim that all of the modern errors have their root in the Reformation, maintained that the socialists and communists were promoting Protestantism only in order to weaken Catholic resistance to their own "wicked theories." In his view,

the goal of this most iniquitous plot is to drive people to overthrow the entire order of human affairs and to draw them over to the wicked theories of this Socialism and Communism, by confusing them with perverted teachings. But these enemies realize that they cannot hope for any agreement with the Catholic Church, which allows neither tampering with truths proposed by faith, nor adding any new human fictions to them. This is why they try to draw the Italian people over to Protestantism...They

know full well that the chief principle of the Protestant
tenets, i.e., that the holy scriptures are to be understood by
the personal judgment of the individual, will greatly assist
their cause.[125]

In turn, Pio Nono saw the weakening of morals and the
increase of vice as crippling the moral character and spiritual resistance of the Italian people, leading them to become "maddened by
draughts from the poisoned goblet of Babylon [and to] take up arms
against their mother the Church." Urging the instruction of the laity
in "Christian doctrine and the law of the Lord," he added,
"Hopefully, they are not too weakened by long license in manifold
and increasing vices."[126]

On the one hand, Pio Nono failed to address both the positive
and negative aspects of the objective side of modern liberalism, that
is, the creative power of liberal democracy and industrial capitalism,
and its accompanying exploitation of workers and nature. Instead, he
reduced liberalism to what he saw as the related dangers of
Protestantism and "Socialism and Communism," with Protestantism
functioning as a Trojan horse for the latter.

On the other hand, the pope powerfully addressed what he saw
as dangers from the subjective side of modern liberalism. He foresaw moral and spiritual corrosion inflicted by modern ideologies on
the psychological self, the family, and the entire societal community. In spiritual response, in addition to the Christian education of
youth, Pius IX stressed frequent reception of the sacraments of
penance and the Eucharist, as well as prayer and fasting. Also, as
had become customary, he warned against "the new technique of
book-production," though in a new note he limited his warning to its
"misuse" and in positive fashion called for clerics to publish their
own works of "sound doctrine."[127]

Returning to the theme of "Socialism and Communism," Pio
Nono made the first modern papal reference to the new organizing
of "workers," though only as an aside and negatively at that:

The final goal shared by these teachings, whether of
Communism or Socialism, even if approached differently,
is to excite by continuous disturbances workers and others,

especially those of the lower class, whom they have deceived by their lies and deluded by the promise of a happier condition. They are preparing them for plundering, stealing, and usurping first the Church's and then everyone's property. And then they will profane all law, human and divine, to destroy divine worship and to subvert the entire ordering of civil societies.[128]

His use of the phrase "even if approached differently" in reference to socialism and communism shows that he was already aware of the difference between the two. (Socialism eventually proved itself a democratic movement, while communism became dictatorial. In addition, socialists accepted both private and public property, while communists sought to abolish private property entirely.) Remarkably Pio Nono foresaw at this early date the danger of totalitarianism. He argued that, should the "perverted theories of Socialism and Communism" triumph, the result would be that "in the end some few, enriched by the plunder of many, will seize supreme control to the ruin of all."[129]

In response to agitation among "workers and others" in "the lower class," Pius insisted on the lawfulness of established authority as from God. Further, he condemned the "coveting or worse the seizure of others' goods" and encouraged "the poor and all the wretched to remember their great debt to the Catholic religion" and to be content with their fate, because Christ will reward them on judgment day.

> Let Our poor recall the teachings of Christ Himself that they should not be sad at their condition, since their very poverty makes lighter their journey to salvation, provided that they bear their need with patience and are poor not alone in possessions, but in spirit too.[130]

Also, overlooking his predecessor's condemnation of slavery, the pope cited a reference of Augustine that "the Catholic Church… teaches slaves to remain true to their masters." Further, he noted that the modern attack on the church had actually stripped it of institutions that in the old society had cared extensively for the poor.[131]

Though the encyclical was written to the Italian bishops, Pio Nono's ecclesial response focused heavily on priests and religious—reflecting the zealot party's close alliance with religious and the lower clergy (thus bypassing the bishops) in their populist outreach. His ecclesial recommendations began with religious, suggesting their centrality in the expanding ultramontanist strategy. He highlighted for the first time in a modern encyclical the distinction between the "regular" clergy and the "secular" clergy. (Members of religious orders take vows of poverty, chastity, and obedience and do not report immediately to bishops but rather to their own superiors. Secular or diocesan priests take no such vows, though they are obliged by church law to maintain celibacy, and they report directly to bishops.) He referred to the recent "Decrees of Our Congregation on the State of Regular Clergy" (meaning those under the rules of religious orders), published in the prior year, and then stressed strong ecclesial control over the education of secular clerics.[132]

Next came a section emphasizing ecclesial control over the education of youth, including the use of the Roman Catechism ("published by a decree of the Council of Trent") and the use of "only books approved by the Holy See." Finally, he urged "the political leaders of Italy to support the bishops by protecting both the spiritual and temporal rights of the church against the dangers of Protestantism and Socialism and Communism." He ended with his now customary appeal to the virgin warrior queen, the "Virgin Mary Immaculate," as well as to the apostles Peter and Paul.[133]

There were several new emphases in this encyclical. Rather than focusing on liberalism or rationalism, Pio Nono emphasized the older threat of Protestantism, seen in the social analysis of the zealots as the root of liberalism, and the newer threat of socialism and communism, seen then as the ultimate consequence of liberalism. Also, along with the turn to spiritual inwardness and avoidance of contamination by the world, as developed in his inaugural document, he clearly appealed for support from the growing numbers of members of religious orders and from diocesan priests, since both had direct access to the Catholic laity.

Soon, however, Pio Nono became consumed with the danger to the Papal States from the Italian nationalist movement. All through the post-revolutionary assaults the popes had believed that their spiritual mission depended vitally on the security of their aristocratic power over the papal territories, and this was particularly true of Pio Nono. After the revolutions of 1848, though a man whose charm, compassion, and above all constant humor could disarm his most bitter opponents, he became fiercely determined to defend the Papal States. While personally wearing the face of mercy, he worked closely with the cruel and avaricious Cardinal Antonelli as his indispensable and primary adviser. A rough Neapolitan whose father reportedly had been a bandit, Antonelli executed rebels throughout the Papal States. He also made a fortune for himself and his family, including for his daughter (born to his mistress), and for the papacy as well, again especially through his price-fixing monopoly on corn imports (as noted, the very opposite of laissez-faire).[134]

More Encyclicals on the Papal States. Two 1859 encyclicals alerted the bishops of the world to the wars and revolutions within the Papal States, with the second challenging the attempts of the new Italian government to take control of the papal territories. The first encyclical declared "that temporal power was necessary to this Holy See."[135] A subsequent encyclical in 1860, also on the Papal States, asserted that "God gave the civil power to the Roman Pontiff." It challenged a letter from the emperor of France suggesting that the pope voluntarily surrender this power.[136] An 1863 encyclical directly attacked the government of Piedmont for its designs on the Papal States and even suggested that the pope might be willing to suffer martyrdom in their defense.[137]

Quanta Cura *and the Syllabus of Errors*

In 1864 Pio Nono issued his encyclical *Quanta cura*, to which he appended the condemned propositions of the infamous Syllabus of Errors.[138] The proposal to issue a comprehensive condemnation of all the errors of the modern world had begun in the middle of the nineteenth century. By then it was becoming clear that, in continental Europe and Latin America (though not in the Anglo-American world), whenever liberalism triumphed the church was attacked.

A year after the revolutions of 1848, the idea of a syllabus of errors was first proposed by Cardinal Pecci (later Pope Leo XIII) and was supported by the Jesuit journal *Civiltà cattolica*. A decade later, in 1859, with new attacks from Piedmont on the Italian church and on the Papal States, the idea was revived. Vatican officials asked notable ultramontanist church leaders for input and actually prepared a first draft titled *Syllabus errorum in Europa vigentium*. But the pope liked better a list of eighty-five erroneous propositions prepared by Bishop Gerbert of Perpignan. Many curial cardinals were reportedly not pleased with this alternative, so the project dragged on slowly, until threatening events in 1863 and 1864 gave the project a renewed sense of urgency. But the cardinals still opposed Gerbert's propositions and suggested instead that a summary list be drawn up from Pio Nono's own past condemnations. When that was done, an encyclical was quickly drafted by a Barnabite priest, L. Bilio. To it was appended the list of eighty condemned propositions. Its publishing caused a flurry of both liberal protest and Catholic confusion.[139]

While the Syllabus was not technically an encyclical, it was still attached to one. Aubert summarizes its eighty propositions:

> In it the pope condemned pantheism and rationalism; indifferentism, which regards all religions as equal in value; socialism, which denies the right to private property and subordinates the family to the state; the erroneous concept regarding Christian marriage; Freemasonry; the rejection of the temporal power of the pope; Gallicanism, which wanted to make the exercise of ecclesiastical authority dependent on the authorization by the civil power; statism, which insists on the monopoly of education and dissolves the religious orders; and naturalism, which regards the fact that human societies no longer have respect for religion as progress and which demands laicization of institutions, separation of Church and state, and absolute freedom of religion and the press.[140]

Proposition eighty was the most publicized, since it declared "anathema" the claim that the Roman pontiff should reconcile himself to progress, liberalism, and modern civilization.[141] Absent from the list was any acknowledgment of the exploitation of workers under the economic liberalism of laissez-faire industrial capitalism.

Some have argued that recalling their original reference to an Italian context should soften the intended meaning of these propositions. But, as mentioned earlier, if the propositions were indeed intended to be strictly local, then why did the document speak of "errors of the age" and promulgate its condemnation to all the bishops of the world? The propositions were inevitably read as having universal import, with ultramontanists rejoicing over them and secular liberals ridiculing them. The liberal ridicule was reduced somewhat by the publication of Monsignor Dupanloup's semi-official commentary, which appealed to the now famous "thesis-hypothesis" concept originally proposed by the Jesuits of *Civiltà cattolica*.[142]

Given the polemical battles that surrounded the Syllabus, it is perhaps best to look to the encyclical that introduced them, for it alone offered a reflective analysis. This encyclical set out the task of noting the "chief errors" from which "other evil opinions…spring forth…as from a fountain." It justified this task by claiming that the Catholic Church's salutary influence was to extend to "not only private individuals, but also over nations, peoples, and their sovereign princes."

While today Catholic social teaching no longer endorses the notion of an aristocratic society or of a state-enforced Catholic confessional monopoly, both of which Pio Nono still held to, the encyclical's claim that the church's mission had a communal and public character remains an abiding and fundamental principle at the foundation of Catholic social teaching. (Over one hundred years later, Pope Paul VI would elaborate extensively on this Catholic understanding of evangelization as both personal and societal in his apostolic exhortation *Evangelii nuntiandi*, 8 December 1975.)[143]

The encyclical's thematic structure can be analytically divided into five sections:

- fundamental errors of religion and society;
- derivative errors of political, economic, familial, and ecclesial life;
- the means for promoting these errors;

- Catholic teaching on religion and society; and

- the Catholic theological and spiritual response to these errors.

These five themes were introduced by an indictment of "wicked men" who were "promising liberty whereas they are the slaves of corruption." The indictment also warned of "poisoned pastures" from which bishops must guard their flocks and of "a truly awful storm excited by so many evil opinions."[144]

Fundamental Error of Naturalism. The fundamental error of religion and society was labeled naturalism. This error, the encyclical charged, dared to teach that

> the best constitution of public society and civil progress together require that human society be conducted and governed without regard being had to religion any more than if it did not exist; or, at least, without any distinction being made between the true and false ones.[145]

Derivative Political Errors. According to the encyclical, several corollaries flowed from this fundamental principle. First, it argued, came the erroneous teaching that the civil power had no duty to restrain offenders against the Catholic religion except in the name of public peace. Second, it stated, came the erroneous teaching that citizens had an absolute liberty of conscience, as well as of speech and the press. For the encyclical, these were "liberties of perdition."[146]

The derivative political errors, according to the document, flowed from the fact that, with society no longer guided by "the genuine notion of justice and human right," their place was supplanted by "material force" (a notion from Newtonian physics, and central to the Enlightenment's cosmology and political philosophy[147]). This material force was then expressed as "the people's will" (an apparent reference to Rousseau), seen as manifested through "public opinion" or "in some other way." This material force was wrongly taken as "a supreme law, free from all divine or human control."[148]

Derivative Economic Error. The political analysis led directly to an economic analysis. In a prophetic comment that could be written amid the contemporary cultural crisis of the consumer society of late industrial capitalism, the encyclical noted:

But who does not see and clearly perceive that human society, when set loose from the bonds of religion and true justice, can have, in truth, no other end than the purpose of obtaining and amassing wealth, and that (society under such circumstances) follows no other law in its actions, except the unchastened desire of ministering to its own pleasures and interest?[149]

The document then linked the pursuit of wealth as a guiding principle to the liberal attack on the Catholic religious orders, as well as on church almsgiving and holy days (when working people were exempt from labor):

For this reason, men of this kind pursue with bitter hatred the Religious Orders…and cry out that the same have no legitimate reason for being permitted to exist…and (these wretches) also impiously declare that permission should be refused to citizens and to the Church, "whereby they may openly give alms for the sake of Christian charity"; and that the law should be abrogated "whereby on certain fixed days servile works are prohibited because of God's worship"; and on the most deceptive pretext that the said permission and law are opposed to the principles of the best public economy.[150]

Clearly at this point the encyclical was confronting economic liberalism and its accompanying utilitarian spirit, but it did not explicitly link this critique to the economic sufferings of the growing industrial working class. As mentioned earlier, liberals in the Latin Catholic countries regularly attacked the Catholic Church for absorbing too many economic resources in the service of religious contemplatives who had no "use-value." They also objected to the Catholic religious orders' extensive economic support for the unemployed poor, because this support interfered with the free-labor market. (If church welfare was available, workers would presumably not seek industrial jobs with less than a living wage.) With equal intensity the liberals attempted to end the broad range of religious holidays, during which the community was excused from work.

Derivative Family Error. Next the analysis was extended to family life. It claimed that, just as these "wicked men" wished to banish religion from the public life of the state, so also they wished to banish it from the private life of the family. This error was linked particularly to communism and socialism, but the flow of the narrative implied that these were all a part of the wider false promise of the unguided liberty of naturalism. This false teaching proposed that the family derived its existence exclusively from the civil law and consequently insisted that the right to educate children belonged first not to the parents but to the state. In particular, such proponents sought to banish the church from the education of youth.[151]

Derivative Error on Church and Society. Finally, the church itself was erroneously seen as subject to the state. According to the liberals, the church had no authority to proclaim decrees without prior governmental approbation, and it could never bind the conscience regarding temporal things or restrain anyone by temporal punishments. For the encyclical, this meant that ecclesiastical power was seen as not of divine but rather of civil origin.[152]

Print Medium as Carrier. The medium of all these errors was again the plague of "pestilential books, pamphlets, and newspapers dispersed over the whole world." So dangerous were these books that some, "moved and excited by the spirit of Satan," have even used them, the encyclical noted, to deny the divinity of Christ.[153]

Response of Natural Law and Repentance. The encyclical responded to these errors by proclaiming Catholic teaching, which it also saw as the teaching of the "eternal natural law engraven by God in all men's hearts" and as the conclusion of "right reason." This position held that kingdoms were founded not on the state but on God and that the Creator alone was the true source of freedom.[154] It claimed that this truth cannot be forgotten in our pursuit of freedom, for

> nothing is so deadly, so hastening to a fall, so exposed to all danger, (as that which exists) if, believing this alone to be sufficient for us that we receive free will at our birth, we seek nothing further from the Lord; that is, if forgetting our Creator we abjure his power that we may display our freedom.[155]

Further, in an extremely broad generalization the encyclical claimed that all kingdoms "rest on the foundation of the Catholic faith." Political leaders were called to recognize that "the royal power was given not only for the governance of the world, but most of all for the protection of the Church." (Note that political power was presumed to be "royal.") The "royal will" must be subjected to "Christ's Priests" and not raised "above theirs."[156]

Since the encyclical read the crisis as fundamentally spiritual (perpetrated by "wicked men" and excited by "the spirit of Satan"), the logical response would have to be spiritual. So it proposed a program of prayer and penance:

> Now, amidst such great calamities both of the Church and of civil society, amidst so great a conspiracy against Catholic interests and this Apostolic See, and so great a mass of errors, it is altogether necessary to approach with confidence the throne of grace, that we may obtain mercy and find grace in timely aid.[157]

The document then sought to "excite the piety of all the faithful" to pray and to be "cleansed through the sacrament of Penance," and it offered a plenary indulgence in the form of a Jubilee for the year 1885. Issued on the tenth anniversary of the "Dogmatic Definition of the Immaculate Conception," *Quanta cura* concluded with an appeal to Immaculate Mary, as well as to Peter and Paul.[158]

Selected Encyclicals from 1865 to 1875

Two more encyclicals focused again on the Papal States.

Levate, issued in 1867 to all the Catholic bishops of the world in the face of attack on the Papal States, complained that "evil men" who were "entirely animated by a diabolical spirit" surrounded the pope. It claimed that these men were aided by "officials of the government of Piedmont," who even supplied them with "arms and other goods."[159]

Respicientes, issued in 1870 again to all the bishops, reported that the government of Piedmont, taking advantage of the Franco-Prussian war (with few French troops available to defend the pope), had invaded the Papal States and had even seized the city of Rome to overthrow the pope's temporal rule. This, at last, was the end of the papacy's thousand-year-old temporal power.[160]

In addition to decrying his loss of the temporal power and reflecting the zealot party's concern with expressive symbolism, the pope continued to blame the print media, whose dangers he reported to have experienced directly in his own city.

> Wicked books filled with lies, infamy, and impiety are offered for sale and disseminated widely; numerous magazines are published each day to corrupt minds and upright laws, to show contempt for religion, and to rouse public opinion against Us and this Apostolic See. In addition, filthy and shameful pictures and other things of this kind are published in which sacred things and persons are derided and exposed to public ridicule.[161]

The pope then described the democratic elections held in the Papal States as "a monstrous crime," for they "made use of a ludicrous type of plebiscite in the provinces stolen from Us." After declaring the usurpation of the Papal States "unjust, violent, null, and void," Pio Nono painted the new image of captivity that would encompass the papacy for decades to come. "We protest before God and the whole Catholic world that, while detained in such captivity, We are unable to exercise Our supreme pastoral authority safely, expediently, and freely."[162]

Ubi nos. The following year, in his encyclical *Ubi nos* issued again to all the bishops, Pio Nono once more lamented the loss of the Papal States. He thanked the Catholic people of the world for their sympathy and support, and rejected the "Guarantees" of the papacy offered by the Piedmont government. Patriarchally, he described the people of Rome as his "children" and worried about their future. And clerically he denounced the fact that "lay" powers were now attempting to control the church. In turn, matrifocally he described Christian rulers not as members of the church but as its "sons."[163] Similarly, in a later 1874 encyclical to the bishops of the Austrian Empire, he cited Ambrose the Great to repeat his clericalized view of the church. "The palace belongs to the emperor, the Church to the priest."[164]

Finally, in *Ubi nos*, the pope apocalyptically portrayed the loss of the Papal States as an institutional repetition of the crucifixion of Jesus. He groaned that "now indeed is the hour of wickedness and the power of darkness." Yet without understanding how, he nonetheless believed that out of this would come some kind of resurrection. "But it is the final hour and the power quickly passes away. Christ the strength of God and the wisdom of God is with us, and He is on our side. Have confidence: He has overcome the world."[165]

Intriguingly, with this encyclical and with the ten more encyclicals that would follow before his death, Pio Nono no longer continued his devotional custom of concluding with an appeal to his virgin warrior queen, the Immaculate Mary. Instead, he turned to themes of Christ, the church, and the Trinity. His great mother figure did not save him, at least not in the way he had hoped. No longer appealing to her strength, he now appeared to draw on a divine power deeper than the maternal symbol.

Next came two encyclicals commemorating the twenty-fifth anniversary of his pontificate.

Beneficia Dei. In the first of these, *Beneficia Dei*, issued in 1871 to all the bishops of the world, Pius IX reviewed both the accomplishments of his papacy and the crises that it had suffered, and reflected tragically on the recent Paris Commune.[166] In speaking of the commune, he described the communards as "God-forsaken scum," condemned their murder of the Archbishop of Paris, and lamented that he saw "so many sons in revolt."[167]

Yet overall there was in this document a surprising sense of spiritual calm and confidence, as if Pio Nono had passed through the turbulent storm to a peaceful place. Writing of the "church militant...prevailing," he could not have been referring any longer to the temporal power or legal privileges, for most of that was now gone. Rather, he must have had in mind the growing spiritual renewal sweeping many Western European Catholic communities. Where once he had constantly spewed vicious invectives against "wicked men" and "diabolical schemes," now he wrote of his soul returning to the "Prince of Shepherds," in whose "bosom there is refreshment from the evils of this troubled and painful life and a blessed haven of eternal calm and peace."

Clearly that "calm and peace" had already entered his inner spirit. He ended by noting that the document was issued on the feast of the Most Holy Trinity.[168]

Saepe venerabiles fratres. The next encyclical, *Saepe venerabiles fratres*, issued in the same year and sent to all the bishops of "the Catholic World," was apparently a spontaneous and surprised expression of gratitude for the great wave of sympathy and support that Pio Nono was still receiving. He noted that the bishops and Catholic people had "redoubled" their prayer for him and for the church.[169]

This sympathy touched him deeply and gave him greater confidence in the ultimate triumph of the church, though there was no sense any longer that this triumph would be temporal. He was especially moved that "the poor as well as the rich" had contributed financially to support him. In response, he called for still greater unity in the church, to provide a "full phalanx" of strength against the enemies of God. But, again, he no longer seemed to fear these enemies or to rage against them. Rather, with his new sense of confident spiritual power, he proclaimed, "The more madly impiety persecutes and oppresses it, and the more cunningly it attempts to deprive the Church of all human aid, the more wonderfully God strengthens the Church."[170]

The Eve of a Strategic Shift

The story of Pius IX remains one of the most intriguing of the entire history of the papacy. In his person the thousand-year-old aristocratic-royal model of the papacy met its collapse. Yet at the same time, and in his very own person, he planted the seeds for a modern spiritual and populist renewal of the papacy.

This new model would be a papacy stripped of coercive-instrumental power over society but vastly enriched in symbolic-expressive power. This new style of power would in turn be based on modern industrial technologies of communication and transportation, and populist lay and religious mobilization, but also on increasingly absolute control over the church's institutional life. The cultural and political offensive of early or local capitalism had provoked this transformation, though the pope who experienced it scarcely addressed its economic revolution.

Shortly before his death Pio Nono seemed to have realized the need for a new strategy, for he reportedly shared the following reflection:

> I hope my successor will be as much attached to the Church as I have been and will have as keen a desire to do good. Beyond that, I can see that everything has changed; my system and my policies have had their day, but I am too old to change my course; that will be the task of my successor.[171]

Pio Nono was indeed correct. With the death of the old pope, the entire classical papal paradigm came to its end. With the election of Leo XIII in 1878, a new modern papal strategic period was born. Dramatically shifting the policies of the prior period, yet also building on the insights of his predecessors, the new pope would launch what Michael Schuck has called the Leonine strategy, destined in its own cycle to last over seventy years. It is to that strategy that we now turn.

Part II.

Modern Foreground

The Leonine Encyclicals and National Capitalism
1878–1958

*Modern Papal Promotion of
an Anti-Socialist and Social-Welfare Revision
of Liberalism in Support of
a New Bourgeois Christian Civilization
for the North Atlantic Nations*

4

The Leonine Papal Strategy of Reforming National Capitalism

Leo XIII's Appeal to Moderate Liberals Against Secular Socialists

---

This chapter examines how the papacy responded strategically to the middle or national stage of modern industrial capitalism, alternately described as the era of social-welfare liberalism.[1]

This national stage of industrial capitalism spanned approximately eighty years, from 1880 to 1960, while the papal strategy for this period ran from the election of Leo XIII in 1878 to the death of Pius XII in 1958. Following the categorization of Michael Schuck, this entire papal strategy may be described as "Leonine." Pope Leo XIII established a Catholic institutional strategy that would not be fundamentally changed during the tenure of the next four popes.[2]

As developed earlier, within the historical context of early or local capitalism (based on the factory revolution), and particularly in the wake of the French Revolution, the papacy in continental Western Europe had been responding primarily to cultural and political attacks on Catholic aristocratic property and power, including the power and property of the clerical aristocracy. These attacks came from a rising lay bourgeoisie guided by the modern liberal philosophy of the modern European Enlightenment, riding a revolutionary wave of liberal democracy, and constructing a secularizing laissez-faire liberal state.[3] The continental European liberal attacks emerged on the terrain of politics and culture, since there had been only limited industrial penetration into the Catholic lands. For most of Catholic Europe, economic modernization would come only after the political and cultural defeat of the clerical and lay aristocracies.

In industrial capitalism's more powerful national stage (precipitated by the machine revolution in the second half of the nineteenth century), the relationship of ecclesial strategy to industrial capitalism became quite direct. For the Leonine popes faced increasing industrial capitalist penetration, accompanied by a growing Catholic working class and by a growing Catholic middle class, with both linked to industrial modernization. These popes also faced a growing socialist movement, controlled by radical bourgeois intellectuals and militantly competing for the allegiance of the working class.

In strategic response Leo XIII and his four successors in the Leonine period legitimated a reformed capitalist political economy. They also encouraged an expanding range of parallel Catholic social structures and movements to compete with secular liberal and socialist initiatives. In the prior period Pius IX had labeled the liberal threat one of "Christendom in apostasy." In this period the French Christian Democratic philosopher Jacques Maritain would speak of a "New Christendom," that is, a new form of Christian civilization adapted to a reformed industrial capitalist and liberally democratic society.[4]

This reforming and anti-socialist Catholic-liberal alliance took shape over many decades and became an important part of wider efforts to revise the original laissez-faire version of the liberal ideology. Papal legitimization of this reform supported both a new interventionist national state and national labor unions as important correctives to the economic libertarianism of laissez-faire. At the same time, the Leonine popes resisted the opposite threat of socialism—in the name of private property (albeit as seen with a strongly social function), and in the name of a limited state (though seen as one positively committed to the common good). They also strongly supported cultural freedom for the Catholic Church and stressed the priority of the family to the state.[5]

To repeat, during the period of national capitalism the Leonine papacy accepted the social-welfare model as a viable foundation for societal reform and for ecclesial evangelization. Again, this contrasted with the preceding period of local capitalism, during which the pre-Leonine papacy had completely rejected modern liberalism.

Leo's four successors—Pius X (1903–14), Benedict XV (1914–22), Pius XI (1922–39), and Pius XII (1939–58)—all made tactical modifications to Leo's original design, but the Leonine strategy still held.[6]

The mature achievement of this adaptive strategy climaxed during the post–World War II years in the middle of the twentieth century, when the Cold War's Catholic-liberal alliance proved so strong. At that time the papacy perceived the United States, by then the predominant industrial capitalist "superpower," as geopolitically central for the defense of "Christian civilization" against the strategic threat of militantly atheistic Soviet communism. Yet even then the seeds for a breakdown of the modern Leonine strategy were already being planted by the nascent cybernetic technologies and newly developing global scale of industrial capitalism's third stage.[7] The next pope, John XXIII (1958–63), would seek a distinct strategic response to the full emergence of global capitalism, but that is the subject of the next book.

The number of papal encyclicals for the period of national capitalism was enormous. Whereas the pre-Leonine strategy spanned ninety years and generated only fifty-three encyclicals, the new Leonine strategy spanned eighty-one years and generated one hundred and eighty-five documents. In Claudia Carlin's five-volume collection of the contemporary papal encyclicals from 1740 to 1981, the documents of the pre-Leonine and Johannine (or post-Leonine) periods each occupy only one volume, while those of the Leonine strategy encompass three full volumes.[8] Clearly, at least until 1981, the texts of the Leonine strategy represented the dominant set of the contemporary encyclical tradition.

The Need for a New Strategy

Again, during the period of local capitalism, the pre-Leonine popes had sought to defend the Catholic Church as it came under attack from continental European liberalism. With the triumph of liberal power in national capitalism, the danger became just the opposite, namely, that the Catholic Church might be pushed to the margins of European society. So, whereas the old strategy had rejected the liberal world of local capitalism in the name of restoring the ancien régime, a new strategy was needed to make the Catholic Church, in the language of British sociologist William McSweeney, "relevant" to the triumph of liberalism in industrial capitalism's national stage.[9]

Again, Pio Nono, the last pope of the pre-Leonine period, had recognized at the end of his life that the external societal situation had changed.[10] The papacy was no longer able to resist the consolidation of modern liberal bourgeois political and economic power. The old aristocratic world had been vanquished, and the new bourgeoisie was already reshaping society in its own image. A fresh papal strategy was needed, one that would undertake a rapprochement with modern democratic liberalism and with the industrial capitalist experience, though without compromising essential Catholic principles.

The Bourgeois Triumph in National Capitalism

As noted in Chapter 2, the consolidation of bourgeois power in national capitalism was signaled by the dawn of a new technological-economic stage, the machine age, as the fruit of the second wave of the Industrial Revolution. This stage was based on advanced metallurgy, on important developments in chemistry (particularly petrochemicals), and on early electricity. By its creation of national railroad systems, as well as of steamships and telecommunications, this second wave of the Industrial Revolution brought forth integrated "national economies" supported by the expanding conquest of industrial colonialism (with the machine gun as the crucial weapon).

So vast was the scale and cost of the now-mechanized factories (in effect, a series of powerful machines connected by an internal rail system, known as the "assembly line") that control came under giant monopolistic or oligopolistic national corporations. Guided by expanding bureaucratic structures called management, these corporations employed masses of industrial workers for mass production in service of a new mass consumption.

This technological-economic revolution of national capitalism led to dramatic changes both in the form of the liberal state and in its underlying liberal ideology. Drawing especially on the German tradition, there emerged a semi-organic revision of the laissez-faire liberal philosophy, which in turn supported a corporatist reform of the liberal state. Central to this reform was the eventual acceptance of state intervention into the economy on behalf of the common good and eventual legal authorization for labor unions. In political terms the new ideological form came to be known as social-welfare liberalism.

In this new national capitalist context, the papacy's internal pastoral policy needed to address the new fact that the European Catholic laity, once composed largely of a majority of peasants ruled by a small aristocratic class, was increasingly being drawn into the expanding industrial working class and professional-technical-commercial middle class. An anti-modern Catholic ghetto, totally disconnected from the new bourgeois societal reality, would not hold the allegiance of the Catholic laity in the modern liberal world.

Finally, and perhaps most important, a new competitor had appeared on the scene, namely, socialism (and communism, as part of the general socialist movement). It was radicalizing the earlier bourgeois attack on Catholicism and attacking the ancient institution of the family. Still worse, it was attracting large numbers of Catholics within the new industrial working class, who were then turning antireligious. Pio Nono had recognized that socialism presented the most dangerous rising force, but he had not separated his resistance against socialism from his overall resistance to what he saw as the wider liberal "barbarism."[11]

Now, however, socialism appeared as clearly distinct from and opposed to moderate liberalism.[12] The distinctive threat required a strategic shift that separated out socialism as the acute and unique danger, distinct from liberalism and one that endangered even more seriously the foundations of church and society. Identifying socialism as a separate enemy provided the common ground for a Catholic reforming alliance with the moderate wing of modern liberal bourgeoisie.[13]

The Election of Leo XIII

At the conclave following the death of Pius IX, almost all of the Catholic cardinals were present for the first time in history, thanks to capitalism's creation of the steamship and railroad. Also for the first time, the College of Cardinals was no longer a largely aristocratic body. Thanks to changes by Pius IX, sons of the urban middle class or of the more affluent tier of the rural peasantry were more typical.[14]

Yet the cardinal electors quickly chose as the next pope one of the few remaining aristocrats, Gioacchino Vincenzo Pecci, Cardinal Archbishop of Perugia.[15] Pecci was a moderate who stood between "zealot" and "liberal" candidates, though more inclined toward the "liberal" side. Of advanced age and in poor health, he was apparently viewed by some in the same way that the later John XXIII would be by his electors: as a caretaker who would neither make great changes nor live very long.[16] Pecci took the name Leo XIII, after his patron Leo XII.

Once the aristocratic cardinal assumed the papacy, it quickly became clear that a new strategy was being born. Leo's primary goal remained the same as that of Pius IX, namely, the restoration of the Davidic-Christic paradigm of evangelization by ultramontanist centralization in papal clerical power. But with Leo the pursuit of that goal shifted from defense to offense, that is, from retreat to outreach, at least in external societal policy.[17]

Leo was prepared to form a tactical alliance with moderate elements of consolidated liberal power, in order to fight what he saw as the greater strategic danger of socialism.[18] Noting this dramatic policy shift and comparing the new pope with his predecessor, the French Le Monde commented, "Where Pius IX opened an abyss, Leo XII traversed it with a bridge."[19]

As a young aristocratic cleric, Pecci had caught the attention of the papal court and had been sent first on missions within Italy, and then, as papal nuncio, to Belgium. In Belgium, the scene of the first major continental industrialization of a Catholic territory and of the first successful Catholic-liberal political coalition (against Protestant Dutch power), the young clerical diplomat had met both the political and economic faces of the new industrial capitalist society. But at that time, disastrously failing to understand the new political and economic realities, he had been recalled to Rome. Despite his diplomatic failure, Pecci would later become the first pope ever to have had direct contact with the Industrial Revolution.[20]

Incurring the abiding hostility of the papal secretary of state Cardinal Antonelli, yet apparently retaining the affection of Pius IX, the future pope was then exiled to the post of Archbishop of Perugia.

Remaining there for thirty-one years, he devoted his life to pastoral and intellectual work and became beloved by the local people, though he still had enough influence in Rome to be named a cardinal. Spoken of as a man who kept "a foot in both camps," he was said to be progressive in social policy but conservative in ecclesial policy—a papal pattern that would continue through the entire Leonine strategy and even beyond it.[21]

Drawing on his constant studies of religion and science, Pecci published late in his years at Perugia a series of pastoral letters that, while conceived from a traditionalist and even triumphalist framework, had nonetheless called for reconciliation between the Catholic Church and modern civilization. In particular, his letter of 1877 had caught wide attention, for it diplomatically supported both the Syllabus of Errors and modern science, as well as the needs of the industrial working class.[22]

A turning point in Pecci's life, the letter had precipitated a call to Rome for the key curial position of *camerlengo* or papal chamberlain. At the pope's death he became the Vatican's senior administrator and the one who prepared the conclave to elect the next pope. Himself elected pope at that conclave, Pecci immediately sought to implement the vision of his pastoral letters, which called for the reconciliation of a traditional church with modern civilization.

Dualist Diplomatic and Pastoral Policies

As we will see, two very different sets of policy marked Leo's strategy at its deepest level.

- *External Diplomatic Policy for Society.* First, for outer-oriented societal or diplomatic policy, Leo would cooperate with moderate liberals in reforming the political-economic side of modern liberalism, both as a defense against socialism and as a potential societal base for both social reform and social evangelization. He would, in effect, attempt a modern revival in bourgeois form of the now collapsed aristocratic Christian civilization.

- *Internal Pastoral Policy for Church.* Second, in an opposite pattern, for ecclesial or pastoral policy Leo would attempt to prevent the church's internal life from being contaminated by the cultural-spiritual side of modern liberalism. He would do this especially by maintaining an intellectually segregated clerical and religious culture and by keeping strict hierarchical control over lay members, even as they were mobilized to defend the church and to reform society.

Thus Leo shifted external societal-diplomatic policy to the offensive but kept internal ecclesial-pastoral policy defensive and began to impose strict theological uniformity. Yet amid the external diplomatic engagement with liberalism that Leo's new strategy fostered, it would prove difficult to isolate internal Catholic pastoral and intellectual life from the wider liberal cultural ferment. As a result, over the long run, papal strategic security regularly had to resort to internal pastoral and intellectual repression.[23]

The strategic problematic became how to adapt the classical aristocratic paradigm of Catholic tradition and order to the modern liberal bourgeois paradigm of secular progress and freedom, without losing the church's internal polity structure of a clerical aristocracy to liberal democratization or lay secularization. The chosen structural solution was to compete externally on the reform liberal terrain through the creation or expansion of parallel structures (modern Catholic social-welfare institutions and movements) while ideologically exercising tight control over Catholic theological-pastoral life.

The phrase "parallel structures" above refers to the network of Catholic institutions and movements created or expanded to compete with liberal or socialist initiatives in the same areas. These included Catholic education at every level from primary school to universities; Catholic health and charitable services; utilization of modern printing for Catholic newspapers and book publishing; the utilization of modern transportation for Catholic pilgrimages; and Catholic associations of workers (eventually including Catholic unions), of employers, of specialized professionals, of women, of families, and of youth.[24] Activist lay associations would later be officially given the name Catholic Action.[25] These parallel structures also included explicitly Christian-Democratic political parties.[26]

Within Leo's papacy these Catholic parallel structures did not develop all at once. For example, though Leo approved the vague concept of Christian Democracy, he nonetheless tried to block actual Catholic political parties, apart from the special cases of Belgium and Germany. (Apparently he remained in his heart a monarchist.[27]) Further, the arena of Social Catholicism stood throughout the period as contested terrain, always subject to great tensions within the episcopacy and, in spite of supportive magisterial pronouncements, never comfortably embraced by the full Catholic leadership.[28]

Another new element in Leo's strategy was heightened affirmation of the family as the foundation of society, though this theme was more developed by his successors.[29] In industrial capitalism's limited local stage, liberals had tried to secularize marriage and the education of youth, but apart from a few radicals they had never significantly questioned the validity of the family or its right to private property. Now in industrial capitalism's more powerful national stage, many socialist intellectuals publicly argued that the family itself was oppressive and needed to be eliminated, along with private property.[30]

Chart 2.
Elements of the Leonine Strategy

Primary Enemy:	Socialism (and Communism)
Primary Ally:	Moderate Bourgeoisie (reformist wing)
Cultural Program:	Philosophy of Thomas Aquinas
Political Program:	Christian Democracy (or Catholic Action)
Economic Program:	Social Catholicism
Ecclesial Program:	Parallel Structures (plus centralized ideological control)

Upon his election Leo XIII immediately began to implement his "grand design" for reconciliation of the traditional church and modern society.[31] Viewed analytically, this design contained three main lines of strategy: the first cultural, the second political, and the third economic. For each of these three lines of strategy Leo drew on already developing Catholic movements, namely, the Thomist revival, Christian Democracy, and Social Catholicism. All three movements found a common center in the strategic enemy of socialism, which Leo proposed as the threatening basis for a united front between traditional Catholicism and moderate liberalism.[32] Later it would become clear that yet another line of strategy needed to be added, namely, tighter control over the internal ideological life of the church itself.

Leaving aside the last element, since it only emerged full-blown in the next papacy, let us now review in more detail each of the other elements of Leo's grand strategy. I begin with the proposed common enemy, and develop at most length the element of Social Catholicism, since its themes are central to this study.

Socialism: The Primary Strategic Enemy

Through the first half of the nineteenth century the socialist movement had been a collection of assorted and relatively unorganized ideologies, all marginal to real social power. But the wave of revolutions arising in 1848 had revealed hidden continental networks of socialist activity (sometimes actually more anarchist than socialist, though the two were not well distinguished in the popular mind). Throughout the rest of the nineteenth century the strength of the socialist movement only increased.

Growing Threat of Socialist Revolution

When the International Workingmen's Association (popularly known as the First International) emerged in 1864, one of its key organizers, the German philosopher Karl Marx, was becoming widely known across socialist circles and his strain of "scientific" socialism was rising. Also on the working-class front, the democratic socialist Ferdinand Lassalle had already organized a significant labor party in Germany, while pragmatic trade unions were growing rapidly in Britain. Then 1870 saw the insurrection of the Paris Commune, which executed the Catholic Archbishop of Paris.[33] Further, as several decades of increasingly mechanized industrial development swept over Belgium, France, and Germany, the Catholic working class increased rapidly and with it the appeal of the socialists.[34]

The possibility that the socialists might gain state power represented a more severe threat than liberal power to the institutional security of the Catholic Church. For the most part, liberals had only attempted to secularize society, while leaving religion free as a private institution (albeit stripped of political and economic power). But most socialists were boldly announcing that they wished to destroy religion, especially the Catholic Church. The most famous anti-Catholic declaration was Frederick Engels's unfulfilled death sentence:

> Before profane feudalism could be successfully attacked in each country and in detail, this, its sacred central organization, had to be destroyed...Every struggle against feudalism, at that time, had to take on a religious disguise, had to be directed against the [Catholic] Church.[35]

The Common Enemy of Church and State

Elected in the wake of the Paris Commune, Leo XIII defined socialism as the strategic danger. Again, the danger was clear, certainly to church leaders but also to social elites, since socialists were plotting to overthrow the whole bourgeois social order. Shortly after the new pope's election, two assassination attempts were made against the German emperor.[36]

The socialist danger provided Leo with an opportunity for diplomatic rapprochement with the "new princes" of the bourgeois order. In this regard, McSweeney noted:

> The threat of socialism facing European governments offered an opportunity for an exchange of services between Church and state, to their mutual benefit. Throughout his pontificate, Leo was deeply concerned, almost obsessed, by the evils of modern society which he saw embodied in socialism. He was convinced that the Church had an essential political role to play in the modern world and that the Church alone was capable of restoring the ruins of society.[37]

Simply to defend themselves against the socialist threat, Leo proposed, these bourgeois leaders needed the weight of Catholic citizens. But more important, Leo argued, the whole new bourgeois order needed religious legitimization. For this, it needed a viable social philosophy, which could turn modern society away from the rebellious philosophical errors that had accompanied its birth. Such a philosophy would have the task of returning modern society to a more stable organic-hierarchical self-understanding, albeit with democratic and industrial modifications. In addition, Leo believed, such a reformed society would have to accept the central public role of the Catholic religion. A Catholic reform of liberalism (supported by the Catholic people, grounded on a Christian philosophy, and guided by the public voice of the Catholic Church) would constitute, Leo claimed, society's strongest defense against the threat of revolutionary socialism.

The British historian Derek Holmes has cited a letter of Leo to the German emperor, William II, that clearly stated this hope and Leo's proposal that an alliance between the papacy and Germany (the ascendant European power) could lead this reform. After comparing the German emperor to Charlemagne, Leo wrote: "I dreamed that you, the actual Emperor of Germany, had received from me, Pope Leo XIII, the mission to combat socialistic and atheistic ideas, and to recall Europe to Christianity."[38]

The task of carrying out this reform fell to the next three planks in Leo's program of Catholic-liberal reconciliation.

Thomism:
The Leonine Philosophical Program

In a bold decision Leo established the intellectual base of the new papal strategy by ordering that the future of Catholic intellectual life be grounded on a revival of the philosophical-theological system of the medieval scholastics in general and Thomas Aquinas in particular.

For over a century the social analysis of the papal encyclicals had traced the roots of the contemporary European crisis to what it saw as the false philosophical teachings of the Enlightenment, and before that to what it saw as the theological heresies of the Protestant

Reformation. It followed, therefore, that a Catholic rapprochement with modern civilization would have to proceed from "correct" teachings in both the philosophical and theological arenas.

In the first year after his election, with his 1879 encyclical *Aeterni patris*, Leo announced his decision to make Thomism the dominant Catholic intellectual ground.

The Thomist Revival

The Catholic intellectual hegemony that Leo established for Thomism had roots in the papacy of Pius IX. Following the shock of the revolutions of 1848, Pio Nono had asked a group of pro-Thomist Jesuits to establish a new journal to aid the papacy. Founded in Naples but later moved to Rome and named *Civiltà Cattolica*, this publication became a key center for developing and propagating the papal strategy of ultramontanism. Totally opposed to anything "modern," the Jesuits of this journal aggressively promoted a neo-Thomist revival as part of an attack against "modernism" and "Americanism."[39]

At the Jesuits' Roman College, the young Gioacchino Pecci had been a student of Taparelli d'Angello, a founder of the new journal (along with Carolo Maria Curci, who had also been a student of Taparelli's along with Pecci). Taparelli became the Jesuit provincial at Naples and the superior at the Jesuit scholasticate. There he influenced another key figure in the Thomist revival, Matteo Liberatore, reportedly a principal drafter of Leo's future social encyclical, *Rerum novarum*. In addition, Pecci's Jesuit brother, Giuseppe, embraced Thomism while studying at the Jesuit college at Modena. Later as Archbishop of Perugia, Pecci brought his brother to the diocesan seminary, as well as the future Cardinal Zigliara, a major figure in the restoration of Thomism. Also, a close friend of Liberatore's was Joseph Kleutgen, appointed to the Jesuits' Roman College in 1843 and an important collaborator with *Civiltà Cattolica*. According to McCool, Kleutgen was later probably one of the drafters of *Aeterni patris*, Leo's encyclical on Thomism. He also reportedly drafted the final version of Vatican I's *Dei Filius*. The stage was set for a papal neo-Thomist offensive.[40]

Thus the revival of Thomism had been developing since the 1840s, particularly among Italian and German theologians, though initially these Thomists represented only one competing Catholic school. A dominant figure, already mentioned, was Joseph Kleutgen, a German Jesuit resident in Rome from 1843 and appointed in 1851 as a consultor to the Congregation of the Index. Backed up by Leo's papal authority, Thomists soon took control of the Catholic seminary system, with vigorous support from the religious orders, particularly the Jesuits and the Dominicans. Gradually in Catholic institutions, authoritarian restrictions began to reduce the pluralistic university theologies to a single neoscholastic model centered in Thomism.[41]

Until its crisis in the post–World War II period, neoscholasticism presided as the official philosophy of Catholic education. Carrying its own limited internal pluralism, it contained both subordinate Augustinian-Franciscan strains and the dominant Thomist strain.

The dominant Thomist strain eventually split into two distinct schools. On one side, there emerged transcendental Thomism, which returned to dialogue with Kant, the archenemy of the initial Thomist revival. On the other side, there continued an attempt in political philosophy to adapt classical Thomism to modern democratic societies (as the philosophical basis of Christian Democratic parties). This political wing of Thomism, particularly as seen in the writings of Jacques Maritain, kept closest to the other Leonine programs of Social Catholicism and Christian Democracy, whereas transcendental Thomism seemed to distance itself from the social struggle.[42]

Strategic Advantages of Thomism

From the perspective of the Leonine analysis, there were four strategic advantages to the Thomist system.

Epistemological Realism. First, the root of modern Enlightenment's philosophical errors was perceived as epistemological—the loss of moderately realist communion between the perceiving subject and the perceived object. Thomists insisted on the moderately realist character of human knowledge as capable of perceiving the essence of external objective realities. They saw the subject-object split as flowing indirectly from the earlier Protestant "rebellious" rejection of the visible church and of the objective authority of papal leadership in the name of subjective conscience. In strategic response the Thomist revival asserted as its fundamental point of defense against Enlightenment philosophies a moderately "realist" philosophical claim for the intellect's capability of objectively valid knowledge.

The modern liberal epistemological split between subject and object had appeared in different strands in British empiricism and continental rationalism. The modern subjectivist epistemology of René Descartes had confined knowledge to the inner self, whose only reach beyond the self was mathematical (quantitative and non-sensuous). The modern subjectivist epistemology of Immanuel Kant had portrayed reason as transcendental subjective activity before an unknowable objective world. The British tradition had tended to reduce knowledge to subjective consciousness of quantifiable impressions from sensory stimulations. Such modern subjectivist epistemological models, according to the Thomists, eventually undermined all objective authority and were a main root of the modern cultural crisis.

Again, the Thomists ultimately traced the epistemological break with objective reality to the Reformation's rejection of papal authority and more widely of a visible church. In response, they claimed, Thomism recovered both objectivity for epistemology and hierarchical institutional authority for social philosophy, but only when the influence of sin upon reason was recognized and the redeeming role of the church as well, including its theological oversight of philosophy.[43]

Community and Authority. Second, modern Thomists viewed the modern claim of autonomous subjectivity (again theologically in Protestantism and philosophically in liberalism) as leading to a priority of the subjective individual over objective institutions and thus to the universal erosion of both social community and social authority. In strategic response, therefore, the Thomist revival set forth its communitarian and hierarchical understanding of human society. In the Thomist paradigm the individual emerges only within the fabric of rooted community under legitimate authority. The Thomist position thus claimed a middle social ground between the atomized capitalist individual and the massified socialist collectivity.[44]

Ethics and Natural Law. Third, in another consequence of the Enlightenment's modern epistemological split of subject and object, Thomists saw modern ethics as increasingly polarized on one side into a literary-humanistic spirit characterized by emotive and relativistic subjectivity, and on the other side into a technological-scientific spirit marked by mechanistic and determinist objectivity. They saw both sides as errors flowing first from the Reformation's rejection of natural theology in favor of voluntarist and emotive faith, and second from the Enlightenment's related mechanistic paradigm of the rationality of the cosmos. In strategic response, therefore, the third advantage of Thomism seemed to be its affirmation of an ethics grounded in an intelligible and objective natural law yet expressed in the free subject within organic community.[45]

Public Religion. Fourth, Thomists saw the Reformation's uprooting of supernatural faith from its Catholic complementary relationship with natural reason as precipitating the opposite reaction of the Enlightenment's claim simply to eliminate the supernatural, a position described in many encyclicals as naturalism. The tragic result, according to this analysis, was the separation of faith and reason, leading to the privatization of religion and the secularization of society. In strategic response Thomists affirmed a hierarchically complementary relationship between reason and faith, and between natural and supernatural spheres, and consequently promised to restore religion to a public position in society and thereby to safeguard society.[46]

Thus Leo XIII found in Thomism a fundamental philosophical instrument that he believed capable of correcting an interrelated series of philosophical errors in modern culture. Again, these perceived errors were the fragmenting polarization of (1) subject and object, (2) individual and community, (3) mind and will, (4) faith and reason, and (5) religion and society. In addition, since the underlying Thomist cosmology was also boldly hierarchical and theocratic, its philosophical paradigm also supported the ecclesial authority of the pope over the church, as well as his proposed spiritual-moral authority over society. Further, the organic spirit of this hierarchical authority could be extended in reforming but antirevolutionary fashion to liberal democracy on behalf of the hierarchical political order of "ruler and ruled," as well as to industrial capitalism on behalf of justice to the hierarchical economic order of employer and employee.[47]

Following the analysis of Pierre Thibault, McSweeney commented on the self-consciously strategic role for the wider society in Leo's revival of Thomism:

> Contrary to popular thinking, the revival of Thomism by Pope Leo XIII was not a matter of peripheral interest in Church history, affecting only clerics and their training like the later and uncharacteristic imposition of Latin in the seminaries by Pope John XXIII. It was the center of a political strategy intended to bring about the restoration of a Christian social order, an organic hierarchic society united by common values and common faith under the temporal kingship of secular rulers and under the ultimate authority of the pope.[48]

According to this perspective, with a correct philosophy Leo would be able to provide moral guidance for both the culture and the state, as well as for the economy. But this would no longer be done in the classical paradigm of the defeated aristocratic world, where popes had claimed direct spiritual-political authority over lay princes (though such claims were seldom successful without powerful military allies). Rather, the papacy's moral authority would now be exercised indirectly in a new modern bourgeois paradigm, through the controlled mobilization of lay Catholics on major strategic fronts, organized through the parallel structures of modern institutions and movements, and using the new industrial technologies of mass communications and mass transportation. For this, Leo would legitimate the developing Catholic movement of Christian Democracy and its related movement of Catholic Action.[49]

Christian Democracy: The Leonine Political Program

Since the French Revolution, an ecclesial debate had continued over how to deal with the new democratic movements.[50]

On one side, as we saw earlier, the "zealot" faction of the papal bureaucracy had rejected any compromise with the French Revolution and had looked initially to restoration of absolutist monarchies. But a later generation of zealots had learned the populist technique of tapping the spiritual energy of lay Catholic protest through modern means of communications and transportation, particularly through a Catholic press and pilgrimages to papal Rome and Marian shrines.

On the other side, as we also saw earlier, the "politician" or "liberal" faction (again, they were not really liberals, but conservative accommodationists) favored diplomatic compromise with the new bourgeois democratic governments by means of elite concordats.

The second generation of the zealot party had supported grassroots Catholic lay movements when they were useful in populist struggle against secularizing liberal or socialist powers. The progressive politician party had preferred to go clerically over the heads of the Catholic laity to negotiate directly with government leaders as fellow elites.

A Cautious Populism

In the Leonine period papal tactics oscillated between zealot-populist and politician-elite, sometimes under the same pope.

Prior to being elected pope, Pecci had remained "open to both sides"; as pope he continued the delicate balance between the zealots and the politicians, but he employed that balance in favor of the politician party's reconciliation with the "new princes" of the liberal society.[51] Eventually he justified this as part of the search for a Christian Democracy, though during his pontificate the meaning of Christian Democracy was limited.

While the first wave of Christian Democracy had emerged during local capitalism in nineteenth century France with Lamennais and had suffered severe papal condemnation, a more successful second generation of Christian Democracy emerged with the advent of national capitalism. The second-generation zealots proved open to this populist movement because, after the total defeat of premodern aristocratic power, modern democratic mobilization of its lay membership was the only significant means remaining for church elites to pressure the new bourgeois political elites. In addition, grass-roots middle-class laity, often under the leadership of local priests, were themselves organizing in a democratic manner.[52]

The German Experience

Leo XIII faced his first major democratic political challenge in Germany with Chancellor Bismarck's *Kulturkampf* or "culture-war" against German Catholics. With Germany recently integrated as a nation, Bismarck thought it necessary to gain state control over all religions. This led him to mount a political attack on the Catholic Church, which was strong in the newly admitted Southern provinces. But Bismarck soon found himself weakened by fighting on two political fronts: one against intransigent Catholics, and another against the growing socialist movement. Still worse, in the politics of parliamentary voting the Catholic Zentrum or Center Party (the democratic political organ of German Catholics and forerunner of the German Christian Democratic Party) often allied with the socialists against Bismarck, particularly when his repressive legislation could be used against either group.[53]

Against this backdrop Leo launched a two-pronged diplomatic game. On the one hand, he sent letters to the German emperor expressing his desire to normalize relations with the German government and hinted that the Catholic Church could be an important ally in the battle against socialism. The emperor, disturbed by a recent attempt on his life, was potentially open to papal support. On the other hand, Leo directed the Center Party to keep up its pressure against Bismarck and implicitly allowed the party to work in coalition with socialists in the parliament, in order to strengthen his diplomatic hand in negotiations with Bismarck.[54]

Eventually Bismarck realized that the culture war against Catholics had been a serious mistake and that he needed to isolate the more dangerous enemy of socialism. Leo negotiated with Bismarck the end of the *Kulturkampf*. But, having used the Catholic lay Center Party for his goal of strengthening papal influence over the German government, Leo then bypassed the party's lay leaders, who had struggled for years in defense of Catholicism. He awarded high papal honors to Bismarck, but none to any Catholic lay leader of the Zentrum.[55]

Drawing on a secret dispatch from the papal nuncio in Vienna, the British diplomatic historian Anthony Rhodes cites the reported comments of Herr Windthorst, leader of the Center Party, and then adds his own remark:

> "It is with rancour…that the Zentrum has been made to stand aside while the Emperor and the Pope deal directly with one another, as they did in the old days before Parliamentary government was the rule." To make matters worse, Leo XIII then bestowed on Bismarck the highest honor of the Catholic Church for lay men, that of Cavaliere del Ordine di Cristo ("Knight of the Order of Christ"), a distinction not accorded to Windthorst.[56]

To explain why, McSweeney cites the analysis of Karl Von Aretin:

> Neither the French liberal Catholics nor later the leaders of the German Centre Party understood what the papacy disliked above all was the position of Catholic parties as mediators between state and church, and that Rome preferred to keep control of diplomatic negotiations at all stages. The papacy looked upon the Catholic political parties as the successors of the hated episcopal power structures of the eighteenth century, and feared an alliance between the state and its Catholic citizens over which Rome would have no control and which would also be against its system of centralization.[57]

The French Experience

When this second wave of Catholic democratic political energy also arose in France (often called the Second Christian Democracy), particularly from the leadership of the Catholic industrialist Leon Harmel and the *abbés democrates*, Leo opposed the creation of a

French Catholic Party. Yet he did support France's democratic government.[58]

In a special letter, *Au milieu des sollicitudes* (1892), Leo told French Catholics to rally in support of the Republic. Although Leo himself favored monarchy as the ideal government, he feared that intransigent French Catholics would lose everything and so attempted to redirect them toward republicanism. In the same year, in a press interview for a popular Parisian paper, he drew a parallel between the French Republic and what he saw as the favorable situation of the United States.[59] Rhodes cites Leo's letter:

> I am of the opinion that all French citizens should unite in supporting the government France has given herself. A republic is a legitimate form of government as any other. Look at the United States of America! There you have a Republic which grows stronger every day—and that in spite of unbridled liberty. And the Catholic Church there? It develops and flourishes. It has no quarrel with the State. What is good for the United States can be good for France too.[60]

Yet due to the strongly monarchist character of the French church, Leo's policy of French *Ralliement* failed. Since the time of the discredited Christian Democracy of Lamennais, much of the French church had bitterly clung to its monarchist heritage and vainly longed for a king. Meanwhile the republican government had entered into another wave of secularization, with an acute struggle over the control of education.[61]

Leo's letter had stunned the French Catholic community, which refused to follow his recommendation. The pope's failed policy of *Ralliement* was set back even more by the notorious *Affaire Dreyfus*, which reignited monarchist-republican antagonism. In one notable exception, however, leading lay Catholic social-activist and militant monarchist Comte de Mun accepted Leo's call to democracy, though his own class then ostracized him. Meanwhile French liberals, reacting against the intransigence of Catholics, moved toward the socialists, forming a virulently anti-clerical coalition aimed at breaking diplomatically with Rome and establishing complete separation of church and state. Thus the French equivalent of the German *Kulturkampf* temporarily succeeded, but only because French Catholics were antidemocratic. Decades later, however, French socialists and radicals would admit their failure to destroy French Catholicism. In 1925 Catholicism would be reestablished as the official religion of France.[62]

The Italian Experience

The most difficult expression of the second wave of Christian Democracy occurred in Italy, where Leo desperately needed to mobilize the Catholic laity to defend the church against nationalist and secularist political forces. In contradictory fashion, however, he also wished to restore the papacy's ancient role of an aristocratic kingship. Thus in his own native Italy, Leo remained officially obstinate on the "Roman Question" (the papacy's political status within Italy), and he continued to forbid Catholic participation in democratic electoral politics. Nonetheless, he did support the controlled mobilization of Italian lay Catholics in the defensive ecclesial movements of Catholic Action.

Much later, in the post–World War II period, Christian Democracy would prove the conservative strain, while major elements of Catholic Action would break beyond the conservative framework and move in the radical direction of Christian-Marist dialogue, and still later in Latin America in the direction of liberation theology. But that is a story for the next book.

Meanwhile a new generation of Italian Catholics, and particularly two activist priests, supported the formation of an Italian Christian Democratic Party. One of the priests was Romulo Murri, who had studied under an Italian socialist and proposed an "alliance of the people and the church," something much more radical than Leo's plan. The other was Luigi Sturzo, a Sicilian priest famous for organizing peasants in the south, and, after World War I, the founder of the Italian Popular Party, the precursor of the Italian Christian Democratic Party. But Leo held these initiatives in check, and blocked the creation of an Italian Catholic party. Later Pius X excommunicated Murri, who then left the clerical state to marry.

Like his predecessor Pius IX, Leo was holding out for restoration of the papacy's temporal power, at least over the city of Rome and with a path to the sea. Officially he refused to recognize or negotiate with the Italian government, and publicly he ignored the government's various proposals to establish an autonomous papal enclave within the city, though he did allow private conversations through intermediaries. He even ordered a Jesuit author who published a book proposing a solution to the Roman Question similar to the one later accepted in the Lateran Treaty to be expelled from the Jesuits.[63]

Leo's protracted negotiations with Bismarck seemed motivated in part by the false hope of obtaining Germany's support for restoration of his own kingly rule over the lost Papal States, though not by war. Leo also seemed to dream that a Catholic reconciliation with the French republic would allow France to again become the supportive ally of the papacy's restored temporal power.

But the emergent Italian nationalism proved too strong for the pope, even among Italian Catholics, and neither France nor Germany desired to intervene. So, like his predecessor, Leo remained a prisoner of the Vatican, though his prison was no longer a place of retreat but instead a platform for dialogue with the world.[64]

An Inconsistent Policy

Although apparently by instinct and by philosophy an aristocratic monarchist, Leo nonetheless sought in different ways for different places to adapt Catholicism to democratic political realities. For example, he accepted the pioneering liberal-Catholic alliance in Belgium and, as we have seen, initially spoke with praise of the experience of Catholics within America's liberal democracy. But he also condemned the Irish Fenian movement for independence from England (he considered it socialist) and, as noted, opposed Catholic participation in the democratic politics of his native Italy, since it threatened the restoration of his own monarchical power.[65]

Overall, the pope's personal preference in lay mobilization leaned toward hierarchically controlled Catholic Action rather than toward lay-led and semi-autonomous Christian-Democratic political parties. Yet even in this restricted sense, Catholic Action can be understood as a central element in the Leonine strategy's attempt to mobilize a grass-roots lay force to create the new democratic Christian civilization. Eventually Leo officially referred to the Catholic Action movement as a form of Christian Democracy. Tightly controlled by the hierarchy, Catholic Action was to stop short of partisan politics, yet was still to defend and advance the political interests of the church in a democratic and secular society. After Leo's time, however, the inner-ecclesial and tightly controlled model of Catholic Action found vigorous competition from a growing international network of lay-led and relatively autonomous Christian-Democratic political parties.[66]

Leo's overall church-state position was that the church should remain officially neutral on the form of government, provided the government supported religion and morality. Officially neutral, though again probably in his heart still an aristocratic monarchist, Leo abandoned the nineteenth-century papal rejection of democracy.[67]

Thus the Catholic papacy, which for nearly a hundred years after the French Revolution had opposed the wave of democracy that emerged in local capitalism, now began to build its strategy on democracy for the stage of national capitalism. From this time forward, the young Christian-Democratic movement, including hierarchically controlled lay movements and semi-autonomous lay-led Catholic political parties, would become a growing component in modern Catholic life.[68]

But a legitimization of democracy alone would prove insufficient to combat the socialists. For that Leo would need to add to his philosophical and political programs an economic component.

Social Catholicism: The Leonine Economic Program

The phrase *Social Catholicism* refers to the organized response by Catholic Christians to the harsh impact of capitalist industrialization upon the working class.[69]

Although during local capitalism Pope Gregory XVI had explicitly condemned the first wave of Social Catholicism in France, the encyclical corpus of that strategic period had ignored the social question. Pius IX had addressed workers in only one document, and then but briefly to urge them to be content with their lot, since "the Catholic Church teaches...slaves to remain true to their masters." Certainly both Gregory XVI and Pius IX had been aware of the new "social question," but their encyclicals avoided addressing it, presumably because the impending scale of the coming economic transformation had remained beyond their imagination, and their aristocratic frame of reference prevented them from conceiving any active role for protesting workers' movements. Instead their attention had been focused on the political question, that is, the turbulent conflict of church and state, and on the underlying cultural threat of the Enlightenment.

The great French Catholic historian Henri Daniel-Rops noted this striking omission. Speaking of the social activities of local church leaders among the new working classes of Belgium, France, Germany, and even Spain, he sadly commented:

> All this activity, it must be noted, was accomplished by laymen or priests working on their own. What of the hierarchy? Here is the black spot in the whole story; there appears to have been a wide gulf of ignorance and obtuseness between the small groups of Social Catholics and those who were responsible for the Church. The highest authority was silent: Gregory XVI's encyclical *Mirari vos* condemned all forms of liberalism except one, which it did not even name—economic liberalism, which left the worker at the mercy of capitalist power. When Cardinal Mastai-Ferretti became Pope Pius IX (1846), it was remembered that as a young canon in charge of St. Michael's hospice he had some original ideas (e.g., workers' participation in profits) and that as Bishop of Spoleto he had created a fund for waifs; it is said also that his library contained many books on social problems, especially on the amelioration of working-class conditions. But he was so much preoccupied with political questions that the first stages of his pontificate afforded little or no evidence of an interest in social affairs.[70]

Leo XIII, author of the historic 1891 social encyclical *Rerum novarum*, became the first pope ever to address the plight of modern industrial workers, albeit more than one hundred and thirty years after the start of the Industrial Revolution.

Conservative Aristocratic Roots

The movement of Social Catholicism had initial roots in a conservative aristocratic Catholic intellectual response to economic liberalism, even before industrialization reached the continent. Conservative Social Catholics held up a romantic vision of the Middle Ages: a family-centered agricultural system with urban craft guilds and communal corporations.[71] The romantic-conservative approach became dominant among Catholics vocal and active on the social question at the local level. Challenging all of liberalism, including its economic doctrine, these conservatives assumed that the Enlightenment's mechanistic paradigm needed to be resisted and the old organic-hierarchical paradigm defended, with a special role in society for the Catholic religion and for the aristocracy.[72]

Social Catholicism began after 1815, when local capitalism first penetrated Belgium, France, and Germany. Belgium had been the first continental European nation to industrialize, no doubt because of its proximity to England and its rich deposits of coal and iron, as well as its strong traditions of banking and artisanship. France followed more slowly, and only in cities with large-scale craft production like Lyons. Germany came next, and by the 1880s, at the start of national capitalism, it had become a major industrial power aspiring to global leadership in the world capitalist system.[73]

Social Catholicism supported a doctrine of hierarchical class harmony between capital and labor, even while taking up the defense of workers. For most of the century paternalistic experiments in Social Catholicism developed in France, but they were largely ineffective and continued to be dominated by a model of workers' clubs controlled by the upper classes (again, mostly aristocratic, but sometimes bourgeois), amid a sea of unchurched proletarian workers.

The main early French spokesperson for aristocratic conservatism was the Viscount de Bonald (1754–1840). He attacked the growing modern cities and the bourgeoisie, whose interests were served, he claimed, at the expense of the moral and physical health of the working class.[74] In a similar style, his son, the Archbishop of Lyon, Cardinal Louis de Bonald, in the 1830s accused the employers of that city of exploiting the workers by treating them as "nothing more than a machine."[75] In a work on Christian economics another conservative French nobleman, Alban de Villeneuve-Bargemont (1784–1850), contrasted the English liberal and the French "Christian" models and recommended keeping much of the population on the land. In 1840 he was the first member of the French parliament to urge the government to play a role in social reform.[76] Léonarde Simonde de Sismondi also rejected industrialism, advocated a conservative return to the land, defended state support for mutual-aid societies and credit unions, and advocated participation of the lower classes in administering their own associations, as with the old corporations of tradesmen.[77]

Through much of the nineteenth century the main leadership for Social Catholicism remained aristocratic. For example, Armand de Melun (1807–77), a lawyer turned "full-time voluntary worker for the poor," set up a series of workers' clubs and workshops for the unemployed, all on a *patronage* model.[78] Different from what we will see later as Kolping's model of workers controlling their own clubs, these initiatives were set up and directed by members of the *classes dirigeantes*. Since organizations of workers were illegal in France, any other model would have provoked police intervention. Indeed, the sermons of Francois Ledreuille, a member of the working-class who had gone to seminary and been ordained by the Archbishop of Paris, quickly provoked police anxiety.[79]

In 1844 and 1846, to professionalize and to connect various charitable activities, de Melun also founded a school of thought and action centered in a journal for the social question, *Annales de la Charité*, and an organization to pursue charitable activities, the Society for Charitable Economy.[80] Rejecting both liberalism (meaning laissez-faire) and socialism, this school supported state regulation of the economy. In a similar charitable style, St. Vincent de Paul conferences grew up across Belgium, France, and Germany.[81]

So Social Catholicism was not predominately the creation of liberal bourgeois Catholics, who were few in number, and certainly not of radicalized working-class Catholics; rather, it arose first from aristocratic Catholics. Among the few liberal Catholics, however, some like Charles de Montalembert even opposed social reform in the name of early liberalism's economic philosophy of laissez-faire. Yet over time Social Catholicism would be liberated of its conservative and paternalist assumptions and move toward accepting the independent leadership and organization of the working class itself, and also toward revisionist liberal and even vaguely socialist perspectives.[82]

Progressive Developments in Germany

Despite its conservative ethos, German Catholicism proved a fertile testing ground for progressive developments in Social Catholicism.

Adolf Kolping (1813–65), a former tradesman turned priest, organized the first truly working-class Catholic movement in Germany. He founded a wide network of workers' clubs for young male, unmarried journeymen (a network extending even to the United States). Kolping's model retained a priest-adviser but allowed only workers into these clubs, thus rejecting the reigning French paternalist model by which workers would be organized under the leadership and control of the "superior" or "directing classes." Kolping was able to develop a separate Catholic workers' movement without the "directing classes," because in Germany the employers were largely Protestant.[83]

A wide variety of other German figures also contributed to a non-paternalistic model of Social Catholicism. Franz Baader (1765–1841) criticized Adam Smith's self-interest model of the common good and proposed that German priests become social advocates on behalf of the proletariat without property. Franz Josef Buss (1803–78) worked for legislation in the German parliament to limit the working day to fourteen hours, with schooling required for children in the factories. Joseph Gorres (1776–1848), a lay liberal who later would catalyze the German Catholic social-rights movement, began a church-based charity organization.[84]

The greatest Social Catholic leader in Germany was Wilhelm Emmanuel von Kettler (1811–77), a Westphalian landed noble turned first civil servant, then priest, and finally Bishop of Mainz. In an 1849 book entitled *The Great Social Questions of the Present* Kettler criticized the theory of economic liberalism from a romantically conservative perspective and countered with Thomas Aquinas's theory of property, which defended private property but claimed it had a social responsibility. A historical thinker, Kettler challenged the Enlightenment's autonomous individualism, which he saw as leading to the opposite extreme of communism. Later, in an 1864 book entitled *The Labor Problem and Christianity*, Kettler reflected on the limitations of charitable and clericalist approaches. Shortly thereafter he endorsed what would become the model of the new social-welfare stage, namely, the combination of benevolent government intervention and workers' unions on the British model. Influenced by the moderate German democratic socialist Ferdinand Lassalle, he even drew near to the independent labor movement. Over time, Kettler would have strong influence on Leo XIII.[85]

Soon a group of young priests in Aachen began to organize a Catholic labor movement. But until the end of the *Kulturkampf*, Bismarck's anti-socialist and anti-Catholic legislation impeded the growth of either independent or Catholic labor unions in Germany. To undermine the socialist threat, the German chancellor pioneered one of the new planks that Kettler supported, namely, the interventionist policies of a reforming social-welfare state.[86]

In the next generation German intellectual leadership for the social Catholic movement fell to a young priest, Franz Hitze (1851–1921), editor of the magazine *Arbeiterwohl*, published by an association of Catholic employers and priests. Later Hitze became professor of social ethics at Münster. Although originally a corporativist, he ceased to reject industrial capitalist society and instead realistically took it as a given fact, while seeking to mitigate its abuses. By this time Germany's industrial power was indeed mighty, already displacing France as the preeminent industrial nation on the continent and threatening to replace Britain as the leading world-capitalist center. Hitze promoted workers' associations on the Kolping model (without employers but under clerical direction) and, as a deputy in the Reichstag, pressed the Catholic Center Party toward reforming social legislation.[87]

Progressive Developments in Belgium and France

In France, as in Belgium, alongside the dominant romantically conservative strain of Social Catholicism, there also emerged a progressive strain.

In Belgium, Edouard Ducpétiaux (1804–68), the government's inspector general of prisons and charitable institutions, conducted field studies on the condition of workers and proposed means of relieving their suffering. The coalition of liberals and Catholics in Belgium enabled the Catholic Church to keep a significant public presence in state-sponsored social-welfare activities.[88]

In France, as we saw in the last chapter, the great early founder of a progressive stream of Social Catholicism had been the Abbé Lamennais, condemned by two encyclicals of Gregory XVI. He had begun as a conservative but then had embraced Christian Democracy in the name of ultramontanism, as well as Social Catholicism. Later he espoused Christian Socialism.[89]

Also in France, Frédéric Ozanam (1813–53), eventually a professor at the Sorbonne and an early and strong proponent of Christian Democracy, promoted a progressive Social Catholicism by insisting that the great problems of modern society were not primarily political but social. He proposed a massive Christian program of charitable assistance through the Society of Vincent de Paul, which he and friends had founded in their student days.[90]

The liberal Catholic Charles de Coux (1787–1864), a Frenchman raised in America, offered Lamennais's articles on social reform for publication in *L'Avenir*. He was appointed to a teaching position in political economy at the Belgian Catholic University of Louvain. De Coux's proposals included population control (by voluntary sexual restraint), support for workers' coalitions, and universal male suffrage. Misner cites de Coux's key proposal, "Give the worker the right to vote, and this undercover warfare that drains our economy will end by itself." Later, however, de Coux abandoned his social concern and espoused a liberal economics based on Ricardo's "iron law of wages."[91]

In a more radical vein, Philippe Buchez (1796–1865), the key figure in nineteenth-century Christian socialism, saw the true goal of the French Revolution as a Christian democratic socialist republic.

Together with a group of artisans, he produced *L'Atelier*, a Christian socialist periodical published throughout the 1840s. Initially called Christian Democracy, its Christian socialism was a pre-Marxist movement. For Buchez, the solution to unfettered competition and to the unpropertied situation of the working class was the creation of producer cooperatives *(ateliers nationaux)*, as well as profit-sharing in capitalist enterprises. Workers, he claimed, had to be rejoined with their tools and had to be supported by legal freedom.[92]

But the early Catholic liberal and socialist alternatives were never fully developed, partly due to the papal condemnation of liberal Catholicism following the revolutions of 1830, and also due to the harsh Catholic reaction against Christian Socialism after the revolutions of 1848. In general, for Catholic leaders liberalism would continue to mean the threatening Enlightenment philosophy of autonomous religious, cultural, and political freedom, with surprisingly little Catholic attention to the liberal economic freedom of laissez-faire. Also socialism came to be identified negatively with philosophies of violent revolution challenging private property, the family, and religion.

Yet Catholic social-liberal voices did not disappear with condemnations of Lamennais. In the wake of the revolutions of 1848, Henri Lacordaire, Frédéric Ozanam, Charles de Coux, and the Abbé Henry Marget, among others, set up a Catholic daily newspaper, *L'Ère Nouvelle*, as the successor to Lamennais's *L'Avenir*. While Lacordaire wished to avoid the social question, Ozanam insisted that "behind the social revolution was a political revolution…the arrival of the working class." Under Marget's editorship, following Lacordaire's resignation, the journal became a bold advocate for the working class. But lacking wider support in the French church, the enterprise failed in less than a year. The Catholic reaction against the revolution had worked against them. Further, strong voices like Montalembert and de Tocqueville condemned the social component of the revolution.[93]

The small group of Christian Democrats concerned with the social question found their leading voice in Frédéric Arnaud de l'Ariège (1819–78), a disciple of Buchez and a Catholic lawyer who had taken up the theme of the working class's right to employment. Arnaud and another Christian-Democratic disciple of Buchez,

Pierre Pradie (1816–?), realizing that neither charity nor legislation alone would resolve the social question, began to support workers' right of free association and proclaimed the need to undertake a class struggle by means of unions. But even this small first French wave of Christian Democracy and Social Catholicism soon faded.[94]

An important progressive outgrowth of the early paternalistic school of French Social Catholicism was the movement of "Christian factories," some owned by benevolent Catholic entrepreneurs and others organized by Catholic sisters as workshops for the unemployed. A key leader among these entrepreneurs, Leon Harmel (1829–1915), later outgrew the paternalistic model and developed what he called the "Christian corporation," that is, new economic ventures structured on a model of workers' self-management. Pioneering France's "second Christian Democracy," Harmel began in 1887 to organize pilgrimages of workers to Rome, thus impressing upon the pope the reality of the social question and the strategic importance of the evangelization of the working class.[95]

Still more progressive initiatives came from conservative French roots. During the Franco-Prussian war, two young noble French military officers, Count Albert de Mun (1841–1914) and Count René de la Tour du Pin (1834–1924), had been imprisoned in Aachen, and there had been exposed to German Social Catholicism. Once freed, they returned to France to take part as officers in the military suppression of workers during the Paris Commune of 1871. Haunted forever by the terrible memory of that bloody event, de Mun gave over his life to the social regeneration of France.[96]

Together with la Tour du Pin and Maurice Maignen, de Mun founded a paternalistic organization called the Oeuvre des Cercles Catholique d'Ouvriers, as well as the Association Catholique de la Jeunesse Française. La Tour du Pin focused more on the theoretical side of Catholic social thought, first in the *Revue de l'Association Catholique,* and later in the international Fribourg union, and thus emerged as a leading theoretician of Catholic social thought. Both staunch monarchists, the two military officers developed close relationships with leading Catholic ultramontanists, including de Maistre, de Bonald, Donoso Cortés, and Veuillot, as well as with the empirical student of family life

Frédérick Le Play, and with the Christian entrepreneur Harmel. Like Kettler, de Mun and his *Cercles* of young Catholics endorsed state intervention on behalf of workers. Because of international competition, the two figures also supported the idea of an international convention to limit working hours. [97]

The resulting combination of the paternalistic strain of the Catholic nobility and the entrepreneurial strain of Harmel's "Christian corporation" helped to form the growing Catholic social orientation called corporativism, which again appealed to a romantic medieval model.

When la Tour du Pin was sent to Vienna as French military attaché, he established a close working relationship between his French school of Catholic social thought and the Austrian school of corporativist Catholic thought led by Baron Karl von Vogelsang (1818–90). Centered in the newspaper *Das Vaterland,* the Austrian school traced the contemporary social crisis to the Enlightenment's fostering of atomized individuals, a mechanical state, property denied any social responsibility, and free rein for economic competition. In response, it proposed a comprehensive program of social reform, which it called Christian Socialism, culminating in a "social monarchy." The fragmented or horizontal class conflict of modern liberalism was to be replaced by a vertical or hierarchical organism of large industry, small crafts and shops, and agriculture. The group also supported state social-welfare legislation. Tragically, the Austrian movement also carried a poisonous anti-Semitism.[98]

La Tour du Pin carried the ideas of the Austrian corporativist school back to France and there argued that the strategy of the Christian corporation, with the idea taken especially from Harmel, needed to be supplemented by the Christian corporativist state. In this comprehensive perspective the whole corporativist vision— employing organic but free associations and thus standing midway between atomized liberalism and massified socialism—embraced the full range of economic, political, cultural, and religious life. While the practical application was never fully clear, it implied that a viable society could be built out of intermediary organic groupings, rather than from atomistic individuals or collectivized masses.[99]

In the judgment of Paul Miser, a leading historical scholar of these developments, the corporativist idea was hindered by a static interpretation of society. Even so, this corporativist vision would have strong influence on the next generation of Christian Democracy. In the coming century, however, European fascist regimes would also use corporativist language for totalitarian purposes.[100]

As proletarian urbanization exploded in the industrializing countries of Western Europe, unfortunately few new Catholic churches were built for urban working-class families. The Catholic clergy, almost exclusively of middle-class or peasant roots, had little understanding of the working-class reality. Thus it was not so much the continental European working class that abandoned the Catholic Church; rather, the continental European Catholic Church largely failed to be present within the creation of the industrial working class.[101]

Progressive Developments in England and America

Paul Misner points out that the 1880s (again, the start of capitalism's national stage) marked a turning point in the social question. With industrialization dramatically expanding, industrial workers were beginning to create effective organizations. A wave of strikes spread across France, Belgium, England, and Germany.[102]

In England and America, two important centers of national capitalism, the industrial working class contained a large Irish immigrant population. Coming from a church historically unified as an impoverished peasantry oppressed by a foreign and Protestant conqueror, and so used to resisting economic oppression from English imperialism, the Irish immigrants carried a model of evangelization that never lost its working class. The Vatican ultramontanists strongly supported this Irish model for the English-speaking countries.

In England, Cardinal Manning, an Anglican convert to Catholicism and a key ultramontanist adviser of the late Pius IX, declared that in the future the church would "no longer have to do with Princes and Parliaments, but with the masses." He later provided support and arbitration for the 1889 British dock strike.[103]

In the United States the Irish-American Cardinal James Gibbons of Baltimore, leading a largely working-class immigrant Catholic community, defended the early union movement known as the Knights of Labor against papal condemnation as a secret society.

In his famous 1887 "Memorial" presented to Rome, Gibbons cited Manning's words above and then added his own: "To lose the heart of the people would be a misfortune for which the friendship of the few rich and powerful would be no compensation."[104]

Gibbons even used language of class warfare. He described "the struggle of the great masses of the people against the iron-clad mail power which…often refuses them the simple rights of humanity and justice." He spoke of "being alarmed at the prospect of the Church being presented before our age as the friend of the powerful rich and the enemy of the helpless poor." He warned that "such an alliance, or even apparent alliance, [would] have done the Church untold harm." Echoing the romanticists' appeal to the Middle Ages, Gibbons repeated the claim of the nineteenth-century papal encyclicals that the roots of working-class suffering could be traced to the Reformation:

> Ever since the Reformation the democratic and co-operative institutions of medieval Europe have been upon their death-bed. In the year 1500 most Englishmen, for instance, owned their own homes, but by 1600 between two-thirds and three-fourths only were still in possession of their own lands. By 1700 one-half still had the economic buttress of a home behind them; but by the year 1900 less than one-tenth of the population possessed all the land of the country.
>
> And what is true of real property is true also of the means of production. Trade and business in the Middle Ages were conducted on the principles of mutual help and assistance, and unlimited competition was never thought of. But with the breaking down of the corporate feeling of united Christendom, methods of business were introduced which would have seemed deeply immoral 100 years before.[105]

From this point on, across the Atlantic nations and now outward to the entire planet, there was a richly developing tradition of Catholic social teaching and action.[106] Unfortunately, there will not be space in this study to chronicle its subsequent history beyond these early foundations. So let us now turn, at last, to Leo's document that would institutionalize Social Catholicism within the contemporary church.

Finally, a Social Encyclical

In Rome, despite the long silence on the social question, intellectual strategists within the papal bureaucracy had been eager to find an economic middle road between liberal individualism and socialist collectivism. These were the twin errors denounced by Juan Donoso Cortés in his 1851 *Essay on Catholicism, Liberalism, and Socialism*. Like the popes, Donoso Cortés saw socialism as the radical offspring of the Enlightenment. Though the Papal States' ancient artisan guilds or corporations had been suppressed following the French Revolution, a commission of cardinals appointed by Pius IX had proposed reestablishing them. Seen as free associations, they were judged to represent a middle way between what was perceived as liberalism's destructive freedom of individualism and socialism's collectivist suppression of authentic communal freedom.[107]

In 1886 there began an influential series of Catholic congresses at Liège, a body later to become famous for new developments among French and Belgian Christian democrats. In 1885 the Swiss Bishop Mermillod (one of the very few European bishops of working-class origin) convened for the first time the famous Fribourg Union (Union catholique d'études sociales et économiques) to study the social question. Members included La Tour du Pin, Prince Karl zu Lowenstein of Germany, a representative from the Austrian corporativist school of Vogelsang, and delegates from Italy and Switzerland. This was the time when Harmel organized workers' pilgrimages to Rome. It was also the time when de Mun founded the French Catholic student association to prepare young Catholics for future leadership in French politics.[108]

While early in his pontificate Leo XIII had concentrated on the political issues of democracy and church-state relations, he had long been aware of the need for Catholic leadership in the economic arena, particularly as the movement of Social Catholicism grew and as the socialist threat intensified. In the early 1880s Leo had encouraged formation of a study group called the Roman Committee of Social Studies under the presidency of Cardinal Jacobini, prefect of propaganda, and including members of the Roman aristocracy, as well as Bishop Mermillod. The Swiss bishop's Fribourg Union, founded later, was an international version of this Roman study group.[109]

For some time it was known in these circles that Leo wished to prepare an official statement on the social question of the working class. In 1888, in the wake of a long economic depression, Leo requested that the Fribourg Union prepare a report on the fruit of its work. Leo also received reports from leading Catholic theorists: one on minimum wage from the Jesuit moral theologian August Lehmkuhl; another on credit and interest from Henri Lorin; and a study on the corporativist organization of society, perhaps from La Tour du Pin. Beginning in 1889, Matteo Liberatore, one of the Jesuit pioneers of the Thomist revival, published a series of major articles in *Civiltà Cattolica* on the moral principles of political economy. Soon after, Leo asked him to write the first draft of an encyclical on the same theme. Reportedly, the Dominican cardinal Tommaso Zigliara also cooperated in this first draft, and Leo's secretaries, Bocali and Volpini, put the encyclical in its final form (according to Misner, toned down in terms of state-intervention), while Cardinal Mazzella did a final critical reading.[110]

The final product, issued in 1891 and bearing the Latin title *Rerum novarum* (meaning "of new things" and referring to the Industrial Revolution), became the Magna Charta of modern papal social teaching.[111] Appearing one hundred and thirty-one years after the Industrial Revolution, forty-three years after *The Communist Manifesto*, and thirteen years after Leo's own election to the papacy, this, his thirty-eighth encyclical, was the first significant papal statement on industrial capitalism. It had taken the birth of national capitalism to summon a papal response, but even then it was the more radical threat of socialism that gave that response its urgency.[112]

Noting that this encyclical emerged soon after the second wave of the Industrial Revolution, Misner commented:

> [*Rerum novarum*] galvanized the *pusillus grex* of social Catholics just at the moment when industrialization was swinging into high gear for the sustained development of a second generation of industries (electrical, steel, chemical, automotive) in many parts of the continent.[113]

Leo XIII's encyclical dramatically legitimated the social-welfare reform of modern industrial capitalism. On the political side it affirmed the principle of the interventionist or regulatory state, as rooted in the classical Catholic-Aristotelian understanding of politics in service of the common good, though it insisted on limitation of the state's role. On the economic side it affirmed the correlative rights and duties of both capital and labor, as rooted in the classical Catholic understanding of an organic-hierarchical society. It also provided surprising affirmation for the principle of workers' unions, though the affirmation was surrounded by major caveats.[114]

Misner cites Jarlot in claiming that the affirmation of unions was a last-minute addition, influenced perhaps by Cardinal Gibbons of Baltimore (again, famous for his defense of the Knights of Labor), and perhaps also by Giuseppe Toniolo.[115] One wonders whether also Cardinal Manning, once close to the papal court of Pius IX, might not also have brought some influence to bear.

While *Rerum novarum* took elements from various schools of Catholic social thought (for example, the Fribourg Union, the Liège School, the Angers School), it nonetheless left several key issues in deliberate ambiguity. These ambiguous themes included the question of a family wage, the scale of state intervention, issues of finance and investment, proposals for a corporativist society, and the acceptability of inter-confessional or religiously neutral unions.[116]

With the addition of Leo's encyclical on the social question, so long in coming and so powerful in impact, the three foundational pieces for Catholic anti-socialist strategy within the national stage of industrial capitalism were complete. Again, these were (1) the Thomist revival; (2) Christian Democracy; and (3) Social Catholicism. Subsequent popes would offer various societal or ecclesial adjustments to this foundation, sometimes to expand the strategic program and sometimes to contract it, but none would shift the basic design. In particular, *Rerum novarum* would be taken as the capstone of the programmatic architecture, as Leo's successors would issue updating encyclicals on its fortieth, seventieth, eightieth, and one-hundredth anniversaries.[117]

While the new strategy proved successful in restoring Catholicism to a public role in Western European society, it actually failed in terms of Leo's original hopes. The pope had dreamed that

Christian civilization would be restored in modern form, with the papacy reestablished as an official international spiritual power and institutionally accepted by European governments as the supranational arbiter of international law and foundation of civilization's morality. But his vision of a modernized bourgeois version of the ancient imperial-aristocratic structure of Christendom proved an empty dream.

The twentieth century would experience two horrendous industrial wars, the totalitarianisms of both anti-Semitic fascism and Russian atheistic communism, capitalism's hedonistic materialism in the First World, massive poverty and oppression throughout the Third World, and eventually a profound ecological crisis across the entire planet. In these traumas modern civilization would reveal itself as anything but Christian.

Before his death Leo apparently realized that his dream of a modernized Christendom would not come to fruition. He partially backed away from the growing Catholic movements encouraged by his rapprochement with liberalism. In an 1899 letter to the bishops of the United States, *Testem benevolentiae*, he condemned what was called the false teaching of "Americanism."[118] In a 1901 encyclical, *Graves de communi re*, he reined in the notion of Christian Democracy.[119] Finally, in 1902 he wrote what the French Catholic historian Roger Aubert called "a bitter letter," a document that the great German Protestant scholar Adolf von Harnack described as "the testimonial of Leo XIII." This was *Praeclara gratulationis*. In the vitriolic style of the pre-Leonine popes, it bemoaned "the insults inflicted upon the church."[120]

Though Leo's modernizing achievements did not match his theocratic dreams, he nonetheless successfully established a viable strategy for Catholic Christianity in the national stage of modern industrial capitalism. Yet his efforts at modernization would create new strategic threats to the internal ideological life of Catholicism— a challenge that his successor would vigorously seek to counter.[121]

Having reviewed Leo's strategic "grand design," we examine in the next chapter the actual texts of his rich encyclicals. After that, we will examine how his successors modified the Leonine strategy, and finally, how the whole strategy began to break down in the post–World War II period.

The Foundational Encyclicals of Leo XIII

The Grand Design for a Modern Bourgeois Adaptation of Christian Civilization

———————

This chapter examines the encyclicals of Pope Leo XIII (1878–1903), the founder of the modern stage of contemporary Catholic social teaching and of the wider modernizing Leonine papal strategy for the period of national capitalism. As already noted, so firmly did Leo establish the new strategic model that despite modifications it held for sixty years, throughout the pontificates of his four successors. A later chapter will examine the encyclicals of these successors, namely, Pius X, Benedict XV, Pius XI, and Pius XII.[1]

Since Leo XIII issued eighty-six encyclicals during his twenty-six years as pope, the corpus of his letters is too vast to permit examining here every document in full detail. Fortunately, a clear articulation of the most innovating dimensions of his strategy can be found in ten key documents issued during his first fourteen years. This chapter will examine those ten in detail and also offer a brief review of the remaining encyclicals in Leo's legacy. The ten key encyclicals include:

- *Inscrutabili Dei concilio*, his 1878 inaugural text;

- *Quod apostolici muneris*, also in 1878, on socialism;

- *Aeterni patris*, in 1879, the next year, on Thomism;

- *Arcanum*, in 1880, on family;

- four encyclicals on politics, namely, *Diuturnum* in 1881, *Immortale Dei* in 1885, *Libertas* in 1888, and *Sapientiae Christianae* in 1890;

- *Humanum genus*, in 1884, on Freemasonry; and

- *Rerum novarum*, in 1891, his single but stunning encyclical on economics.

These ten encyclicals embody Leo XIII's "grand design."

Toward the end of his pontificate, Leo began to show reservations about the optimistic side of his project. For example, he attempted to rein in Christian Democracy by tighter episcopal control. But these reservations by no means abandoned his strategic plan.[2]

The encyclicals of Leo XIII, as well as of those of his successors within the Leonine strategy, need to be read holistically against the horizon of the encyclicals of the pre-Leonine period. As Michael Schuck has already demonstrated, only a reading that embraces the complete corpus of papal encyclicals since 1740 can fully appreciate its posture of fundamental philosophical and theological opposition to the Enlightenment's mechanistic root metaphor.[3]

There is an additional reason for such a holistic reading. It has to do with the progressive-versus-conservative polarization that continues to haunt contemporary Catholicism. Progressive Catholics frequently play down the pre-Leonine strategy's spiritual-cultural resistance to modern secularization and play up the Leonine strategy's political-economic teachings on justice and peace. Meanwhile, conservative Catholics often do the reverse by playing down the Leonine strategy's modern social teachings on justice and peace and playing up the pre-Leonine religious resistance to modern secularization. In the ensuing debate progressives often accuse conservatives of forgetting the socially prophetic side of the gospel, while conservatives often accuse progressives of reducing the gospel's spiritual message to ethics.

It is important to recall, therefore, that while Leo XIII launched a new strategy that sought to adapt Catholic Christianity to the modern political-economic context, he did not abandon the cultural-religious critique of secularizing modernity developed in the prior stage. Neither did he simply take that cultural critique for granted. Rather, he gave it even more coherence and sharpness, thanks to the intellectual systematization provided by Thomism. Hence the modern Leonine political-economic teachings on industrial capitalism need to be seen as still grounded in the pre-Leonine cultural-religious critique of the modern secular Enlightenment.

To repeat, a complete reading of the Leonine corpus needs to address the encyclical tradition's full range of social teachings as based on a foundational critique of the modern Enlightenment. That critique, however, has both strengths and weaknesses, with the weaknesses revealing a nostalgic longing for theocratic power over society, and with the strengths opening on a post-Enlightenment vision. But more on this in the sequel book on postmodern Catholic social teaching.

Leo's Appeal to Liberal Leaders: Restore the Church's Role in Civilization

Leo XIII's first two encyclicals, *Inscrutabili Dei concilio* and *Quod apostolici muneris,* both issued in 1878 during his first year as pope, immediately disclosed the core of his strategic shift. This core included the separation of socialism from liberalism, with socialism seen as a greater danger, and an appeal to the "new princes" of the consolidated liberal order to ally themselves with the church for their own protection against the socialist threat.[4]

As we saw earlier, at the conclusion of the prior strategy Pius IX, although also preoccupied with socialism, had ultimately not distinguished socialism from liberalism as a separate strategic danger. Therefore, he could not have conceived of a Catholic-liberal coalition against the socialists. In addition, during much of Pius IX's pontificate, the industrial working class in the Catholic Latin countries, particularly in Italy, remained relatively small, and so socialist competition with Catholic evangelization had not yet become an acute problem for the papacy.

Despite the shift, Leo's strategic focus on socialism remained consistent within the earlier ultramontanist analysis of the crisis of modern European civilization, seen as flowing from the marginalization of the church from the heart of Western culture.

Socialism and the Crisis of Civilization

Inscrutabili Dei concilio. Leo's 1878 inaugural encyclical, *Inscrutabili*, opened with a summary description of the modern crisis. The result of this "plague," the pope charged, would be more upheaval and "final disaster." Repeating the ultramontanist analysis, he claimed that the root cause of the modern crisis was the attack on the Catholic Church, beginning with the attack on the Bishop of Rome. The ultimate result was the destruction of the very foundations of human society.[5]

According to Leo's Eurocentric perspective, the Catholic Church, acting like a "mother" to "the nations," particularly through the Roman pontiffs, had long ago freed "the nations" from savagery and slavery, and restored humans to their "original dignity." It had done this through its teaching of primary truths and higher morality, through its patronage of the arts and sciences, and through its charitable institutions. All of this had led, Leo claimed, to great "progress" and "prosperity" (note the liberal terms), particularly in Italy, for so long "preeminent" among the nations. In Leo's view the popes had provided a center for an ennobled Christian civilization and had saved human society from "its former superstition and barbarism." But those who were attacking the church's power threatened to "bring the standing and peace of the State to the very brink of ruin." As a result, he warned, "our epoch is rushing wildly along the straight road to destruction."[6]

In response to this crisis, Leo announced that he would pursue a twofold strategy, one external-societal and the other internal-ecclesial:

- *External Diplomatic Policy.* Externally, in society, he would seek with contemporary political leaders a church-state alliance, aimed at restoring the societal role of the Roman pontiff and at defending the peace and security of the state against the socialist threat.

- *Internal Pastoral Policy.* Internally, in church life, he would seek a closer union between the pope and the Catholic people. He would do this by means of the education of youth in harmony with Catholic teaching and "chiefly in philosophy," and by means of a defense of the Christian family, particularly its sacred sacramental character and its need for protection against divorce.

The result of this strategy, Leo predicted, would be a renewal of individual character, of the domestic society of the family, and of the civil society of the state.[7]

Appealing to the "princes," Leo highlighted how the church could support their authority and build up among the peoples "the way of justice and peace," as well as "a happy era of prosperity and glory."

> We address ourselves to princes and chief rulers of the nations, and earnestly beseech them in the august name of the Most High God, not to refuse the Church's aid, proffered them in a season of such need, but with united and friendly aims, to join themselves to her as the source of authority and salvation…God grant that…they may give their whole thought and care to mitigating the evils by which the Church and its visible head are harassed, and so it may at last come to pass that the peoples whom they govern may enter on the way of justice and peace, and rejoice in a happy era of prosperity and glory.[8]

Then, speaking to the Catholic bishops and noting that Christ "founded the church for the welfare of the peoples," he urged the bishops to continue to build up the internal unity of the church, and he expressed his optimism for the future. "This perfect union We regard as not merely an impregnable bulwark against hostile attacks, but also as an auspicious and happy omen, presaging better times for the church."[9]

In this inaugural encyclical, Leo was vague about who the enemies were, but this vagueness was quickly clarified in his next encyclical, issued only eight months later.

Quod apostolici muneris. In his second 1878 encyclical, *Quod apostolici muneris*, Leo blamed the "socialists" for the "increasing evils" of the already described "deadly plague," and he warned of the socialists' intention to overthrow the new bourgeois rulers:

> We speak of that sect of men who, under various and almost barbarous names, are called socialists, communists, or nihilists, and who, spread all over the world, and bound together by the closest ties in a wicked confederacy, no longer seek the shelter of secret meetings, but, openly and boldly marching forth in the light of day, strive to bring to a head what they have long been planning—the overthrow of all civil society whatsoever.[10]

Before exploring Leo's analysis of socialism, let us first look at his more basic analysis of the modern problem, since for him socialism was simply its most contemporary and pernicious expression. For his fullest analysis, we need to turn to his later encyclical, *Humanum genus* (1884). While aimed at mobilizing grass-roots Catholics to combat Freemasonry, particularly in Italy, this encyclical also presented a more extensive theological and philosophical reflection of the modern problem as Leo saw it.[11]

Humanum genus: *False Philosophical Teachings*

The Two Cities. According to *Humanum genus*, the modern problem was ultimately rooted in the human race's ancient fall from communion with God into sin and in the consequent separation of humanity into two parts, "the Kingdom of God" and "the Kingdom of Satan." As Leo noted, this division was long ago articulated by Augustine as two cities, the city of God and the city of this world, which in turn resulted from two loves, the love of God and the love of self.[12]

It was clear from Leo's overall program, however, that these two cities were not to remain set in irreconcilable polarization. Rather, the city of this world was to be rescued from Satan by the church's spiritual mission to create a Christian civilization that would direct the nations and their civil societies to their proper "temporal end." This was to be done through the twofold political task of the promotion of the common good and the restraint of evil, and by means of religion, justice, and virtue, with all assisted by the gospel's healing of human reason and the human will.

According to Leo, this ancient problem of the human city falling under the kingdom of Satan was now reappearing and consequently undermining the foundations of Christian civilization, thus threatening to return Western culture to barbarism and paganism. Leo further charged that the contemporary source of this reappearance of the kingdom of Satan was Freemasonry.[13]

In the prior strategy the modern crisis had been portrayed as the fruit of liberalism. But Leo, presumably because he was seeking reconciliation with moderate liberals, did not mention liberalism. Rather, he narrowed the blame to the Freemasons (before the triumph of liberalism its necessarily clandestine promoters in the repressive Latin countries), and he cast his charge against them as an appeal to contemporary liberal rulers:

> In this insane and wicked endeavor we may almost see the implacable hatred and spirit of revenge with which Satan himself is inflamed against Jesus Christ. So also the studious endeavor of the freemasons to destroy the chief foundations of justice and honesty, and to cooperate with those who would wish, as if they were mere animals, to do what they please, tends only to the ignominious and disgraceful ruin of the human race.[14]

Leo proposed that the various bodies of Freemasonry, though differing in name and ceremonies, were united as a "sect" by common and destructive teachings that could be grouped into three main areas: (1) the fundamentally false doctrine of *naturalism*, culminating in socialism, (2) a erroneous understanding of the *family* ("domestic society"), and (3) a misguided doctrine of *politics* ("civil society"). The secrecy grounding these false teachings recalled, Leo claimed, the ancient sect of the Manichees.[15] Let us look at his analysis of each of these areas.

The False Teaching of Naturalism. In his analysis of what he saw as the ultimately destructive goals of this "sect," Leo traced the root cause to the philosophical idea of "naturalism." In his judgment, the Freemasons were seeking

> the utter overthrow of that whole religious and political order of the world which the Christian teaching has produced, and the substitution of a new state of things in

accordance with their ideas, of which the foundations and laws shall be drawn from mere naturalism.[16]

The philosophy of naturalism, coming from the modern European Enlightenment, denied any supernatural dimension to reality and implicitly denied the reality of sin, as well as society's need for the aid of the Catholic Church. The leading claim of this naturalism was that reason alone "ought in all things to be mistress and guide." As a result, Leo proposed, naturalists claimed that no religious teachings could be accepted apart from those reached by reason alone, nor should any teacher be accepted simply on the principle of authority. In this false teaching, according to Leo, the Catholic Church was seen as the primary enemy, and Masonic attacks on the church took three forms: (1) assaults in speech and in print; (2) the subjection of the church to the state, and (3) the stripping of all power and property from the church.[17]

The very logic of naturalism, Leo further proposed, pushed this false doctrine beyond its initial position. Having overthrown supernatural truth, the naturalists soon began to lose their bearings even in the order of natural truth. First, he argued, there emerged a skepticism or agnosticism about "the existence of God, the immaterial nature of the soul, and its immortality." With the loss of certainty concerning these fundamental natural truths, he continued, there quickly followed a degeneration of public and private morality. In particular, there was no longer certain knowledge about "what constitutes justice and injustice, or upon what principle morality was founded."[18]

> For, wherever, by removing Christian education, this teaching has begun more completely to rule, there goodness and integrity of morals have begun quickly to perish, monstrous and shameful opinions have grown up, and the audacity of evil deeds has risen to a high degree.[19]

With the loss of moral orientation, Leo further argued, the passions began to rebel against right reason and to be allured toward hedonistic pleasure, expressed as the license of personal vice. Some Freemasons, he claimed, had even proposed that the multitude should be encouraged to indulge themselves "with a boundless license of vice, as, when this had been done, it would easily come under their power and authority for any acts of daring."[20]

Derivative Errors on Marriage and Family. Naturalism's resulting disorientation of reason and the will, according to Leo, led to what he saw as the first destructive consequence, namely, the undermining of the domestic society of marriage and the family.[21]

Though addressed briefly in *Humanum genus*, Leo's analysis of the crisis of domestic society was spelled out in detail in his earlier encyclical on Christian marriage, *Arcanum* (1880), issued in his third year as pope. He had begun that encyclical by recalling that Jesus came among humans to renew the earth and to restore whatever in human society had fallen into ruin. While this renewal was largely in the supernatural order of grace, "nonetheless some of its precious and salutary fruits were bestowed abundantly in the order of nature," specifically in regard to the civil society of the state and the domestic society of the family.[22]

Regarding family (which Leo saw as having its origin in marriage, with society then being an outgrowth of family[23]), he argued that God had designed marriage as monogamous and indissoluble. But God's original teaching on marriage, he proposed, "began to be corrupted by degrees, and to disappear among the heathen; and became even among the Jewish race clouded in a measure and obscured."[24] Pagans had allowed polygamy, turned women into slaves and property, and sometimes even allowed the husband to murder the wife, while Jews had allowed divorce. By contrast, Leo argued, Jesus had restored marriage to its original position of permanent monogamy, and the church had guarded this restoration through its legislation.[25]

Although repeating the apostle Paul's patriarchal teaching on the husband as head of the wife and the wife as subject to the husband, Leo nonetheless insisted (using the modern language of equality, rights, and freedom) that the relationship of husband and wife was grounded in "mutual love" and an "equality of rights." He pointed out that the church had defended the "freedom" of sons and daughters against the power of their fathers to marry those whom they wished with "rightful freedom." Further, he noted, the Catholic Church has defined Christian marriage as a sacred sacrament. All of this, he proposed, had worked to the betterment of both the family and the state.[26]

But, Leo continued, many false teachers had aimed at the destruction of Christian marriage: "Gnostics, Manichaeans, and Montanists; and in our own time Mormons, St. Simonians, phalansterians, and communists." These last three movements, linked respectively with Saint-Simon, Charles Fourier, and Karl Marx, were all socialist. The first step of the naturalists, Leo stated, was to remove matrimony from the sanctity and legal jurisdiction of the church by means of civil marriages, and the second step was to provide easy divorce—a practice, he noted, that had begun in Protestant countries.[27]

In *Humanum genus* Leo implicitly linked this secularization of marriage with the commercial spirit of capitalism. Naturalists claimed, he lamented, that marriage simply "belongs to the genus of commercial contracts, which can rightly be revoked by the will of those who made them." Also in *Humanum genus*, he further lamented that civil rulers of the state were attempting to gain total control over the education of youth. (In Catholic Europe education had been traditionally the province of the family and the church.) The result, he charged, was "that in the education of youth nothing is to be taught in the matter of religion as of certain and fixed opinion.[28]

In *Arcanum* Leo bemoaned the consequences of this erosion of marriage as sacred and indissoluble. "A veritable torrent of evil has flowed from this source, not only into private families, but also into States."[29]

> Mutual kindness is weakened; deplorable inducements to unfaithfulness are supplied; harm is done to the education and training of children; occasion is afforded for the breaking up of homes; the seeds of dissension are sown among families; the dignity of womanhood is lessened and brought low, and women run the risk of being deserted after having ministered to the pleasures of men...Nothing has such power to lay waste families and destroy the mainstay of kingdoms.[30]

Derivative Errors on Politics. The second consequence of naturalism, according to *Humanum genus*, was its false teaching on politics.[31] Here Leo offered a brief summary of an analysis he stated more extensively in his encyclicals on politics.

The political errors of the naturalists, according to Leo, were to be found in the claim that authority was not ultimately from God. A related false claim was that the state had no need to acknowledge God as the source of all political power, or the Catholic Church as the one true religion. But Leo denounced these perceived errors not simply on their own, as had been the case with Pius IX, but more importantly because he saw them as opening the door to still worse dangers.[32] Thus he charged that the doctrines of the Freemasons "prepare the way for not a few bolder men who are hurrying on even to worse things, in their endeavor to obtain equality and community of all goods by the destruction of every distinction of rank and property."[33] These "bolder men" were, of course, the socialists.

Quod apostolici muneris: *Radicalization in Socialism*

According to Leo's 1878 encyclical on socialism, *Quod apostolici muneris*, the socialists radicalized the modern problem in three basic ways: (1) by their refusal of "obedience to the higher powers," (2) by their claim for "absolute equality of all men in rights and duties," and (3) by their debasing of "the natural union of man and woman." Leo's focus was thus on the nature of authority and on its expression in domestic and civil society.[34]

Rejection of the Church's Authority. The errors of the socialists, Leo claimed, were simply the most current expression of "that most deadly war which from the sixteenth century down has been waged by innovators against the Catholic faith" (the Reformation). Later this "deadly war" took expression in the teachings of "a set of men who gloried in the name of philosophers" (the Enlightenment). Now that "war" has "grown in intensity" and has led to "a new species of impiety." Seeking to "overthrow the supernatural order" and falsely usurping "the name of reason," this campaign has recently reached the working class, which was threatening "to attack the homes and fortunes of the rich" (socialism).[35] Leo conveniently left out from his social analysis any reference to those two great modern historical steps between the Enlightenment and socialism, namely, the creation of liberal democratic governments and the emergence of the Industrial Revolution.

Sadly, Leo charged, civic leaders rejected the very church whose "doctrines and precepts" had as their "special object…the uprooting of the evil growth of socialism." For socialism, he maintained, was a special distortion of the gospel itself, since the gospel proclaimed the equality of "men" according to their same nature and dignity as "sons of God," all called to the same end and to be judged by the same law.[36]

False Teaching on Society. Elaborating his own "true" political theory, Leo added that there also existed an "inequality of rights and of power," of "princes and their subjects," rooted in the same God "from whom all paternity in heaven and earth is named." But this inequality should be governed by "mutual rights and duties," which recognize that "there is no power but from God."[37] Articulating the organic-hierarchical model so central to the papal tradition, Leo stated that God

> has appointed that there should be various orders in civil society, differing in dignity, rights, and power, whereby the State, like the Church, should be one body, consisting of many members, some nobler than others, but all necessary to each other and solicitous for the common good.[38]

Even in cases where this power was wielded tyrannically, Leo assured the new bourgeois rulers, Catholic teaching prohibited an insurrection "on private authority," for fear that public order would be even more radically disturbed. Rather, such injustices were to be addressed by patience and prayer.[39]

False Teaching on Family. Regarding family life, which Leo described as "the cornerstone of all society and government," he charged that the socialists wished to dissolve almost completely the union of husband and wife. This led, he argued, to the weakening of the authority of the father over his children and of the duties of the children toward the parents. But he did not elaborate at length on the socialists' error concerning family life.[40]

Leo linked politics (civil society) and family (domestic society) by means of the institution of private property, which, he claimed, the socialists also wanted to destroy in the name of a pure community of goods that would recognize no inequality.[41] But while defending private property, he also insisted on its social function and on the obligation of almsgiving:

> She [the church] is constantly pressing on the rich that most grave precept to give what remains to the poor; and she holds over their heads the divine sentence that unless they succor the needy they will be repaid by eternal torments…Who does not see that this is the best method of arranging the old struggle between the rich and the poor?[42]

Appeal to Liberal Political Leaders. Then again came Leo's strategic appeal to the "princes tossed about by the fury of the tempest." "Moved by the extreme peril that is on them" and "for their own safety's sake," Leo argued, they needed to "welcome and give ear to the Church." For the "public prosperity of kingdoms" was closely bound up with "the Church of Christ." Indeed the church "has the power to ward off the plague of socialism." Therefore, Leo argued, let the princes "restore the church to the condition and liberty in which she may exert her healing force for the benefit of all society."[43]

The Church and Workers. Finally, influenced by his concern with the working class, Leo turned internally to the church's pastoral life. Since "the recruits of socialism are especially sought among artisans and workmen," he urged the bishops to "encourage societies of artisans and workmen, which, constituted under the guardianship of religion, may tend to make all associates contented with their lot and move them to a quiet and peaceful life."[44] Though a modern pope was finally beginning to address the working class, Leo was still a long way from his later landmark encyclical, *Rerum novarum.*

Summary of Leo's Social Analysis

To summarize Leo's analysis, we may say that he saw the liberal society as rushing headlong into a fatal crisis. For him, the root of this crisis was in the four-hundred-year-old modern European cultural-spiritual war against the Catholic Church. According to this analysis, the war began in the Reformation, was intensified by the philosophers of the Enlightenment, was advanced by Freemasonry, was institutionalized with liberal state power (though again Leo diplomatically avoided speaking directly of liberalism), and now was being threatened with total disaster from the socialists.

Reaching out strategically to the new leaders of the consolidated liberal political order, Leo warned them that their own security stood endangered by the advancing anti-authoritarian logic of the modern rebellion, now led by the socialists. To avoid this catastrophe, he urged the liberal rulers to restore the power of the church, in order that their own power might be secure and their peoples prosper. This restoration would not require rejecting democracy, but it would mean publicly acknowledging again the realities of God, sin, and supernatural healing, and particularly the public role of the Catholic Church.

Under the church's tutelage, Leo maintained, all authority would be defended by celebrating its roots in God. Then the domestic society of family would be restored, especially through the reaffirmation of the religious character of marriage, the prohibition of divorce, and the return to religious education of youth, all of which would reestablish the moral ground of society. Finally, in civil society the political leaders themselves would be protected by the church's divine legitimization of their own authority, as well as by the church's extinguishing the spirit of rebellion through the restoration of religion and morals. Underlying all this was the classical organic-hierarchical root metaphor.

As we saw earlier, to carry out this program Leo would ultimately embrace three new movements in contemporary Catholicism, each corresponding to one of the three structural-functional regions of society:

- *Culture*—the philosophy of Thomism, in order to challenge the Enlightenment's mechanistic philosophy, seen as climaxing in socialism;

- *Politics*—Christian Democracy, in order to develop the Catholic-liberal coalition against socialism; and

- *Economics*—Social Catholicism, in order to compete with socialism for the loyalty of the working class.

Also, as we already saw, to promote the Thomist revival Leo issued one year after his election the encyclical *Aeterni patris*. To promote Christian Democracy, at least in a limited way, he issued four major encyclicals on politics: *Diuturnum* (1881), *Immortale Dei* (1885), *Libertas* (1888), and *Sapientiae Christianae* (1890). And to promote Social Catholicism, he issued in 1891 his most famous encyclical, *Rerum novarum*. Let us now examine each of these texts.

The Leonine Cultural Program: *Aeterni patris* and the Thomist Revival

For Leo, the philosophy of Thomas Aquinas provided an intellectual key to the whole modern crisis and architectural principles for his strategic "grand design." The importance of Leo's encyclical on Thomism, *Aeterni patris*, was signaled by its position as third in line right after his inaugural encyclical and his quickly following one on socialism. The text of *Aeterni patris* may be divided into three sections:

- relationship of faith and reason;

- history of philosophy in relation to Christianity; and

- restoration of the philosophy of Thomas Aquinas.[45]

The Relationship of Faith and Reason

Regarding faith and reason, Leo argued that the "bitter strife of these days" had its origin in "false conclusions concerning things divine and human," and that these false conclusions had grown through three steps. First, they had "originated in the schools of *philosophy*"; second, they had "crept into the orders of the *state*"; and third they were now "accepted by the common consent of the *masses*" (italics added). As we have seen, the first step was, of course, the modern European Enlightenment; the second was the rise of secular liberal governments, following the French Revolution; and the third was the spread of socialism among industrial workers.[46]

Leo's earlier analysis of socialism as the most critical danger had been based on his judgment that these "false conclusions" were now reaching the "masses" (that is, the industrial working class) in the form of socialism. Thus the final disaster of the modern trajectory was imminent; the revolution would soon devour its own children, that is, the liberal rulers themselves.

To avoid this ultimate threat, Leo proposed restoring the traditional Catholic understanding of the relationship of faith and reason, in which reason found its completion in faith and, without usurping the role of reason, faith provided guidance for all intellectual endeavors from philosophy to the sciences.[47] Arguing that Christian thinkers had purified and deepened the rich truths discovered by ancient "pagan sages," Leo wrote:

> And, assuredly, the God of all goodness, in all that pertains to divine things, has not only manifested by the light of faith those truths which human intelligence could not attain of itself, but others, also, not altogether unattainable by reason, that by the help of divine authority they may be made known to all at once and without any admixture of error.[48]

Grounding this hierarchically organic understanding of faith and reason, Leo claimed, was the principle of analogy, namely, that higher spiritual truths are known through the truth of lower material creation.[49] In support of this claim, he cited Paul in Romans 1:20: "For, as the Apostle says, the invisible things of Him, from the creation of the world, are clearly seen, being understood by the things that are made."[50]

In particular, Leo argued, through the Christian use of philosophy, reason had demonstrated three important truths in relation to faith:

- first, that God exists, since the Creator is disclosed though the greatness and beauty of the creature;

- second, that the gospel deserves "reasonable consent," because of the signs and wonders that accompany it as "established proofs";

- third, that the church carries a divine mission, as shown by "its wonderful spread, its marvelous sanctity, and its inexhaustible fecundity in all places, as well as of its Catholic unity and unshaken stability."

Hence for the pope, reason was an important apologetic weapon for defending religion and the church against attack by enemies.[51]

In addition, Leo maintained, reason needed to approach the search for truth with a profound humility concerning its own limitations, because the supernatural order surpasses its natural powers. So too, he noted, Catholic philosophers would know that, if they came to a conclusion opposed to revealed truth, then somehow both faith and reason had been violated. Thus, Leo argued, the study of philosophy needed to be conducted in obedience to the faith, for, as Vatican Council I declared, "Faith frees and saves reason from error, and endows it with manifold knowledge."[52] Leo did not entertain the alternative possibility that God-given reason might also correct certain historical distortions in the human understanding of faith.

Christianity and History of Philosophy

Leo traced the historical path of Christian philosophy from its origins in pre-Christian "philosophers of old," to the early Christian apologists, to the great thinkers of the early Christian empire, and finally to the Scholastics of the Middle Ages, "in particular, the 'angelic' Saint Thomas and the 'seraphic' Saint Bonaventure." He noted the great schools and universities that once flourished in Christian Europe and pointed out that Aquinas had been celebrated by many popes and ecumenical councils, particularly by the Council of Trent, where his writings were placed on the high altar, together with the Bible and pontifical decrees. Citing Cajetan, he called Aquinas "the chief and master of all towers" and proposed that Aquinas "in a certain way seems to have inherited the intellect of all."[53]

In recent times, however, Leo charged, "a novel system of philosophy has succeeded," and this novel system had its roots in the Reformation. For "it pleased the struggling innovators of the sixteenth century to philosophize without any respect for faith." The result, he wrote, had been the multiplication of philosophies with "differing and clashing" conclusions "about those matters even which are the most important in human knowledge," all leading to doubt and instability across society. This doubt and instability, he implied, was at the root of the contemporary crisis of society.[54]

Papal Restoration of Thomism

Climaxing his argument about the hierarchically organic character of faith and reason, and his review of the growth and then undermining of Christian philosophy, Leo concluded by commanding across Catholic institutions the restoration of "the renowned teaching of Thomas Aquinas." His purpose was to provide guidance for the education of youth, as well as to "heal" the minds of those who have been "alienated from the faith, hate Catholic institutions, [and] claim reason as their sole mistress and guide."[55]

The fruit of this restoration, Leo claimed, would be peace and security for domestic and civil society. Further, he proposed, the teaching of Thomas would disclose "the true meaning of liberty" and have "very great and invincible force to overturn those principles of the new order which are well known to be dangerous to the peaceful order of things and to public safety."[56]

This "true meaning of liberty" then brings us to the second strategic movement that Leo moved to center stage, namely, Christian Democracy.

The Leonine Political Program:
Four Encyclicals on Christian Democracy

Applying Thomism to the political sphere, Leo published four encyclicals on the church and contemporary states. These documents provided strategic guidance, along the lines of Thomist principles, for the Catholic Church's reconciliation with modern democracy. Seeking to reform democratic governments according to Thomist teaching, Leo legitimized Christian Democracy, a movement long ago proposed by Lamennais and condemned by the popes of that time. In contrast to Lamennais, however, Leo proposed democracy as only one legitimate political path among others.

Though Christian Democracy was Leo's alternative to liberal democracy, and part of his antidote to socialism, it was probably not his ideal political regime.

Actually, in these four encyclicals Leo never used the phrase Christian Democracy. Indeed, his first official use of the term did not appear until his 1901 encyclical, *Graves de communi re*, and then he used it in a very wide sense.[57]

Despite the absence of any explicit mention of the phrase before that document, Leo's four earlier encyclicals on politics implicitly gave official approval to the political concept of Christian Democracy. As we will soon see, these documents accepted modern democracy as one legitimate political path and combined that acceptance with Thomist guidelines for how the democratic state "should be governed according to the principles of Christian philosophy," in contrast to the "false teachings" of "naturalism."

But Leo avoided the explicit phrase *Christian Democracy* for as long as he could. Presumably to have invoked it would have recalled Lamennais, provoked the wrath of the "integralists" (the ecclesial right wing), and perhaps conveyed the impression that democracy was being held up as the ideal form of Christian government.

Diuturnum: *The Divine Origin of Civil Power*

Leo's first political encyclical, *Diuturnum*, published in 1881, has been given the English name *On the Origin of Civil Power*.[58] The pope again recounted his story of the war against the authority of the church, and quickly pointed out that the same war had now been directed against the authority of the "sovereign princes," including the recent murder of the emperor of Russia (Alexander II, who had been a liberal social reformer). Since the sixteenth century, Leo argued, the spirit of human rebellion had attempted to lessen "the majesty" of political power, and as a result "not only has the multitude striven after a liberty greater than is just, but it has seen fit to fashion the origin and construction of the civil society of men in accordance with its own will."[59]

The false teachings on the origin of civil power had begun, Leo again charged, with the "so-called Reformation," as was testified to, he claimed, by the "sudden uprisings and boldest rebellions [that] immediately followed in Germany." The second stage of "false teachings" emerged "in the last century," when "heresy" moved to "false philosophy" (the Enlightenment) and a false doctrine of liberty was proclaimed. Now, he warned, "we have reached the limit of horrors, to wit, communism, socialism, nihilism, hideous deformities of the civil society of men and almost its ruin." From the Reformation to the Enlightenment to socialism: Leo had repeated his social analysis, though again without mentioning liberalism.[60]

Leo proposed that, before the modern rebellion, the Christian religion had provided "a wonderful force" for promoting restraint, obedience, and tranquility for the state. But recently false teachers, he argued, had undermined this achievement by claiming that all power comes from the people and that rulers of the state exercise this power not on their own but only as delegated by the people. In Leo's view, such teaching denied that "the right to rule is from God, as from a natural and necessary principle."[61]

Yet in rejecting this "false teaching" Leo did not thereby reject democracy, an important nuance that distinguished his strategy from that of his predecessor. Rather, for the first time a Catholic pope accepted the notion that "in certain cases" (again, democracy was not being proposed as *the* way) "those who may be placed over the State may...be chosen by the will and decision of the multitude." But, he insisted, though the ruler be designated by this choice, "the rights of ruling are not thereby conferred," nor is the authority received simply the delegation of the people, but real authority is vested in the person of the "ruler."[62] (Note that Leo still used classical aristocratic language for political leaders: rulers, princes, and so on.)

Leo accepted democracy on practical grounds as one among many legitimate forms of government that may suit either the "dispositions" or "customs" of a people. But he offered no philosophical evaluation of democracy as an ideal, since presumably he still held in theory that monarchy was the best form. His general criteria for the legitimacy of government applied to democracy as to any other form, namely, that "it be just, and that it tend to the common advantage."[63]

In this encyclical Leo also developed his argument for a Catholic view of the nature of society as the ground for authority within it. Opposing the modern liberal doctrine of social contract, he claimed that society was a natural institution and not the fruit of an arbitrary agreement. Indeed, tradition had long maintained this, he asserted, but reason also showed that society was necessary, for, without the association of society, individuals could not meet their needs. Further, he claimed, the very "faculty of language" as a medium of social intercourse showed that humans were willed by God, the author of nature, to live in a civil society. Thus, he argued, humans had been created for "a natural community of life" seeking the "common good."[64]

But, according to Leo, a natural society could not be conceived without someone "to govern the wills of individuals" and "to make, as it were, one out of many, and to impel them to the common good." Within this "natural community," he noted, "necessity compels that some should have pre-eminence, lest society, devoid of a prince or head by which it is ruled, should come to dissolution and be prevented from attaining the end for which it was created and instituted."[65]

Hence, those who administer the state must "be able to compel the citizens to obedience," and it is "clearly a sin in the latter not to obey." The only legitimate reason to disobey divinely constituted authority would be if anything should be demanded "which is openly repugnant to the natural or the divine law." Indeed, Leo pointed out, "Christians of old" obeyed pagan emperors even when they were persecuted by them, provided their commands were not against the divine or natural law.[66]

In a patriarchal perspective Leo argued that the authority of the "prince," like the authority of the fathers of families, partook of the authority of God, from "whom all authority in heaven and earth is named." Therefore, he stated, it was fitting, in order to enhance the dignity of authority, that its divine character be acknowledged as carrying an aura of religious "majesty." Without this religious majesty, Leo claimed, civil power alone would have, as Saint Thomas taught, "a weak foundation." To offset this weakness, he noted, the Roman pontiffs had historically been able to enhance the aura of ruler's majesty and thereby to ensure the prince's own safety and the security of the state. "For this reason, the Roman Pontiffs are to be regarded as having greatly served the public good."[67]

Approaching the end of this letter, Leo restated his strategic appeal: "To princes and other rulers of the State we have offered the protection of religion." He again repeated the appeal: "Our present object is to make rulers understand that this protection, which is stronger than any, is again offered to them." He made clear that he was not rejecting liberty, since he maintained that the church has never been "opposed to honest liberty." Finally, for a third time he reached out to the rulers by proclaiming that "it is God who gives safety to kings."[68]

Immortale Dei: *Relations of Church and State*

Four years later, in 1885, Leo issued another encyclical on politics, *Immortale Dei*, a document that he identified in his later encyclicals as his most important statement in this area.[69] This encyclical repeated the analysis and teaching of his prior document on politics, *Diuturnum*, but it did so in more systematic fashion, at greater length, and with the main stress on the relationship of church and state. Overall, it had less the tone of diplomatic outreach and more that of an Olympian pronouncement.

One point receiving sharp stress in *Immortale* was the obligation of the state to publicly profess religion, the "one true religion" of the Catholic Church. As in *Aeterni patris*, Leo maintained on grounds of reason that it was "not difficult to find which is the true religion," because "proofs are abundant and striking." But, reflecting his earlier reputation as "a man with a foot in both camps," he then conceded that in particular cases rulers should not be condemned for allowing various religions to have a place in the state, provided it was for the sake of "securing some greater good or hindering some great evil." Further, he pointed out, "no one shall be forced to embrace the Catholic faith against his will."[70]

Nonetheless, Leo's defense of the role of the church in public life assumed a stronger theocratic air than in *Diuturnum*. Thus he spoke of the church's authority as "the most exalted of all" and of its "unrestrained authority in regard to things sacred," including the "true power of making laws" and "the twofold right of judging and punishing." Still, he argued, the two powers of church and state were, by Divine design, to be exercised in harmony, like the harmony of the cosmos and "the union of the soul and the body."[71]

As with *Diuturnum*, Leo attempted to reclaim liberty from liberalism for the Catholic religion. True liberty, he maintained, was not to be an exercise in license for "the multitude," but to have "truth and goodness for its object," and the "Church of Christ is the true and sole teacher of virtue and guardian of morals." Perhaps under strong pressure from the ecclesial right wing, Leo even recalled Gregory XVI's encyclical *Mirari vos*, which condemned Lamennais, and Pius IX's condemnation of false opinions in the Syllabus of Errors (both notoriously antiliberal documents). Yet in diplomatic fashion he still did not mention the word *liberalism*.[72]

No doubt referring to the Italian situation, Leo noted by way of exception that "in some places" it was "by no means expedient for Catholics to engage in public affairs or to take an active part in politics."[73] Yet he still legitimized democracy as one possible form of government: "In matters purely political, as, for instance, the best form of government, and this or that system of administration, a difference of opinion is lawful."[74]

Libertas: *The Relationship of Liberty and Law*

Three years later and after completing ten years as pope, Leo issued his third encyclical on politics, *Libertas* (1888).[75] Perhaps because he was under still strong pressure from the ecclesial right in the context of growing attacks against the papacy by Italian liberals, Leo for the first time actually used the word *liberalism*. In a condemnatory style, he identified it with the error of naturalism or rationalism.[76] Liberalism, he claimed, would lead "straight to tyranny," prefaced by "tumult and sedition…among the people," as was daily evidenced, he pointed out, "in the conflict of the socialists."[77]

But, again in the style of "the man with a foot in both camps," he also noted that there were "some adherents of liberalism who do not subscribe to these opinions" and who "would have liberty ruled and directed by right reason, and consequently subject to the natural law and to the divine eternal law."[78]

In addition to repeating the teachings of *Diuturnum* and *Immortale Dei*, *Libertas* presented a distinctive emphasis on the classic Thomistic teaching on law (the linkage of eternal law, natural law, and human law) as related to right reason. Perhaps he made this emphasis because he saw the new Italian laws governing relations with the Vatican as threatening the church.[79] In returning to the Thomist approach to law, Leo triumphalistically insisted that there was nothing new in authentic liberty, for the church had always defended it. Further, he stated that whatever was actually new in modern liberty was in fact erroneous.

> We have shown that whatsoever is good in those liberties is as ancient as truth itself, and that the Church has always most willingly approved and practiced that good; but whatsoever has been added as new is, to tell the plain truth, of a vitiated kind, the fruit of the disorders of the age, and of an insatiate longing after liberty.[80]

Thus, in his outreach to liberalism, Leo's strategic goal was not so much to update the church for the modern liberal age, as to return the modern liberal age to its ancient Christian roots.

Also, with this document and in zealot-like fashion, Leo condemned the separation of church and state, linked liberalism's modern revolt against authority with Satan, and rejected freedom of religion. He proposed that liberty of speech, of the press, of teaching, and of conscience could only exist in relation to the truth, so that error had no rights and could not be tolerated. The basis of this position, he argued, was that "evil of itself, being a privation of the good, is opposed to the common welfare." But diplomatically he noted that the church "does not forbid the public authority to tolerate what is at variance with truth and justice," just as Thomas taught that God, "in allowing evil to exist in the world," does not thereby will evil.[81]

Finally, Leo dramatically reversed Proposition 80 of Pius IX's Syllabus of Errors, even though he had earlier cited his own agreement with Pius's condemnations of political liberalism:

> Lastly, there remain those who, while they do not approve the separation of Church and State, think nevertheless that the Church ought to adapt herself to the times and conform to what is required by the modern system of

government. Such an opinion is sound, if it is to be understood of some equitable adjustment consistent with truth
and justice.[82]

Yet with his characteristic even-handedness, Leo also commented,
"But it [this adaptation] is not so in regard to practices and doctrines
which a perversion of morals and a warped judgment have unlaw-
fully introduced."[83]

Then, softening his harsh rejection of modern moral liberties,
he concluded with a series of pragmatic exceptions. First, he
accepted the toleration of freedom of "thought, speech, or writing, or
of worship" wherever there was "just cause," but only in moderation
so as to "prevent its degenerating into license and excess." Second,
he stated, "it is lawful to seek...a change of government," on grounds
of "unjust oppression of the people on the one hand, or a deprivation
of the liberty of the Church on the other." And lastly, he declared, "it
is not wrong to prefer a democratic form of government, if only the
Catholic doctrine be maintained as to the origin and exercise of
power."[84]

Thus a document that began in a tone recalling the theocratic
style of the Vatican's zealot party ended on pragmatic grounds in the
style of its politician party.[85]

Sapientiae Christianae: *Catholics in Public Life*

Two years later, in 1890, Leo XIII's fourth encyclical letter on
politics appeared: *Sapientiae Christianae*. In this encyclical the
pope defined in greater detail the duties of Catholics in relation to
public life.[86]

This encyclical on politics had a different character from the
prior three. The earlier ones were written in a clearly philosophical
genre, reflecting the strong influence of neo-Thomist hands. By
contrast, this one had a homiletic and spiritual character, appealing more to the Bible than to Aquinas. Perhaps this shift in sources
reflected the re-ascendancy of the older zealot party, a group that
used spiritual rather than philosophical language and that under
the name of integralism would emerge preeminent in the next
papacy.

The encyclical opened with the charge that progress in material things, "not inconsiderable indeed," had not been matched by equal progress in the "goods of the soul," and that such progress was "incapable of satisfying our soul." This one-sided progress, Leo noted, had been accompanied by insults heaped on the Catholic Church, and, since the church had historically been the guarantor of morality, "the main foundation of human society" was now in decline. The remedy, he proposed, was "re-establishing in the family circle and throughout the whole range of society the doctrines and practices of the Christian religion."[87]

The remainder of the encyclical elaborated on the duty of lay Christians to place divine law above the laws of the state, to profess "openly and unflinchingly Catholic doctrine" (that is, not to collapse into the privatization of religion), and to maintain the tight unity of the church "as an army drawn up in battle array" in order to defend the church. This new emphasis on the laity reflected the growing importance of mobilization of the faithful, particularly in Italy and more tightly defined later as "Catholic Action."[88]

Leo noted that this turn to the laity had been endorsed by the (First) Vatican Council:

> Such cooperation on the part of the laity has seemed to the Fathers of the Vatican Council so opportune and fruitful of good that they thought well to invite it. "All faithful Christians, but those chiefly who are in a prominent position, or engaged in teaching, we entreat, by the compassion of Jesus Christ, and enjoin by the authority of the same God and Savior, that they bring aid to ward off and eliminate these errors from holy Church and contribute their zealous help in spreading abroad the light of undefiled faith."[89]

The encyclical then offered encouragement for this lay action, in conformity with the relation of church and state as defined in the prior encyclicals. It concluded by stressing the importance of the family for the training of children and of the "right education of youth."[90] In that conclusion it described the foundational role of family so insisted upon in Catholic social teaching since Leo: "The family may be regarded as the cradle of civil society, and it is in great measure within the circle of the family that the destiny of the States is fostered."[91]

But a restoration of the Catholic doctrine on politics, though it was Leo's primary concern, would not be sufficient to counter the socialist threat. As a result, the pope found himself pressed to follow in the logic of his own strategy the very historical movement of the modern error: from intellectual elites (philosophy) to political elites (the state) to the working class (socialism). And so his strategy moved from Thomism to Christian Democracy to the third and final Catholic movement that Leo came to legitimate, namely, Social Catholicism.

The Leonine Economic Program:
The Papal Acceptance of Social Catholicism

Before *Rerum novarum* was issued in 1891, Leo XIII had many times expressed his concern with the social question of the working class, though mostly in brief comments in encyclicals on other issues. Again, these expressions of concern had sometimes been negative, as he traced the degeneration of the modern error from the Reformation, to false philosophical teachings (the Enlightenment), to the achievement of state power (liberal democratic governments), to the sedition of the masses (socialism). The closer he came to *Rerum novarum*, however, the greater became his attention to the workers' question, and the more he began to shift his economic response from traditional expressions of piety and charity to modern calls for justice.

Earlier Economic Statements

Leo's first mention of workers in his encyclicals came in his 1878 document on socialism. There he warned that the expanding modern rebellion had reached the "lowest class." "Weary of their wretched home or workshop," Leo saw the workers as "eager to attack the homes and fortunes of the rich." But other than his appeal to "rulers" to restore the church to power and to repress secret societies, Leo's only response was to encourage almsgiving. He demanded that the rich give their surplus wealth to the poor, as "this is the best method of arranging the old struggle between the rich and poor."[92]

Several brief references followed in subsequent documents. In *Aeterni patris*, Leo's 1879 encyclical on Thomism, he again claimed that the false conclusions at the root of the modern revolt had passed from schools of philosophy to the orders of the state and now to the masses. But he offered no remedy apart from the education of youth, guided by Thomist philosophy.[93] In an 1882 encyclical letter to the bishops of Italy, *Etsi nos*, he referred to the "associations" being promoted by Social Catholicism, especially among young men and workmen, and encouraged them in their mission "to relieve poverty."[94]

In the same year, in *Auspicato concessum*, an encyclical on the upcoming seventh centenary of Saint Francis of Assisi, Leo charged that the Albigensians of Francis's time had paved the way for the materialistic socialists of the present time.[95] These socialists, he lamented, "approve of violence and sedition among the people, they attempt agrarian outbreaks, they flatter the desires of the proletariat, and they weaken the foundations of domestic and public order."[96]

In response, Leo offered the traditional aristocratic solution of charity by the rich and patient suffering by the poor.

> The question that politicians so laboriously aim at solving, viz., the relations which exist between the rich and poor, would be thoroughly solved if they had this as a fixed principle, viz., that poverty is not wanting in dignity; that the rich should be merciful and munificent, and the poor content with their lot and labour; and since neither was born for these changeable goods, the one is to attain heaven by liberality and the other by patience.[97]

In the same document Leo commended the way of penance of the Third Order of Saint Francis, the lay wing of the Franciscans.[98] Two years later, in *Humanum genus* (1884), his encyclical on Freemasonry, he again commended the Third Order of Saint Francis. In the following year he encouraged it yet once more in *Quod auctoritate*, an encyclical celebrating his fiftieth anniversary as a priest.[99]

Also in *Humanum genus* (seven years before *Rerum novarum*), Leo issued a call for restoration of the ancient craft guilds. The guilds had been suppressed in the Papal States and throughout much of Western Europe by the economic liberalization of the French Revolution and its extension in the Napoleonic conquest. In urging their restoration Leo noted that these associations of workers were designed "for the protection, under the guidance of religion, both of their temporal interests and of their morality." He saw them as countering the socialist threat: "If our ancestors, by long use and experience, felt the benefit of these guilds, our age perhaps will feel it the more by reason of the opportunity which they will give of crushing the power of the sects."[100]

Along with the guilds, Leo also encouraged the formation of other kinds of associations for workers, especially the St. Vincent de Paul Society, founded by the early Christian Democrat Frédérick Ozanam.[101]

Other occasional references to workers continued to appear. In his 1885 encyclical on politics, *Immortale Dei*, Leo cited the progression of the false philosophy from the Reformation to its current spread among the workers, but he did not refer to associations or guilds.[102] In *Jampridem*, an 1886 letter to the bishops of Prussia, he noted the "worker question, which preoccupies civil authorities," as well as the need to "block sectarians" and to seek "reform."[103]

In this last document, for the first time and perhaps influenced by the pioneering artisan clubs of German worker-turned-priest Adolf Kolping, Leo referred to the experience of priests ministering among the working class. Again a key goal for Leo was to counter the socialist threat.

> It is amazing how human society can profit from the work of the Church's ministers in these cases. We have been able to observe this in the conflagrations and catastrophes which have afflicted past times. In effect, the priests have almost daily contact with the lower classes by virtue of their ministry. They are accustomed to conversing familiarly and intimately with them and know thoroughly the labors and the sorrows of the people from this class. They see clearly their wounded hearts; drawing suitable aids

and arguments from religious sources, they are able to give consolation and remedies to the weak in spirit. Thus they lessen the present evils, revive broken strength, and restrain minds hurtling toward seditious plots.[104]

Despite the anti-socialist conclusion, such deep compassion may have reflected the special pastoral commitment of the German church to the working class. Indications of such personal warmth toward workers were found in no other papal document prior to *Rerum novarum*.

In *Exeunte iam anno* (1888), an encyclical on Christian life, Leo made his first reference to economic liberty.[105] This was Leo's first encyclical addressed not only to bishops but also to "all the Faithful"—presumably reflecting the growing importance of the lay mobilization for his strategy. Arguing that there was an increasing degeneration of public and private morals, he added:

> Hence arises an unbridled greed for money, which blinds those whom it has led captive, and in the fulfillment of its passion hurries them madly along, often without regard for justice or injustice, and not seldom accompanied by a disgraceful contempt for the poverty of their neighbor…They call self-love liberty.[106]

In the same document, he noted how this degeneration of morals was linked to "rationalism, materialism, atheism," which in turn have "begotten socialism, communism, nihilism."[107]

In the following year, 1889, Leo issued *Quaquam pluries*, an encyclical on Saint Joseph the worker. To "workmen" he commended Joseph for having "passed his life in labor, and won by the toil of the artisan the needful support of his family."[108] Joseph was recommended as an antidote to socialism:

> Let the poor, then, if they would be wise, not trust to the promises of seditious men, but rather to the example and patronage of Blessed Joseph, and to the maternal charity of the Church, which each day takes an increasing compassion on their lot.[109]

In *Dall'alto dell'apostolico seggio*, an 1890 encyclical on
Freemasonry, this time to the bishops, clergy, and people of Italy and
written in Italian (again presumably aiming at lay appeal), Leo
claimed that the church alone had the solution to the modern crisis
and included in this crisis the social question. "The social questions,
which now so greatly occupy men's minds, would find their way to
the best and most complete solution, by the practical application of
the gospel precepts of charity and justice."[110]

Also in 1890, in *In ipso*, an encyclical to the bishops of Austria,
Leo commented:

> It is the cause of workers, who sorely need the support of
> religion both for the honorable accomplishment of their
> labors and for the alleviation of their sufferings. Their
> cause is closely connected with the social question; the
> more difficulties it encounters, the more pressing is its
> need for attention. If the bishops direct their attention to
> this question, if they see to it that justice and charity influ-
> ence all classes of society and are deeply imprinted in
> souls, if by their authority and activity they come to the
> aid of the lowly condition of workers, they will have
> deserved well of the Church and society alike.[111]

All of this was still far from *Rerum novarum*.

Rerum novarum: *Magna Charta of Social Catholicism*

In 1891 Leo finally published *Rerum novarum*, no doubt his
greatest encyclical, often called the Magna Charta of Social
Catholicism. The title means "of new things," but in English it is
often given the name *On the Condition of the Working Class*. "New
things" refers, of course, to the Industrial Revolution. Leo was the
first modern pope to address it directly—some one hundred and
thirty one years after it began.[112]

If length of the text had any meaning, this encyclical was Leo's
longest. Of his eighty-six encyclicals in the Carlin collection of
English translations, only nine exceed ten pages, with most others
running in the two-to-six-page range. Of those longer documents, six
range between eleven and fourteen pages (*Aeterni patris, Arcanum,*

Humanum genus, *Immortale Dei*, *Libertas*, and *Sapientie Christianae*—all seen here as key strategic documents), while two later documents range between sixteen and twenty pages (*Providentissimus Deus* in 1893 on the study of the Bible, and *Satis cognitum* in 1896 on the unity of the church). Exceeding all these was *Rerum novarum*, with twenty-two pages.

Rerum novarum came late in Leo's strategic design—long after his initial warning on socialism, his defense of the family, his attack on Freemasonry, and his four major encyclicals on the church and politics. The four earlier letters on politics suggest that Leo originally conceived his strategy as aimed primarily at political elites. But as the machine revolution of industrial capitalism's national stage unfolded, and as the ranks of the industrial working class grew dramatically, presumably Leo was pressured to address the social question in a direct and substantial way. Certainly he was pressured by growing socialist competition for the loyalty of the expanding working class, by the need for pastoral engagement with the new working class in the local churches (particularly acute in America, England, Germany, Belgium, and France), and by his own turn to the laity for support against the state.

The text of *Rerum novarum* may be divided into seven parts:

- an opening statement of the economic problem;

- a critique of socialism as a false remedy;

- the correct remedy offered by the church;

- the role of the church itself in this remedy;

- the role of the state in this remedy;

- the role of employers and workers in this remedy; and

- a concluding summary.

The Economic Problem. In the first part, the opening statement of the problem, Leo noted that the spirit of revolutionary change had now "passed beyond the sphere of politics and made its influence felt in the cognate sphere of economics." Explaining why this had happened, he noted phenomena associated with the rise of industrial capitalism:

> The elements of conflict now raging are unmistakable, in the vast expansion of industrial pursuits and the marvelous discoveries of science; in the changed relations between masters and workmen; in the enormous fortunes of some few individuals, and the utter poverty of the masses; in the increased self-reliance and closer mutual combination of the working classes.[113]

But faithful to his spiritual-cultural analysis, he added a religious note by including "the prevailing moral degeneracy."[114]

In light of this urgent situation, just as in the past he had felt compelled to issue letters bearing on political matters, so now Leo declared: "We have thought it expedient to speak on the condition of the working classes." But he warned: "It is no easy matter to define the relative rights and mutual duties of the rich and of the poor, of capital and of labor." He further warned that "crafty agitators" were taking advantage of the situation "to stir up the people to revolt."[115]

A proximate cause of the problem, Leo proposed, was that in the last century "the ancient workingmen's guilds were abolished, and no other protective organization took their place." Thus, just as laws set aside religion, so too

> by degrees it has come to pass that workingmen have been surrendered, isolated and helpless, to the hard-heartedness of employers and the greed of unchecked competition. The mischief has been increased by rapacious usury, which, although more than once condemned by the Church, is nevertheless, under a different guise, but with like injustice, still practiced by covetous and grasping men. To this must be added that the hiring of labor and the conduct of trade are concentrated in the hands of comparatively few; so that a small number of very rich men have been able to lay upon the teeming masses of the laboring poor a yoke little better than slavery itself.[116]

Socialism as a False Remedy. In the second part of *Rerum novarum* Leo argued that the socialists had proposed a false remedy to the social question: "Working on the poor man's envy of the rich," they have striven "to do away with private property," so that all should become "common property" and be "administered by the State." But, Leo argued, this false solution was wrong because it would hurt the worker, the family, and the wider society.[117]

First, Leo claimed, in the socialist solution of state-administered community property "the working man himself would be the first to suffer." For workers would not be able to invest savings in land, would lose "the workingman's little estate" and "the liberty of disposing of his wages, and thereby the hope and possibility of increasing his resources and of bettering his condition."[118]

Such a loss would be against justice, Leo argued, since the right to possess property was rooted in the fact that humans have reason, in contrast to other animals. The possession of reason gave humans the power of choice, he maintained, and the right to hold things in stable and permanent possession, because through reason humans can link the future with the present and "lay provision for the future." Leo then elaborated a traditional claim that labor's transformation of natural resources, so necessary to meet human needs and especially over the long term, gave a real title to property. To work the land and to transform it, and then to turn it over to someone else for ownership, would be unjust. Leo further noted that this practice of private property had been consecrated by the tradition "of all ages," had been confirmed by civil laws derived from the natural law, and had been defended by divine sanction in Deuteronomy 5:21.[119]

In developing this argument about the right to private property, Leo made two interesting claims that went beyond the property issue. On the one hand, in an ecological way he linked human property to nature and particularly to land, by saying that the supplies that humans need come from the earth and its fruit. Clearly Leo's normative model of labor was in direct relation to the earth. Even if a worker did not work directly with the land, he argued, at least his savings could enable the worker to purchase a "little estate" for permanently sharing the fruits of nature.

On the other hand, he asserted that "Man precedes the State," and that, therefore, humans "possesses, prior to the State, the right of providing for substance." In the face of modern state encroachments on religion, family, and even the individual, Leo laid down the defensive principle that the state is a secondary institution and must remain limited. This claim that "man precedes the State" would become even more important with his successors, as frighteningly totalitarian states would push state encroachment to an absolute scope.[120]

Second, Leo argued that the socialist solution violated these same rights in a much stronger way in regard to the family. The family, he claimed, is "a true society, and one older than any State," and consequently "it has rights and duties peculiar to itself which are quite independent of the State."

The right of property was particularly important here, Leo argued, though he ascribed the right not to the family as a whole, but rather, following the patriarchal Roman model, to the *paterfamilias*. Only the father, "in his capacity as head of the family," must "provide food and all necessities for those whom he has begotten." The father's personality, he then argued, was extended in his children, who carried on the right to his property. While Leo's patriarchal model would prove problematic in the future, his claim that the family was "prior to the community" and had rights that were "founded more immediately in nature" would again be an important resource against the looming threat of totalitarianism.

Leo concluded his section on family by again challenging the socialists, who, he stated, "in setting aside the parent and setting up a State supervision, act against natural justice, and destroy the structure of the home."[121]

Third, against the socialist remedy of state-administered community property, Leo made an argument frequently repeated later in reference to industrial communism, namely, that the whole civil society would be afflicted by a loss of motivation, and equality would become nothing more than "one dead level." Thus he prophesied

> to how intolerable and hateful a slavery citizen would be subjected. The door would be thrown open to envy, to mutual invective, and to discord; the sources of wealth themselves would run dry, for no one would have any interest in exerting his talents or his industry; and that ideal equality about which they entertain pleasant dreams

would be in reality the leveling down of all to a like condition of misery and degradation.[122]

The Church's True Remedy. In the third part of *Rerum
novarum*, in contrast to the "false remedy" of the socialists, Leo
offered what he proposed was the church's true remedy. "No practical solution of this question will be found," he declared, "apart from
the intervention of religion and of the Church." And again, "It is we
who are the chief guardian of religion." And once more, "All striving
of men will be vain if they leave out the Church."[123]

To preface his proposal for a solution, Leo began by unfolding
his philosophy of society. Against the mechanistic idea of individual
equality, he upheld what he claimed was nature's own celebration of
"manifold differences" among people—"in capacity, skill, health,
strength," with "unequal fortune" being "a necessary result of
unequal condition." These natural differences actually aided the
whole community, for different people needed to play different parts
in community life.[124]

Regarding "bodily labor," Leo argued that not work but only
unhappiness in work was the result of sin. Yet to attempt to restruc-
ture society so as to eliminate all suffering in work would represent
"lying promises" that would only "bring forth worse evils than the
present."[125]

"The great mistake" in this deception, Leo claimed, was to
assume that the social classes were naturally hostile, "that the
wealthy and the working men are intended by nature to live in
mutual conflict." He again appealed to the organic-hierarchical paradigm for society:

> Just as the symmetry of the human frame is the result of
> the suitable arrangement of the different parts of the body,
> so in a State it is ordained by nature that these two classes
> should dwell in harmony and agreement, so as to main-
> tain the balance of the body politic.[126]

Then came the clearest articulation of the foundational ethical
principle for his solution: "Each needs the other; capital cannot do

without labor, nor labor without capital."[127] Here, Leo proposed, the church could be of great aid.

> There is no intermediary more powerful than religion (whereof the Church is the interpreter and guardian) in drawing the rich and the working class together, by reminding each of its duties to the other, and especially of the obligation of justice.[128]

Leo then spelled out the duties of justice on the one hand for "the proletarian and the worker," and on the other hand for "the wealthy owner and the employer." Since the recounting of these reciprocal duties is so central to the encyclical, I will mostly cite his words. On the one side, the worker was obliged

> to perform the work which has been freely and equitably agreed upon; never to injure the property, nor to outrage the person, of an employer; never to resort to violence in defending their own cause, nor to engage in riot or disorder; and to have nothing to do with men of evil principles, who work upon the people with artful promises of great result, and excite foolish hopes which usually end in useless regrets and grievous loss.[129]

On the other side, the employers were obliged

> not to look upon their work people as their bondsmen, but to respect in every man in his dignity as a person ennobled by Christian character...to see that the worker has time for his religious duties; that he be not exposed to corrupting influences and dangerous occasions; and that he not be led away to neglect his home and family, or to squander his earnings. Furthermore, the employer must never tax his work people beyond their strength, or employ them in work unsuited to their sex and age.[130]

With special emphasis, Leo noted the employer's obligation to pay a just wage:

His great and principal duty is to give everyone what is just. Doubtless, before deciding whether wages are fair, many things have to be considered; but wealthy owners and all masters of labor should be mindful of this—that to exercise pressure upon the indigent and the destitute for the sake of gain, and to gather one's profit out of the need of another, is condemned by all laws, human and divine. To defraud anyone of wages that are his due is a great crime which cries to the avenging anger of Heaven.[131]

Finally, he elaborated on the just wage:

Lastly, the rich must religiously refrain from cutting down the workmen's earnings, whether by force, by fraud, or by usurious dealing; and with all the greater reason because the laboring man is, as a rule, weak and unprotected, and because his slender means should in proportion to their scantiness be accounted sacred.[132]

Along with his modern call for justice, Leo held up the traditional perspective of charity, which maintained that the rich would be saved by munificent almsgiving and the poor by patient suffering. Regarding the rich, he harshly warned that "riches do not bring freedom from sorrow and are of no avail for eternal happiness, but rather are obstacles." He further warned that "the rich should tremble at the threatenings of Jesus Christ."[133]

Then Leo repeated the "most excellent rule for the right use of money," the rule that distinguished between the possession of money and its use. He repeated the teaching of Aquinas that defended the right of private property but insisted on its social nature, namely, that after one's own needs (or one's family's needs) were met according to one's station in life, then the remainder must be given to the poor. Anyone who possessed "temporal blessings" was but "the steward of God's providence, for the benefit of others."[134]

Regarding the poor, Leo reminded his readers that "in God's sight poverty is no disgrace" and that workers should not be ashamed of "earning their bread by labor." For Christ, "whereas He was rich, for our sakes became poor," and "being the Son of God, and God

Himself, chose to seem and to be considered the son of a carpenter."
Indeed he "did not disdain to spend a great part of His life as a carpenter Himself." Thus, "God Himself seems to incline rather to
those who suffer misfortune" and "displays the tenderest charity
toward the lowly and the oppressed."[135]

Such a perspective on riches and poverty, Leo maintained,
would make the pride of the rich disappear and enable "rich and
poor to join hands in friendly concord." The two classes would then
be "not only united in the bonds of friendship, but also in those of
brotherly love." They would understand that they had "the same
common Father, who is God" and "the same common end, which is
God himself."[136]

The Role of the Church. In the fourth section of *Rerum
novarum* Leo spelled out the role of the church in applying this
remedy. The church's basic role, he maintained, was "to teach and
to educate men" which it did through the intermediary of "her bishops and clergy."[137] This contribution of the church was unique,
because it alone "can reach the innermost heart and conscience,
and bring men to act from a motive of duty, to control their passions
and appetites, to love God and their fellow men with a love that is
outstanding."[138]

Leo then noted how in the past "civil society was renovated in
every part by Christian institutions." So too, "if human society is to
be healed now, in no other way can it be healed save by a return to
Christian life and Christian institutions." Only the church, he
claimed, could "restore" society to a path of class harmony. This
restoration would not be just spiritual, for the restoration of Christian
morality would inevitably promote "temporal prosperity" in two
ways, by restraining the greed for excessive possession and the thirst
for pleasure.[139]

In addition, Leo pointed out, the church "intervenes directly
in behalf of the poor" through its many "associations which she
knows to be efficient for the relief of poverty." This direct assistance
to the poor goes back to the beginning, when Christians shared their
goods with each other, to the ancient order of deacons, and to the
subsequent patrimony of the church, which has been "guarded with
religious care as the inheritance of the poor." Then, warning about
the secularizing tendency of the liberal state, Leo condemned the

current tendency to substitute for these charitable activities of the church "a system of relief organized by the State."[140]

The Role of the State. In the fifth part of *Rerum novarum*, after condemning what he saw as the state's usurpation of the role of the church in caring for the poor, Leo turned to the proper role of the state in the new context. This was an especially long part of the encyclical, no doubt because of Leo's great interest in politics. He articulated both a positive role for the state, in contrast to the negative understanding of laissez-faire liberalism, and yet limited that role, in contrast to the expansive ambitions of actual modern liberal states. It may be simplest to list his several points, with a brief comment on each.

- *Forms of Government.* First, Leo again made clear that he was not endorsing any particular form of government, and that any form of government was acceptable, provided it conformed to "right reason and natural law" and to the principles that he had laid out in *Immortale Dei.*[141]

- *The Common Good.* Second, the fundamental task of the state, Leo maintained, was "to serve the common good." In addition to the many functions associated with the modern state, he insisted that this also included "moral rule, well-regulated family life, [and] respect for religion and justice." Further, the more the state could do "for the benefit of the working class by the general laws of the country, the less need there will be to seek for special means to relieve them."[142]

- *Justice and Differences.* Third, Leo proposed, the commonwealth needed to be understood in an organic manner with all classes, and especially the working class that formed the majority, making up real parts of its body. In this organic context "the first and chief" duty of rulers "is to act with strict justice—with that justice which is called *distributive*—toward each and every class alike." Leo further noted that it was "only by the labor of working men that States grow rich," and therefore the state must especially watch over the interests of the working class. But he also argued that there were natural "differences and inequalities" in the citizenry, which were then expressed as class differences, no matter what the form of government, and that the state needs to respect these inequalities. (This is why the traditional Catholic theory, going back to Aristotle, had argued that distributive justice was to be guided by an equity proportionate to the station in life of the various classes.[143])

- **A *Limited State*.** Fifth, Leo also argued for a limited state. Thus he wrote, "The state must not absorb the individual or the family." In this regard, he noted, the object of the government of the state should not be "the advantage of the ruler," but "the benefit of those over whom the ruler is placed." For the ruler's power to rule came from God, as a participation in divine sovereignty, and so needed to be exercised with the same "fatherly solicitude" with which God guided both the community as a whole and each individual in it.[144]

Leo offered extensive comments on how "the public authority" needed to intervene or "to step in," whenever "the general interest or any particular class suffers, or was threatened with harm," provided that need could not be met in another way. The areas of state intervention that Leo mentioned included religious observance and family life, moral standards, justice, the development of youth, and military service. In particular, he saw "a strike of workers" as an occasion for state intervention, if there were "imminent danger of disturbance to the public peace," as well as "danger to morals through the mixing of the sexes," and work-place dangers to health. In such cases "it would be right to invoke the aid and authority of the law," though "the law must not undertake more, nor proceed further, than was required for the remedy of the evil."[145]

Also, Leo argued, the state had the obligation to protect rights, and especially the rights of the poor:

> The poor and badly off have a claim to especial consideration. The richer class have many ways of shielding themselves, and stand less in need of help from the State; whereas the mass of the poor have no resources of their own to fall back upon, and must chiefly depend upon the assistance of the State. And it is for this reason that wage-earners, since they mostly belong in the mass of the

needy, should be specially cared for and protected by the government.[146]

At the same time, Leo also stressed the duty of the state "of safe-guarding private property." Here he warned of the danger of socialist revolution.

> Most true it is that by far the larger part of the workers prefers to better themselves by honest labor rather than by doing any wrong to others. But there are not a few who are imbued with evil principles and eager for revolutionary change, whose main purpose is to stir up disorder and incite their fellows to acts of violence. The authority of the law should intervene to put restraint upon such fire-brands, to save the working classes from being led astray by their maneuvers, and to protect lawful owners from spoliation.[147]

Leo recognized that workers sometimes resort to strikes for just reasons, but he urged the state to prevent strikes by eliminating the conditions that generate them.

> When working people have recourse to a strike and become voluntarily idle, it is frequently because the hours of labor are too long, or the work too hard, or because they consider their wages insufficient...The laws should fore-stall and prevent such troubles from arising; they should lend their influence and authority to the removal in good time of the causes which lead to conflicts between employers and employed.[148]

Then Leo offered several long paragraphs on the duty of the state to protect the "interests" of the worker, particularly "the inter-ests of his soul," since the worker "is made after the image and like-ness of God." The pope stressed the transcendence of human dignity over all the rest of creation, and condemned anything that would diminish the dignity of the worker. He then added the state's duty to protect "the obligation of the cessation from work on Sundays and certain holy days." He urged the state "to save unfortunate working people from the cruelty of the greedy, who use human beings as mere instruments for money-making" through "excessive labor," and even employ children and women in workshops and factories. Regarding children, Leo noted, they should not be allowed to work in these places "until their bodies and minds are sufficiently developed." Regarding women, he argued in a traditionalist manner that they "are not suited for certain occupations," and that "a woman is by nature fitted for home-work."[149]

Leo rejected the liberal economic teaching that wages, "as we are told, are regulated by free consent." This leaves out, he insisted, several "important considerations," namely, that labor is both personal and necessary. In a direct challenge to the laissez-faire liberal teaching, he held up what would later be called the principle of the "living wage." "There underlies a dictate of natural justice more imperious and ancient than any bargain between man and man, namely, that wages ought not to be insufficient to support a frugal and well-behaved wage-earner." Such a living wage could be determined, he said, by appropriate societal boards, with the state providing "sanction and protection" for their decisions.[150]

Apparently without canonizing the added notion of a "family wage" (the question would remain ambiguous in Catholic social doctrine well after *Rerum novarum*), he noted that, if a worker's wage were sufficient "comfortably to support himself, his wife, and his children," the worker would be able to save, and could thereby procure a modest income, apparently from a small farm that "would add to the produce of the earth and to the wealth of the community." He encouraged working people to obtain "a share in the land," both in order to bridge the gap between rich and poor, and because "men always work harder and more readily...on what belongs to them," as well as to avoid the perils of immigration. (Leo was especially concerned about the spiritual fate of Italians migrating to America, where they faced Protestant missionary outreach.)[151]

Role of Employers and Workers. In the sixth part of *Rerum novarum* Leo addressed the role of "employers and workmen...of themselves," that is, independent of church and state.[152] Here he wrote first of "associations...which drew the two classes together," presumably the paternalistic clubs of employers and workers so long developed in France. The task of these organizations, he said, was "mutual help." He also mentioned "benevolent foundations" established to help workers, their widows, or their orphans, in cases of calamity.[153]

Then came the most dramatic section of the encyclical, its legitimization of unions. At the start of industrial capitalism's national stage, many looked upon unions as subversive. So for the pope to support them was truly shocking.

> The most important of all these are workingmen's unions, for these virtually include all the rest. History attests what excellent results were brought about by the artificers' guilds of olden times. They were the means of affording not only many advantages to the workmen, but in no small degree of promoting the advancement of art, as numerous monuments remain to bear witness. These unions should be suited to the requirements of our age — an age of wider education, of different habits, and of far more numerous requirements in daily life. It is gratifying to know that there are actually in existence not a few associations of this nature, consisting either of workmen alone, or of workmen and employers together, but it were greatly to be desired that they should become more numerous and more efficient.[154]

While Leo argued that unions were needed because of the weakness of individual workers in defending themselves, he also argued that unions were a natural form of human community. He stated that they existed "of their own right," that is, even apart from the need to defend the workers against exploitation from ruthless employers.

> It is this natural impulse which binds men together in civil society; and it is likewise this which leads them to join together in associations which are, it is true, lesser and not independent societies, but, nevertheless, real societies.[155]

Further, he argued, societies like unions, which are formed within "the bosom of the commonwealth," even though they are called "private," are nonetheless part of the commonwealth and as such cannot be prohibited by public authority:

> For, to enter into a "society" of this kind is the natural right of man; and the State has for its office to protect natural rights, not to destroy them; and, if it forbids its citizens to form associations, it contradicts the very principle of its own existence, for both they and it exist in virtue of the like principle, namely, the natural tendency of man to dwell in society.[156]

Here he compared these unions with the various "confraternities, societies, and religious orders" that arose in times past within the church. In those times, Leo noted, rulers of state had tried to repress or control these organizations, but the church had defended their autonomy from the state, and their resulting freedom had brought many benefits to society.[157]

On the negative side, Leo warned that many associations of workers are "in the hands of secret leaders, and are managed on principles ill-according with Christianity and the public well-being." He argued that Christian workers should not join "associations in which their religion will be exposed to peril," but rather should "form associations among themselves and unite their forces so as to shake off courageously the yoke of so unrighteous and intolerable an oppression."[158]

Thus, to fight socialist unions, Leo implicitly encouraged Christian unions. He also encouraged various discussion groups, made up of "men of eminence," to promote practical action on behalf of workers.[159]

Final Summary. The sixth and final section of *Rerum novarum* was Leo's summary. Here he emphasized again workers' associations and the three themes of body, soul, and property, with particular emphasis on the religious foundation of these associations and the need to reestablish Christian morals. Thus ended the most important encyclical of Leo's pontificate, and the foundational one for the economic dimension of the modern social teachings contained in the papal encyclicals.[160]

The Remaining Encyclicals

Though this chapter cannot analyze in detail the remainder of Leo XIII's eighty-six encyclicals, it may be helpful to give a brief sense of the flavor of these documents.[161]

More than half of the total remaining corpus, forty-seven encyclicals in total, addressed particular nations, provinces within nations, or regional clusters of nations. Of these, four encyclicals were about Italy, with three of them focusing on Freemasonry. Yet another general encyclical, addressed to all the bishops of the world and referred to earlier in this chapter, also addressed Freemasonry, namely, *Humanum genus.*[162] Four encyclicals were addressed to the United States: the first about Italian immigrants; the second about the newly founded Catholic University of America; the third about Catholicism in general in the United States; and the fourth also about the church in general in the United States.

The third, *Longinqua* (1895), while affirming the fruits of the American model of separation of church and state, warned that "it would be very erroneous to draw the conclusion that in America is to be sought the type of the most desirable status of the church." The encyclical commended the freedom of association of the working class (the right to form unions) but recommended that "Catholics ought to prefer to associate with Catholics." With no recognition of the richness of non-European cultures, it also referred to America's "savage tribes" and encouraged missionary outreach to "the Indians and Negroes…the greatest portion for whom have not yet dispelled the darkness of superstition."[163]

Among the remaining national encyclicals, a highly significant one was Leo's letter to French Catholics recommending that they "rally" to the Republic, that one hundred years after the French Revolution they should accept its democratic legacy (*Au milieu des sollicitudes*, 1892).[164]

Yet another national encyclical rejected as unlawful the use of the "boycott" by Irish peasants to protest unjust treatment by rural landlords (*Saepe nos*, 1888).[165]

A letter to Brazil condemned the institution of slavery, affirmed the unity of the whole human race, and claimed that the popes had always been great enemies of slavery, especially since the European encounter with the "New World." (The papal record in regard to the Atlantic slave system was less noble than Leo claimed.)[166]

At least twenty encyclicals addressed themes that might be categorized as spiritual. Eleven of these were on the Rosary. Three were on particular saints: Cyril and Methodius; Francis of Assisi; and Joseph, who was portrayed as patron of workers.

One thirteen-page long spiritual document on the Bible (*Providentissimus Deus*, 1893) condemned "higher criticism" and called for a battle against "rationalist" attacks on interpretation. It also commended the study of the Latin Vulgate version in seminaries and religious houses. But it never suggested promoting the Bible among the laity in vernacular translations.[167]

Another on the Holy Spirit (*Divinum illus munus*, 1897), written toward the end of Leo's life, described the goals of his papacy somewhat differently from his earlier documents. The first goal, it stated, was the restoration of Christian society, a theme frequently addressed in earlier encyclicals. The second goal, it claimed, had been the "reunion of all those who have fallen away from the Catholic Church either by heresy or by schism. Yet this had not been a major theme in Leo's inaugural programmatic encyclical." And neither had the theme of reunion been stressed in his repeated anti-Reformation polemic.[168]

Another spiritual encyclical promoted the consecration of the whole human race to "the Sacred Heart of Jesus," as an act of reparation for the sins of the age and to "draw tighter the bonds which naturally connect public affairs with God (*Annum sacrum*, 1899).[169]

Still another on the Eucharist commended the frequent reception of this sacrament as a means for healing the evils of the age "to the recovery and advantage of the whole body politic (*Mirae caritatis*, 1902).[170]

Leo's last spiritual encyclical (*Tametsi futura prospcientibus*, 1900), on the theme of Christ the King and Redeemer, looked back at the battles of the now completed nineteenth century and sounded an optimistic note of "consolation and hope." It saw "a renewed interest in spiritual matters and a revival of Christian faith and piety [as] influences of great moment for the common good."[171] Throughout this document, the pope proclaimed a Davidic-Christic paradigm of evangelization, though one no longer on the defensive.

Without resting secure, Leo was nonetheless acknowledging that the new strategy had taken root.

Three encyclicals addressed the missions: one on mission societies (*Sancta Dei civitas*, 1880); a second condemning the African slave trade (*Catholicae ecclesiae*, 1890); and a third encouraging seminaries for a native clergy in "the Orient," largely India (*Ad extremas*, 1893).

Three more were on the Eastern churches and Christian unity. One of these three was exclusively on Christian unity (*Satis cognitum*, 1896). This was among Leo's longest documents (twenty pages), implying that it was of great importance.[172] This text came late in his papacy, suggesting that Christian unity became a mature theme only later in his pontificate. In an earlier foreshadowing of this emphasis, Leo's 1888 encyclical *Quod anniversarius*, issued for the fiftieth anniversary of his ordination as a priest, had warmly stated: "We hope to obtain that all nations and all peoples, united in the faith by one bond of charity, may soon form one flock under one shepherd."[173] *Satis cognitum* also spoke warmly of Christian love but still offered a triumphalistic view of the Catholic Church and admitted of no human failings in the Catholic legacy.

Last Encyclical on Christian Democracy

The final encyclical to mention here, though analyzed earlier, is *Graves de communi re* (1901), written a few years before Leo's death and the first papal encyclical finally to endorse the phrase "Christian Democracy." This text both climaxed Leo's legitimization of a Catholic form of modern democracy and revealed the now strong papal desire to tighten episcopal control over the mobilization of the Catholic laity through the centralized structures of "Catholic Action."[174]

Leo began the document by recalling the "grave discussions on economical questions" that had been disturbing countries for some time, and by repeating his claim that these problems had been rooted in the "bad philosophical and ethical teaching that is now widespread among the people." He noted too the explosion of "mechanical inventions" and "rapidity of communications," and in turn the great "struggle between capital and labor." But the greatest problem amid all these changes, he argued, was still the danger of "socialism," which he saw as threatening property, the social order, morality, and religion itself. His response to this acute threat and to the wider social crisis, he pointed out, was *Rerum novarum*.[175]

Leo then chronicled the many good things that had followed this foundational document of modern Catholic social teaching: defense of the proletariat; new institutions to support the poor; rural banks and cooperatives; and associations of working people, including unions. He reflected on the various names proposed for these activities: initially, "Christian Socialism"; then "the popular Christian Movement"; also "Social Christianity"; and finally "Christian Democracy." He chose the name Christian Democracy.[176]

Leo listed the objections to this name: it canonized popular government and "disparaged" other forms; it restricted religion to social concern; it attacked legitimate power; and it suggested support for Social Democracy (that is, moderate secular socialism). He countered by declaring that Christian Democracy had nothing in common with social democracy; that it was above the "passions and vicissitudes" of all party politics; that it sought to embrace all classes, rich and poor; and finally, that it stood in respectful obedience to lawful rulers. Thus, for Leo, Christian Democracy meant the Catholic social movement mobilized to undercut socialism by itself challenging the great social question of the age. And this entailed an acceptance of the modern political form of popular democracy as well as engagement with the social question.[177]

Then Leo deepened his analysis by insisting that the "social question" was not simply "economic," but more fundamentally "a moral and religious matter." It was, he declared, a failure of both justice and charity. He commended Catholic associations of workers to deepen both morality and religion, as part of the struggle with the social question. He insisted on what today is called "the option for the poor," repeating the words that Jesus cited from Isaiah: "The blind see, the lame walk, the lepers are cleansed, the deaf hear, the dead rise again, the poor have the Gospel preached to them." So too he recalled the terrifying message of the last judgment from Matthew 25:35–36, that people will be rewarded or condemned by how they treated the hungry, the thirsty, the strangers, the naked, the sick, and the imprisoned. Justice and charity were "so linked with each other," he stated, "under the equable and sweet law of Christ, as to form an admirable cohesive power in human society." Both rich and poor had to work together for the common good.[178]

Returning toward the end of this encyclical to the threat of socialism, Leo warned of dissension and division among Catholics in the social movement. Hence he insisted that "the action of Catholics" (that is, Catholic Action) of all associations "move together under one primary and directing force." In Italy, he declared, the center is "the Institute of Catholic Congresses and Reunions." For other countries he demanded the same unity, that "the charge of controlling the common action of Catholics [be] under the authority and direction of the bishops of the country."[179]

Later, after Leo was gone, the phrase *Christian Democracy* would be used more specifically for the Catholic political parties and allied movements. Later, too, the phrase *Social Catholicism* would come to refer to what Leo meant by the social side of Christian Democracy. Finally, especially with the next pope, Pius X, the phrase *Catholic Action* would be emphasized as the name for lay movements organized under strong episcopal control for the defense of church interests.[180]

Leo's final encyclical on Christian Democracy ended with a plea to the bishops to use the church to build up unity between rich and poor.

Despite his adaptation to modern democracy and the modern social question, Leo's paradigm of evangelization remained classically aristocratic. The church was seen as an institution (described as "she") above the people and exercising its ministry in the form of "control."

> Let it become more evident that the tranquility of order and the true prosperity flourish especially among those peoples whom the Church controls and influences; and that she holds it as her sacred duty to admonish every one of what the law of God enjoins, to unite the rich and the poor in the bonds of fraternal charity, and to lift up and strengthen men's souls in the time when adversity presses heavily upon them.[181]

In reviewing the encyclicals of Pope Leo XIII, we have seen that this pope launched a fresh strategic phase in the history of modern Catholicism, yet one with strong roots in the prior strategy. On the one hand, he affirmed the critiques of liberalism made by his predecessors in the pre-Leonine period. On the other hand, he reached out to moderate liberals in a spirit of alliance and reform, and did so in order to form a common front against what he perceived as the more serious strategic threat of socialism. The truly innovating movements that he supported at the heart of his strategy were Thomism, Christian Democracy, and Social Catholicism. In addition, he also considered Christian unity one of his major goals.

In the next chapter, we will see how these programs of Leo's "grand design" evolved in the encyclicals of his successors throughout the remaining years of the modern Leonine strategy.

6

Modification and Breakdown of the Leonine Strategy

The Crisis of Modern European Bourgeois Civilization

As we have seen, Leo XIII's strategy for national capitalism attempted to create an anti-socialist reforming Catholic coalition with moderate liberals as the basis for a modern bourgeois adaptation of classical Christian civilization. Again, partly in the language of later usage, this strategy employed three external strategic programs:

- *Thomism* — promotion of the hierarchically organic teachings of Thomism as the philosophical ground for church and society.

- *Christian Democracy* — external diplomatic acceptance of moderately liberal democratic regimes and careful internal pastoral mobilization of lay Catholics to pressure these regimes in the direction of Catholic teaching.

- *Social Catholicism* — church support for the rights of the growing industrial working class and its unions, and for supportive but moderate social-welfare governmental policies.

Implicitly the strategy contained a fourth program, namely, the attempt to keep modern liberal culture from contaminating the internal life of the Catholic Church. In extreme form this became known as the campaign against modernism. Leo had begun his new strategy by optimistically assuming the old Christian civilization could soon be restored, albeit with modifications adapted to the new bourgeois context. Conservative or "integralist" voices in the papal bureaucracy, however, questioned this optimistic assumption. In particular, they called for tighter controls over modernizing dissidents in the inner ecclesial world of biblical and theological studies (ecclesial modernism), as well as in the outer societal world of political and economic engagement (social modernism). Toward the end of Leo's papacy, these voices seemed to have more influence over the aging pope, and in the next papacy they would have the upper hand.

Four more popes carried on the modern Leonine strategy: Pius X (1903–14), Benedict XV (1914–22), Pius XI (1922–39), and Pius XII (1939–58). The first three would make significant modifications to the strategy but not abandon it, with Pius X dramatically reigning in "modernism." The last, Pius XII, conducted himself as the most aristocratically triumphant of all the Leonine popes. Beneath his feet, however, the foundations of the modern Leonine strategy were already crumbling. Yet paradoxically, like Pius IX at the end of the pre-Leonine period, Pius XII would plant important seeds for a fresh post-Leonine and postmodern strategy.

Pius X:
The Internal Threat of Modernism

In 1903 Giuseppe Sarto was elected as Leo XIII's successor. He took the name Pius X, in memory of the quientessentially antiliberal Pius IX.

At the deepest level the new pope did not abandon the substance of Leo XIII's papal strategy for national capitalism, for he did not seek to restore the ancien régime. But he did modify the strategic orientation in two ways. First, he shifted from an optimistic view of the modern world to one that was profoundly pessimistic about its spiritual dangers. Second, he consequently downplayed external diplomatic rapprochement with the new liberal society and tried to strengthen the internal life of the church, both by a spiritual campaign for pastoral renewal and by a repressive campaign against "modernism."[1]

Campaign for Pastoral Renewal

Later canonized as a saint, Pius X had a simple and pious side that led him to feel at home in internal pastoral life and uncomfortable with external secular diplomacy. He creatively encouraged frequent communion, reformed the breviary, reemphasized the importance of seminaries, and encouraged priestly spirituality. He also began a reform of the Code of Canon Law, cut the Vatican bureaucracy in half, and reorganized it both financially and structurally. (Leo XIII had apparently left the Vatican in financial shambles and rife with organizational disarray and clerical nepotism.) He also appealed to the laity for help in religious instruction (through the Confraternity of Christian Doctrine) and in restoring Christian teaching to the family, the school, and the social classes (through Catholic Action).[2]

In an unpopular early legislative document, Pius X prohibited the use of the vernacular in the Mass (it had already begun to creep in) and directed that women singers be replaced by boys and the piano by the organ. He also forbade popular religious hymns in favor of Gregorian chant (for example, the beloved Christmas hymn "Adeste Fideles" was judged to be not "liturgical"). In addition, he began to reverse the internationalization of the Sacred College of Cardinals, which Leo XIII had initiated, in order to restore its earlier Italian character.[3]

Apparently possessing the psychic gifts of healing and of foreseeing the future, this pope spoke as early as 1910 of a *guerrone* (huge war) soon to engulf Europe, the likes of which people had never experienced. This huge war, he claimed, would come as a punishment from God, so that Europe might atone for its sins of attacking the church.[4]

Campaign Against Modernism

Pius X also had a repressive side, for he launched a massive inner-church campaign against modernism.[5] A term originally used in the Counter-Reformation, *modernism* came to mean a vague collection of teachings seen as bringing modern liberal innovations into the traditional understanding of the Bible and Christian theology as well as of the hierarchical order of church and society. Calling modernism "the synthesis of all heresies," this pope condemned the writings of leading Catholic theologians and biblical scholars (for example, Alfred Loisy and George Tyrell), brought Catholic Action under tight ecclesiastical control, and severely disciplined leading Christian Democratic activists (for example, Romulo Murri and Marc Sangnier). Seeing the social question more as a matter of personal morality and charity than of a corporate struggle for justice, he even supported for a long time the French proto-fascist movement known as Action Française.[6]

Toward the end of the papacy of Pius X, the pull toward the right became very strong and anti-union. Under pressure from French Catholic capitalists who were opposed to the pro-labor activities of the French Jesuits of Action Populaire, the pope contemplated condemning the very principle of unions as part of "social modernism." As a trial balloon, the Jesuits of *Civiltà Cattolica* (still closely allied with the pope) published in the spring of 1914 a series of anti-union articles. Pius X's secretary of state, Cardinal Merry del Val, also worked extensively to undermine pro-union arguments. The main objections offered by conservative voices against unions were that they rejected the principle of social hierarchy and emphasized justice over charity. Only a massive counter-campaign by Gusave Desbuquois of Action Populaire, particularly his appeal to *Rerum novarum*, held off the threatened condemnation through to Pius's death in 1914.[7]

The driving ideological group behind Pius X's campaign against modernism was the so-called integralists, heirs of the nineteenth-century *zeloti*. The secret organizational instrument behind their power was the Sodalitium Pianum, a body of clerical spies organized with the pope's support by Monsignor Umberto Benigni, later to become a secular spy for Benito Mussolini. This group mounted a campaign of ideological repression across global Catholicism. A secret internal policy document defined the group as counterrevolutionary and totally opposed to liberalism, democracy, anti-militarism, and any social involvement by the clergy. Members used code names, with Cardinal Merry Del Val as "Miss Romey" and Pius X as "Lady Micheline." Only the following pope, Benedict XV (as a cardinal himself a target of the anti-modernist campaign), put a stop to the wave of ecclesiastical repression.[8]

Two major documents condemning modernism issued from the papacy of Pius X. The first was a July 1907 decree of the Holy Office known as *Lamentabili*; the second was a September 1907 encyclical known as *Pascendi*.[9] All clergy, prior to ordination to major orders or before assuming a church office, were required to take a special oath against modernism. Excommunications were frequent.

Despite these negative expressions, Pius X did not repudiate the strategy of Leo XIII. Like Leo, he continued to see socialism as the main enemy and to pursue a liberal coalition to counter it. But in Pius's case, the liberal coalition leaned center-right rather than center-left. More than Leo, this pope tried to mobilize the laity on behalf of the church's pastoral ministry and the Vatican's defensive political interests. In particular cases he even relaxed the infamous *non expedit* (a ban in Italy prohibiting Catholics from voting or from running for office), so Catholics could vote in democratic elections against socialist candidates.

As a whole, like Leo, Pius X accepted bourgeois society, though he tilted the Leonine Catholic-liberal coalition to a center-right direction. He clearly differed from Leo in his attempt to condemn unions. Paradoxically, his hostility to "social modernism" constituted an implicit acceptance of economic liberalism. In addition, perhaps because he had been Archbishop of Venice, a diocese outside the papal territories, he proved less hostile to the new Italian state than had Pius IX and Leo XIII. He also differed from Leo in the consistently vitriolic and apocalyptic tone of his encyclicals. Lastly, he tilted Christian Democracy in the more tightly controlled direction of Catholic Action.

But despite these differences, three of the four elements of the Leonine strategy still held under Pius X: (1) identifying socialism as the primary enemy; (2) using Thomism as the philosophical base for a challenge to liberalism; and (3) mobilizing the laity as a pressure group within a democratic society. What did not hold was Social Christianity, which tended to be identified as social modernism. In addition, Pius made more visible a latent element of the Leonine pattern, that is, resistance against the penetration of modern liberal culture into the church's internal intellectual and pastoral life.

Benedict XV:
The Devastation of Industrial Warfare

In September 1914 Giacomo della Chiesa became Pope Benedict XV. A small and frail figure, the Romans nicknamed him *Il Piccoletto* (the midget).[10] Walking for the first time into his new office, he reportedly found on the papal desk an unopened letter to his predecessor denouncing him (della Chiesa) as a modernist. Soon thereafter, the ecclesial spy ring known as the *Sodalitium Pianum* was terminated, Monsignor Benigni was dismissed, and Cardinal Merry Del Val was relieved of his position as secretary of state. The repressive integralist campaign came to a halt.[11]

New Papal Theme of Peace

Benedict assumed the papacy just as World War I was beginning. He immediately recognized the horrendous terror of modern warfare and the cruel sufferings it brought on families, especially on children. Though sympathetic to the central European powers and obsessed with a fear of Russia, he nonetheless maintained strict papal neutrality.

Ascribing the war to the breakdown of Christian civilization, Benedict offered to serve as mediator among the contending powers. But this ancient diplomatic role of the papacy was not accepted. After the war he was explicitly excluded from the 1919 peace settlement, though he maintained a secret representative at the proceedings.[12]

Benedict showed little resentment at this loss of the papacy's traditional role of preeminence in European diplomacy. Instead, he continued to appeal morally for peace; focused his energies on the victims of the war, especially children; and organized massive campaigns of war relief. So generous was this pope's financial support for victims of the war that he nearly bankrupted the Vatican.[13]

As the British historian Derek Holmes noted, upon the death of Benedict XV the Vatican treasury was so depleted that a loan had to be obtained to pay for the conclave to elect his successor. From this time forward, Holmes also noted, the Vatican became increasingly dependent on the generosity of the North American church. Thus there emerged what would become two new traits of the twentieth-century papacy: (1) a supranational papal voice crying out on behalf of peace and aiding the victims of modern war; and (2) financial dependence on the North America church.[14]

Support for Christian Democracy

During Benedict's pontificate Italian Catholics were finally allowed a Catholic (though officially nondenominational) political party, the Partito Popolare Italiano, founded by Luigi Sturtzo. This was a precursor of the post-World War II Italian Christian Democratic Party. So ended the *non expedit* that had restrained Catholic voters in Italy since the time of Pius IX. With the new party Catholics were immediately in a strong position in the Italian parliament. Their unity broke down, however, during the 1921 elections, when socialists and fascists met in direct confrontation. The Vatican refused to support a popular alliance with the socialists and instead pressured for coalition with the fascists, who showed themselves hostile to Freemasons and offered state support for church institutions.[15]

Despite its continuing hospitality to socialism, the Vatican under Benedict XV opportunistically saw in communist repression of the Russian Orthodox Church an opening for Catholic inroads. Papal diplomats began negotiations with the new Soviet government and provided massive socialist assistance to war victims there. For a while the Soviet communists saw dialogue with the Vatican as a route to international diplomatic recognition of their new regime. But in 1927, when the Soviets received official recognition from Britain and the United States, they no longer needed the Vatican and broke off dialogue.[16]

Toward a Post-Colonial World Church

Benedict XV enthusiastically supported missionary outreach and began a long-term Catholic disengagement from industrial colonialism. In early industrial colonialism many European governments that had persecuted the Catholic Church at home had nonetheless protected their Catholic missionaries abroad, since they aided colonial domestication of local populations. This colonialist character of the early industrial missionary movement, as well as what Holmes calls the "territorial feudalism" of the religious orders (different orders controlling different geographic areas), had prevented the formation of native leadership for the new churches. Benedict challenged this colonial structure of the missions and established the first turning point toward what would later be known as a post-European world church. He reorganized missionary activity, encouraged native clergies, and began to put in place native bishops.[17]

Benedict's strategic innovations were thus threefold: first, establishment of the modern papacy as a supranational voice against militarism and on behalf of peace and victims of war; second, initial decolonization of the Catholic missions; and third, strong support for the precursors of modern Christian Democratic political parties. He also proved open to critical studies of the Bible, and some four hundred years after the Reformation had first promoted printing the Bible in the language of the people, this Catholic pope encouraged use of the vernacular Bible by Catholic families.

Despite these distinct emphases, Benedict XV still held fast to the Leonine strategy. He continued to see socialism as the primary strategic enemy, supported Scholasticism and especially Thomism, and deepened the overall commitment to Christian Democracy. In regard to Social Catholicism, many of his encyclicals referred to the class struggle, but his main response to the social question seems to have been a condemnation of materialism and a spiritual ministry to the working class. None of his encyclicals ever mentioned *Rerum novarum*, perhaps in part because the urgency of the great problems from the war and its aftermath displaced the workers' question.

Pius XI:
The Terror of State Totalitarianism

In 1922, following the death of Benedict XV, the cardinals, unable to give a majority either to Cardinal Gasparri (Benedict's accommodationist secretary of state) or to Cardinal Merry Del Val (Pius X's intransigent secretary of state), chose as pope Ambrogio Damiano Achille Ratti. He took the name Pius XI. Although he had spent much of his prior life as a librarian, he became the first pope to tackle the new realities of industrial warfare, totalitarianism, and the maturing of national capitalism.

While the primary threat of Russian communism dominated his papacy, Pius XI also had to contend with two additional societal threats. The second threat was the now mature national corporate model of industrial power. The third was European fascism, an alternative form of national capitalism and itself a new modern ideology alongside socialism and liberalism. His response to each of these threats would differ in intensity.[18]

Condemnation of Atheistic Communism

Born of a simple family in Lombardy and the prefect of the Vatican Library, Achille Ratti was chosen because, during his brief experience as papal nuncio in Poland, he had seen firsthand the military and ideological threat of Russian communism. The cardinals judged Russian communism to be the single greatest danger to the contemporary church. Linking the longstanding papal goal of the restoration of Christian civilization with his new papal concern for peace, Pius XI took as his motto "The peace of Christ in the Kingdom of Christ."[19]

In response to the primary threat of Russian communism, Pius XI issued his 1937 encyclical, *Divini redemptoris*, a systemic and unqualified condemnation of "atheistic communism."

Challenge to National Capitalism

The second stage of modern industrial capitalism had brought forth a truly national economy, as giant corporate actors achieved a national level for financing, production, and marketing—thanks to the new national grids of transportation and communications. At the same time national governments in the industrial countries dramatically expanded internal political power over their own populations, particularly through new persuasive techniques in mass communications. Further, governments assembled enormous information systems in expansive national bureaucracies and cultivated sophisticated nationwide police-intelligence structures. Last, these industrial nation-states achieved unprecedented projection of external military power by means of rapid industrial transport of troops by rail and ship, as well as by new industrial weapons of mass destruction, including tanks, long-range artillery, automatic weapons, battleships, submarines, and air-borne fighters and bombers.[20]

The most extreme form of this new industrial-political-military power has been labeled totalitarianism. It appeared both in the communist movement, established as a state power in Russia, and in the new ideology of fascism, taking state power in several European countries, including Germany, Italy, and Spain.[21]

In addition, as the world-market system began to mature, threatening international political-economic clashes began to arise among the competing major industrial capitalist nations. The collision of these forces intensified during the 1920s, and more so as the Great Depression unfolded the 1930s.[22]

In response to the new corporate form of capitalism and its international clashes, Pius XI boldly updated Leo XIII's historic encyclical *Rerum novarum* with his own 1931 encyclical *Quadragesimo anno*. This update unequivocally condemned "economic liberalism," offered still stronger support to workers, directly challenged the new national concentrations of capital, highlighted the principle of subsidiarity, and proposed a corporativist alternative to both liberal and socialist models of society. This pope criticized national capitalism more boldly than had Leo XIII, but he did not reject it.[23]

Ambiguity Regarding Fascism

Pius XI's response to fascism, the third threat, was still more nuanced. On the one hand, he regularly criticized fundamental aspects of fascism's state-oriented ideology, and in his 1937 encyclical *Mit brennender Sorge* even issued a blistering condemnation of major policies of Hitler's "national socialism." On the other hand, he seems to have preferred a strategic alliance by which moderate fascists and church leaders would work together against liberal individualism and socialist collectivism, as well as against the anticlericalism of both.[24]

Even when it became clear that both German and Italian forms of fascism were anything but moderate, and that both were turning against the church, Pius XI held back from a total break. Despite their threatening attacks, he continued to treat this right-wing ideology as a lesser evil than the communist menace. Initially, according to Holmes, "Achille Ratti regarded the forces of democracy as too weak and indifferent to the issues involved to be able to defend Christian Civilization against the threat of Communism." That certainly remained his perception in the Italian case. Toward the end of his life, however, he became increasingly hostile to Nazism in Germany, even though his adviser, Cardinal Pacelli, constantly recommended diplomatic compromise.[25]

In establishing his initial coalition with Italian and German fascism, Pius XI abandoned Benedict XV's strong support for Christian Democrat political parties. In return for promises of governmental cooperation with the papacy to reestablish Christian civilization, he ordered that both the German Zentrum (the Catholic Center Party) and the Italian Partido Popolare (the Catholic Popular Party) be disbanded. While not completely naive about the fascist danger, he apparently saw fascism as the only movement providing an opening for the papacy's program of spiritual-cultural restoration of Christian civilization, since only the fascists offered official support to church institutions (at least initially). Thus he returned politically, though not economically and theologically, to the center-right model of Pius X. In place of Catholic political parties, he placed all his confidence in tightly controlled Catholic Action as the main vehicle for the restoration of Christian civilization.[26]

Yet Pius XI did not immediately support Spanish fascism and, returning to Leo XIII's policy of *Ralliement*, he condemned the French fascist movement, Action Française. Regarding Spain, the Vatican initially did not side with the fascists, but rather with the new Republic, whose popular front included a new Catholic republican party, Acción Popular, based on the principles of *Quadragesimo anno*. Apparently the Spanish political situation was viewed as similar to that of France during the time of Leo XIII, when an intransigently monarchist church appeared threatened with being marginalized by a democratic triumph.[27]

Apart from Spain and France, Pius XI presumably assumed that over the long term fascism's negative side could be undercut by the organized work of Catholic Action. But once the fascists achieved a political monopoly in Italy, and even more so in Germany, the stage was set for brutal attacks on Catholic Action and on the church itself. This was in part thanks to the pope's clearing away the Catholic political parties as forces of resistance. (In contrast to the Vatican tendency to work with Hitler and to sacrifice the Zentrum party, the German bishops had been hostile to Hitler and supportive of the Zentrum, but they deferred to the pope's position.) Yet this pope failed to foresee the new European reign of terror, a tragedy that would be crushed only at the price of a second world war.[28]

In Italy, the bishops as a whole seemed supportive of Mussolini's brand of fascism, especially of his military invasions of Africa. Holmes cited the pro-fascist Italian Cardinal Schuster, Archbishop of Milan, as proclaiming: "On the plains of Ethiopia, the Italian standard carries forward in triumph the Cross of Christ, smashes the chains of slavery, and opens the way for the missionaries of the Gospel." In the wake of the Italian invasion, Protestant missionaries were expelled, and the leader of the Ethiopian Coptic Church was beheaded.[29]

Rejection of a Coalition with Democratic Socialism

In Europe the only feasible alternative to a center-right Catholic-fascist alliance would have been a center-left alliance between Catholic political parties (particularly the Zentrum in Germany and the Partito Popolare in Italy) and democratic socialists who were themselves increasingly anti-communist. In his encyclical *Quadragesimo anno* Pius XI recognized that many socialists had clearly rejected dictatorial communism and had moderated their formerly radical positions on property, family, and religion. Indeed, in both Germany and Italy Christian democrats and democratic socialists were frequently cooperating on tactical issues. But Pius XI firmly rejected such a center-left political coalition.[30]

Faithful to the fundamentally anti-socialist base of the Leonine strategy, Pius XI blocked any broad anti-fascist coalition between progressive Catholics and democratic socialists. Further, uneasy with Catholic parties, he preferred the elite diplomatic strategy of having papal diplomats negotiate legal concordats directly with national governments. His guide in this tactic of concordats was Eugenio Pacelli, the future Pius XII.[31]

Pacelli's most famous and controversial concordat was with Adolf Hitler. Rhodes noted that a secret clause in the concordat with

Hitler sealed an agreement between the Nazis and the Vatican to form a "common front" against Russia. On Pius XI's reliance on concordats rather than lay parties, Holmes wrote:

> Pius XI has often been criticized for his failure to support the Catholic Centre Party in Germany and the Catholic Popular Party in Italy. And History may well record that his greatest error was to reverse the policy of his predecessor, Benedict XV, who preferred to put his trust in these Catholic political parties rather than in the good faith of countries with whom the Church made Concordats. The whole foreign policy of Pius XI was based on the many Concordats he made, eighteen in all, a record for any Papal regime.[32]

According to Peter Kent, throughout the 1930s Pius XI became more hostile to Nazism than to communism, but Pacelli, his secretary of state, pressed for a more pro-German stance. After Ratti's death, Pacelli, elected as the new pope, would immediately tone down his predecessor's intensified anti-Nazi policy.[33]

An interesting sidebar on these two popes is the story of a proposed papal encyclical condemning racism and anti-Semitism, which was never published. In 1938 Pius XI asked the American Jesuit John LaFarge, founder of the National Catholic Conference for Interracial Justice, to prepare an encyclical on the two themes. Collaborating with LaFarge were two other Jesuits notable in the field of social justice: Gustav Grundlach, eventually the main social adviser to Pius XII, and Gustave Desbuqois of Action Populaire in Paris. Grundlach later claimed that the militantly anti-Bolshevik Polish Jesuit general, Vladimir Ledochowski, deliberately delayed transmission of the draft to the pope. The draft, titled *Humani generis unitas*, only reached Pius XI's office a few weeks before his death, and the pope himself may never have seen it. In any case, he died before it could be published. The next pope, Pacelli, who had a very different view of Germany than did Ratti, did not publish it, though there is no definite conclusion about why. Paradoxically, some have judged that it was best that the document was never published, since, despite good intentions, it actually contained strongly anti-Semitic aspects, for example, blaming the Jews for the death of Jesus.[34]

At least for the early Pius XI, and certainly for his successor Pius XII, a Catholic-fascist coalition could have made sense in the light of the Leonine papacy's longstanding social analysis of modern culture. In that analysis liberalism was seen as the foundational enemy, with socialism and communism seen as the children of liberalism and becoming the more radical and primary danger. In response to what was perceived as the more radical threat, Leo XIII had shifted papal strategy by seeking an anti-socialist coalition with the moderate wing of the liberal bourgeoisie on behalf of an organic-hierarchical reform of liberalism that would open on a modernized Christian civilization. Pius XI's proposed solution of an organic-hierarchical corporativism (with roots in the Austrian school of Social Catholicism) was a logical development of Leo's original strategy. In a certain sense fascism could have been initially seen as an organic-hierarchical revision of the modern bourgeois project, and initially a pro-Catholic one. But the reality of fascism would prove terrifyingly different.

Settlement of the Roman Question

A key strategic gain that Pius XI achieved by his coalition with Italian fascism was resolution of the Roman Question. Since the papacy's loss of the Papal States during the pontificate of Pius IX, modern popes had felt themselves prisoners of the Vatican and institutionally impeded from fully conducting their mission. The temporal power of the papacy, even if it were never to be restored on the same scale as the now lost Papal States, was seen as the institutional foundation for the papacy's presumed supranational mission as leader of a potentially restored Christian civilization. It was also seen as an indispensable defense against nationalist encroachments on local churches and even on the papacy itself.

In 1927 Benito Mussolini and Cardinal Gasparri, Pius XI's secretary of state, concluded the Lateran Treaty, which established the Vatican City State of 107.8 acres as an autonomous sovereign power. The two also signed a concordat that reestablished the Catholic Church as the official religion of Italy and provided important financial benefits for the Italian church, including a state salary for the clergy. In compensation for the loss of the Papal States, the Italian government gave to the Vatican in Italian *lire* the foundation of a large modern capitalist investment fund that James Gollin estimated to be worth at 1929 rates approximately $92.1 million. Vatican officials later developed that grant, over time augmented by funds from other sources, into an enormous capitalist portfolio.[35]

For over a thousand years the economic basis of the papacy had been feudal, with support coming from agricultural and mercantile revenues from the rural lands of the Papal States. After 1870, when the Italian government seized the Papal States, the papacy had lost not only its temporal power but also its economic foundation, and it gradually came to depend on external donations, particularly "Peter's Pence," with major revenues from the North American church. By the death of Benedict XV (as we saw, an extremely generous pope who gave away practically all the Vatican's liquid assets to victims of war), the papacy was nearly bankrupt.

Because of Pius XI's arrangement with Mussolini, the Vatican overcame its financial crisis and accomplished the transition from an economic foundation formerly based on premodern agricultural lands to a new one based on modern capitalist investments. During the next forty years the Vatican would become one of the major capitalist investors in the emerging world-market system. Thus yet another result of the Leonine strategy was the economic transformation of the papacy into an important economic actor in the modern capitalist world.[36]

Faithful to the Leonine Strategy

Pius XI held to the basic strategic lines of Leo XIII. As was clear in his rejection of a Catholic coalition with even democratic socialists, he maintained the strategic primacy of a battle against socialism, even to the point of allowing what appeared to be a tactical alliance with fascism when moderate liberalism appeared not strong enough to resist communism. He also strongly supported the organic-hierarchical teachings of Thomas Aquinas and issued his own encyclical reaffirming Leo XIII's *Aeterni patris* (*Studiorum ducem*, 1923). With language of militant support for the working class and vehement denunciation of the capitalist class, Pius XI also intensified Leo's position on the social question. He did this by issuing his own landmark social encyclical *Quadragesimo anno,* creatively updating *Rerum novarum* in light of the maturing of the national stage of industrial capitalism. Even his apparent tactical support of fascist governments can be conceived broadly within the framework of Leo's opening to Christian Democracy, since both Hitler and Mussolini initially rose politically through apparently democratic means and promised to aid in the reconstruction of Christian civilization.

Restoring Christian civilization was a foundational goal for Pius XI, as it had been for his immediate predecessors. In this pope's view, as also with his predecessors, this meant in ideal form restoring public authority for the Catholic Church as the single official religion of a nation, plus accepting the papacy's claimed public supranational authority as the spiritual-diplomatic mediator among nations.

In the statement of this goal, as with all the Leonine and pre-Leonine popes, there was a tendency to identify the kingdom of God uncritically with the church, and particularly with papal authority. Amid bitter papal denunciations of the sins of society, it remained inadmissible for the popes to acknowledge any institutional inadequacy on the part of the church. The church was seen as perfect and pure, insulated from and looking down from above upon a world of sin. That model of a pure church—standing in judgment over a sinful world and seeking the restoration of Christian civilization—would hold through one more pope.[37]

Pius XII:
The Strategic Conclusion

When Pius XI died in 1939, the cardinals quickly elected as pope his secretary of state, Eugenio Maria Giuseppe Giovani Pacelli. A member of a Roman family with several generations of service in the papal bureaucracy, he took the name Pius XII. Pacelli had been a key diplomat for Pius XI and had conducted the famous negations for the concordat with Hitler, while his brother, a layman and attorney, had played a central role in the negotiation of the Lateran Agreements with Mussolini. Different from the strong-willed Pius XI, Pacelli had been and would remain quintessentially a diplomat, never taking the stance of bold leader, and always seeking compromise. As Pope Pius XII he cultivated the image of an ascetic aristocrat, well informed on every subject and in detached yet complete command. During his pontificate, however, the ground began to tremble beneath the whole Leonine strategy, foreboding a strategic earthquake.[38]

Pius XII presided over the Catholic Church during perhaps the most turbulent and terrifying societal events of all Christian history. It was the time not simply of mature national capitalism, but also of the totalitarian systems of German fascism and Russian communism, all colliding with each other in a second and even more horrendous world war. It was the time of the blasphemous *shoah* of the Jews, and of the millions of others who died with them in the monstrous Nazi death camps. It was the time of the cataclysmic terror of modern "advanced" weaponry, including the mass civilian atomic bombing of Hiroshima and Nagasaki and the mass civilian saturation bombings of Dresden and other European cities. It later became the time of the fierce ideological struggles of the Cold War, both within Europe and later beyond it in the Third World. It became the time of the shift of global leadership from the old nations of Europe to the young and predominately Protestant "Anglo-Saxon" nation of the United States. It became the time of the birth of the United Nations, the advocate of a new truly global "world order" that would prove less and less European. Finally, it became the time when the modernizing and even left-leaning calls for lay-oriented inner-church reform, held at bay for so long, began to gain power—a development due in part to the new solidarity that had been forged among socialist and Catholic intellectuals and activists in their common resistance to European fascism.[39]

Pacelli and German Fascism

In regard to German fascism, commentators on Pius XII's papacy have been divided. Critics have seen him as a weakly, transcendent figure, unwilling to condemn Hitler and Nazism, and above all as failing adequately to denounce the genocide of the Jews. Supporters have argued that his reluctance to speak out publicly was based on the diplomatic calculation that to do so would bring still worse suffering. In retaliation, these supporters argued, the Nazis would have turned even more harshly on Jews in general, on Catholic Christians, on the papacy itself, and especially on Catholic Jews. According to Holmes:

> A former Israeli Consul in Italy has claimed that: "...the Catholic Church saved more Jewish lives during the war than all the other churches, religious institutions and rescue organizations put together. Its record stands in startling contrast to the achievements of the International Red Cross and the Western Democracies...The Holy See, the Nuncios, and the entire Catholic Church saved more than 400,000 Jews from certain death."[40]

Perhaps the most scholarly supportive perspective on Pius XII is the work by British diplomatic historian Anthony Rhodes, *The Vatican in the Age of Dictators*. The study was based on extensive original research in the archives of the British and German foreign offices, as well as in official Vatican diplomatic documents. Rhodes acknowledges the limitations of the personality of Eugenio Pacelli and of the historical situation. He also acknowledges that, both as a cardinal and later as pope, Pacelli made a tragic mistake in suppressing the anti-fascist Catholic political parties of Germany and Italy. Nonetheless, Rhodes concludes that Pius XII acted nobly in both diplomatic and covert attempts to save as many Jews as possible.[41]

A highly critical study of the same experience by another author who had brief access to the Vatican archives is John Cornwell's *Hitler's Pope: The Secret History of Pius XII*. Cornwell concludes that the pope, whom he refers to by his pre-papal name of Pacelli, was profoundly anti-Semitic, that his alliance with Hitler undermined German Catholic resistance to fascism, that he minimized the persecution of the Jews, and that his silence was mainly motivated by his desire to preserve the ultramontanist institutional power of the modern papacy. Cornwell's book has been strongly criticized, however, as being sensationalist and lacking real scholarship. Even Cornwell's book acknowledges that as early as 1939 Pacelli had become involved in a plot to assassinate Hitler (by acting as an emissary for the conspiring German generals to the allied leaders)—a bizarre activity for someone who, according to Cornwall, was "Hitler's pope."[42]

Though initially uncritical toward fascism, Pius XII was not naive. He came to understand the danger to the church from fascist attacks in Germany and Italy. But his analysis was constrained by the ancient construct of Christian civilization and by his preference for the elite diplomatic model of relating church and society.

In a radio speech of 29 June 1941, apparently reflecting his presumption of a future German victory, Pius XII broadcast the following statement in support of the Axis powers:

> Certainly in the midst of surrounding darkness and storm, signs of light appear which lift our hearts with great and holy expectations—these are the magnanimous acts of valour which now defend the foundations of Christian culture, as well as the confident hope in victory.[43]

Rhodes notes that, until the American government unexpectedly announced that it planned to destroy European fascism, Pius XII continued to receive leading Nazis and even to send birthday cards to Hitler. Only after a dramatic American intervention by President Roosevelt's ambassador, Myron Taylor, did the magnanimous papal policy toward Germany finally stop.[44]

The fascists had been willing through concordats to grant official status to the Catholic Church in public life, so apparently in Pius's initial view they provided the legal ground out of which Christian civilization could one day be restored and the modern world could thereby be healed of its systemic ills. In particular, with the Lateran Agreements the Italian fascists had restored the economic independence and political sovereignty of the papacy, in the pope's view an indispensable precondition for the restoration of Christian civilization. Neither liberals nor socialists had been willing even to consider such official public restoration, and so, presumably again in his view, these other political streams prohibited the restoration of Christian civilization and thus prohibited the Christian resolution of what he saw as the root crises of modern liberal culture.

Certainly Pius XII had to calculate the damage to the church from fascist harassment, and even the danger of large-scale persecution. But so long as fascist attacks did not eliminate the restored legal or public role of the Catholic Church, then he apparently believed that the foundations for a restoration of Christian civilization remained safe, even if the full edifice could not be built until later. Presumably the pope and his advisers judged that with time fascism would be tempered or fall, but that the restored legal role of the church and of the papacy would survive. The Leonine strategy of restoring the old power of the papacy by adapting to new modern conditions was still seen as feasible.

Another motive for Pius XII's acceptance of German fascism, in addition to his apparently initial hope of using fascism as a tool for restoring Christian civilization, was his increasing fear of communism. Soviet power was now threatening Western Europe, both externally by its growing military power and internally by its expanding political parties and front organizations. Fascism, it seemed, provided the only antidote to communist subversion or invasion. According to this analysis, should fascism be defeated, the resulting political vacuum would probably be filled by communism. Further, whatever their evils, the fascists might militarily destroy communist power in Russia and perhaps themselves be crippled in the process. Therefore, German and Italian fascism may have appeared, at least initially, as the lesser evil to be temporarily and conditionally tolerated in pursuit of the broader aim of the restoration of Christian civilization. Rhodes has cited the words of the pope's close aide Montini (later Pope Paul VI) to the German ambassador, "Certainly the Pope did not want Germany to be defeated, because this would open the way to atheistic Communism in Europe" [45]

Yet three new tremors were shaking the ground on which the Leonine strategy stood. The first two came from within Europe, one in the form of fascism's increasingly demonic face, and the other in the form of a new grass-roots Christian-socialist rapprochement. The third came from across the Atlantic in the form of the emerging non-European superpower of the United States.

Fascist Evils

Again, the first tremor that shook Pius XII's conclusion of the Leonine strategy was the increasingly demonic face of fascism.

As noted, in Germany most of the Catholic bishops had initially been critical of Hitler, but under Vatican prodding they had accepted the new regime. By contrast, in Italy there had been immediate and broad episcopal support for Mussolini. When both fascist regimes began their imperialist military campaigns (the Germans invading Eastern Europe and the Italians invading Africa), both episcopacies largely blessed the campaigns, though the Italians did so with far greater enthusiasm. But it was not long before major doubts were voiced about the viability of Christian civilization under fascism.[46]

There were several reasons for these growing doubts. First, the more the German and Italian fascists grew in power, the more they stepped up their attacks on the Catholic Church and the more clearly they proclaimed their idolatry of the state. Second, social atrocities committed in the name of fascism increased dramatically, especially with the growing attacks on the Jews.

Despite this increase of fascist militarism, of anti-Catholicism, and of social persecution, Pius XII for a long time attempted to combine a policy of political neutrality with diplomatic intervention. He reportedly did so in order to seek peace, to diminish church attacks, and to protect as many Jews as possible. After agreeing to send a conciliatory letter to Hitler, he expressed the sincerity of his efforts but also his awareness that the tactic might not work. Finalizing the form of the letter, he announced to a gathering of the German cardinals: "So we have taken the risk of trying again. Now we shall see. If they want a fight, we are not afraid. But the world shall see that we have tried everything to live in peace with Germany."[47]

Pressures for an Opening to the Left

While church leaders debated their doubts about the legitimacy of fascism, grass-roots members of the Catholic laity, religious orders, and lower clergy threw themselves headlong into the European resistance against fascism, frequently at the risk of their lives. Generally led by socialists or communists, the anti-fascist resistance brought Catholic Christians into close working contact with those whom the Leonine strategy had considered the primary enemy. In that cooperation new bonds of friendship emerged between Catholic militants and militants of the secular left. Over time, the experience of the resistance led many activist Catholics to reassess the anti-socialist character of the external face of the Leonine strategy and the often still premodern forms of scholarship and ministry that its internal face required.[48]

Thus, while the papal leadership still held up the Leonine dream of a modernized European Christian civilization, important figures within European Catholicism's lower clergy, members of religious orders, and lay intellectuals and activists implicitly began the search for a different strategy. In this second major tremor beneath the Leonine strategy, these figures explored an *apertura a sinestra* (opening to the left), a development that would have transformative implications for the wider society and for the internal life of the church itself.

Hegemony of the United States

The third tremor that shook Pius XII's continuation of the Leonine strategy was the rise of the United States to global industrial-military and eventually political-cultural hegemony within the democratic world. The new power of the United States appeared during World War II and emerged full-blown after the war.

At the start of the war Pius XII, like many European analysts, apparently assumed that the Axis forces would triumph because of the superiority of German scientific, industrial, and military power. He also seemed to assume that Germany, in alliance with the rest of central Europe, would again emerge as the center of European history. Leo XIII's alliance with Bismarck had favored Central Europe, even though Leo himself had been a Francophile, and Pius XII was clearly a Germanophile. Soon after his election as pope, he had apparently regarded himself in a situation like that of Leo XIII before Bismarck—possibly facing the potential to end this new *Kulturkampf*. The vision of a restored German-Vatican alliance, under the spiritual leadership of a modernized papacy, seemed to captivate his diplomatic imagination.[49]

Yet both Leo XIII and Pius XII fundamentally misread the geopolitical future. The Second World War would devastate Germany, leave the region industrially crippled for years to come, and turn global capitalist hegemony over to the United States. Early in the war the pope came to understand this unexpected shift.

On 20 September 1942, Myron Taylor, President Roosevelt's personal envoy to the Vatican, began a series of meetings with Pius XII. Taylor informed the pope that America and its allies had decided to destroy Nazism in Europe, to fight until Germany accepted an unconditional surrender, and to grant communist Russia a major role in the postwar world order. A few excerpts from Roosevelt's message to the pope reveal the strength of his determination, as well as the powerful future for the growing American military-industrial complex:

> The United States will prosecute the war until the Axis collapses...We know that no nation or combination of nations can stand against us in the field...The entire industry of the world's greatest industrial nation is now directed to one objective—to manufacture, by mass production methods in which we excel, the implements of war...The world has never seen such an avalanche of war weapons, manned by skilled mechanics and stout-hearted freemen, as we shall loose in 1943 and 1944 against the Axis...[Our] offensive will rise in irresistible crescendo, more and more rapidly, more and more powerfully, until totalitarianism, with its menace to religion and freedom, is finally and utterly crushed.[50]

Pius XII must have listened carefully to Taylor's words. As a master diplomat well versed in geopolitics, the pope would have recognized immediately that both the European order, and indeed the whole world order, was about to shift. His geopolitical vision of a strategic alliance between Germany and the Vatican on behalf of a restored and modernized Christian civilization was being cast into the dustbin of history. Highlighting the depth of this change for the papal self-understanding, Rhodes commented:

> The Pope's great dream that as a new Innocent XI he might unify the nations of the Christian West against the Infidel and save Vienna, Budapest and Warsaw as Innocent had saved those cities from the Turks—but this time from the Bolshevists—was over.[51]

Pius XII must have also listened carefully because, since the start of the war, the flow of financial support to the Vatican from the European Catholic countries had all but stopped. Yet vast sums were now flowing to the Vatican from the United States, reportedly from Catholic groups, but in reality mostly from secret government funds drawn on by Roosevelt.[52] Soon after the dramatic meeting with Taylor, the pope and the Vatican began to speak of Hitler as the most dangerous enemy, to be defeated with the aid of Soviet Russia.[53]

Rhodes also repeated the negative comment of Monsignor Tardini, a key adviser to Pius XII: "The Americans are preparing to reorganize Europe as they think fit...This desire on their part may cause enormous damage to Europe."[54] The American government certainly did not base its anti-fascist strategy on the renewal of a Christian civilization centered in a Germanic-Vatican alliance.

Perhaps a powerful motive in the American decision to destroy Germany was economic. Germany had originally been the primary candidate to succeed Britain as the leading economic power in industrial capitalism's new national stage. Thus Germany was America's primary economic competitor for leadership of the international industrial capitalist system. To destroy Germany's military machine would also mean destroying its industrial power. The defeat would assure global economic and political hegemony for the United States. Was it simply a coincidence that Roosevelt's representative to the Vatican, Myron Taylor, had earlier held the position of chairman of the board of United States Steel, one of the largest industrial corporations in the American nation's new military-industrial complex?[55]

For conservative European Catholic elites, America symbolized a combination of the feared Protestant and liberal threats.

Charges of the reputed heresy called Americanism had been a pre-monition of the later and more extensive campaign against mod-ernism.[56] The Vatican bureaucracy presumably assumed that the American cultural style would threaten the spiritually aristocratic model of the Catholic higher clergy and with it the triumphalistic hierarchical model of Catholic evangelization. An intrusion of mod-ern American culture into the culturally premodern theological and organizational style of the European Catholic Church would create powerful pressures for a more decentralized and lay-centered church, and perhaps even for a democratic model of evangelization, as found in the Protestant churches of liberal North America. That must have been a frightening prospect for senior Vatican officials.

With the United States Against Socialism

To repeat, the first two strategic tremors came from the fascist crisis and from European Catholics who joined the socialist-led resistance against fascism. This led to the threat of an external Catholic opening to socialism. Meanwhile, the third strategic tremor came from the Americanization of the post–World War II international world order. This threat carried not only a derailing of the papacy's vision of a Germanic-Vatican alliance at the heart of a restored Christian civilization, but also the heightened danger of an internal American-style liberalization of Catholicism's theo-logical consciousness and organizational structure. Again, these three strategic tremors must have appeared to the integralist wing of the Vatican bureaucracy as threatening to unleash all that the anti-modernists had fought so hard to repress.

Yet faced with the greater danger from the *apertura a sinestra*, Vatican policy turned toward the United States and against the European Catholic-socialist coalition. Thus to the end, Pius XII revised yet preserved Leo XIII's European-oriented vision of an anti-socialist Christian civilization. He did it by turning in the American direction.

Strategic cooperation with the Americans was also important because, with the postwar revival of an Italian Catholic political party (now named the Italian Christian Democratic Party), many Italian Catholic lay leaders had grown sympathetic to a center-left alliance and were determined to defend themselves from Vatican control. Since the Vatican could no longer itself directly control the Italian Catholic party, American financial and intelligence support proved an indispensable ally in pushing the party's line away from the left.[57]

Shifting tactics from Europe to North America, Pius XII remained faithful to the foundational Leonine strategy of an anti-socialist coalition with the moderate bourgeoisie. The resulting American-oriented revision of the Leonine strategy continued into the post–World War II period, as the Vatican and US intelligence agencies jointly undertook a major campaign to prevent a communist electoral victory in Italy. Later, with the official declaration of the Cold War, the Vatican-American alliance against Soviet communism flourished.[58]

At the same time, there was a strong papal attempt to avoid being totally reconstituted by American hegemony. Throughout the rise of industrial capitalism, papal social analysis had claimed that the foundational modern philosophical threat to Christian civilization was subjectively "individualistic" liberalism and that beneath liberalism lay the religious "rebellion" of Protestantism. The United States was now the global center of modern liberalism, and the most dynamic wing of modern Protestantism. If the modern crisis were to be overcome, inevitably this would mean challenging the rising culture of the United States, but not yet.

The papacy did have a strategic opening that could be used over the long term to relativize American geopolitical hegemony and to attempt to protect Catholicism's traditional theological consciousness and institutional structures from liberal and Protestant modernization. This opening was found in the vast regions of the post-colonial world where Catholic missionary outreach was still expanding. Turning to this young Catholic constituency, the European papacy could resist being overwhelmed by a new wave of "Americanism" and instead could ally itself with a new "world church" increasingly rooted in Africa, Asia, and Latin America.[59]

Thus Pius XII began dramatically to transform the College of Cardinals into an international body, though he continued Italian episcopal control over the Vatican bureaucracy. He also expanded the promotion of native clergy and native hierarchies, as was undertaken earlier by Benedict XV and Pius XI.[60] The fruit of this line of strategy would not blossom, however, until the next strategic stage.

Summary of Pius XII's Modification

Overall, like his immediate predecessors, Pius XII still held to the Leonine strategy; he modified it only to ensure its continued viability. First, the primary enemy remained socialism. Second, the philosophical base of strategic response remained Thomism. Third, the pope continued Leo's coalition program of Christian Democracy, that is, a reforming alliance with the modern democratic bourgeoisie and a controlled mobilization of the laity to protect church interests amid the bourgeois culture, though now he was using American support to restrain European Christian Democratic parties from alliance with the left.

As we have seen, however, under Pius XII the shape of this papal-bourgeois alliance shifted dramatically in response to turbulent changes in the historical context. Initially the alliance had for him meant a guarded legitimization of German and Italian fascism (initially rising to power within bourgeois democracies). Later, when it became clear that Germany would be totally defeated, it meant a strategic turn to the United States, the preeminent bourgeois power in the world. At the same time, in postwar Europe it meant a major struggle to exert powerful but indirect influence (again, with assistance from American intelligence services) over Christian Democratic parties, in order to prevent them from turning to the left.

The final element in the Leonine strategy, namely Social Catholicism, also still held under Pius XII. While this pope produced no major encyclical on the social question, his frequent speeches, allocutions, and radio addresses were filled with attempts to apply Catholic social teaching to every aspect of contemporary moral life. Yet, despite this attempt at technical sophistication, Pius XII's approach appeared to lack the passionate commitment to the working class found in Leo XIII and Pius XI. Rather, one senses a cool, even remote detachment, reflecting his cultivated posture as a transcendent spiritual aristocrat.

Following the death of Pius XII in 1958, the full impact of the tremors beneath his pontificate erupted in the second earthquake of papal strategy in the history of modern industrial capitalism. In the first earthquake, revealed after the election of Leo XIII, the ground of Catholic strategy had suddenly shifted from total rejection of liberalism to reforming dialogue with its moderate wing in order to fight socialism. The societal context of this first strategic shift had been the emergence of the second technological wave of the Industrial Revolution, namely, the machine revolution of the national stage of modern industrial capitalism. Now, in this second strategic earthquake appearing with the election of John XIII as successor to Pius XII, the once dreaded *apertura a sinestra*, that is, a reforming dialogue with socialism (again, something against which all popes since Leo had struggled), suddenly became papal policy. The societal context of this reforming dialogue was the third technological wave of the Industrial Revolution, namely, the electronic revolution of the global stage of modern industrial capitalism. But that is a matter for the next book.

In an appendix to this chapter, let us briefly examine the vision of a new Christian civilization as articulated by the preeminent Christian-Democrat philosopher Jacques Maritain. Then, in the next chapter, we will review the codification, modification, and conclusion of the Leonine strategy as documented in the texts of the papal encyclicals of Leo XIII and his Leonine successors from Pius X to Pius XII.

Appendix:
The Neo-Christendom of Jacques Maritain

In the later years of the Leonine strategy, a creative model for this adaptation of classical Christian civilization was proposed by the Catholic lay philosopher Jacques Maritain. He called it a "New Christendom," meaning adapted to modern bourgeois society in contrast to the "Old Christendom" of premodern society. While Maritain's model captured the imagination of the more progressive side of the late Leonine strategy and perhaps best articulated where the overall strategy was headed, his model was not completely accepted by the late Leonine papacy. Rather, his ideas seemed to function as a transition point, a way station between the Leonine and post-Leonine strategies.

Because Maritain played such a central role in the post–World War II period as ideological guide for Christian Democratic parties, as well as for large sectors of Catholic social action, and indeed for the whole Catholic rapprochement with liberalism, it may be helpful to review here his most basic ideas of political philosophy.

Maritain's Life

Brought up as a young man in a liberal Protestant French environment, but influenced by Henri Bergson and Leon Bloy, Maritain converted to Catholicism, together with his Russian Jewish wife, who was a poet. Initially he had leaned politically to the right. But after the pope condemned the early French fascist movement called Action Française, to which he had been sympathetic, the young philosopher threw himself headlong into the study of political philosophy. He soon became one of the most brilliant and creative figures in the Catholic attempt to reconcile classical and modern political thought and practice.

From the 1930s to Vatican Council II, Maritain was the dominant thinker influencing the progressive wings of Social Catholicism and Christian democracy. Internationalist in outlook, he rooted his thought globally in the social practice of Christian Democratic parties, Catholic trade unions, and movements of Catholic intellectuals. He became a close friend and adviser to Monsignor Giovanni Battista Montini, a key Vatican figure during the pontificate of Pius XII (and later to become Pope Paul VI).[61] Toward the close of his life, Maritain taught in the United States at Princeton University, though he would have preferred the University of Chicago. While Maritain published over fifty books, his social ideas were most clearly outlined in his 1936 seminal work *Integral Humanism.*[62]

Analogy of Christendom

The key resource in Maritain's attempt to link the classical and modern perspectives was the Thomist philosophical concept of analogy. Aristotle, on whom Aquinas drew, had seen the classical freedom of the Greek *polis* as a non-historical ideal resting on a fragile platform and easily lost. By contrast, modernity had rejected any fixed classical ideal and committed itself to a pragmatic linear drive of progressive freedom. A non-historical ideal and historical progress—how to connect these two contrasting notions of freedom? Maritain's solution was what he called the "concrete historical ideal."

In Maritain's view, the task was neither equivocally to reject the past nor univocally to return to it, but rather to realize a fresh model at once analogously similar to the past ideal yet historically different from it. In his view, history was indeed developmental; that is, truly new social forms emerged in progressive fashion, but they were not uprooted from their past traditions and so analogously resembled those past traditions. Whereas traditionalists looked only backward and progressives looked only forward, Maritain tried to move in both directions at once.

In describing the movement of history Maritain proposed a novel periodization that only recently has begun to gain acceptance. He separated the medieval period from its classical roots and connected it with modernity as part of a single cycle. In addition, he suggested that modernity was now exhausted. Like his contemporary, Catholic theologian Romano Guardini, Maritain proposed that the modern world was ending; unlike Guardini, he did not use the word *postmodern*. Instead, he argued that a new stage of Western culture was beginning.

In his wide panorama Maritain described three phases for Western culture: (1) the pagan classical era; (2) the era of the "Old Christendom," comprising the medieval realization of its ideal and the modern fall from that ideal; and (3) the "New Christendom," which was now beginning but which had roots in the medieval period. Again, in Maritain's view, the medieval and modern worlds were two phases in a single cycle, with the former being the ascendant or constructive side and the latter (flowing from Renaissance humanism and from Reformation Protestantism) being the descendant or deconstructive side.

The Old Christendom

In Maritain's analysis, at the root of the decline of the historical ideal of the Old Christendom were Martin Luther, René Descartes, and Jean Jacques Rousseau.[63] According to his interpretation, the theologian Luther destroyed the connection between Christianity and its natural intellectual ground in philosophy; the scientist Descartes turned philosophy into a mechanistic, mathematical enterprise completely separate from religion; and the political philosopher Rousseau celebrated pure nature with no role for sin. All three, he claimed, culminated in Immanuel Kant, the most prominent and foundational modern continental European liberal and Protestant philosopher..

For Maritain, the whole modern process was a logical progression of decay of the historical ideal. He further claimed that these three figures—Luther, Descartes, and Rousseau—led directly to the great crisis of his time, the rise of totalitarian and atheistic communism.

According to Maritain, the heart of the modern fall was the loss of philosophy as the ground of Western culture, or at least the loss of what he saw as the ideal philosophy, the moderate realism of Thomas Aquinas. This led, he claimed, to an imbalance between freedom and grace, with the religious stream (especially in Protestantism but also in Catholic Molinism) losing any sense of freedom, and with the secular scientific stream losing any sense of sin and grace. Yet Aquinas's thought, Maritain argued, was not completely lost, for he had covertly influenced the rise of modern participatory democratic theory, particularly in America, even more than Locke. According to Maritain, the modern idea of democracy had germinated in the medieval cities, the home of the early bourgeoisie.

For example, in classical times the Benedictine order, a rural feudal movement led by an aristocratic founder, had structured the authority of its abbot as a benevolent Roman *paterfamilias* (father of the family) who was "superior" to the members. In medieval times, however, the Dominican order, an urban movement linked to the emerging bourgeoisie, had constituted its elected prior as a *primus inter pares* (first among equals)—not a father to sons, but a brother to brothers. The Dominican prior was elected by his peers, and for a limited term of office.

Spanish Dominican theologians, Maritain claimed, were the strongest voices in the early formulation of modern democratic theory. Some even argued that the Spanish *conquista* constituted an unjust war and that the Spanish empire in the Americas was an illegitimate government, since the Amerindians had been unjustly attacked and had never given consent to their domination. The Constitution of the United States, Maritain further claimed, owed much to these Dominican roots. He even cited a story that Jefferson had studied the constitution of the Dominican order.

In sum, for Maritain, the fundamental problem leading to the modern decline of Christian civilization was theoretical rather than practical, namely, the loss of the moderately realistic philosophy as found in Aquinas. His solution was at root also theoretical, namely, the analogous articulation of a new theory for a new age. Political practice to achieve this would be the application, or better the incarnation, of that philosophy.

The New Christendom

In addition to its expansion of democracy, the practical historical ideal of the New Christendom would be different from the old version in two related ways: first, in the relation between the temporal and spiritual orders; and second, in the relation of the clergy and the laity.

In the Old Christendom the relation of the spiritual and temporal had been theocratic, with temporal politics considered as a ministerial service to the church's spiritual mission. The old historical ideal attempted to have direct theocratic control over the culture. By contrast, in the New Christendom the autonomy of the political, discovered by Machiavelli, would be respected, and Christians would only attempt to "animate" the "temporal order," that is, to influence it indirectly through persuasion and formation of the culture. In particular, the "temporal order" would be marked by religious pluralism, and people would be united in basics—not by doctrine or philosophy, but by practical reason. Thus, Maritain commented, the United Nations Charter of Human Rights was accepted by most member-states, but the philosophical reasons for accepting it differed.

Second, in the Old Christendom laypeople were understood to exist in a lower "state of life" than that of the clergy and religious. The clergy and religious, in turn, attempted to exercise direct theocratic control over the lay society. Thus the old ideal was a sacral form of government. By contrast, in the New Christendom there would be Christian lay influence within a secular and pluralistic form of government. The clergy and religious would be restricted to church functions and would be guides for the laity but would not exercise direct influence over society.

Christian influence upon society would be exercised only through lay movements and organizations—explicitly through Christian Democratic parties and Catholic trade unions, or implicitly through the Catholic lay presence in secular parties and unions. In addition, the New Christendom would carry a lay model of spirituality, stressing the vocational character of work and the special role of the sacrament of marriage.

During the Cold War period Maritain's vision and program achieved dramatic influence within young Christian Democratic parties. But with the new period of social and ecclesial history that began seminally in the late 1950s and became revealed more fully in the 1960s, his model of a New Christendom began to break down. As an old man, he so acknowledged in his charming but sad lament, *The Peasant of Garonne: An Old Layman Questions Himself About the Present Time.*[64]

The Leonine Encyclicals of Pius X, Benedict XV, Pius XI, and Pius XII

Modernism, Industrial Warfare, Economic Dictatorship, and Political Totalitarianism

The Leonine strategy of creating a modern bourgeois adaptation of classical Christian civilization for the national stage of modern industrial capitalism encompassed the pontificates of Leo XIII and his four successors, Pius X, Benedict XV, Pius XI, and Pius XII. Of these successors, the first three made significant modifications to the strategy, while the fourth presided over the strategy's conclusion. This chapter examines the encyclicals of these successors.

The Encyclicals of Pius X: Resistance Against Modern Secular Culture

During his twelve years as pope, Pius X (1903–14) issued sixteen encyclicals.[1] They were largely aimed at strengthening the internal spiritual life of the Catholic community and at resisting within the church what he saw as the external philosophical and theological threat of modern liberal culture, which he termed "modernism."

Initial Programmatic Documents

E Supremi. Pius X's inaugural encyclical, *E Supremi* (1903), announced the motto of his pontificate as "restoring all things in Christ" (Eph 1:10). The document lamented "the disastrous state of human society today," identified this state of society as a "perversity" that was a "foretaste" or perhaps even "a beginning of those evils which are reserved for the last days." The answer, the new pope announced, was to restore "God's dominion over man and all things." This was to be done, he argued, by "bringing (human society) back to the discipline of the Church," with the "principal way" being the restoration of the "empire of God" in the souls of those who have been "led away by reason and liberty."[2]

According to the encyclical, the restoration was to be accomplished by proclaiming the church's religious teaching, especially on marriage, youth, property, the state, and social classes. This was to be implemented primarily by priests and laity mobilized for religious instruction programs, and by Catholic voluntary associations, later widely known as Catholic Action.

> For it is not priests alone, but all the faithful without exception, who must concern themselves with the interests of God and souls—not, of course, according to their own views, but always under the direction and orders of their bishops...Our predecessors have long since approved and blessed those Catholics who have banded together in societies of various kinds, but always religious in their aim.[3]

In this response to the modern crisis, Pius X made no mention of justice or of Social Catholicism as endorsed by Leo XIII, but rather addressed the social question exclusively in terms of charity. Foreseeing the day when religion would be restored to public life, he described how the social question would be handled:

> For when these conditions have been secured, the upper and wealthy classes will learn to be just and charitable to the lowly, and these will be able to bear with tranquility and patience the trials of a very hard lot.[4]

Ad diem illum laetissimum. Next followed an encyclical on the Immaculate Conception, *Ad diem illum laetissimum* (1904), which blamed the crisis of the times on "Rationalism and Materialism" as "repudiating all respect and obedience for the authority of the Church, and even of any human power." Such repudiation of church authority, the document continued, was "the origin of Anarchism."[5]

Jacunda sane. Also in 1904, Pius X issued *Jacunda sane,* an encyclical on Pope Gregory the Great, who had presided over the church while the Roman Empire crumbled and who had served as the personal model for his papacy. Describing the contemporary world as "laying the axe to the root of the tree," that is, as attacking the church as the root of Christian civilization, he decried "this error" (the attack on the church) as the chief one of our times and the source "whence all others spring." The fundamental form of this attack, he claimed, was denial of "supernatural order," promoted chiefly through "historical criticism."[6]

Then, prefiguring his pending attack on modernism, Pius X offered his solution of force to this attack on the church, which he traced to a loss of philosophical ground.

> But these errors will never be effectively refuted, unless by bringing about a change of front, that is to say, unless those in error be forced to leave the field of criticism, in which they consider themselves firmly entrenched, for the legitimate field of philosophy through the abandonment of which they have fallen into their errors.[7]

The pope also declared here his criticism of what would later be called social modernism, again with no reference to Leo XIII's promotion of Social Catholicism:

> And so too are all they seriously mistaken who, occupying themselves with the welfare of the people, and especially upholding the cause of the lower classes, seek to promote above all else the material well-being of the body and of life, but are utterly silent about their spiritual welfare and

the very serious duties which their profession as
Christians enjoins upon them.[8]

He also warned of activist priests who were not under firm episcopal control and hinted of a coming ecclesial repression:

> They will exercise the sacerdotal ministry not for the sal-
> vation but for the ruin of the Christian people. For they
> will provoke discord, and excite rebellion, more or less
> tacit, thus offering to the world the sad spectacle of some-
> thing like division amongst us, whereas in truth those
> deplorable incidents are but the pride and unruliness of a
> few. Oh! Let those who stir up discord be altogether
> removed from every office.[9]

Two more encyclicals further spelled out Pius X's program of
emphasis on religious instruction and Catholic Action.

Acerbo nimis. The first letter, written in 1905, described religious knowledge as the primary antidote to the sinful rebellion of the
human will and called for every parish in the world to establish a
Confraternity of Christian Doctrine, charged with using "lay
helpers" to teach the catechism to youth.[10]

Il fermo proposito. The second letter, also written in 1905,
though only to the bishops of Italy, mandated "Catholic Action"
associations, "promoted chiefly by lay Catholics," as the principal
means to solve the "social question." It called upon these associations
to restore "Christian civilization" in the family, the school, and society by "re-establishing the principle of authority," and to do so with
special concern for "the agricultural and working classes."[11]

Pius X's model was clearly that of Christian civilization, with
the church as its guardian: "The Church has consequently become
the guardian and protector of Christian society." He lamented the
"raids continually made on the peaceful conquests of the church."
He called for the church to "study every possible means she can use
in regaining the losses in the kingdom already conquered," in order
"to restore all things in Christ."[12]

> "To restore all things in Christ" includes not only what
> properly pertains to the divine mission of the Church,

namely, leading souls to God, but also what We have already explained as following from that divine mission, namely, Christian civilization in each and every one of the elements composing it.[13]

Again, central to this restoration was to be controlled mobilization of the laity under the name of Catholic Action. While its main cultural-spiritual theme was to be authority, it was to include both religious formation and the passage of just laws.

Those chosen bands of [lay] Catholics who aim to unite all their forces in combating anti-Christian civilization by every just and lawful means...seek to restore Jesus Christ to the family, the school, and the society by re-establishing the principle that human authority represents the authority of God. They take to heart the interests of the people, especially those of the working and agricultural classes, not only by inculcating in the hearts of everybody a true religious spirit...[but also by making] public laws conformable to justice and amend or suppress those which are not...All these works, sustained and promoted chiefly by lay Catholics and whose form varies according to the needs of each country, constitute what is generally known by a distinctive and surely a very noble name: "Catholic Action," or the "Action of Catholics."[14]

In this encyclical, Pius X for the first time explicitly mentioned Leo XIII's 1891 social encyclical *Rerum novarum* and defined the object of Catholic Action as "the practical solution of the social question according to Christian principles." He also supported the creation of a "Catholic Union," which would "gather all Catholics, and especially the masses, around a common center of doctrine, propaganda, and social organization." All other activities of Catholics concerned with economic life were to be integrated with such centers.[15]

The pope even announced that "in particular cases" a "dispensation" could be given to the church law forbidding Catholics in Italy to take part in electoral politics. Indeed, he announced that "it was a duty of all Catholics to prepare themselves prudently and seriously for political life," and some may even "as a true Catholic, accept and fulfill public office." All such efforts, he declared, needed to be "united in the work of restoring Christian civilization under its various aspects."[16]

Yet he warned that these efforts also had to be under strict episcopal control. "With extreme regret," he lamented, it was necessary for him to condemn a tendency of some Catholics, including clergy, to operate outside episcopal control. The purpose of this tightly controlled mobilization was "to protect the masses from the invasion of Socialism, saving them at the same time from both economic ruin and moral and religious chaos."[17]

Next there appeared four more encyclicals on various themes but particularly on the problem of the separation of church and state triggered by the French government's abrogation of its concordat with the Vatican. In the first, *Vehementer nos* (1906), Pius X proclaimed that "the thesis" of separation of church and state was absolutely false and "an obvious negation of the supernatural order."[18]

The Encyclical on Modernism

Then there came Pius X's most famous document, *Pascendi Domini gregis*, on modernism, issued in 1907 to all the Catholic bishops of the world.[19]

The encyclical on modernism began with the pope's "divine mandate" to "guard with the greatest vigilance the deposit of faith," and with the consequent "rejecting of all novelties."[20] Next it sounded the alarm that the enemies of the church were no longer external; now "they lie hid, a thing to be deeply deplored and feared, in her very bosom and heart, and are the more mischievous, the less conspicuously they appear." Belonging both to the laity and to the priesthood, it claimed, these enemies "vaunt themselves as reformers of the church." Further, it argued, these enemies were insidiously disguising their attack by fragmenting it into countless apparently unconnected themes, which now need to be connected in the full light of day.[21]

But since the Modernists (as they are commonly called) employ a very clever artifice, namely, to present their doctrines without order and systematic arrangement into one whole, scattered and disjointed one from another, so as to appear to be in doubt and uncertainty, while they are in reality firm and steadfast, it will be of advantage, Venerable Brethren, to bring their teachings together here into one group, and to point out the connection between them, and thus to pass an examination of the sources of the errors, and to prescribe remedies for adverting them.[22]

In attempting to connect disparate parts of what was perceived as a threatening teaching, the encyclical described the typical modernist as simultaneously "a philosopher, a believer, a theologian, an historian, a critic, an apologist, a reformer." The document went on to investigate each of the roles and the connection among them, with special emphasis on the role of philosopher as the control point.[23]

The encyclical's description of the movement's reputed underlying philosophy seemed to be a synthesis of Kantian subjectivity ("agnosticism" before external reality, with knowledge limited to "phenomena"), Bergsonian evolution ("vital immanence"), and Jamesean religious psychology ("religious consciousness"). This alleged philosophical synthesis was then viewed as undermining belief in God, authentic revelation, the church itself, the social bond, objective morality, and all authority. The analysis of modernism concluded by describing it as the "synthesis of all heresies," aiming "at the destruction not of the Catholic religion alone but of all religion."[24]

Opposed to this proposed synthesis was the Roman Thomist position, which represented a premodern philosophical understanding of transcendence without modern historical consciousness. This position had no place for the evolutionary development of human society, church structures, and theological dogma. Building on this point, Gabriel Daly has cited the argument of the Catholic modernist George Tyrrell that there was a necessary connection between the hierarchical transcendence of the Roman version of Thomism and the clerical authoritarianism of the church at the time:

[Tyrrell] argues that Roman authoritarianism is given theological color by a concept of transcendence which is in effect deistic: an absent God who communicates in a "telegraphic" manner with his vicegerents on earth… "Sacerdotalism," i.e., the clerical abuse of authority, is the direct result of the lack of a theology of immanence.[25]

Clearly the principle of evolution would require not only a foundational shift in philosophy and theology, but also in the structure and process of the church itself. This was the very thing that the Leonine strategy had hoped to avoid. Therefore the encyclical warned:

> First of all they lay down the general principle that in a living religion everything is subject to change, and must change, and in this way they pass to what may be said to be, among the chief of their doctrines, that of Evolution. To the laws of evolution everything is subject—dogma, Church, worship, the Books we revere as sacred, even faith itself, and the penalty of disobedience is death.[26]

Further, since the acceptance of the philosophical principle of immanence would be inevitably tied to an attempt to recover the originally lay character of the Christian movement, the encyclical warned of a lay danger as well. "Note here, Venerable Brethren, the appearance of that most pernicious doctrine which would make of the laity a factor of progress in the Church." For Pius X, the laity were most welcome as "helpers" of the clergy, but, unless closely contained, the lay movement itself would prove subversive of the whole Leonine strategy's attempt to preserve within the ecclesial institution the spiritually aristocratic character of the clerical state.[27]

Pius X even claimed that his condemnation of modernism was nothing new, that it had long ago been condemned by Pius IX in his Syllabus of Errors.[28]

In a section describing "the Modernist as Reformer," the document once more warned of the lay danger. The section decried the call for democratization of the church and for other reforms like abrogation of mandatory celibacy. Then it charged that modernists wished that "a share in ecclesiastical government should therefore be given to the lower ranks of the clergy, and even to the laity, and that authority should be decentralized." These modernist reformers, it claimed, were linked with the principles of "the Americanists" (referring to Leo XIII's condemnation of the reputed heresy of "Americanism").[29]

In seeking to disclose the causes of modernism, the encyclical distinguished proximate and remote causes, with the former seen as a perversion of mind and the latter as curiosity and pride. In intellectual terms, according to the text, the root problem was ignorance of Scholasticism, which "has left (the modernists) without the means of being able to recognize confusion of thought, and to refute sophistry." "Unfortunately," the text continued, the modernists, "in their efforts to undermine tradition and the magisterium," make great "efforts to win new recruits" and "seize upon chairs in the seminaries and universities."[30] The Leonine strategy's fear of liberal contamination within the church itself had become acute.

The remedies for modernism, according to *Pascendi's* concluding section, included seven techniques:

- study of Thomist philosophy, along with the natural sciences;

- exclusion of modernists from seminaries and Catholic universities, and from candidacy for holy orders;

- episcopal vigilance to prevent the reading of modernist publications;

- episcopal censorship of local church publications (thus the requirement of an *Imprimatur* and *Nihil obstat*, as well as the naming of official censors);

- forbidding of congresses of priests;

- establishment of diocesan "watch dog" committees, to be called the Council of Vigilance; and

- three-year reports by all bishops to the Vatican on their battle against modernism.[31]

The anti-modernist philosophical campaign, begun in positive form with the papal campaign for Thomism during the papacy of Pius IX and made strategically central during the papacy of Leo XIII, now took on a repressive spirit that would hover over Catholic theology until the time of Vatican Council II. Such was perhaps the inevitable price of the Leonine attempt to establish an external Catholic diplomatic-political rapprochement with the modern liberal world while trying to prevent the modern liberal world from contaminating the internal theological-pastoral life of the church itself.

Subsequent Documents

Five more encyclicals followed the condemnation of modernism in *Pascendi*. *Communium rerum* (1909) celebrated Saint Anselm, the French evangelizer of England, perhaps because modernism seemed more rooted in Anglo-Saxon cultures and from there seemed to influence France and the rest of continental Europe.[32] *Editae saepe* (1910) honored Saint Charles Borromeo, the great apostle of the Counter-Reformation, which presumably Pius saw continuing in his day.[33] *Iamdudum* (1911) criticized the separation of church and state in Portugal.[34]

The last, *Lacrimabili statu* (1912), admirably and zealously defended the native peoples of South America against "the crimes and outrages committed against them." Though a very brief letter, it described the pope as "moved by the deplorable conditions of the Indians in Lower America." Decrying the past servitude and enslavement of the native peoples, the pope repeated an earlier papal condemnation:[35]

> We…condemn and declare guilty of grave crime whosoever…shall dare or presume to reduce the said Indians to slavery, to sell them, to buy them, to exchange or give them, to separate them from their wives and children, to deprive them of goods and chattels, to transport and send them to other places, or in any way whatsoever to rob them of freedom and hold them in slavery; or to give counsel, help, favour, and work on any pretext of colour to them that do these things, or to preach or teach that it is lawful, or to co-operate therewith in any way whatever.[36]

Pius X's final encyclical, *Singulari quadam* (1912), tentatively accepted the inter-confessional character of workers' associations and trade unions in Germany, but only as a matter of practical expediency.[37]

Still Within the Leonine Strategy

In spite of its anti-modernist drive and internal pastoral emphasis, Pius X continued the Leonine strategy. His documents still saw
socialism as the primary strategic enemy, though his tactics for protecting church and society were more negative than Leo's had been.
According to this pope the purpose of Catholic Action was "to protect the masses from the invasion of Socialism, saving them at the
same time from both economic ruin and moral and religious
chaos."[38]

Pius X also kept the grounding in Thomism, even enforcing it
more rigorously, but he focused negatively on its internal enemies in
the "modernist" movement rather than on its external contribution
to a reform of liberalism. Still, he sustained the coalition with the
modern liberal bourgeoisie, though he shifted from a center-left
alliance to a center-right one, and he even began a papal flirtation
with the fascist ideological current within the bourgeois experience.
He also continued to reach out to the working class, though not primarily through support of the rights of labor. Instead, he stressed the
pastoral dimensions of popular religious education, a renewal of lay
spirituality (for example, frequent communion), and Catholic lay
associations in the style of Catholic Action aimed at restoring Christ
spiritually to civil society, including by legislation.

Leo XIII had stressed his positive hope for the new social context, had given priority to an offensive diplomatic outreach to moderately liberal political elites, and had moderately supported the
social struggle of the working class. By contrast, Pius X stressed negative fears of the internal contamination of church life by modern
culture and gave priority to a defensive internal pastoral renewal of
the Catholic Christian community. He vigorously supported the turn
to the laity for religious education, spiritual renewal, and Catholic
Action, albeit under strict hierarchical control. Though the two
popes differed in tactics and tone, both sought the same goals of
resisting socialism and of restoring Christian civilization within the
new bourgeois context.

The Encyclicals of Benedict XV:
The Modern Papacy as Promoter of World Peace

During his nine years as pope, Benedict XV (1914–22) issued twelve encyclical letters. With this pope the tone of papal encyclicals shifted to one of love, compassion, and mercy, and placed a new emphasis on peace.

Inaugural Encyclical

Benedict XV's inaugural letter, *Ad beatissimi apostolorum* (1914), appealed in a loving tone to all humankind. With a compassionate lament, it bemoaned "the sad conditions of human society...filled with bitter sorrow" and afflicted in war by "the most awful weapons military science has devised." Using these weapons, he grieved, "the greatest and wealthiest nations of the earth...strive to destroy one another with refinements of horror." Anticipating the same language that would later become famous with the early postmodern encyclical of the future Pope John XXIII, Pius X spoke of Christ's gift of "peace on earth to men of good will" (Luke 2:14).[39]

The cause of the terrible war, in Benedict's view, was that "the practices and precepts of Christian wisdom ceased to be observed in the ruling of states." This led, he declared, to four major problems:

- the loss of "brotherly love," leading to racial and class hatred;

- the loss of respect for ruling authorities, with that authority, according to Benedict, having its "natural origin...in the family";

- the stirring up of class hatred among the poor against the rich, due to a wrong sense of equality provoked by socialists; and

- the materialistic desire for money and pleasure, with the still deeper root, caused by the loss of awareness of humanity's supernatural goal.

In response to these crises, Benedict proclaimed that the keynote of his pontificate was "to strive in every possible way that the charity of Jesus Christ should once more rule supreme." Whereas Pius X's goal had emphasized the restoration of authority, this pope's goal emphasized the restoration of love. Reading his words here and throughout his encyclical corpus, one cannot help but note the compassionate strain that warms every text, in contrast to the often-vitriolic language of his predecessor.[40]

In the same encyclical, Benedict softened the fear of modernism. While officially decrying "the monstrous errors of Modernism" and renewing its condemnation,[41] he nonetheless affirmed a limited pluralism in the Catholic Church.

> As regards matters in which without harm to faith or discipline—in the absence of any authoritative intervention of the Apostolic See—there is room for divergent opinions; it is clearly the right of everyone to express and defend his own opinion.[42]

Then he called for a halt to the use of "certain appellations" that were being used "to distinguish one group of Catholics from another"—presumably the names "integralist" and "modernist."[43]

Benedict concluded with a call for the clergy to be loyal to bishops, for the bishops to take leadership, and for the "abnormal position of the Head of the Church" (referring to the Roman Question) to be restored to its normal state.[44]

Subsequent Documents

Next came *Humani generis redemptionem* (1917), an encyclical on preaching the word of God, which surprisingly made almost no reference to the society within which the church functions.[45] Following that, *Quod iam diu* (1918), an unusually short encyclical of only three paragraphs, welcomed the upcoming peace conference and called for "a just and lasting peace" that would be "founded on the Christian principles of Justice."[46] Another encyclical, *In hac tanta* (1919), addressed the twelve-hundredth anniversary of the evangelization of the peoples of Germany by Saint Boniface, with no reference to the war through which Germany had just passed.[47] Yet another very brief encyclical, only five paragraphs long, *Paterno iam diu* (1920), expressed the pope's great concern in the wake of the war for the children of Central Europe and noted the great generosity of the "Episcopate of the United States of America" in sending relief.[48]

In 1920, Benedict XV issued *Pacem Dei mujus pulcherrimum,* a longer call for peace among nations. He warned that there could be "no stable peace or lasting treaties...unless there be a return of mutual charity to appease hate and banish enmity." He insisted that the gospel's call for forgiveness and reconciliation applies not just to individuals but also to nations. He even offered to suspend the former ban against Vatican receptions of heads of Catholic states (issued in protest over the loss of the Papal States) in order to work for peace.[49]

Without mentioning explicitly the League of Nations, he urged that "all States...should be united in one league, or rather a sort of family of peoples." He also called for a campaign of disarmament:

> What specially amongst other reasons, calls for such an association of nations, is the need generally recognized of making every effort to abolish or reduce the enormous burden of the military expenditure which states can no longer bear, in order to prevent these disastrous wars or at least to remove the danger of them as far as possible.[50]

A 1920 encyclical on Saint Jerome *(Spiritus paraclitus)* addressed the Bible and, for the first time ever, "warmly commended" the use of "critical methods" for its study, thus reversing Leo XIII's rejection of "higher criticism" and Pius X's rejection of "historical criticism." Also, the reading of the Bible, presumably in the vernacular, was now strongly encouraged for Christian families.[51]

Another 1920 letter celebrated Saint Ephrem the Syrian *(Principi apostolorum Petro).*[52] Yet another 1920 document again lamented the postwar suffering of children in Central Europe and praised the Save the Children Fund.[53]

Two 1921 documents, *Sacra propediem* and *Fausto appetente die,* celebrated the Franciscan third order, a lay association, and Saint Dominic, who also founded a lay third order. The former warned against the love of riches and pleasure, and decried immodest clothing and (apparently noting the new music and dance of the Roaring Twenties) "those exotic and barbarous dances recently imported into fashionable circles." The latter largely extolled Thomas Aquinas's piety and fidelity to the Holy See.[54]

Also a 1921 encyclical, *In praeclara summorum*, celebrated the centenary of the lay Catholic writer Dante. It used the figure of Dante to recommend the Scholastic method, particularly the philosophy of Saint Thomas Aquinas. It warned against the return of "Paganism."[55]

Continuing the Leonine Strategy

Under Benedict XV the Leonine strategy held in its basic lines. Socialism was still the strategic enemy, although greater attention was given to the pressing problem of the Great War. Thomism was still the favored philosophy, as seen in the encyclicals on Dante and Dominic, though the repressive style of Pius X was softened. Christian Democracy advanced dramatically in Italy with the creation of a Catholic political party, officially "interdenominational." The "social question" of the workers and the economic class struggle were still major concerns, though Benedict's way of dealing with them seemed more like that of Pius X, namely, as a matter of religious reform and the defense of authority. With the next pope, however, Social Catholicism would again come to center stage.

The Encyclicals of Pius XI:
Economic Dictatorship and State Totalitarianism

While not matching the output of Leo XIII's eighty-six encyclicals in twenty-six years, Pius XI (1922–39) was nonetheless a prolific writer; he produced thirty encyclicals in eighteen years. His documents focused on what he saw as the social and spiritual crisis of Christian civilization. The greatest challenge, in his view, was "atheistic communism," and every aspect of his teaching was part of his strategic response to the communist threat. More than any prior pope, and in even stronger language than Leo XIII, he insisted on the rights of workers and saw the spread of communism as succeeding mainly because of the failure of Christian employers to follow the dictates of justice in the work place.[56]

Inaugural Document

Pius XI's first encyclical, *Ubi arcano Dei consilio* (1922), announced his program of "re-establishment of the Kingdom of Christ by peace in Christ," a two-part theme that combined the older goal of ecclesial restoration with the new concern over modern war. In his opening social analysis, the pope spoke of five levels of disrupted peace:

- among nations;
- between classes;
- among political parties;
- in threats to the family; and
- in the moral disorientation of individuals.

Along with resulting social disorders like unemployment, he warned of the growing spiritual hurt to people, particularly from the recent "Great War." This social and spiritual disorder, he claimed, was dragging Christian civilization back into a barbarism worse than that from which it was once saved.[57]

Next Pius moved to what he saw as the root causes of the disorder. These included:

- the recent war;
- obsession with materialism; and
- most profoundly, the rejection of God and Jesus Christ.

This last cause he linked to the false claim that all authority comes only from humans, a claim that then led, he argued, to the secularization of family and school and to the loss of any adequate religious-moral ground for social order.[58]

> Because men have forsaken God and Jesus Christ, they have sunk to the depths of evil...It was a quite general desire that both our laws and our government should exist without recognizing God or Jesus Christ, on the theory

that all authority comes from men, not from God. Because of such an assumption, these theorists fell very short of being able to bestow upon law not only those sanctions which it must possess but also that secure basis for the supreme criterion of justice which even a pagan philosopher like Cicero saw clearly could not be derived except from the divine law. Authority itself lost its hold on mankind...Society, quite logically and inevitably, was shaken to its very depths and even threatened with destruction, since there was left to it no longer a stable foundation, everything having been reduced to a series of conflicts, to the domination of the majority, or to the supremacy of special interests.[59]

The remedy, according to the pope, was to restore the peace of Christ and its roots in justice. In his view, this was possible only if the church were restored to its public position of authority as moral and spiritual guide over the individual, the family, and the society. The instrument of this remedy was to be Catholic Action, through which the laity assisted the clergy in its mission. The section on remedies also contained an isolated condemnation of "social modernism" and "theological modernism," though there was no elaboration on the phrases (as if the condemnations had been extraneously inserted into the text).[60]

Programmatic Encyclicals

Francis de Sales. Pius XI's second encyclical, *Rerum omnium perturbationem*, issued in 1923 to celebrate the third centenary of the death of Saint Francis de Sales, offered a spiritual response to the great social crisis of the times. In this document the pope noted again "the great disorders with which the world struggles today," and argued that "the root of these evils lies in the souls of men." He portrayed these evils as flowing from "the unmeasured desires of mankind, desires which are the fundamental cause of wars and dissentions, which act, too, as a dissolving force in social life and in international relations." To heal these evils, he continued, we need "to have recourse to the assistance of the Divine Healer Jesus Christ, by the means which he has placed at the disposal of His Holy Church."[61]

In calling all people to "the Divine Healer," the pope emphasized that Saint Francis de Sales had rejected the classical spiritual claim of two ways of life: a so-called higher way of perfection for the monastic or religious vocation, and a so-called lower way of imperfection for others. Prefiguring the Second Vatican Council's rejection of this concept of two ways and its proclamation that the call to holiness is one and universal, Pius insisted: "We cannot accept the belief that this command of Christ ('Be ye therefore perfect as your heavenly Father is perfect.' Matt. V, 48) concerns only a select and privileged group of souls." He thereby radically challenged a long Platonic dualistic distortion of the teachings of Jesus by spiritual theologians. He also rooted the social crisis in a deeper spiritual crisis and laid a spiritual foundation for mobilization of the laity.[62]

In reviewing the life of de Sales, the first Counter-Reformation Catholic bishop to return to Calvinist Geneva, Pius XI resurrected the nineteenth-century Catholic argument that traced the modern social crisis back to the Reformation. But rather than responding harshly, as had been the case since the rise of ultramontanism, he pointed out that de Sales, despite his naturally choleric temperament, had been a model of meekness, cheerfulness, and love toward the "heretics" of Geneva, and indeed toward all people. The pope also pointed to de Sales's constant visits to prisons. Yet he reminded readers that de Sales never hesitated to confront the powerful when he found them unjust, including the local senate and the local prince.[63]

Finally, Pius XI used the example of de Sales to support Catholic use of the print medium. After summarizing the saint's key books *(An Introduction to the Devout Life, Treatise on the Love of God,* and *Controversies),* he named him "a Doctor of the Church, to be the Heavenly Patron of all Writers." Relinking his spirituality to the laity, the pope also indicated that de Sales could be an inspiration for "the apostolate, as it is called, of the clergy and the laity which has for its end the bettering of the world."[64]

Thomas Aquinas. In 1923 Pius XI issued *Studiorem ducem,* an encyclical on Saint Thomas Aquinas in preparation for the six-hundredth anniversary of his death. The document was not so intellectually dramatic as had been Leo XIII's *Aterni patris*, but it confirmed the abiding centrality of Thomism for the Leonine strategy.[65]

Pius began the text by addressing Thomas's devotion to the virtues, particularly chastity, "aversion for fleeing possessions and a contempt for honors," humility in the devotion to truth, and above all wisdom, all of which culminated in "charity." He emphasized the connection of Thomas's intellectual life to his immersion in prayer, such that "he would frequently fast, [and] spend whole nights in prayer." Then he described Thomas's great commitment to philosophy, and in turn to theology, as the complementary wisdoms of reason and faith.[66]

In terms of the Leonine strategy Pius argued that Thomas's philosophy challenged "the root of the errors and opinions of modern philosophers." Those errors, he continued, were grounded in a false epistemological claim that "it is not being itself which is perceived in the act of intellection, but some modification of the percipient." The "logical consequence" of this epistemological error, he argued, is agnosticism, which was condemned in Pius X's encyclical on modernism, *Pascendi*. Thomas taught, the pope reminded his readers, that we can indeed know God's creation and not just our own inner sensations or thoughts, and that through reason's knowledge of creation, as the First Vatican Council affirmed, we can truly know God.[67]

Pius XI then turned to theology, where he emphasized the role of moral theology in giving "rules and precepts of life not only for individuals, but also for civil and domestic society which is the object of moral science, both economic and political." Hence for the pope, Thomas's moral wisdom provided the solution for the great modern social problems. This was particularly true, he maintained, for the great scourge of war:

> Hence those superb chapters in the second part of the Summa Theologica on paternal or domestic government, the lawful power of the State or the nation, the natural and international law, peace and war, justice and property, laws and the obedience they command, the duty of helping citizens in their need and co-operating with all to

secure the prosperity of the State, both in the natural and supernatural order. If these precepts were religiously and inviolably observed in private life and public affairs, and in the duties of mutual obligation between nations, nothing else would be required to secure mankind than "peace of Christ in the Kingdom of Christ" which the world so ardently longs for.[68]

Finally, referring implicitly to Pius X's anti-modernist encyclical *Pascendi*, the pope proposed that Thomas's wisdom was the antidote to modernism, which, like Pius X, he saw as the root of all modern evils:

> Again, if we are to avoid the errors which are the source and fountain-head of all the miseries of our time, the teaching of Aquinas must be adhered to more rigorously than ever. For Thomas refutes the theories propounded by Modernists in every sphere, in philosophy...in dogmatic theology...in exegesis...in the science of morals, in sociology and law...in the theory of asceticism...It is clear therefore why Modernists are so amply justified in fearing no Doctor of the Church so much as Thomas Aquinas.[69]

After his encyclicals on Francis de Sales and on Thomas Aquinas, Pius XI issued in 1923 *Ecclesiam Dei*, a document on Saint Josaphat, a saint and martyr of the Slavic rite. It appealed to the Orthodox "schismatics" to return to Christian unity with the "rock of Peter." The next year he issued *Maximam gravissimamque*, a letter to the French bishops on "diocesan cultural associations."[70]

Christ the King. Then came Pius XI's 1925 encyclical *Quas primas*, establishing the feast of Christ the King. This was the central symbol of Christian civilization, reflecting a Davidic or Christic model of evangelization. According to the encyclical,

> [the] manifold evils in the world were due to the fact that the majority of men had thrust Jesus Christ and his holy law out of their lives; that these had no place either in private affairs or in politics; and...as long as these individuals and states refused to submit to the rule of our Savior,

there would be no really hopeful prospect of a lasting peace among nations.[71]

Therefore, the pope called for "the restoration of the Empire of Our Lord" and public recognition of "the Kingship of Our Lord Jesus Christ" and of the public authority of the Catholic Church, which is the "Kingdom of God on earth." Calling particularly for obedience to the Lord, he decried anticlericalism as a plague that infects society.[72]

Various Documents. Next came a series of encyclicals that addressed various matters. These included *Rerum ecclesiae* in 1926, on the Catholic missions (strongly supporting the promotion of native clergy); *Rite expiates,* also in 1926, on Francis of Assisi (seen as modeling the Christian alternative to the modern materialistic desire for riches); *Iniquis afflictisque,* again in 1926, on the persecution of Catholics in Mexico; *Mortalium animos* in 1928, on Christian unity and relations with Protestant churches (forbidding Catholic participation in ecumenical meetings); *Miserentissimus Redemptor,* also in 1928, on reparation to the Sacred Heart; *Rerum orientalium,* again in 1928, on oriental studies and the hope for unity with the Orthodox churches; and *Mens nostra* in 1929, on the spiritual exercises of Ignatius Loyola and Francis de Sales.[73]

The Lateran Treaty. Quinquagesimo ante, in 1929, celebrated the fiftieth anniversary of his ordination as a priest and rejoiced at the Lateran Treaty. This agreement with the fascist government of Mussolini, the document stated, had ended the "Roman Question" by establishing Vatican sovereignty (as if it were an independent nation) and by financially compensating the papacy for loss of the Papal States. The treaty laid the economic and political foundation for a truly modern papacy. The pope interpreted this agreement as "restoring the peace of Christ to Italy."

Soon after came two of Pius XI's very important encyclicals: one on Christian education, and the other on Christian marriage.

Christian Education. In his 1929 letter on education, *Reppresentanti in terra,* Pius XI built on the long struggle of the modern papacy to resist the state-sponsored secularization of the education of youth. Now, in the face of rising totalitarianisms, the Catholic struggles to retain control over the education of youth moved to center stage. Distinguishing the claims over youth among the three different societies of family, state, and church, Pius gave educational priority to the family. But he also argued that it needs the complementary support of the state, though never in a way by which the state would destroy the family's foundational responsibility. He further argued that the church has a supernatural claim over both familial and state-sponsored education, and that the role of each of these societies must be honored in due proportion. In this document Pius XI held up a patriarchal model of the family and saw children as an extension of the person of the father and under his authority, with no mention of the mother at this point. He condemned nationalistic and militaristic approaches to education, as well as "pedagogic naturalism" (which, he argued, denied sin and grace), coeducation, and religiously "neutral" schools.[74]

Christian Marriage. After an encyclical on Saint Augustine, Pius turned to Christian marriage. In his 1930 encyclical *Casti connubii*, he sketched the Catholic position on marriage as "the principle and foundation of domestic society and therefore of all human interaction," yet also "raised…to the rank of a truly and great sacrament of the New Law." In this document the pope countered the liberal position that society is simply an aggregate of individuals loosely bonded by the feeling of sympathy. (This was the mechanistic-emotive philosophy made famous by the Scottish philosopher Adam Smith and known more widely on the ethical side as moral-sense theory.) In this view, marriage was seen simply as a private contract. He also countered the statist theory that all associations, including the family, are subordinate to the civil government (a theory found more in the Latin stream of liberalism).[75]

This document constituted the first modern papal statement offering a central ecclesial role to the spirituality of marriage—testimony to the growing strategic importance of the laity. But it still affirmed a patriarchal model of marriage by stressing the teaching of Paul on the wife's subjection and obedience to her husband (Eph 5:22–23), and it decried the emancipation of women as a crime:

> The same false teachers who try to dim the luster of conjugal faith and purity do not scruple to do away with the honorable and trusting obedience which the woman owes

to the man. Many of them even go further and assert that such a subjection of one party to the other is unworthy of human dignity, that the rights of husband and wife are equal; wherefore, they boldly proclaim the emancipation of women has been or ought to be effected...(We have already said that this is not an emancipation but a crime).[76]

The document noted especially the new danger to family life from propaganda being delivered into the home by cinema and radio. Here, the pope claimed, "the sanctity of marriage is trampled upon and derided." The text also condemned unmarried unions, divorce, abortion, and the new "science" of "eugenics." This encyclical is also the source of the now classic statement of contemporary Catholic teaching on the two ends of marriage as procreation of children and mutual support, as well as on the inadmissibility of deliberately frustrating the begetting of children.[77]

In discussing mutual support in marriage, the pope argued that its function was not private but needed to spill over into the wider society:

> This outward expression of love in the home demands not only mutual help but must go further; it must have as its primary purpose that man and wife help each other day by day in forming and perfecting themselves in the interior life, so that through their partnership in life they may advance ever more and more in virtue, and above all that they may grow in true love toward God and toward their neighbor.[78]

Quadragesimo anno *on Social Justice*

Pius XI's next encyclical, *Quadragesimo anno* (1931), often called in English *On Reconstruction of the Social Order*, his most famous social document, was a fortieth-anniversary reflection on Leo XIII's 1891 foundational social encyclical *Rerum novarum*, now updated in light of new political-economic developments.[79] In the long list of key documents of papal social teaching, this one stands second in line after *Rerum novarum*. The encyclical itself is divided into three main parts, plus an introduction and conclusion:

- review of the benefits of *Rerum novarum*;
- defense and development of the church's social teaching; and
- analysis of the root of the social problem and its remedy in Christian moral reform.

Introduction

Pius XI set the stage by recalling the modern industrial division of labor into two social classes in terms even more sympathetic to workers than Leo XIII's original document:

> From toward the close of the nineteenth century, the new kind of economic life that had arisen and the new developments of industry had gone to the point in most countries that human society was becoming divided more and more into two classes. One class, very small in number, was enjoying almost all the advantages which modern inventions so abundantly provided; the other, embracing the huge multitude of working people, oppressed by wretched poverty, was vainly seeking escape from the straits wherein it stood.[80]

In this introduction Pius XI immediately rejected the socialist solution. But, unlike Leo XIII—even while appealing to him—he wrote not of a reform of moderate liberalism but formally identified liberalism as an equal danger:

> [Leo] sought no help from either Liberalism or Socialism, for the one had proved that it was utterly unable to solve the social problem, and the other, proposing a remedy far worse than the evil itself, would have plunged human society into greater dangers.[81]

Pius described Leo as having "boldly attacked and overturned the idols of Liberalism," and instead as having proclaimed a "new social philosophy," rooted in "the treasury of right reason and Divine Revelation."[82]

Benefits of Rerum novarum

In describing the benefits of Leo XIII's social encyclical, Pius identified three areas that had been helped: (1) the church; (2) the state; and (3) the production system of employer and workers.

The Church. Pius claimed that the encyclical had aided the popes in their "defense especially of the poor and the weak," and that thanks to the document "scholars, both priests and laymen" had developed "a social and economic science in accord with the conditions of our times." He commended "courses instituted at Catholic universities, colleges and seminaries," as well as "social congresses and [social study] weeks." As a result, he boasted, "Catholic principles on the social question have...passed into the patrimony of all human society," such that "after the terrible war," the "leading nations" attempted to "restore peace on the basis of a thorough reform of social conditions, [based on] the norms agreed upon to regulate in accordance with justice and equity the labor of workers." The pope also argued that Leo's teachings had been "widely diffused in the minds of men," that the "souls of workers" had been filled with "the Christian spirit," and that "new organizations" of "workers draftsmen, farmers, and employees of every kind" had been founded "frequently under the leadership of priests."[83]

The State. Pius XI proposed that Leo's teaching had helped governments move beyond "the confines imposed by Liberalism." Describing the liberal philosophy of government in negative laissez-faire terms as seeking only legal order, he described Leo as showing how the state needs positively through its laws to promote the common good. In that process, he added, "chief consideration ought to be given to the weak and the poor." Describing "the principles of Liberalism as tottering," he added that "good Catholics" had been "champions of social legislation" in their legislatures. Finally, he rejoiced that "a new branch of law" had emerged "to protect vigorously the sacred rights of workers," including "the protection of life, health, strength, family, homes, workshops, wages and labor hazards, in fine, everything which pertains to the condition of wage workers, with special concern for women and children."[84]

Employers and Workers. Pius XI celebrated the creation of "associations that embrace either workers alone or workers and employers together." He recalled the hostility that formerly was directed to "workers' associations" by "those at the helm of State, plainly imbued with Liberalism."[85] Such political leaders, he highlighted,

> were showing little favor to workers' associations of this type; nay, rather they were going out of their way to recognize similar organizations of other classes and show favor to them, they were with criminal injustice denying the natural right to form associations to those who needed it most to defend themselves from ill treatment at the hands of the powerful.[86]

Leo's encyclical, the pope continued, "encouraged Christian workers to found mutual associations according to their various occupations." Such endeavors, he added, also protected them from "socialist organizations," which claimed "to be the sole defenders and champions of the lowly and oppressed." Such associations were to be "founded upon religion," so as to increase "the goods of body, of soul, and of property." In certain situations, however, he acknowledged that workers were "almost forced" to join "secular labor unions," but this was permissible provided they truly professed "justice and equity and [gave] Catholic members full freedom to care for their own conscience and obey the laws of the Church." In such situations, he declared:

> Side by side with these [secular] unions there should always be associations zealously engaged in imbuing and forming their members in the teaching of religion and morality so that they in turn may be able to permeate the unions with that good spirit.[87]

Pius XI expressed his regret that the spirit of forming Christian unions was not matched by zeal for employers to form their own Christian associations. He developed this theme of employers' associations no further, apparently because there was little to praise.[88]

The pope concluded the first part of his document by naming Leo XIII's *Rerum novarum* "the *Magna Charta* upon which all Christian activity in the social field ought to be based, as on a foundation." Acknowledging, however, that both doubts as to "the correct meaning of some parts of Leo's Encyclical" and certain "controversies" that have arisen in regard to it, he then turned to a defense of the church's authority to teach in the social arena.[89]

Defense of Church Social Teaching

Pius XI began by defending the authority of the church to teach in socio-economic matters. The laws of economics, he argued, are "based on the very nature of material things," and God is "the author of nature." Therefore economics, he continued, needs to be placed in its "proper place in the universal order of purposes," so that it may be oriented to "the final end of all things, that is God."[90]

Right of Property. The first theme that Pius XI addressed in his defense of church teaching was "ownership, or the right of property." Following Aquinas, he argued that property had both an individual and a social character. When both were honored, he stated, society avoided the "twin shipwrecks" of "individualism" and "collectivism," which were promoted by the two wings of "social modernism." Because of property's dual character, "the right of property is distinct from its use." It is the task of "public authority" to define in details the duties of its use on behalf of "the common good." Further, he proposed, while "it is grossly unjust for a State to exhaust private wealth through the weigh imposts and taxes," the opposite is also true, namely, "a person's superfluous income...is not left wholly to his own free determination." Rather, he emphasized, "the rich are bound by a very grave precept to practice almsgiving, beneficence, and munificence."[91]

Capital and Labor. While historically unclaimed property may be acquired by occupancy or labor, Pius noted, "work that is hired out" does not entitle one to ownership of that which is worked. Nonetheless, he continued, the claim of "Manchesterian Liberals" that the labor-contract is to be determined only by the free market is false. Because of this false claim, "capital has too long been able to appropriate too much to itself...hardly leaving to the worker enough to restore and renew his strength." On the contrary, as Leo XIII stated, "Neither capital can do without labor, nor labor without capital." Again, the pope cited Leo's words, "However the earth may be apportioned among private owners, it does not cease to serve the common interests of all." Then, adding in his own words a new phrase to the terminology of justice, he proclaimed, "By this law of *social justice*, one class is forbidden to exclude the other class from sharing in the benefits" (italics added.)[92]

> To each, therefore, must be given his share of goods, and the distribution of created goods, which, as every discerning person knows, is laboring today under the gravest evils due to the huge disparity between the few exceedingly rich and the unnumbered propertyless, must be effectively called back to and brought into conformity with the norms of the common good, that is, social justice.[93]

The Propertyless. Pius XI lamented that "in our age of 'industrialism'" so many workers were without ownership, especially in Asia:

> Since manufacturing and industry have so rapidly pervaded and occupied countless regions not only in the countries called new, but also in the realms of the Far East that have been civilized from antiquity, the number of the non-owning poor has increased enormously and their groans cry to God from the earth. Added to them is the huge army of rural wage workers, pushed to the lowest level of existence and deprived of all hope of ever acquiring "some property in land," and, therefore, permanently bound to the status of non-owning worker unless suitable and effective remedies are applied…The immense multitude of the non-owning workers on the one hand and the enormous riches of certain very wealthy men on the other establish an unanswerable argument that the riches which are so abundantly produced in our age of "industrialism," as it is called, are not rightly distributed and equitably made available to the various classes of the people.[94]

The pope warned that, unless there were a rapid and socially just distribution of property, "let no one persuade himself that public order, peace, and the tranquility of human society can be effectively defended against the agitators of revolutions."[95]

Just Wages and Salaries. While defending the hiring contract as not essentially unjust of itself, Pius nonetheless demanded that the pay be just. To determine what was just, he argued, required addressing three factors, plus one recommended enhancement:

- *Family Wage.* "The worker must be paid a wage sufficient to support him and his family." Mothers, he continued, "should work primarily in the home or in its immediate vicinity." He decried as "an intolerable abuse, and so to be abolished at all cost, for mothers on account of the father's low wage to be forced to engage of gainful occupations outside the home to the neglect of their proper cares and duties, especially the training of children."

- *Condition of Business.* The pope acknowledged that, in determining wage levels, it would be unjust to raise wages to a level that would destroy a business. But it would be wrong, he insisted, to underpay workers in order to sell a product at less than a just price.

- *Public Economic Good.* Workers' pay, he argued, needs to be set at a level that would not increase unemployment. Opportunity to work, he continued, needs to be provided for all those who are willing to work. Further, its level should be sufficient to allow the worker eventually "to attain gradually to the possession of a moderate amount of wealth." There should be "a right proportion among wages and salaries" that is "closely connected [with] a right proportion in the prices at which goods are sold by the various occupations."

- *Workers' Participation.* Finally, the pope considered it advisable that "the work-contract be somewhat supplemented by a partnership-contract" (sharing in ownership and/or management). In this way, he argued, "workers and other employees thus become sharers in ownership or management, or participate in some fashion in the profits received."[96]

Reconstruction of the Social Order. Pius XI next turned to the social order itself, which he said was greater than the preceding questions yet strongly influenced them. Two things were necessary, he claimed: (1) reform of institutions; and (2) correction of morals. Under these two headings the pope offered three lengthy descriptions of institutional reforms and a brief statement on moral reform.

- ***Subsidiarity.*** The pope's first concern under institutions was with the state. Here he worried that "individualism" had eroded the "rich social life which was once highly developed through associations of various kinds." What was left, he lamented, was only the naked relationship of individuals and the state, with the state forced to take over "all the burdens which the wrecked associations once bore." As a result, "the state has been overwhelmed and crushed by almost infinite tasks and duties." In response, the pope offered his now famous principle of "subsidiarity."[97]

So important is this principle in the Catholic social tradition, that it may be helpful to cite the pope's words in full:

> Just as it is gravely wrong to take from individuals what they can accomplish by their own initiative and industry and give it to the community, so also it is an injustice and at the same time a grave evil and disturbance of right order to assign to a greater and higher association what lesser and subordinate organizations can do. For every social activity ought of its very nature to furnish help to the members of the body social, and never destroy and absorb them.
>
> The supreme authority of the State ought, therefore, to let subordinate groups handle matters and concerns of lesser importance, which would otherwise dissipate its efforts greatly. Thereby the State will more freely, powerfully, and effectively do all those things that belong to it alone because it alone can do them: directing, watching, urging, restraining, as occasion requires and necessity demands. Therefore, those in power should be sure that the more perfectly a graduated order is kept

among the various associations, in observance of the principle of "subsidiary function," the stronger the social authority and effectiveness will be and the happier and more prosperous the condition of the State.[98]

- **Industries and Professions.** In what would later be a controversial and unclear teaching of this encyclical, Pius XI called for associations between the individual and the state to be established in the economic arena. He likened these to the earlier guilds, which had organized workers into functional associations. Such economic associations were not to operate simply on the principle of competition, found in the free market, but rather from a "harmonious" arrangement of their social functions. The associations were to pursue the interests of their whole area of work, and to do so freely.[99]

- **Directing Authority.** Pius XI warned that "the right ordering of economic life cannot be left to a free competition of forces" (something that he called "this evil individualistic spirit"). Rather it was necessary that "economic life be again subjected to and governed by a true and effective directing principle." Such a "directing principle" would be quite different from "economic dictatorship." There was needed "a juridical and social order which will, as it were, give form and shape to all economic life." This principle needs also to be expanded, he argued, to the level of nations through international treaties. Such an authority, described in the document as "a system of syndicates and corporations," would have the following characteristics: (1) It would give "monopoly privilege" to "free syndicates" of workers or employers to make binding labor agreements; (2) delegates from workers' and employers' syndicates would form governing "corporations" for their industry, with strikes and lockouts forbidden, and with appeal to a higher governing "magistracy"; and (3) all would be governed by "Catholic principles."[100]

- **Reform of Morality.** Actually, Pius XI said little here about the reform of morals, except to appeal to "right reason" and to warn against the danger of socialism, as arising from the failure of the current economic system.

The precise nature of Pius XI corporativist vision remains to this day an unsettled question. Further, the vision became obscured by the authoritarian corporativist reality of fascism.

Next the pope turned to the great changes that, he claimed, had developed in "the economic system and Socialism...since Leo XIII's time."

Root Causes of the Social Crisis and Its Remedy

Pius XI began this third section by offering his analysis of historical changes since Leo's time in terms of three themes: (1) the capitalist world; (2) socialism; and (3) "the Christian reform of morals."

Interestingly, the pope did not emphasize the word *capitalist* but usually wrote non-ideologically of "this economic system" or "the contemporary economic regime." The word *capitalist* or *capitalistic* appeared only three times in the document, and all within a limited section (pars. 103, 104, 112), while the words *socialist, socialism, communist,* and *communism* appeared fifty-seven times. Nonetheless, this document represents, I believe, the first papal use of an explicit ideological reference to capitalism.

Changes in Capitalism. Pius XI began by appealing to Leo XIII to declare that "this economic system" was not itself unjust, but needed to be reformed:

> With all his energy Leo XIII sought to adjust [reform] this economic system according to the norms of right order; hence, it is evident that this system is not to be condemned in itself. And surely it is not of its own nature vicious. But it does violate right order when capital hires workers, that is, the non-owning working class, with a view to and under such terms that it directs business and even the whole economic system according to its own will and advantage, scorning the human dignity of the workers, the social character of economic activity and social justice itself, and the common good.[101]

The pope then noted that the "capitalist" economic regime was not the only alternative, and pointed to "agriculture, wherein the greater portion of mankind honorably and honestly procures its livelihood," although it too is "crushed with hardships and difficulties." Nonetheless, he continued, with "the diffusion of modern industry throughout the world, the 'capitalist' economic regime has spread everywhere." Hence, in addressing this regime, Pius XI made clear that he was not speaking simply to the old industrial regions, but to "all mankind."[102]

The pope then addressed the changes in the "capitalist" regime since the time of Leo XIII. "In the first place," he pointed to the management revolution and what he called an "economic dictatorship." Since this is a classic statement of this pope, it may be helpful to cite the full text:

> It is obvious that not only is wealth concentrated in our times but an immense power and despotic economic dictatorship is consolidated in the hands of a few, who often are not owners but only the trustees and managing directors of invested funds which they administer according to their own arbitrary will and pleasure.
>
> This dictatorship is being most forcibly exercised by those who, since they hold the money and completely control it, control credit also and rule the lending of money. Hence they regulate, so to speak, the life-blood whereby the entire economic system lives, and have so firmly in their grasp the soul, as it were, of economic life that no one can breathe against their will.[103]

The cause of this "economic dictatorship," the pope claimed, was the "unlimited freedom of struggle among competitors...which lets only the strongest survive." As a result, he continued, "this is the same as saying those who fight the most violently, those who give least heed to conscience."[104] The resulting "accumulation of might and of power," he then argued, "generates three kinds of conflict":

- "the struggle for economic supremacy itself;

- "the bitter fight to gain supremacy over the State to use its resources and authority"; and

- "the conflict between States themselves."[105]

In the pope's analysis, the ultimate result is the paradoxical destruction of the free market by unbridled competition and the degradation of the state into an instrument for greed. In addition, he stated, the destructive pattern expands to the international level in two forms:

- "economic nationalism or even economic imperialism"; and

- "a no less deadly and accursed internationalism of finance or international imperialism, whose country is where profit is."[106]

Pope Pius XI's remedy was to be found, of course, in "Christian social philosophy," which "avoids the reefs of individualism and collectivism." The competitive freedom of the market, he proposed, needs to be "brought under public authority" and there guided by "the norm of social justice."[107]

Changes in Socialism. This encyclical also contained a landmark analysis of socialism, in which for the first time a modern pope reflected upon the strategic split in the movement of the left. In the time of Leo XIII, the pope noted, the two sections of socialism were not radically separate, but in his time they had often become "bitterly hostile" to each other.

On one side, the pope described "communism" as the result of changes within the socialist movement paralleling similar changes "within the capitalist economic system." Presumably he meant that just as the modern nationalist stage of capitalism had produced what he called a nationalist "economic dictatorship," so the nationalist stage of socialism had produced in the communist state a political dictatorship. Pius XI virulently condemned this dictatorial or communist side of the split. Communism, he further lamented, had inflicted "horrible slaughter and destruction" upon "vast regions of eastern Europe and Asia," sought "unrelenting class warfare and absolute extermination of private property," and remained "openly hostile to Holy Church and to God himself."[108]

The other stream, he noted, "kept the name Socialism" but had become more moderate by rejecting violence, modifying the class struggle and the attack on private property, and even

> inclines toward and in a certain way approaches the truths which Christian tradition has always held sacred; for it

cannot be denied that its demands at times come very near those that Christian reformers of society justly insist upon.[109]

But, in face of the question of whether Christians and socialists might meet in some middle ground, and acknowledging that many Catholics were asking this question, he responded negatively that it was "a vain hope!"[110] Rejecting any compromise or coalition, he declared:

> We make this pronouncement: Whether considered as a doctrine, or an historical fact, or a movement, Socialism, if it remains truly Socialism, even after it has yielded to truth and justice on the points which we have mentioned, cannot be reconciled with the teachings of the Catholic Church because its concept of society itself is utterly foreign to Catholic truth.[111]

Yet, Pius XI maintained, the socialist position on the class struggle and property, though modified, is still far from the Christian position. Even were moderate socialism to modify further its doctrines in these areas so as to become identical with Catholic teaching, the pope insisted that it could not be accepted.

For the pope, the reason that socialism remained "utterly foreign" was that it ignored "the sublime end of both man and society" and affirmed that "human association has been instituted for the sake of material advantage alone." In this perspective, the pope continued, an efficiently "socialized" division of labor became the only criterion for economic organization. As a result, people were required "to surrender themselves entirely to society," including if necessary their liberty, and there was no place for "true social authority, which...descends from God alone, the Creator and last end of all." Therefore, he again dramatically proclaimed, "no one can be at the same time a good Catholic and a true socialist."[112]

Pius XI continued his condemnation of socialism by warning of "a certain new kind of socialist activity" that attempts to pervade "morality and culture," that seeks to train "the mind and character," and that in particular aims at "children of a tender age." The pope then repeated the now classical papal social analysis of the slide from the Enlightenment into communism: "Let all remember that Liberalism is the father of this Socialism that is pervading morality and culture, and that Bolshevism will be its heir."[113]

The pope concluded his reflections on socialism by lamenting that "not a few of Our sons…have gone over to the ranks of Socialism." He rejected the excuse that the church had abandoned the poor and pointed to the great legacy of Leo's encyclical on labor. Then he invited those who had left the church for socialism to return.[114]

The Spiritual Root of the Crisis. For Pius XI, the "ardently desired social restoration" could only proceed from "a renewal of the Christian spirit." In his analysis, "the present economic system" (that is, capitalism) labored "under the gravest of evils," while "Communism and Socialism" had wandered "far from the precepts of the Gospel." "Only a return to Christian life and institutions" could heal society. So serious was the crisis that it threatened the "loss of souls."[115]

For Pius XI, the root cause of the crisis of economic and social life, and of the resulting "apostasy of great numbers of Christian workers from the faith," was "the disordered passions of the soul," which are the "result of original sin." These "disordered passions" have expressed themselves as an "unquenchable thirst for riches and temporal goods, which has at times impelled men to break God's laws and trample on the rights of their neighbors." Such "disordered passion" had always been present to some degree, but the pope saw them as acutely aggravated by the "present system of economic life."[116]

> The easy gains that a market unrestricted by any law opens to everybody attracts large numbers to buying and selling goods, and they, their one aim being to make quick profits with the least expenditure of work, raise or lower prices by their uncontrolled business dealings so rapidly according to their own caprice and greed that they nullify the wisest forecasts of producers. The laws passed to promote corporate business, while dividing and limiting the risk of business, have given occasion to the most sordid

license. For We observe that consciences are little affected by this reduced obligation of accountability; that furthermore, by hiding under the shelter of a joint name, the worst of injustices and frauds are perpetrated; and that, too, directors of business companies, forgetful of their trust, betray the rights of those whose savings they have undertaken to administer. Lastly, We must not omit to mention those crafty men who, wholly unconcerned about any honest usefulness of their work, do not scruple to stimulate the baser human desires and, when they are aroused, use them for their own profits.[117]

Such economic license emerged, the pope claimed, precisely because the "new form of economic life" arose along with "the principles of rationalism," which then created "a body of economic teaching far removed from the true moral law." As a result, he continued, "completely free rein was given to human passions." Thus, for Pius XI, the spiritual and moral crisis at the root of the modern social question was the direct fruit of the applications of Enlightenment rationalism to the economic arena. Then, when the "rulers of economic life" charted a destructive course, "the rank and file of workers everywhere" rushed "headlong into the same chasm, and all the more so, because very many managers treated their workers like mere tools, with no concern at all for their souls."[118]

The solution, the pope proclaimed, is to return to the teaching of the gospels, which the church preaches. "All created goods under God [needs to] be considered as mere instruments to be used only in so far as they conduce to the attainment of the supreme end." He continued, "The sordid love of wealth, which is the shame and great sin of our age, will be opposed...by the gentle yet effective law of Christian moderation."[119]

Conclusion of *Quadragesimo anno*

Finally, the pope insisted that justice, while essential, could not do without charity. Justice, he argued, can "remove the causes of social conflict," but only charity can "bring about the union of hearts and minds." Such was the perspective that needed to guide his "restoration of human society in Christ." He rejoiced that "workers themselves" were taking up this challenge. He appealed through the clergy to "lay apostles of both workers and employers" for all to take up "an intensive study of the social question," to form "Christian organizations" and "study groups guided by principles in harmony with the Faith," to promote "Workers' Retreats," and for all to be united "under the leadership and guidance of the Church…to contribute…to the Christian reconstruction of human society which Leo XIII inaugurated through his immortal encyclical, *On the Condition of Workers.*"[120]

The Rise of Totalitarianism

Italian Fascism. After his great encyclical on social justice, Pius XI published in 1931 *Non abbiamo bisogno,* a militant document condemning the persecution of Catholic Action by Italian fascists. In bitter language the pope decried the fascist tendency toward "a real pagan worship of the State" ("Statolatry"), and the fascist attempt "to monopolize completely the young." Nonetheless, despite these strong denouncements, he thanked the fascists for "putting out of existence Socialism and anti-religious organizations," and insisted that "in everything We have said up to the present, We have not said that We wished to condemn the [Fascist] party as such." He also spoke warmly of "Our dear sons who are members of the party."[121]

Pius XI kept up his steady stream of encyclical letters. Two more addressed the economic crisis, including a condemnation of the new arms race. One was on the Council of Ephesus. Two defended the church in Mexico and Spain. One was on the priesthood. Another was on motion pictures—again recognizing the new medium's tremendous power for cultural propaganda.[122] Then he issued two more anti-totalitarian encyclicals that are still well known, namely, his sequential condemnations of Nazism and Soviet Communism, promulgated only five days apart.

German Fascism. Pius XI's 1937 encyclical *Mit brennender Sorge,* on the church and the German *Reich,* was the final result of year after year of the pope's anger over the Nazis' persecution of the Catholic Church in Germany. To outmaneuver Nazi censorship, the document was clandestinely printed, secretly delivered to every church in Germany by a vast team of motorcyclists, and dramatically read aloud in all churches, and in cathedrals by the bishops themselves. Speaking of a "war of extermination," it accused the Nazis of systematically violating the government concordat with the Vatican, of turning to pantheism and paganism, and of reverting to a "so-called pre-Christian Germanic conception of substituting a dark and impersonal deity for a personal God." It further warned that, should persecution continue, "then the Church of God will defend her rights and her freedom in the name of the Almighty whose arm has not shortened." Yet it was only a condemnation of policies, not a systemic condemnation of German fascism.[123]

Russian Communism. By contrast, Pius XI's second 1937 letter, *Divini Redemptoris*, was unquestionably a systemic and absolute rejection of communism. In its analysis, Christ the Savior was seen as having come to set up "a new universal civilization, the Christian Civilization." But the "modern revolution," now expressed as "Bolshevistic and atheistic communism," threatened to push this civilization back "into a barbarism greater than that which oppressed the greater part of the world at the coming of the Redeemer."[124]

According to this encyclical and following the established papal social analysis, the modern revolution originally arose from "intellectuals" who arrogantly sought "to free civilization from the bonds of morality and religion" (the Enlightenment). "That school of philosophy which for centuries had sought to divorce science from the life of Faith and the Church" had produced "the atheistic movements existing among the masses of the Machine Age." The heart of this new stage of the modern movement was seen as "dialectical and historical materialism," which taught that "there is in the world only one reality, matter, the blind forces of which evolve into plant, animal, and man." In this teaching, the pope claimed, there was no room for God or for the individual. In addition, he lamented, private property was to be eradicated, and marriage and family were seen as purely civil institutions. As a result, for this philosophy human society had "only one mission: the production of material things by means of collective labor." Unfortunately, the pope warned, an opening for this teaching "had already been prepared...by the religious and moral destitution in which wage-earners had been left by liberal economics."[125]

According to Pius XI, society was seeing in communism "for the first time in human history…a struggle, cold-blooded in purpose and mapped out to the least detail, between man and 'all that is called God.' Communism is by its nature anti-religious." Again, by contrast, the prior encyclical challenging Nazism had implied that, although fascism had proved itself anti-Christian in practice, it need not be so by its nature. There was no such possibility, the pope claimed, for communism.[126]

Further, repeating again the established papal social analysis, the pope charged that the roots of communism were found in liberalism:

> There would be today neither Socialism nor Communism if the rulers of the nations had not scorned the teachings and maternal warnings of the Church. On the bases of liberalism and laicism they wished to build other social edifices which, powerful and imposing as they seemed at first, all too soon revealed the weakness of their foundations, and today are crumbling one after another before our eyes, as everything must crumble that is not grounded on the one corner stone which is Christ Jesus.[127]

As mentioned earlier, the pope saw the threatened breakdown of Christian civilization as not simply due to enemies of Catholicism, but also to certain Catholic employers who (following the laissez-faire form of the liberal ideology) resisted justice for workers.

> It is unfortunately true that the manner of acting in certain Catholic circles has done much to shake the faith of the working-classes in the religion of Jesus Christ. These groups have refused to understand that Christian charity demands the recognition of certain rights to the working-man, which the Church has explicitly acknowledged. What is to be thought of the action of those Catholic employers who in one place succeeded in preventing the reading of Our Encyclical *Quadragesimo anno* in their own local churches? Or of those Catholic industrialists who even to this day have shown themselves hostile to a

labor movement that we ourselves recommended? Is it not deplorable that the right of private property defended by the Church should so often have been used as a weapon to defraud the workingman of his just salary and his social rights?[128]

Nonetheless, Pius XI insisted that, despite its seductive power "communism is intrinsically wrong, and no one who would save Christian civilization may collaborate with it in any undertaking whatsoever."[129]

Before his death, Pius XI issued two more encyclicals, one again addressing the religious situation in Mexico, and the other on the Rosary as a means of fighting communism.[130]

The Leonine Legacy of Pius XI. Faithful to the path of his predecessors and in the face of the new challenge of the national stage of capitalism and its offspring of state communism, Pius XI held to the Leonine strategy. The entire socialist project, despite the moderation of one of its wings, remained for him the most immediate and dangerous enemy. As a result, he made no concessions even to democratic socialism. Further, Thomism was still the philosophical and theological basis of the papal program and the official intellectual guide for all the church. In addition, the acceptance of Christian Democracy also held, though it again shifted away from lay parties to episcopally controlled Catholic Action and to papal diplomacy with bourgeoisie political elites. In addition, the papal-bourgeois political alliance in Italy and Germany had moved center-right toward the dangerous ground of fascism. Finally, the commitment to Social Catholicism remained central and became even more important than it had been for Leo XIII, for this pope's sympathies were unquestionably with the working class.

Pius XI was the first pope to contend with the full-blown power of state totalitarianism, in both left-wing and right-wing forms. He conducted his battle against totalitarianism at the levels of spirituality and politics, though he treated the left-wing variant as a systemic evil and the right-wing variant as redeemable, even if afflicted with evil policies. His successor would contend with yet a more terrifying danger—the escalation of the ideological struggle to the level of a yet more "advanced" industrial war.

Strategic Conclusion:
The Encyclicals of Pius XII

Pius XII (1939–58), the successor to Pius XI and the last pope of the Leonine strategy, issued forty-one encyclicals in twenty years, an average of slightly more than two per year. Leo XIII had issued an average of more than three per year, Benedict XV an average of a little more than one per year, Pius X also an average of a little more than one per year, and Pius XI an average of a little more than one and a half per year. Thus, if frequency means anything, Pius XII ranked second among the Leonine popes after Leo XIII himself in the use of the encyclical medium. Pius XII was also the first pope to make major use of the new communications technology of radio. Indeed, while he issued no encyclical addressed exclusively to the social question (though many of his documents include ample references to it), he regularly used radio to apply Catholic social teaching to technically specific areas.[131]

Initial Documents

Continuing the Davidic-Christic mode of his predecessors, Pius XII placed his inaugural encyclical *Summi pontificatus* (1939) "under the seal of Christ the King." According to its analysis, the modern age was marked by technical progress but also by spiritual emptiness and moral disorientation, leading inevitably to "a drift toward chaos" and "the tempest of war."[132]

The immediate historical root of this crisis, Pius XII claimed, was "the forgetfulness of natural law" as the foundation of the social order within and among nations, as well as of the self and the family. But the deeper root, he further claimed, was "the abandonment of that Christian teaching of which the Chair of Peter is the depository and exponent." That teaching, and its guarantee in the papacy, he argued, had formerly given "spiritual cohesion" to Europe. But now, with Christ and the church excluded from public life, modern "progress" was withdrawing "man, the family, and the state" from "the beneficent and regenerating effects of the idea of God and the teaching of the Church." As a result, he continued, Christian civilization was in decline, and there were appearing "signs of a corrupt and corrupting paganism." Thus, he lamented, Europe was filled with "convulsions and wars," and "pessimism."[133]

Pius XII highlighted two errors as central to the new situation. The first was the denial of the solidarity of humanity as one family, with that denial embodied especially in nationalism and racism. The second was the deification of a state that claimed for itself "that absolute autonomy which belongs exclusively to the Supreme Maker." Where human solidarity was denied, he argued, there could be no social order—international, national, or domestic. Where the state was deified, he insisted, civil authority had no limit, authority came to rest only on autonomous utilitarian claims like materialism, the peace and prosperity of nations was undermined, and the family became its victim.[134]

From these errors of the modern age, Pius XII claimed, there flowed a general crisis of human civilization:

> Today, Venerable Brethren, all men are looking with ter-
> ror into the abyss to which they have been brought by the
> errors and principles which We have mentioned, and by
> their practical consequences. Gone are the proud illu-
> sions of limitless progress…What used to appear on the
> outside as order, was nothing but an invasion of disorder:
> confusion in the principles of moral life. These princi-
> ples, once divorced from the majesty of the Divine law,
> have tainted every field of human activity.[135]

In response to the denial of human solidarity, Pius XII countered that all humans were made in the image of God and came from one original couple. Further, he stressed the equal rights of people of all civilizations, and he linked this equality to importance in the global church of the development of native clergy and national bishops.[136]

In response to the deification of the state, Pius XII responded that the function of the state is to serve the common good as defined by natural law. He insisted that "man and the family are by nature anterior to the state." And he called for a "new international order," based on justice and prosperity and standing on the "solid rock of natural law and Divine Revelation." [137]

Pius XII described the future task as one of "regeneration." He called for "adapting (the church) to the altered conditions of the times and to the new needs of the human race," and doing so "in every region of the world."[138]

In addition, in this task he appealed especially to the laity to collaborate "in the Apostolate of the Hierarchy" in order to "bring back to Christ the masses that have been separated from him," and to do so under the standard of "Christ the King." For the first time in the modern encyclical tradition, it seems, a papal encyclical spoke of a special ministry of the laity, even while retaining the old language of "collaboration" with the mission of the hierarchy.[139]

> This collaboration of the laity with the priesthood in all classes, categories and groups reveals precious industry and to the laity is entrusted a mission than which noble and loyal hearts could desire none higher nor more consoling. This apostolic work, carried out according to the mind of the Church, consecrates as a kind of "Minister to Christ."[140]

For Pius XII, the family was central to this lay ministry. "When churches are closed, when the Image of the Crucified is taken from the schools," he wrote, then "the family remains the providential and, in a certain sense, impregnable refuge of Christian life."[141]

The goal of this lay ministry, according to Pius XII, was to restore the church's public role in society:

> What torrents of benefits would be showered on the world; what light, order, what peace would accrue to social life; what unique and precious energies would contribute towards the betterment of mankind, if men would everywhere concede to the Church, teacher of justice and love, that liberty of action to which, in virtue of the Divine Mandate, she has a sacred and indisputable right! What calamities could be averted, what happiness and tranquility assured, if the social and international forces working to establish peace would let themselves be permeated by

the deep lessons of the Gospel of Love in their struggle against individual and collective egoism![142]

Yet, the pope warned, should the "rulers of the peoples" not heed this call and fail to "turn their gaze with renewed hope to the Church, to rock of truth and of charity, to that Chair of Peter," and to Christ who "alone is the 'Corner Stone' (Ephesians ii. 20) on which man and society can find stability and salvation," then "the nations swept into the whirlpool of war are perhaps as yet only at the 'beginnings of sorrows' (Saint Matthew xxiv. 8)." He even foresaw "the horrors of a world conflagration," yet promised that, despite present and future suffering, "Christ the King is never so near as in the hour of trial."[143]

> The Catholic Church, the City of God…with the zeal of a mother, stands as a blessed vision of peace above the storm of error and passion awaiting the moment when the all-powerful Hand of Christ the King shall quiet the tempest and banish the spirits of discord which have provoked it.[144]

Next came *Sertum laetitiae*, a 1938 encyclical on the fiftieth anniversary of the hierarchy in the United States. In this document Pius XII expressed his special affection for "the Negro people." He also welcomed the many associations of the laity and warned against the dangers of materialism and egoism, particularly regarding the family. In addition, he supported the use of the "Marconi Radio" and commended the struggle for social justice, especially for a just wage and a family wage, and supported workers' unions.[145] The past shadow of a reputed heresy of "Americanism," cast across the United States since the time of Leo XIII, had now apparently been eclipsed.

Then, after *Saeculo exeunte octavo*, a 1940 encyclical celebrating the eight-hundredth anniversary of the independence of Portugal, which stressed Portugal's contribution to missionary activity, this pope issued perhaps his most famous document.[146]

The Mystical Body of Christ

In 1943, in the midst of World War II, Pius XII published *Mystici Corporis Christi*, his longest and landmark encyclical on the Catholic Church as the "Mystical Body of Christ."[147]

Since the time of the Council of Trent, and including the First Vatican Council, the dominant understanding of the church had been the legalistic and institutional model of a juridically perfect society, articulated especially by Jesuit Cardinal Robert Bellarmine.[148] Strategically, this legal-institutional model had served multiple purposes. First, in the face of Protestant theological attacks on the visible nature of the church, it had insisted on the principle of institutional visibility. Second, in the face of rationalist legal attacks on the public role of the church in society, it had defended the church's legal status as a "perfect society" and also had provided the legal justification for contractual negotiations (concordats) with civil governments. Third, in the face of both kinds of attacks it had strengthened the principle of hierarchical authority so central to the Counter-Reformation and ultramontanist movements. Now, however, Pius XII opened a strategic door to a different understanding of the church, one that was mystically organic and partially lay in character.

With ancient biblical and patristic roots retrieved particularly by the romantically oriented Tübingen school, this mystical model was promoted in the twentieth century especially by Belgian Jesuit Emile Mersch.[149] His theological turn to a mystical and organic unity supported the growing papal stress on the solidarity and communion of all the national churches in the late colonial or post-colonial world. It also provided a richer understanding of the importance of the laity in both the church's pastoral life and in its external mission, and provided a sacramental image for the spiritual unity of all humanity.

In this encyclical, after summarizing the crisis-oriented social analysis proposed in his inaugural encyclical, Pius XII held up as an ecclesial response the metaphor of the church as the "Mystical Body of Christ." But he carefully continued to affirm the institutional model's stress on the principle of hierarchy. He insisted that "those who exercise sacred power in this Body are its *first and chief* members," and that the members of the laity only *"collaborate* with the ecclesiastical hierarchy" (italics added). Further, he excluded from this mystical body not only unbelievers and those who have formally separated themselves from Catholic communion, but also those who have been separated by ecclesiastical authority. Emphasizing the role of the papacy, he wrote that, while Christ governs the church invisibly, he does so "in a visible and normal way through His Vicar on earth." Further, he insisted that the bishops of "individual Christian communities" were "subordinate to the…Roman Pontiff" and received their power of jurisdiction from him.[150]

Despite his many qualifications, and always careful to guard the privileged place of the hierarchy, Pius XII nonetheless granted a significant theological and spiritual place to the laity in this mystical communion of the church. Just as in the biological analogy the head needs the other members of the body, he declared, so "Christ has need of all His members." Christ is present in and assists all members, though "*in proportion* to their various duties and offices" (italics added). And again, "It is He, who while He is personally present and divinely active in all the members, nevertheless in the *inferior members* acts also through the ministry of the *higher members*" (italics added). Continuing his lay theme, Pius XII praised the role of Catholic Action and of lay associations, as well as the centrality of the Christian family.[151]

This mystically organic model also placed greater emphasis on the role of the Holy Spirit in the life of the church. While Christ was called the "Head of the Church," the Holy Spirit was given the title of "soul" of the church, meaning "that vital principle by which the whole comity of Christians is sustained by its Founder." Further, the pope referred to the "Spirit of God" as an internal principle that was "vastly superior" to the principle of unity of a physical or moral body.[152]

As the encyclical continued, the pope reaffirmed the institutional model and condemned those who, he claimed, erroneously contrasted an invisible church of the Spirit of Christ with the visible juridical church. Stressing its "perfect" character, he argued: "And if at times there appears in the Church something that indicates the weakness of our human nature, it should not be attributed to her juridical constitution, but rather to the regrettable inclination to evil found in each individual." Thus, he argued, perfection belonged to the church as an institution, but sin and imperfection were to be identified only with individuals and never with the church itself.[153]

The encyclical urged the community of the church to offer supplications on behalf of "kings and princes," as well as of "rulers."[154] (Note that in the mid-twentieth-century age of democracies and dictatorships, a papal encyclical was still using pre-modern aristocratic political titles.) Also, in addition to the institutional and mystical models, throughout the encyclical a strong underlying metaphor for the church remained that of a "mother" with her lay "children."[155]

Additional Documents

Also in 1943, approximately three months after *Mystici Corporis Christi*, Pius XII issued his major encyclical on biblical studies, *Divino afflante Spiritu*.[156] Recalling Leo XIII's 1893 letter on biblical studies, *Providentissimus Deus*, Pius XII dramatically approved modern critical biblical studies. (Leo's document had rejected "higher studies" of the Bible.) Noting the fruit of recent archeological excavations and of improved translations, Pius supported textual criticism and form criticism, encouraged modern vernacular translations, and in general promoted the study of the Bible by the whole church, including laity, especially by families.

Next came *Orientalis ecclesiae*, a 1944 letter on Saint Cyril, some fifteen centuries earlier the Patriarch of Alexandria.[157]

In 1945, the year of World War II's end, Pius XII issued a very brief encyclical on peace, *Communium interpretes dolorum*. In it, he blamed the war on rejection of God and called for a renewal of Christian morals for both private and public life, and for a renewal marked by both justice and peace.[158] Interestingly, this was Pius XII's first encyclical explicitly on the issue of the war, even though war had raged during most of his pontificate thus far.

Then came another and longer 1945 encyclical, *Orientales omnes ecclesias*, on the fiftieth anniversary of the reunion with Rome of the Ruthenian Church, a Catholic church within the Russian communist orbit.[159] In the following year he issued a brief encyclical, *Quemadmodum*, this time appealing on behalf of the "host of innocent children" left destitute by the "terrible war."[160] Also in 1946 he sent to all the bishops of the world another brief encyclical letter, *Deiparae virginis Mariae*, inquiring about their judgment on defining the assumption of Mary as a dogma of faith.[161]

In 1947 Pius XII issued an encyclical letter on Saint Benedict, *Fulgens radiatur*, in which he described the great founder of Western monasticism as the Catholic Church's solution to the collapse of the Roman Empire. Following Cicero, Pius described the Roman Empire as "more correctly the world's protector rather than its imperial master." He used the example of Benedict, whose work fourteen centuries before had led to the reconstruction of classical European civilization in Christian form, as proof that the church "can build and erect a new society of citizens, peoples, and nations," including the reconciliation of all classes.[162]

Liturgical Movement

In 1947 Pius XII also issued his second-longest encyclical, *Mediator Dei*, in which he canonized the emerging liturgical movement (so central to the later reforms of the Second Vatican Council).[163] Its renewed emphasis on the liturgy, in which the Eucharist was seen as "the fountainhead of all Christian devotion," stressed the fact that "all the faithful," including the laity, were called to participate. This included the singing of popular hymns and the new dialogue Mass (in which the congregation uttered the Latin responses formerly reserved to altar servers).[164]

According to Pius XII, the liturgical renewal was an important response to "the needs of our day...after a long and cruel war that has rent whole peoples asunder with its rivalry and slaughter." The pope saw the liturgy as aiding the postwar spiritual renewal of Catholic Christians, and in turn serving the wider search for world peace. By rendering worship to God, he argued, the people would be made one: "for we, being many, are one body: all that partake of one bread." Thus, he proposed, the liturgical movement would serve as an explicit spiritual antidote to the modern rejection of God and to the modern denial of human solidarity.[165]

But, as with the encyclical on the mystical body of Christ, which also placed great emphasis on lay participation, this liturgical turn to the laity was still surrounded by constant insistence on the superiority of the priestly caste. Reminding his readers that in the Old Law God had established "a sacerdotal tribe...and described the vestments with which the sacred ministers were to be clothed," he implied that the Davidic model of Judaism was normative for Christianity. In the proposed Davidic model of the Catholic liturgy, the laity were to participate, but only "according to their station." The liturgy was described primarily as a mysterious sacrifice conducted by a priesthood separate from the laity. "Table altars" were rejected, as was the vernacular language. This priesthood, the pope insisted, "does not emanate from the Christian community." Rather, the priest is "God's vice-regent in the midst of his flock." And again, "Holy orders sets the priest apart from the rest of the faithful," since the priest alone is "assigned to service in the sanctuary." Yet once more, "The priest performs the sacred liturgy in the name of the Church." Finally, Pius claimed, it was an error to teach that the New Testament applied the word "priesthood" to all the baptized, or to teach that the priests should "concelebrate" with the people. For, the pope insisted, "the people...in no sense represent the divine Redeemer and...can in no way possess the sacerdotal power." Also, as with the encyclical on the mystical body, this document continued the metaphor of the church as "mother" and laity as "her children."[166]

Further, Pius XII admitted that the liturgy had evolved historically. Yet he insisted that control over any changes in the liturgy belonged exclusively to "the Sovereign Pontiff." The responsibility for vigilance against unauthorized innovations belonged to bishops, and private individuals had no authority to make any changes.

Remaining Documents

After the encyclical on the liturgy, Pius XII issued *Optatissima pax* (1947), a brief document on peace between the classes and among nations. On the one hand, he faulted nations for their vast "military expenditures." On the other hand, he warned of "a secret and astute plan" to "embitter and exploit the working man in his distress." In response, he called for prayer and mutual cooperation, where especially the rich would place the common welfare above private advantage. The root cause of all these problems, he claimed, was that "the divine religion of Jesus Christ" no longer governed private, domestic, and public life. Restoring the church's authority, he argued, would replace error with truth and hate with love.[167]

During the next two years Pius XII issued three more brief encyclicals, all on the crisis in Palestine, in which he pleaded for peace in the Middle East and for protection of the Christian holy places there: *Auspicia quaedam* (1948); *In multiplicibus curis* (1948); and *Redemptoris nostri cruciatus* (1949).[168] Then, in 1950, a holy year, another short encyclical, *Anni sacri*, warned of the new "armaments race" and proposed that the root of the arms race was found in public and private atheism, which undermined all morals.[169] In the same year came yet another brief encyclical, *Summi maeroris*, asking for prayers for peace between the classes and among the nations.[170] Again, the pope warned of the terror of modern weapons of war:

> With the progress of time, technology has introduced and prepared such murderous and inhuman weapons as can destroy not only armies and fleets, not only cities, towns and villages, not only the treasurers of religion, of art and culture, but also innocent children with their mothers, those who are sick and the helpless aged.[171]

Once again, the solution was to be found with religion, though this time Pius XII spoke in the modern liberal language of recognizing "the freedom that is due religion." Yet the freedom of religion included not only its "primary purpose of leading souls to eternal salvation," but also the purpose of "safeguarding and protecting the very foundations of the State."[172]

Humani generis

Also in 1950 Pius XII issued *Humani generis*, an encyclical that to some degree recalled Pius IX's Syllabus of Errors and also Pius X's more recent campaign against modernism. In this document he warned against two opposite tendencies toward error, and under each tendency listed a series of false teachings.

The first tendency, he argued, was a monistic and pantheistic interpretation of evolution, which tried to explain the origin of everything by eliminating any notion of a personal God. (Note that he did not reject evolution itself.) This tendency, he argued, appeared most strongly in the communist doctrine of "dialectical materialism," but also in "a new erroneous philosophy" called "existentialism," which, he claimed, rivaled idealism, immanentism, and pragmatism. (These condemnations were all directed to the liberal side of the Cold War divide.) It also led, he claimed, to a completely human-centered "historicism."

The second and opposite tendency, according to the pope, was the attempt, in the name of a common Christian front against atheism (presumably communist), to advocate "eirenism," according to which dogmas would be relativized and adapted to modern immanentism, idealism, or existentialism. This second tendency then led, he claimed, to "despising scholastic theology" and to neglecting "the Teaching Authority of the Church itself." Other false teachings included "polygenism" (that all humans did not spring from one common source) and purely symbolic interpretations of the historical books of the Old Testament. The solution to both these tendencies was fidelity to "the method of Aquinas," which the pope then charged bishops and superiors-general of religious orders to protect.[173]

In 1950 Pius XII also issued yet another brief encyclical, *Mirabile illud,* decrying as "so terrible" the "mechanical equipment and instruments of modern warfare invented by the genius of man." He linked the cost of these armaments with economic suffering of the "poorer classes," and he warned that "new dangers of wars threaten mankind." As before, the papal solution was to follow the moral teachings of the Catholic Church in both public and private life. That would guarantee that "a peaceful stability, founded on right order and justice, would possess the minds and souls of men and would open up a safe path to the attainment of a daily growing measure of prosperity." Again appealing to the liberal doctrine of freedom, he prayed that "due liberty in all nations" would be granted to "the Catholic religion, which is the most secure foundation of human society and civilized culture."[174]

The Catholic Missions and Social Reform

In 1951 Pius XII issued *Evangelii praecones,* a long and major encyclical on evangelization and the Catholic missions.[175] In this document he lauded the spread of the church throughout the world as proclaiming a "brotherly and common fellowship which transcends racial conflicts and national boundaries." He also celebrated the dramatic increase in native clergy and native bishops. He warned, however, of the grave danger of the spread of "atheistic materialism," particularly in Latin America. He insisted that the church's goal, along with bringing "the supernatural light of faith to all peoples," was "to promote the interests of civilization and culture, and fraternal accord among nations." In particular, he praised the role of laity, and especially "the advance guard and forerunners of Catholic Action." And he recalled that the gospel was originally carried along the Roman roads, "not only by Bishops and priests but also by public officials, soldiers and private citizens." He also spoke of the great work of the laity in the Middle Ages, especially through the guilds.[176]

Then, in a section on social justice, Pius XII called for "social reform" and criticized both communism and capitalism, though the latter name was not explicitly used.[177]

> The Church has condemned the various forms of Marxist Socialism; and she condemns them again today…But she cannot ignore or overlook the fact that the worker, in his efforts to better his lot, is opposed by a machinery which is not only not in accordance with nature, but is at variance with God's plan and with the purpose He had in creating the goods of the earth.[178]

In response to these attacks against the worker, Pius XII proclaimed "the dignity of the human person," and "as a natural foundation of life the right to use the goods of the earth." Building on this right, he defended "the fundamental obligation to grant private ownership of property, if possible, to all." Referring to the "economic servitude and dependence" of the worker, he repeated his critique of both communism and capitalism: "Whether this servitude arises from the exploitation of private capital or from state absolutism, the result is the same."[179]

Interestingly, the term *paganism*, used here in reference to the native cultures of the mission areas, carried a more positive sense than had been the custom in earlier papal encyclicals, which had warned of a reversion to the pre-Christian "paganism" of ancient European cultures. In a new note, Pius called for respect for the old and developed cultures of the mission lands and made clear that "European civilization and culture" need not be transplanted to "foreign soil." He based this positive approach to "pagan" cultures on the ancient acceptance of classical European philosophy by Christian theologians.[180]

> Let not the Gospel on being introduced into any new land destroy or extinguish whatever its people possess that is naturally good, just or beautiful…This is the reason the Christian religion has neither scorned nor rejected pagan philosophies. Instead, after freeing them from error and all contamination, she has perfected and completed them by Christian revelation.[181]

Classical European "pagan" philosophy, like the good things in pre-Christian native cultures, was now seen as providing a "natural basis" for evangelization. But this same approach did not apply to the "pagan" philosophies that stemmed from the modern European Enlightenment, namely, liberalism and socialism.

Pius XII concluded this landmark encyclical by dualistically arguing that the world today was divided into "two opposing camps, for Christ or against Christ." Those who were against Christ were the "preachers" of "materialism."[182] Again, he drew on the constant metaphor of the church as "mother," reaching out to her "children."[183]

Concluding Documents

Before his death, Pius XII issued twenty more encyclicals, only three of which appear to be major ones by virtue of length. The seventeen shorter documents addressed the following themes:

- the Council of Chalcedon, and particularly its relation to Roman primacy;
- the Rosary, as a special prayer for social and world peace;

- the persecuted Eastern European church;

- Saint Bernard of Clairvaux, as a model for religious renewal in the face of societal crisis;

- a Marian Year, in honor of the one hundredth anniversary of the papal proclamation of the dogma of the Immaculate Conception;

- Saint Boniface, Anglo-Saxon missionary to the Germanic tribes, and agent of the restoration of Christian civilization;

- the church in communist China and the supranationality of the Catholic Church (also describing "the faithful" as divided into "two classes: the clergy and the laity");

- the queenship of Mary as protector of the persecuted, and Mary as Queen of Peace;

- sacred music (holding up the idea of single-sex boys' choirs, yet allowing mixed choirs but only "as long as the men are completely separated from the women and girls");

- prayer for peace and freedom for Hungary;

- prayer for peace for Poland, Hungary, and the Middle East;

- again, concern for Hungary and condemnation of the Soviet invasion (These last three encyclicals, all addressing the crisis in Hungary, were issued in the short span of nine days.);

- the Catholic missions, especially in Africa (noting that the church had grown well beyond Europe);

- the Polish martyr Saint Andrew Bobola;

- materialism, on the occasion of the one hundredth anniversary of the apparitions at Lourdes (noting that materialism was not confined to communism but also "rages in the love of money which creates ever greater havoc as modern enterprises expand");

- communism and the church in China; and

- again, prayer for the persecuted church (with a special warning about "weapons so powerful that they can ravage and sink into general destruction, not only the vanquished, but the victors with them, and all mankind," and with a critique of both communist political persecution and of capitalist moral seduction, especially through the new media).[184]

The three longer documents addressed the themes of virginity, the Sacred Heart, and the new communications media. Let us look briefly at each.

In 1954 Pius XII issued *Sacra virginitas*, his encyclical on "holy virginity." In this document the pope defended the traditional claim that holy virginity was spiritually superior to marriage. Referring in misogynist language to men "who were not *defiled* with women" (italics added), he argued that holy virginity had a higher purpose, namely, "to aim only at the Divine," whereas "the heart of married persons will remain more or less divided." Further, the pope claimed, "this doctrine of the excellence of virginity and of celibacy and of their superiority over the married state was…revealed by our Divine Redeemer." Based on this superiority, Pius XII argued that the clergy needed to be "separated from the world," and hence that young clergy during their years of training needed "for long years" to "remain in a Seminary or Scholasticate."[185]

Two years later, in 1956, Pius XII issued his third-longest encyclical, *Haurietis aquas*, on devotion to the Sacred Heart. In the nineteenth century the Sacred Heart had been a religious symbol of the Counter-Revolution. But now the pope linked it with the twentieth-century spiritual struggle through "love and reparation" against "the false tenets of *materialism* being propagated in practice and theory" (presumably referring respectively to capitalist practice and communist theory) and against the "unbridled freedom of lust everywhere extolled." The largest section of the encyclical was devoted to showing how this devotion was rooted in the whole history of Christianity, a claim argued by linking this modern devotion with God's love, and then referring to references to God's love throughout the entire tradition of Christianity.[186]

Pius XII's last major encyclical, *Miranda prorsus*, published in 1957, addressed the new communications media, namely, "motion pictures, radio, and television."[187] The pope took a positive approach by celebrating technological developments as gifts of God and by

proposing that these new means of communications would revolu-
tionize both how individuals and society as a whole think and act. He
saw visual images as particularly congruent with the sacramental
approach to God through visible signs. He noted that these new
communications media "bring men into contact with one another
and unite their efforts." He celebrated the power of radio and television to reach into the home, thus inducing "both young and old to
remain at home," and "strengthening the bonds of loyalty and love
within the family circle."[188]

But he also warned of the abuse of these media, since their persuasive power was so great. In the last century with the advent of
industrialization, "machines which were intended to serve man have
actually reduced him to serfdom, to his great loss." Now these new
media, if used wrongly, could "enslave not only the powers of nature
but also those of the soul." The temptation is present, he proposed,
to use these media only for political or economic purposes and to
give them a false freedom to pursue their goals with no reference to
natural law and its guidance of public morals. Further, because of
their power to penetrate the home, he argued, these media, when
badly used, threaten youth.[189]

To counter these threats, Pius XII directed the bishops to set up
special commissions on media, for leaders in public life to establish
committees of vigilance, for the media professions to be guided by
Christian teaching, and for church ministries to take full advantage
of these media. The pope himself established a special commission
in the Vatican to deal with the new media, and he encouraged
Catholic radio stations. He also made great use of Vatican Radio and
in this encyclical promised to expand its role.[190]

With these directives Pius XII was no doubt the first pope to
shift the former concern of papal encyclicals from the dangers of
printed books (an acute concern throughout the pre-Leonine period)
to the new dangers and opportunities of electronic media. Thus, just
as this pope shifted the strategic metaphor from restoration to regeneration, and just as he pointed out both the new dangers of the global
arms race and the new possibilities of a global civilization, so too in
the area of communications he signaled the newly emerging electronic era.

Conclusion of the Leonine Strategy

Pius XII presided over the climax and conclusion of the Leonine strategy and in part laid the ground for a post-Leonine period, just as Pius IX had done at the conclusion of the pre-Leonine period. He emphasized especially a growing role for the laity and a more adequate ecclesiology to support the laity's role, even though he continued to use the non-evangelical metaphor of church as "mother" and laity as her "children." In addition, he supported, albeit cautiously, the liturgical and biblical renewals. And finally, he foresaw the steady emergence of a world civilization and a world church, the centrality of the worldwide struggle for justice and peace, and the implications of a new electronic media.

Yet in all of this Pius XII remained faithful to the Leonine strategy. Socialism, and with it communism, remained his primary enemies, and against them he maintained the papal coalition with the moderate bourgeoisie, though now led by its American wing. He upheld a foundational criticism of liberal capitalism along with those of atheistic communism, although his criticisms of capitalism were never so strong as those against the left. Pius XII also continued to promote Thomism as the official philosophical foundation of the Catholic Church, and in *Humani generis* he tried to fight off new threats to Thomism from materialistic understandings of evolution. Similarly, he also supported Christian Democracy and especially tried to steer Christian Democratic parties away from a center-left coalition with socialists. Finally, although he did not write a major encyclical on the social question, his encyclicals were filled with references to Social Catholicism, which also in prophetic manner he now expanded to a global scale.

In addition, Pius XII gradually adapted his language about church and society toward the liberal model of persuasion and away from the classical model of coercion. Thus he began to speak not of the power of the church over society but rather of its freedom within society. And finally, building on the emphases of Benedict XV and Pius XI, he placed concern with modern militarism, as well as the prayerful search for peace and for a new international order, at the heart of papal strategy.

Paradoxically, in his personal demeanor Pius XII reportedly cultivated an aloof and highly aristocratic style, apparently more so than his immediate predecessors. He also continued ultramontanist Roman centralization and expansion of the role and status of the Bishop of Rome.[191] Despite these tendencies, this pope increased the international stature of the papacy, emphasized the newly emerging world church, and prepared the Catholic Church for a post-Leonine strategic period.

Despite the subtle changes begun under Pius XII, it would prove a great surprise to most, and even a shock, when his successor, John XXIII, shifted the modern Leonine strategy and set the Catholic Church on a very different postmodern course. That turn, however, will have to await the sequel to this book.

8

Conclusion

The Legacy of Modern Catholic Social Teaching and the Postmodern Challenge

---

The preceding chapters have offered a contextual and textual foreground analysis of the modern (or Leonine) phase of contemporary Catholic social teaching (1878–1958), set against a background analysis of its premodern (or pre-Leonine) phase (1740–1878), with the social teaching of both phases officially codified in the papal encyclicals. A future book will explore the postmodern phase of contemporary Catholic social teaching from its inception in 1958 up to 2000, though the postmodern phase continues to unfold.

While Leo XIII's original "grand design" contained only five central elements, the Leonine strategy grew to embrace supplementary elements during its eighty years of duration. We may thus list the following eight central elements as making up the developed Leonine program for church and society:

1. socialism (and communism) as the primary enemy;

2. the moderate bourgeoisie as the primary ally;

3. Thomist philosophy as the cultural program to reform modern liberal society;

4. Christian Democracy (or Catholic Action) as the reforming political program;

5. Social Catholicism (or Social Justice) as the reforming economic program;

6. ecclesial parallel structures (Catholic unions, parties, associations, schools, and so forth) as the carriers of defending church and reforming society;

7. theological defense against ecclesial contamination by liberal modernism; and

8. commitment to peace among nations and care for victims of modern industrial war.

Now at the conclusion of this study, it may be helpful first to summarize the legacy of this modern phase of Catholic social teaching, second to reflect briefly on its internal contradictions, and third to point to the new challenges that the tradition faces in the postmodern turn. But before doing all that, let us first review the model of church-society correlation guiding this whole project.

The Correlation of Catholicism and Capitalism

The emergence and development of contemporary Catholic social teaching has been charted here as the evolving guide for strategic ecclesial responses to the contextual societal evolution of industrial capitalism, seen as the economic fulfillment of the long-term mechanistic-emotive philosophical vision of the modern Western bourgeoisie.

Throughout this period, modern bourgeois civilization has been guided by its underlying ideology of liberalism, which emerged with the European Enlightenment from the cultural application of the early modern mechanistic (or atomistic) scientific paradigm to the structures and processes of society. Additional roots of modern bourgeois civilization may be found in the print revolution and the parallel Protestant Reformation, and still earlier in the *via moderna* of philosophy (empiricist nominalism) and the *devotio moderna* of spirituality (the emotional pietism of psychological interiority), with all arising from the new bourgeois power of medieval European cities gained by the expansion of trade during the Crusades.

Contextual Challenge:
Three Stages of Industrial Capitalism

While modern bourgeois culture came to expression in politics with liberal democracy, it expressed itself economically in the capitalist industrial revolution. (Industrial communism and industrial fascism are seen here as antidemocratic variants of modern bourgeois culture, with the former an extremist form of modern rationalism and the latter an extremist form of modern romanticism.) Industrial capitalism, in turn, has been seen here as going through three distinct historical-structural stages, described as follows.

Stage 1—Local Capitalism

- running roughly from 1740 to 1870;

- rooted in the originally British factory revolution;

- arising more deeply out of the European conquest of the Americas and the related Atlantic slave trade and plantation system;

- precipitating violent early democratic bourgeois revolutions;

- guided politically by the modern liberal philosophy's laissez-faire model of the state; and

- with socialism appearing only as a small and radical movement of protest.

Stage 2—National Capitalism

- running roughly from 1870 to 1960;

- rooted in the machine revolution;

- supported by the new wave of industrial colonialism across the Third World;

- growing especially from German scientific and technological advances, particularly in metallurgy, electrification, and the petrochemical industry;

- revising the classical laissez-faire liberal philosophy into a more social or corporate form (social-welfare liberalism);

- taking political expression in the nationally powerful social-welfare state (with both revisionist liberal and social-democratic variants), as well as in the totalitarian extremes of communism and fascism (seen here as two forms of state capitalism);

- with socialism splitting into the opposed poles of dictatorial communism and democratic socialism and eventually gaining state power in communist form in the Soviet Union and still later in social-democratic form in post–World War II Western Europe; and

- with the United States after World War II emerging as the great capitalist super-power.

Stage 3 — Global Capitalism

- beginning about 1960 and still unfolding;

- rooted in the electronic revolution, which has made possible a neoliberal capitalist "globalization" based on rapid international communications and transportation;

- precipitating a crisis of the social-welfare stage of the liberal state (as well as of dictatorial communism and democratic socialism), and eventually evolving into a new national-security stage of the liberal state;

- fostering ruthless global economic competition under the hegemony of gargantuan transnational corporations with few effective global social or ecological standards;

- linked to growing global division between rich and poor, with the rise of a vast marginalized urban underclass, as well as downward mobility for large sectors of the technical-professional middle class;

- linked also to deepening ecological crises across planetary society, particularly from fossil-fuel technologies guided by the modern mechanistic philosophy;

- precipitating a fundamental spiritual, societal, and ecological breakdown of modern bourgeois civilization across its full ideological range (center, left, and right); and

- opening on a fresh postmodern planetary civilization centered in ecology, reversing the global centralization of the multinational corporations, celebrating the vast diversity of human cultures, and shaped especially by rising energy of women and local peoples.

The third or electronic stage of the Industrial Revolution is, however, a matter for the sequel to this book.

Ecclesial Response:
Three Stages of Papal Strategy

As we saw, these three stages of industrial capitalism correlate with three distinct stages of Catholic social teaching, with each stage of Catholic social teaching representing a distinct papal strategy in relation to the church's surrounding and evolving societal context.

Anti-Modern — The Pre-Leonine Papal Strategy

- beginning with the election of Benedict XIV in 1740 and ending with the death of Pius IX in 1878;

- anti-modern in character and aimed at defending or restoring Europe's aristocratic Christian civilization against the cultural and political assault of the modern European Enlightenment;

- condemning both liberal democracy and industrial capitalism (as well as socialism and communism, with both still seen as minor radical strands within liberalism itself);

- hostile to the rising bourgeoisie and by and large ignoring the sufferings of the young industrial working class;

- still relatively uncritical of the conquest of the Americas and the Atlantic slave system (despite a few notable exceptions);

- maintaining an aristocratic patriarchal vision of church and society, and still hostile to women's emancipation;

- clinging to a structure of hierarchical clerical arrogance offering little positive interpretation of the role of the laity;

- rejecting modern critical methods for study and interpretation of the Bible, and not encouraging widespread reading of vernacular translations by the laity;

- claiming that the Protestant Reformation was at the root of the modern crisis;

- continuing the negative tradition of European Catholic anti-Semitism;

- ultimately collapsing with the loss of the Papal States; and

- yet at the end making use of modern technologies of transportation and communication to birth a modernized papal model marked by a spiritual cult of the person of the pope and centralized bureaucratic power for the Vatican (ultramontanism).

Modern — The Leonine Papal Strategy

- beginning with the election of Leo XIII in 1878 and ending with the death of Pius XII in 1958;

- accepting both liberal democracy and capitalist industrialism;

- reaching out to the expanding industrial working class by support for unions and for social-welfare intervention by a reformed liberal state;

- seeking a modern bourgeois adaptation of premodern European Christian civilization (based on social and moral reform and on restored power for the Catholic Church in European society);

- establishing an anti-socialist (and anti-communist) coalition with moderate liberals, first within Europe and then during the Cold War with the United States;

- being initially supportive of fascism, and later at least tolerant of it, by critiquing only fascist policies and not the fascism itself, in contrast to total condemnation of socialism and communism as systems;

- remaining relatively uncritical of European (including European-American) industrial colonialism;

- still clinging to a patriarchal vision of society and still hostile to women's emancipation;

- although adapting the church to the liberal world in external diplomatic-political policy, schizophrenically resisting liberal influence within the church's internal theological-pastoral policy and thereby attempting to preserve the classical European aristocratic-authoritarian paradigm for church polity and consciousness;

- turning partially to the laity as helpers of the clergy, but only under tight papal and episcopal control and within a still non-evangelical clericalist ideology;

- expanding ecclesial "parallel structures" (for example, Catholic schools, hospitals, political parties, unions) to compete with similar structures on the secular liberal terrain;

- planting seeds of a new ecumenical movement, but still in a triumphalistic and ineffective way;

- opening, albeit cautiously, to scientific study of the Bible and modestly recommending lay reading of the Bible in the vernacular;

- finally experiencing the deep crisis of Western bourgeois civilization as revealed in the attempted racist extermination of the Jews and others in the Nazi death-camps, in the World War II saturation bombing of civilians, and in the atomic bombing by the United States of Japanese cities, and in industrial warfare in general, and in the third-world liberation from colonialism; and

- ultimately planting seeds, albeit slowly and unevenly, for a post-Eurocentric world church and for the internal renewal of Catholic Christianity.

Postmodern — The Johannine Papal Strategy

- beginning with the election of John XXIII in 1958 and still unfolding, though unevenly and in polarized fashion;

- postmodern in character, abandoning completely the triumphal claim of a Eurocentric Christian civilization and instead pointing the church toward service of a new global and multicultural humanistic civilization;

- initially beginning a post-ideological spiritual dialogue with socialists and communists, and later playing a major role in the collapse of Soviet communism;

- undertaking a broad critique of all modern ideologies, including stage-three capitalist neoliberalism;

- placing the church's commitment to justice and peace at the heart of evangelization and supporting especially the poor in the post-colonial world;

- affirming the dignity and power of women in society, but still keeping women marginal from real leadership in church;

- beginning to develop a strong critique of the ecological devastation inflicted by the mechanistic assumptions of modern civilization;

- attempting to integrate clergy, religious, and laity in the common framework of the one people of God;

- strongly and effectively encouraging lay use of Bible in vernacular languages;

- developing a new pastoral model centered in small ecclesial communities (domestic church);

- rejecting officially the long-held tradition of anti-Semitism;

- more humbly and effectively seeking a new Christian ecumenism with Orthodox and Protestant Christians (despite occasional relapses into triumphalism); and

- beginning a deep, long-term, and still unfinished evangelical renewal of the internal life of Catholic Christianity in service of the newly emerging planetary civilization.

Again, detailed analysis of the third strategy belongs to the sequel to this book. Further, although these three Catholic strategic stages may seem clear as ideal types, the history of the papacy (and of the wider church) even for a given historical strategy has never been monolithic. Also, the term *postmodern* is used here in a strictly temporal way, meaning only after the modern, and not in the highly ideological way of deconstructive "postmodernism."

Within the Vatican bureaucracy, as well as in the world episcopacy, there has been and continues to be in effect two "parties" shaping Catholic strategy. As noted earlier, these have been called by some the "politicians" and the "zealots," or alternately "progressives" (or "liberals") and "reactionaries" (or "conservatives"). This latter set of names is not completely appropriate, however, since even the so-called liberals have generally not accepted the mechanistic philosophical assumptions of the modern liberal theory of progress, and the so-called conservatives have often been modern innovators, as, for example, in the case of modern papal centralization of control over the world church, which had no historical precedent prior to the dawn of modern communications and transportation.

The politician party has been traditionally centered in the office of the secretary of state, while the zealot party has been traditionally centered in what is now named the Congregation for the Doctrine (formerly the Holy Office of the Inquisition). The politician party has been historically more concerned with the church's political relevancy to the wider social world. The zealot party has been historically more concerned with the church's internal theological and pastoral life. Each tendency may have served as a corrective to the deficiencies and excesses of the other.

Even though each strategic period had its own distinct papal model, the implementation of that model regularly oscillated between these two poles of so-called progressives and conservatives, or sometimes was stalemated by conflict between the two. Certain popes may be seen clearly to have been representatives of one or the other tendency, but other popes sometimes shifted their orientation first toward one pole and later toward the other. For example, Pius IX clearly became a central figure in the zealot tradition, but he was initially perceived as a liberal. Similarly, Leo XIII clearly began as leaning to the liberal side, and indeed launched a new and long-surviving "strategic opening" to liberalism, but toward the end of his papacy he was drawn toward the conservative side.

The Legacy of Modern Leonine Social Teaching

Let us now summarize the legacy of the modern Leonine social teaching in terms of the three structural-functional regions of society: culture, politics, and economics. In addition, we may add summaries of how the Leonine social teaching viewed modernism in the church, industrial warfare, the family, and the Catholic laity, and also reflect briefly on two related internal contradictions within the Leonine strategy.

The Leonine Cultural Teaching

The popes of Leonine strategy, beginning with Leo himself, largely continued the social analysis from the pre-Leonine period, namely, that the root problem of the crisis of the church in the modern world was spiritual. More specifically the analysis argued that the root problem was the modern attack on "Christian civilization."

This earlier analysis had seen the modern spiritual attack on Christian civilization as unfolding in three sequential and expanding steps, ultimately leading to a fundamental crisis of modern civilization.

- *The Anti-Catholic Theology of the Protestant Reformation.* First, it was claimed, the modern attack on Christian civilization began in theological form with the Protestant Reformation's "rebellion" against the authority of the pope and hence against the Catholic tradition.

- *The Anti-Christian Philosophy of the Liberal Enlightenment.* Second, the modern attack on Christian civilization was seen as spreading in philosophical form to the educated classes with the secular humanism of the modern European Enlightenment (traditionally perceived by the papacy as carried by Freemasons). Thus, the assault expanded to an attack on Christianity itself.

- *The Anti-Divine Ideology of Marxian Socialism.* Third, the modern attack on Christian civilization was seen as eventually infecting the masses in ideological form with the rise of Marxian socialism, carrying a militant atheism (more so in the case of communism).

So, according to the papal analysis, the modern attack on Christian civilization began with the Protestant theological rebellion against the authority of the pope, then expanded into the secular-humanist philosophical rejection of Christianity, and finally reached its peak as a Marxian-socialist ideological rejection of God.

The Leonine popes held what may be called philosophically a hierarchical-organic cosmological interpretation of society. In this interpretation the great theological figure to whom the Leonine popes appealed was Thomas Aquinas, and behind him the philosopher Aristotle. By contrast, the modern liberal philosophy drew implicitly on the pre-Socratic philosopher Democritus to propose a mechanistic or atomistic cosmological interpretation of society.

In the hierarchical-organic interpretation, the whole is greater than the sum of the parts, and the whole is, in turn, kept whole through a spiritual unity ordered by authority. By contrast, in the mechanistic or atomistic interpretation, the parts are freely autonomous with the whole no more than the sum of the parts, with social unity established only by voluntarist contract, and with authority seen as suspect unless flowing from and supporting the freedom of the parts.

The root metaphors of organicism and hierarchy had sources respectively in primal tribal society (organic) and in classical aristocratic society (hierarchical), whereas the root metaphor of mechanism or atomism triumphed only with the rise of the modern Western bourgeoisie. The mechanistic metaphor was first established in modern culture by Newtonian science, then took philosophical expression with the modern European Enlightenment, achieved political expression with liberal democracy, and triumphed economically with industrial capitalism. Its highest value was freedom, including religious freedom, intellectual freedom, political freedom (liberal democracy), and economic freedom (industrial capitalism), but all represent only procedural freedoms devoid of any substantive guidance.[1]

In their social diagnosis the Leonine popes did not differ greatly from their pre-Leonine predecessors, though Leo diplomatically muted this background analysis for the sake of his distinct strategic purposes. What distinguished Leo and his Leonine successors from their premodern predecessors was their strategic response to the perceived attack on Christian civilization. Let us now turn to that response, beginning with the political dimension.

The Leonine Political Teaching

As an ecclesiastic originally trained for elite diplomacy, Leo XIII had realized for two reasons that it was futile to continue the premodern papal strategy of rejecting modern liberal democracy. First, as a political realist, he knew that liberal freedom had won the battle against aristocratic authority, that the liberal political order was now consolidated, and that the classical aristocracy would never return to power. Second, as a theological student of Thomism, he believed that consolidated political power, even if liberal, must hold some legitimacy from God.

So, more than one hundred years after the first modern democratic revolutions in America and France, Leo became the first Catholic pope ever to accept the legitimacy of democratic political authority. He reached out to modern liberal democratic political leaders, whom in nostalgic aristocratic fashion he continued to call "rulers." But Leo accepted democracy only as one legitimate form of government among many, and he probably remained in his heart a monarchist.

Leo also had a third reason for reaching out to modern liberal democratic leaders, and it was perhaps his strongest motive. This reason was his fear of socialism. Presumably following the traditional papal social analysis that the modern rebellion had begun in theology, then spread to philosophy, and now was reaching the masses though socialism, he saw a coalition with moderate continental European liberals (that is, liberals who were not anticlerical and who were open to social reform) as key to resisting the socialist advance. Anti-socialism became for Leo, and remained so for all the Leonine popes, the strategic centerpiece.

Through his political coalition with moderate liberal "rulers," Leo hoped to reform the new liberal European civilization in two ways. First, Leo argued that a partial restoration of hierarchical organicism would prevent modern bourgeois society from disintegrating in the revolutionary chaos that he saw fomented by the socialists (and ultimately collapsing into communism). Thus he warned the new bourgeois "rulers" that the very spirit of rebellion by which they had come to power would soon turn against them, unless the principle of hierarchical authority was reestablished to provide organic unity to society.

Second, Leo argued that religious authority was essential in order to provide spiritual unity for society and spiritual legitimation for the new "rulers." For him, of course, spiritual unity was to be found in Catholicism as the official religion of the society and in the authority of the pope over both religion and society. Were the pope's authority to be accepted by the new European elites, then, he proposed, Christian civilization could be restored in modern democratic form and socialism could be defeated. Implicit in his vision was the assumption that, although the aristocracy could not be formally restored, the hierarchical-organic root metaphor when reapplied to society would gradually undermine what Leo still saw as the multiple theological and philosophical errors of the Reformation, the Enlightenment, and the French Revolution.

For Leo XIII the political front was the most important one. Indeed, he published five major social encyclicals on the church and liberal politics. By contrast, he issued only one on economic life. Though certainly his favorite achievement was the mandated restoration of Thomism within the internal intellectual life of the church, most of his effort was devoted to political rapprochement with the "new princes." So it was also with most of his successors.

Despite Leo's lingering nostalgia for the classical world, his political teaching has had an abiding value. Drawing on Thomas Aquinas's appropriation of Aristotle, Leo rejected classical liberalism's negative political principle of laissez-faire. Instead, he insisted that government had a positive role of pursuing the common good of all, particularly the poor and weak. He also rejected the socialist claim that the means of production should be entrusted to the state, that the distinct classes of employers and employees were inevitably opposed to each other, and that the state should represent exclusively the working class. Rather, he argued, private property was a value to be defended and expanded especially to workers, and that it is the function of the state to join all classes in service of the common good. Against the laissez-faire position, Leo supported reforming social legislation.

Yet Leo still placed his political vision within the framework of Christian civilization, and the succeeding Leonine popes never abandoned this foundational Leonine vision of the restoration of Christian civilization in the political arena. Their appeal to "Christ the King" served as a symbolic call to that restoration. Nonetheless, Leo's successors had to contend with new challenges that he never fully foresaw. Let us look briefly at how this played out in each of his successors within the Leonine strategy.

Pius X. This pope of the "zealot" party was elected to address in a more forceful way the cultural threat of the liberal world to the internal life of the church. Liberalism was seen by the zealot party (now called integralists) as "contaminating" Catholic theological theory and pastoral practice. So Pius X launched a massive and much debated institutional campaign against the penetration of "modernism" into the inner life of the Catholic Church. But he also provided important contributions to the renewal of Catholic lay spiritual life through his encouragement of frequent communion and of popular religious education.

Benedict XV. With most of his prior life spent as a librarian, Benedict XV had to face the terrifying reality of modern industrial warfare, which used enormously powerful weapons of mass destruction and distinguished little between soldiers and civilians. He became the first modern pope to identify the papacy with the theme of peace. He so generously aided victims of World War I that he nearly bankrupted the Vatican. In addition, upon becoming pope he immediately terminated Pius X's right-wing campaign against "modernism."

Pius XI. A figure guided by the German organic-hierarchical vision of social reform, Pius XI confronted the worldwide crisis of capitalism during the Great Depression, as well as the gigantic economic and political structures emerging overall with the maturing of the national stage of modern industrial capitalism. On the economic terrain, he challenged the great concentrations of capital that he called "economic dictatorships," while on the political terrain he confronted the "political dictatorships" of both German fascism and Russian communism. True to the Leonine tradition, he condemned the very system of communism because it was atheistic, but he remained willing to negotiate with fascism because it seemed to offer the promise of restoring Christian civilization, or at least of blocking the communist threat to destroy religion entirely.

Pius XII. The last of the Leonine popes, Pius XII presided over the end of the Leonine strategy. In his papacy the challenges faced by all the prior Leonine popes came to a head. He had to deal with World War II—an even more terrifying modern industrial war than the one experienced by Benedict XV, and one that threatened extermination of the Jews and countless others and inflicted atomic bombings on the people of Japan. He also faced the increasing political terror of both Nazi and Soviet totalitarianism, though again he rejected the Soviet system in principle and until close to the end of World War II tried to negotiate with fascists for the sake of Christian civilization. Further, during his papacy the long heritage of Eurocentrism began to break down, as the United States became the world capitalist center and the most powerful military force on the planet. When the Cold War flared up, the papal rhetoric of Christian civilization took on renewed strength in the cultural battle against Soviet communism. But behind the rhetoric there must have lurked confusion, for the center of the modern world had shifted to a largely Protestant and quintessentially liberal nation.

While the Leonine political teaching accepted democracy, the militantly anti-socialist stance of the Leonine popes led them at various points into alliances with fascist governments, which they either initially believed would restore the Catholic Church to a strong public role or which they saw as important bulwarks against atheistic communism. Indeed, it was through a treaty with a fascist government that the present Vatican City State was created. In addition, the Leonine popes rejected even the possibility of a Catholic alliance with moderate democratic socialists in European parliaments, even though lay Catholic legislators and lay Catholic movements sometimes saw such an alliance as a means of avoiding both communism and fascism.

Though the Leonine popes gave priority to the political arena (except Pius X, who stressed internal theological and pastoral life), the political component of the Leonine strategy would prove insufficient on its own to retain the loyalty of the working classes. Hence the need for a bold initiative on the economic terrain.

The Leonine Economic Teaching

The Leonine economic teaching emerged both from the lobbying of grass-roots Catholic activists and intellectuals and from the papal fear of socialist inroads with the growing Catholic sector of the modern industrial working class. It was this economic teaching that would leave the most powerful and lasting legacy from the Leonine strategy. Amid the plethora of documents from the period, two economic encyclicals stand out, Leo XIII's *Rerum novarum* and Pius XI's *Quadragesimo anno*.

Rerum novarum

Leo XIII's 1891 encyclical *Rerum novarum* (meaning literally "of new things" but often given the title *On the Condition of the Working Class*) stunned both the capitalist and Catholic worlds. Though written more than one hundred and thirty years after the modern Industrial Revolution, it was the first contemporary papal encyclical ever explicitly to address economic life. The dramatic power of this document still stands; indeed, it is called the Magna Charta of contemporary Catholic social teaching. It may be helpful to offer here a brief summary of the main economic teachings of this historic document.

Leo proposed that industrial conflict raged because of the loss of the ancient guilds, which then left modern workers with no means of self-defense. He portrayed socialism as a false remedy to this problem, because it undermined private property and favored an expansive state that took priority over the individual and the family. The result, he proposed, would be general impoverishment and trampling of the rights of the individual and the family.

The true remedy, Leo continued, was the one offered by the church, namely, an organic-hierarchical vision that accepted differences but placed all classes in service of the common good, including the demands of both justice and charity. Within the demands of justice, Leo emphasized the just wage. In turn, Leo saw the church as a key agent of charity, the state as both limited (versus the socialists) and interventionist (versus laissez-faire). The state, he insisted, was obliged to assist the poor and to protect the interests of workers (like all humans, made in the image of God). In addition, Leo shockingly supported the role of unions, ideally Christian unions, as part of the natural form of human community.

Quadragesimo anno

Forty years after *Rerum novarum*, Pius XI issued an updating of Leo's foundational document. *Quadragesimo anno* (1931) continued the rejection of socialism and explicitly addressed liberalism to condemn its classical laissez-faire form. Leo had diplomatically avoided a formal attack on liberalism and had preferred to place the blame for the modern crisis on Freemasons. But Pius XI had no such diplomatic reserve.

Reviewing the benefits of *Rerum novarum*, Pius XI praised all that had been accomplished, particularly the growing orientation of the state to the common good; defense of the poor and the weak; and legislation supporting workers, the family, women, and children. He then defended private property but insisted on its social character, and urged the expansion of ownership to workers by means of a rapid and just distribution of property. In this context he added a new phrase that would become increasingly central to the Catholic tradition, namely, "social justice." He also expanded the definition of just wage to a family wage and called for workers' participation in both management and ownership of business enterprises.

Then, addressing the "social order," Pius XI added another new term to Catholic social teaching: "subsidiarity." Seeing society increasingly structured under an all-powerful state triumphing over individuals devoid of protective associations, he insisted that social activities should be performed by associations at the lowest possible level, with higher levels only providing assistance. Key in his view was to be the role of professional associations, to be given real authority to replace the competition of the free market with social harmony, and to be governed by Catholic principles. In addition, he insisted, such social reforms would have to be accompanied by a reform of morals.

Overall, Pius XI called for a reform of capitalism in light of the great economic changes since the time of Leo XIII. Describing the new great concentrations of wealth as an "economic dictatorship" controlling money and credit and as breeding ever more ruthless competition, he argued that the new economic centralization was causing not only new economic battles but also new political ones, including struggles over the control of the state and even between states. Decrying "economic imperialism" and an "international imperialism" of finance, he proposed bringing the competitive freedom of the market under public authority, where it could be guided by the "norm of social justice."

He also decried a parallel concentration of power on the socialist side, where a new "political dictatorship" brought fierce attacks on whole populations, on private property, and on the church. He acknowledged that democratic socialism was quite different in this regard from dictatorial communism and, in fact, was in many respects quite close to Catholic social teaching. But he still rejected the proposal that Catholics cooperate with socialists.

Last, Pius XI returned to the Leonine strategy's claim of the foundational cause of the modern crisis, namely, its spiritual root. He saw this spiritual root as the sin of greed, flowing ultimately from original sin, but now unleashed in revolutionary fashion by the modern liberal ideology of the unregulated free market. As a result, he claimed, the passions were unbridled, and all kinds of social evils were magnified. The solution, he proposed, was a return to the gospel, which included Catholic teachings on moderation, justice, and charity.

Additional Themes in the Leonine Tradition

Several other themes woven through the full Leonine corpus bear mention in this summary. These are modernism, war and peace, the family, and the laity.

Modernism

As noted, Leo XIII had originally hoped both to embrace the modern world and to convert it into a modern model of Christian civilization. This required accepting the institutions of modernity, especially democratic politics and industrial economics, but also gradually shifting their cosmological foundations and ethical guidance from the mechanistic liberal philosophy of the modern European Enlightenment to the classical organic-hierarchical philosophy of

Thomism. It would also require keeping the internal life of the Catholic community, especially its theological-philosophical theory and its pastoral-spiritual practice, free of ideological contamination by modern liberalism, and a fortiori by modern socialism. Achieving this goal would require periodic resort to internal ecclesiastical repression. As noted, Pius X, with his inquisition-like campaign against "modernism," was the major figure in that repression.

War and Peace

Beginning with Benedict XV, the Leonine popes became known as popes of peace as well as of justice, such that in the wake of Vatican Council II the phrase "justice and peace" became canonized as defining the Catholic social tradition. In their social analysis, he and the subsequent Leonine popes came to see the modern political warfare of states, with all its industrial terror, as flowing from the same philosophical errors of the modern economic warfare between the classes. These popes repeatedly denounced modern warfare as due to a loss of social order and presented themselves both as caring for the victims of war and as peace-loving mediators of disputes between states. Their solution to the crisis of war was again the restoration of the principles of Christian civilization and implicitly of papal authority. Despite this nostalgic perspective, the papal concern for peace and for the victims of war stands out as a shining beacon in the Leonine legacy.

The Family

Though a focus on the family was not central to the encyclicals of Leo XIII, it gradually became clear that the atomistic or mechanistic cosmology of modern liberal culture meant a mounting attack on the integrity and viability of family life, particularly from secular education and media. In response, Pius X greatly strengthened popular religion through his emphasis on frequent communion and grass-roots religious education. The first major document on family, however, did not come until 1930 with Pius XI's encyclical *Casti conubii*. Pius explicitly set the Catholic sacramental and organic understanding of family over against the Enlightenment's mechanistic philosophy, both in its liberal atomistic variant and in its socialist statist variant. In addition, he provided the first modern papal support for a spirituality of marriage, although its perspective was still strongly patriarchal. In addition, in his 1929 letter on education, *Representanti in terra*, Pius XI defended the right of the family to educate its children as prior to the right of the state and as needing the support of the church.

The Laity

Last, it may be helpful to reflect in a bit more detail on the evolving understanding of the laity within the Leonine strategy.

From the pre-Leonine period, the Leonine popes received the negative Platonic legacy of a highly clericalized and dualistic understanding of the church. In this legacy the laity was identified with "the world" and was often seen as an object of suspicion. Throughout the nineteenth century the popes regularly used the adjective *lay* to describe the enemies of the church.

Further, the Leonine papal encyclicals consistently described the church as something apart from the Catholic people. Drawing unconsciously on the still strong Roman cultural tradition of the Mediterranean Magna Mater (the pre-Christian "Great Mother" goddess), the church was identified as the "mother," with the pope as the "father," the bishops as the pope's "brothers," the priests as the "sons," and the laity as the "children." In this non-biblical and non-evangelical ecclesiology, all Christians were external to "mother church."

Nonetheless, as the popes and bishops lost power in society, they were forced to turn to the laity as allies in order to maintain at least indirect ecclesial influence within society. As early as the mid-nineteenth century the bureaucratic strain of ultramontanism had grasped the potential for mobilizing the laity under tight clerical controls. With his acceptance of "Christian Democracy," Leo XIII canonized this turn to the laity, though he continued to use the old ecclesiological language of the church as "mother," and he remained guarded in how he used lay allies.

In the name of Catholic Action, Pius X strongly tightened episcopal control over lay allies, while he described Catholic Action as "laity assisting the hierarchy" in their mission. Pius X also relaxed the papal ban in Italy against Catholics participating in democratic elections, in order to mobilize Catholic lay resistance against socialism, and he strengthened lay spirituality by urging frequent communion and popular religious education.

Next, Pius XI held up as an ideal the lay-oriented spiritual teaching of Francis de Sales, perhaps the first major Catholic theologian in early modern times to abandon the old spiritualistic theologians' non-evangelical tradition of Platonic dualism, which had placed the laity on a "lower level" and portrayed the laity as not called to true holiness (which allegedly pertained only to the religious and clerical states in life). Also, as noted, Pius XI was the first modern pope formally to promote the spirituality of marriage.

The most dramatic lay breakthrough, however, came with Pius XII's 1943 encyclical on the church as the mystical body of Christ (*Mystici Corporis Christi*). Here for the first time in the contemporary encyclical tradition there was an attempt to return to a biblical and evangelical ecclesiology. Now the Leonine strategy's organic-hierarchical metaphor was applied to the church itself. The church was portrayed as the body of Christ, with the laity as an essential part of it. Even so, there were important caveats. The clergy, the document insisted, were the "first and chief" members, or alternately the "higher" members, with the laity declared to be "inferior" members, and with the laity allowed only to "collaborate with the hierarchy." In addition, despite its embrace of the mystical-body model, the encyclical continued to proclaim the traditional image of the church as "mother" with her lay "children" as external to her.

Building on this new opening to the laity, albeit still with great caution, Pius XII's 1947 encyclical on liturgical reform, *Mediator Dei*, called on the laity to "participate" actively in the Eucharist. But it also declared that the clergy constituted a "sacerdotal tribe" set apart from the laity. In addition, it rejected the use of vernacular languages in the liturgy, and the laity was again described as the "children" of "mother church." In yet another encyclical, *Sacra virginitas*, issued in 1954, Pius XII insisted that virginity was spiritually superior to marriage, and he praised men who were not "defiled by women."

Despite these limitations, the Leonine strategy was a great achievement. For its time, at least, it brought renewal to the church and reform to society, and it enabled the Catholic tradition to break partially free of its past imprisonment within the anti-modern heritage of classical aristocratic European culture. By the time of the death of Pius XII, however, the Leonine path was being undermined by new and difficult challenges that would require the creation of yet a new papal strategy for the emerging postmodern global context.

Contradictions Within the Leonine Strategy

Before moving to the postmodern challenge, it may be helpful to conclude this summary of the Leonine strategy by reflecting on two deep contradictions within it. These reflections are offered not to demean the Leonine legacy, for we stand profoundly in its debt, but rather to show that every strategy is indeed limited and inevitably carries seeds of contradiction, as do all historical projects short of the eschaton.

An Authoritarian Church in a Democratic Society

The first contradiction, mentioned earlier in this study, may be found in the attempt to convert the outer liberal society into a new form of Christian civilization, but not to allow the outer liberal society to influence the internal life of the church, which still carried the polity of the aristocratic world.

Where the bourgeois world had opened to historical consciousness, Catholic authorities still clung to a non-historical method in philosophy and theology. The theology of Thomas Aquinas, on which the Leonine strategy was grounded (and the philosophy of Aristotle on which Aquinas had drawn), preceded the modern discovery of developmental or evolutionary processes in geology, biology, and cosmology. The first great theologian to explore the implications of historical development for Catholic theology was the English convert from Anglicanism, John Henry Newman. But while Leo XIII made Newman a cardinal (to redeem him from the suspicion under which he had been cast during the papacy of Pius IX), Newman's developmental approach to theology was not reflected in Leonine theology. Only very late in the strategy would a modern pope even admit to some element of historical evolution in the internal life of the church (Pius XII in his encyclical on the liturgy).

Further, where the bourgeois world had grounded itself on democracy, albeit a highly imperfect one, Catholic authorities vigorously repressed any tendencies to develop democratic practices within the internal life of the church. Just the opposite. Following the French Revolution, with the progressive defeat of the Western European aristocracy, the papacy in a modern innovation centralized clerical authority over the whole church within the Vatican bureaucracy. Having lost its aristocratic status within the premodern social world, the papacy intensified and centralized its authoritarian control over the whole church.

Yet there were ancient traditions of democratic participation in Mediterranean Catholicism on which papacy could have drawn. For example, Augustine and his mentor Ambrose, like most bishops from apostolic times up to that point, were elected to the episcopacy with broad popular voting by the lay people of their dioceses. The fear of internal democracy for church polity was heightened, however, by the still strong external attack on the continental European church — residually from secularizing liberals, and even more threateningly from atheistic strands within socialism. When an institution is under siege, neither democracy nor decentralization is attractive.

Last, even while abandoning the external aristocratic social world, Catholic leaders clung to a spiritually aristocratic understanding of the clerical state. In non-evangelical style, bishops continued to wear classical regal dress and to use the pretentious titles of the aristocratic nobility (your excellency, your eminence, your holiness, and so on). Also, the title *monsignor* (my lord) was spread throughout elite sectors of the presbyterate.

The Appeal to and Fear of the Laity

This internal cultivation for clerical elites of an aristocratic style and polity worked against the goal of lay mobilization, which was the second internal contradiction of the Leonine strategy. On the one hand, Catholic clerical elites reached out to the laity for "assistance" in defending the church's interests in society and also for reforming society. On the other hand, Catholic clerical elites considered themselves institutionally separate from and spiritually above the laity to whom they appealed. In turn, they denied the laity any significant participation in the processes of institutional policy.

It is widely recognized in contemporary nonprofit institutions that appeals for support without participation in decision-making, at least in an advisory manner, are not very effective. Was the failure by Catholic institutional elites to break with a classical clericalist model of spiritualistic superiority and authoritarian control, and the consequent failure to bond in participative solidarity with creative Catholic lay leaders, an important factor in the failure of the Leonine strategy to re-Christianize European society? Or would the demonic forces of evil rising on the European horizon, especially the murderous terrors of Nazi fascism and Soviet communism, have spewed their venom anyway? We can only guess what the answer might be.

In any case, presumably both for some reasons internal to church practice and for other reasons external to it and beyond its control, the brilliant, long-lived, and highly creative Leonine strategy finally came to an end. In external terms, the main reason for the breakdown was the emergence of a distinctly postmodern and post-Eurocentric period in human history, namely, the new global civilization precipitated by the electronic revolution. Let us end this conclusion with a brief reflection on the new challenges presented by the postmodern turn.

Postmodern Global Challenges

The sequel to this book will address at great length the new postmodern context and the attempt by Catholic social teaching to find a creative strategy within it. What is offered here can only point to the postmodern turn and its challenges.

The Postmodern Context of a New Planetary Civilization

The new historical context to which Catholic strategy has begun to respond is the deep cultural shift from a modern, print-based culture, centered in the North Atlantic nations, to a postmodern, electronic-based culture, now giving birth to a truly planetary civilization. As I have proposed elsewhere, the new planetary civilization is called to be ecologically sustainable, economically just, politically democratic, and culturally spiritual.[2]

A Model of Four Stages of Human Culture

As I have also proposed earlier and elsewhere, since its reflective emergence into the Neolithic era, humanity has experienced the maturation of three major cultural eras and is now entering a fourth era.[3]

These four long eras or waves of human evolution might better be seen as concentric circles. For just as a living tree does not lose its inner rings when it grows new ones, so new human cultural eras do not fully eliminate prior ones. Rather, they contribute to a richer whole that includes the legacy of the still living past. These four eras may be described as:

- *The Primal Era:* the original egalitarian, tribal, and matrifocal experience, grounded in speech and cultivating a sacramental spirituality of immanence;

- *The Classical Era:* the aristocratic, imperial, and patriarchal experience, grounded in writing and cultivating a priestly spirituality of transcendence;

- *The Modern Era:* the bourgeois, nationalist, and hyper-masculine experience, grounded in printing and cultivating a psychological spirituality of interiority; and

- *The Postmodern Era:* the as-yet-undefined and still crystallizing planetary experience, grounded in electronics, and potentially cultivating an artistic spirituality of co-creativity between humanity and the rest of the natural world, between women and men, and among all cultures, with the deepest source of co-creativity seen as the Divine Mystery.

Within these four eras, the long primal era may be described as the communal women's revolution. It laid the abiding and indispensable organic foundations for human culture, using biodegradable materials. Similarly, the shorter classical and modern eras, based on early advances in metallurgy, represented two sequential waves in the mechanistic-hierarchical men's revolution, using non-biodegradable stone, metal, and later synthetic materials. The men's revolution awakened humanity to its awesome but potentially destructive mechanistic technological power.

In light of this new cultural shift, it is necessary to define what is meant by the term *postmodern*. In academic circles the term *postmodernism* is used to refer to a novel school of philosophical, artistic, and social-scientific thought, alternately called deconstructionism or sometimes post-structuralism. While I do not wish to exclude this school of thought from the range of postmodern phenomena, my use of the term is broader. Here it simply means, in a literal sense, "after the modern."

Chart 3.
Concentric Circles in the Evolution of Human Culture

ERA	Communication	Society	Gender	Spirituality
PRIMAL 40,000 B.C.E.	Speech	Tribe	Women's Revolution	Immanence
CLASSICAL 5000 B.C.E.	Handwriting	Empire	Men's Revolution-1 (aristocratic)	Transcendence
MODERN 1500 C.E.	Printing	Nation-State	Men's Revolution-2 (bourgeois)	Interiority
POSTMODERN 2000 C.E.	Electronics	Planet	Partnership of Women and Men	Co-Creativity

Contending Strategies for the Postmodern Era

Within the range of postmodern phenomena, I propose that four major cultural strategies are contending to define the postmodern experience. Each of these streams has strengths and weaknesses, and all may contribute to the ultimate definition of *postmodern*, but only one of these streams, I further propose, is "foundational" (though not in the doctrinaire philosophical sense of premodern "foundationalism").

- *Economic Neoliberalism.* First, there is the *ideological* strategy, pursued by some business elites of the new global stage of capitalism, to create a comprehensive globalized market culture. This attempt seeks to reduce all human processes and structures to the modern capitalist financial calculus (what Karl Marx called the "commodity fetish"). While creating invaluable global networks of communication and transportation, this strategy also reveals the objective side of the crisis of modernity by precipitating the marginalization of the poor, the devastation of the ecosystem, and spiritual loss of meaning and hope among many young people.[4]

- *Academic Deconstructionism.* Second, there is the *academic* strategy of many university elites to celebrate diversity and difference, of itself an important contribution. It began originally as a literary movement in Peru in the 1930s, spread to circles of poets in the United States, and now has expanded across the world into philosophy, the arts, and the human sciences. As noted earlier, it is now best known from its French proponents as "deconstructionism" or "post-structuralism." Despite its liberating celebration of diversity and difference, this strategy unfortunately rejects the possibility of broad human meaning articulated in "meta-narratives." As such, it reveals the subjective side of the crisis of modernity and is threatened philosophically with collapse into relativism and even nihilism.[5]

- *Religious Fundamentalism.* Third, there is the *spiritual* strategy of some clerical elites across world religions to restore traditional values as a critique of the modern process of secularization. At the extreme, this attempt has been called fundamentalism, while in more moderate versions it may be called restorationism. Though rightfully pointing to the primacy of spiritual values and rightfully critiquing the culturally destructive results of modern secularization, most sectors of this strategy unfortunately appear to seek a restoration of the premodern patriarchal styles of classical masculine warrior civilizations.[6]

- *New Scientific Cosmology.* Fourth, there is the *scientific* strategy of some elites in the frontiers of physics and biology to articulate a post-Newtonian and so postmodern scientific cosmology that is at once relationally holistic, artistically developmental, and mystically humble. Each new technological stage of scientific observation yields a different cosmology. Primal cosmology was based on the populist observations of folk wisdom. Classical cosmology was based on the systematic observations of a leisured priestly class. Modern cosmology was based on systematized observation by a small scientific class aided by optical magnification (the microscope and the telescope). Now, postmodern cosmology is based on systematized optical observation by an advanced and expanded scientific class aided by electronically enhanced optics (the electronic microscope and the electronic telescope) and by computerized information systems.[7]

Chart 4.
Four Strategies Contending to Shape Postmodern Culture

STRATEGY	VISION	CULTURE	GIFT
Economic Neoliberalism	Bourgeois Colonization of the Entire Planet	Ultramodern Style (Objective Side)	Economic Initiative (But social-ecological crisis)
Academic Deconstruction	Deconstruction of All Meta-narratives	Ultramodern Style (Subjective Side)	Diversity/Difference (But cultural-spiritual crisis)
Religious Fundamentalism	Return to Classical Patriarchal Values	Premodern Style (With Postmodern Technology)	Public Spirituality (But patriarchal)
New Scientific Cosmology	Participation in Evolutionary Holism	Authentically Postmodern Style	Ecological-Mystical Consciousness

The Postmodern Cosmological Vision

We find one creative interpretation of the newly emerging post-modern scientific cosmology, especially for physics and biology, in the writings of theologian Thomas Berry and physicist Brian Swimme. Though there is by no means complete scientific agreement on the philosophical implications of the new cosmology, other scientific exponents advocating a similar interpretation include the late physicist David Bohm, the biologist Rupert Sheldrake, and the physicist Fritjof Capra. Meanwhile, in the humanistic disciplines, important voices also advocating a similar interpretation include cultural analyst Charlene Spretnak, theologian Sallie McFague, and historian Carolyn Merchant.[8]

I propose that this fourth strategy, the new scientific cosmology made possible by the electronic revolution, needs to ground the new planetary civilization. In all stages of human evolution cosmology has always been foundational for culture, including religion and science.

For example, the new scientific cosmology requires a radical revision of the underlying scientific assumptions of modern economic theory. Now economic analysis needs to become a subset of ecological analysis. By contrast, in an alienated manner modern economic theory, whether liberal or Marxian, has seen the natural world only instrumentally as a collection of "resources" for utilitarian human use. In reality, ecological globalization precedes and is deeper than economic globalization. Thus it is not sufficient to add environmental concerns to modern economics, but rather modern economics itself needs to be reconceived within postmodern ecology. The failure to recognize this truth needs to be seen as profoundly unscientific.[9]

The emergence of this new paradigm for science has led to growing dialogue between religion and science—signaling the end of the modern antagonism between the two, and proposing a fresh cosmological ground for the new planetary civilization.[10]

In this postmodern cosmology, again a fruit of the globalizing electronic revolution, we are beginning to glimpse—for the first time ever—the depth and breadth of the evolving human story, of the evolving Earth story, and of the still richer evolving cosmic story. At what might be called the level of natural religion, we are seeing an interpretation of the human story and its spiritual meaning as an integral part of the wider and richer evolutionary story of our garden planet Earth, and of its wider matrix of the entire cosmos. In this postmodern cosmology the universe is seen as relationally holistic across time and space, artistically creative, and mystically immersed in Mystery. In turn, humanity is perceived within the new cosmology as the reflective consciousness of Earth's own evolution, itself part of the wider evolving cosmic process evolution, and in turn part of the wider evolving cosmic process.

New Themes in the Postmodern Era

In their modern Catholic social teaching, the Leonine papacy addressed almost exclusively the social dynamics of *class relation-ships*. In the political dimension of this teaching, the papacy was disengaging from its ancient pro-imperial alliance with the aristocratic class of the old Christian civilization. In its place, it was building a new anti-socialist alliance with the moderate sector of the liberal bourgeoisie, with the hope of creating a modern adaptation of Christian civilization. Meanwhile, in the economic dimension of modern Catholic social teaching, the Leonine papacy was attempting to retain or to win the loyalty of the modern industrial working class in the face of competition from expanding socialist and communist movements.

In the global postmodern era, however, there has come to consciousness in the arena of social relationships a collage-like diversity of social conflicts, including class, but also much wider than that category alone. While this is not the place to explore these diverse conflicts in detail, it may be useful to note a few of the ones that have come to center stage.

The Culture of Death

As human technological intervention into biology increased, and as adequate public philosophical grounds for defending human dignity receded more and more before the triumph of liberal utilitarianism, there arose in early postmodern liberal societies a new attack on life at both ends of the life cycle, namely, the advent of

mass technological abortion and the growing threat of mass technological extermination of the elderly. Such violent elimination of
human life also returned in the United States with the expanded
use of the death penalty in the 1970s, 1980s, and 1990s, and
presently is even being suggested by elite utilitarian ethicists for the
handicapped.

While today the Catholic Church is widely known as being
both anti-abortion and anti-death penalty in the name of a personalist philosophy of human dignity, surprisingly, Catholic social teaching during its modern period did not address these issues in a central
way. The technological means of violent killing in such areas had
not yet been fully developed or widely applied, though the gruesome
shock of the "scientific" Nazi extermination camps, as well as the
advent of "scientific" warfare backed by a military industrial complex
(particularly the atomic bombing of Japanese cities and the "con-
ventional" saturation bombing of European cities), were some of the
first signs of what Pope John Paul II would later call "the culture of
death."

The Oppression of Colonialism

In the wake of World War II there arose across what is now
called the Third World of Africa, Asia, and Latin America a powerful anti-colonial movement that included a rebellion against neocolonialism (that is, external control without a formal colonial
system). These anti-colonial movements were one source of the birth
of a New Left, galvanized around the theme of liberation. The term
liberation had been used, of course, during World War II as a rally-
ing cry for defeating the Axis forces that had invaded and occupied
Western Europe. In the immediate postwar era the spirit of liberation
was extended both to the captive nations under the Soviet empire
and to the nations invaded earlier by Western colonialism and neocolonialism.

Tragically, neither the Leonine popes nor their premodern
predecessors truly challenged the reality of European (including
European-American) colonialism or neocolonialism. They implicitly supported it, for many Catholic missionary orders worked hand
in hand with European military, political, and economic colonialism

and neocolonialism. In the postmodern era, however, major liberation movements in the post-colonial nations, aided by allies in the
First World, would begin a fundamental challenge to the hegemonic
dominance of modern Western economics, politics, and culture.
This challenge is, of course, the source of the many liberation theologies and liberation spiritualities that are springing up and still
spreading across the world.

Ecological Devastation

The most fundamental social conflict to arise in the postmodern era has been over the ecological crisis. No class, race, or gender
is above it. Indeed, it appears to be intimately interwoven with
racism and sexism, as the recognition of "environmental racism" and
the emergence of "ecofeminism" testify. The ecological crisis concerns everyone, for it attacks the very diversity and integrity of God's
beautiful creation, which the First Letter of John tells us that God
loved so much as to give it his only Son (1 John 3:16). Thus, ecology
is not just one more merely human issue or simply a matter of the
distribution among humans of natural "resources."

While the capitalist-versus-socialist debate has focused on the
question of who is to control capital (the economic corporations or
the political party), the new ecological perspective argues that the
question is deeper than capital itself. It is located at the fundamental
cultural level of technological design, in turn shaped by cultural
assumptions. For example, fossil-fuel technologies are seen as
destructive while solar-energy technologies are seen as beneficial.

Further, while the capitalist-versus-socialist debate over market versus state has focused on the class dimension, the ecological
perspective focuses on the community dimension. Many transnational corporations are seen as fostering a corporate model of "development" that destroys local communities through the global
centralization of control, especially over the design of technologies.
By contrast, an ecological model of development would serve the
diversity and integrity of creation by promoting relatively decentralized and relatively self-reliant sustainable communities, especially
by using solar technologies, linked through global electronic
networking.

Modern Catholic social teaching did not address the ecological debate at all. Indeed, until recently modern bourgeois consciousness was scarcely aware of ecology, in contrast to the traditional wisdom of the ancient local peoples of the Earth, who never lost awareness of their ecological roots. But recently the Catholic theological tradition, perhaps because of its strong sacramental orientation with roots in the primal spirituality of immanence, has increasingly been making an ecological perspective central. Nonetheless, in the heritage of official Catholic social teaching there has been and still appears to be a strong fear of the philosophical principle of immanence (that is, God's creative presence in and through the natural world), and a strong patriarchal tendency to totalize the principle of transcendence as "domination." The harmonizing marriage of transcendence and immanence within Catholic social teaching is still a major task.

The Oppression of Racism

The entire modern European project from the 1500s forward (including its European-American expression, both North and South) was founded on the racist attack on the native peoples of the Americas and on the racist exploitation of the Atlantic slave system. Without the great European accumulation of capital from the precious metals stolen very early from the native peoples of the Americas (especially from the great silver mine of Potosí in present-day Bolivia), and without the four hundred years of generating enormous pools of capital from the Atlantic slave system, Europe and later the United States would probably never have emerged as centers of the modern world.

As Enrique Dussel has pointed out, prior to the European invasion of the lands of the ancient local peoples of the Americas, Europe was largely an intellectual, technological, and economic backwater. The great centers of civilization around the Mediterranean basin were in North Africa and at the eastern end of the Mediterranean.[11]

While the racist mercantile colonization of the Americas began in the late fifteenth century, only in the nineteenth century did a similar invasion inflict itself on Africa and Asia, and then in the form of industrial colonialism—thanks to the steamship, the railroad, and the machine gun.

With the anti-colonial spirit of liberation that arose in the post–World War II era, a new spirit of racial liberation began to emerge. For example, the long-lived civil rights movement within the United States took on new energy, and from it grew the Black Power movement as one stream of the New Left. The challenge to racism took on new confidence with the genetic discovery that humanity itself comes from Africa, and thus that all humans probably have African roots.[12] So too there has been developing throughout the early postmodern period a powerful spiritual-cultural awakening of the ancient local peoples of the Americas, who inhabited the two continents for tens of thousands of years before the European invasions and whose consciousness has remained deeply interwoven with the land and its myriad life forms.

Tragically, the Catholic popes were complicit in legitimizing the mercantile colonization of the Americas, as well as in the industrial colonization of Africa and Asia. Further, they did not question the Atlantic slave system until it was close to collapse. Last, the papacy, many bishoprics, and many religious orders dramatically increased their wealth and splendor thanks to revenues that flowed directly or indirectly from colonizing and racist systems. Even today, well into the postmodern period, Catholic social teaching has not adequately faced the truth of this harsh reality.

The Oppression of Sexism

We find yet another of the deep human oppressions not addressed by modern Catholic social teaching in the theme of sexism. It seems hard to believe, for example, that scarcely one hundred years ago women in the United States were not allowed to vote, and that for a long time the Catholic bishops in the United States were bitterly opposed to granting women the right to vote. There were, of course, mitigating factors (for one thing, white Protestant "nativist" groups hoped to use the votes of white Protestant women against Catholic immigrants), but the painful reality still stands.

In my own deep historical analysis briefly summarized earlier, I have argued that both the modern and classical waves of human culture represented first patriarchal and then hyper-masculine attempts to construct human civilization in an exclusively male image. In my expanded analysis I have elsewhere argued that a central and deep root of the present global crisis of spiritual, societal, and ecological life is a profound symbolic imbalance, especially in the sexual symbols, at the foundations of Western culture. Further, in my view, the classical Catholic tradition of spiritualistic theology, so infected with Platonic dualism, has been a key source for this cultural imbalance.

Throughout the modern period of Catholic social teaching, the Leonine popes consistently reflected and defended the patriarchal perceptions of classical society. Nonetheless, they cultivated through their profound Marian devotion indirect access to the feminine face of God. Presumably unconsciously, they held up the maternal symbol flowing from the ancient Mediterranean mother goddess (appearing now as "holy mother church"). Also, they supported the bourgeois "feminine" spirituality of the *devotio moderna*, that is, the modern spirituality of psychological interiority. This was in effect the spirituality of a privatized womb, in contrast to the more powerful and public cosmic womb symbol of the ancient goddess tradition. For both these reasons the modern popes presided over a church that was much more effective in recruiting and retaining women than men. But the women whom it so gathered remained largely within the orbit of privatized "feminine" religion with little public impact, and the church to which they were drawn did not address their oppression. Now, in the postmodern period, women's awakening consciousness is one of the most basic and powerful challenges to the limitations of the modern stage of Catholic social teaching.

A Conclusion on Postmodern Tasks

To conclude, though global Catholicism is now well within the new postmodern era, I have reviewed in this study the abiding legacy of modern Catholic social teaching, along with its premodern background, and briefly pointed to the profound postmodern challenge that it now faces, both within the human experience and within its wider ecological matrix. The modern legacy of Catholic social teaching, though carrying both rich strengths and tragic weaknesses, has become a cherished albeit under-utilized gift both in the postmodern renewal of Catholic Christianity and in the postmodern healing of our wounded world.

Now, in the early stage of the postmodern era, the greatest strategic tasks still before Catholic social teaching in its postmodern phase are

- to reformulate its theological, philosophical, and scientific perceptions in light of the newly emerging postmodern cosmology;

- to find deeper roots in the wellsprings of truly evangelical lay spirituality (free of the impeding legacy of clericalism and neo-Platonic religious dualism); and

- to integrate into its theory and practice a holistic consciousness of the full range of social and ecological oppressions.

The new postmodern stage of Catholic social teaching is only beginning to face these tasks. If Catholic social teaching can embrace the postmodern cosmology of ecological, social, and spiritual co-creation, root itself evangelically in an evangelical lay spirituality, and address the full range of human and ecological challenges, then the power of the Holy Spirit working through this rich tradition will truly be manifest. It is to be hoped that the next book, on the postmodern stage of the tradition, will be of some humble service to that project.

Notes

1. Introduction

1. This corpus up to the year 1981 is conveniently available in English translation in the five-volume collection by Claudia Carlin IHM, *The Papal Encyclicals* (n.l.: Pierian Press, 1981).

2. Two rich studies in this area by scholars from the United States are Marvin L. Krier Mich, *Catholic Social Teachings and Movements* (Mystic, Conn.: Twenty-Third Publications, 1998), and Thomas Bokenkotter, *Church and Revolution: Catholics in the Struggle for Democracy and Social Justice* (New York: Doubleday, 1998).

3. On the tradition of practical or praxis theology, see Johannes van der Ven, *Practical Theology: An Empirical Approach* (Leuven, Belgium: Peeters Press, 1998). For the concept of a strategic theology and also a praxis theology, see John A. Coleman, *An American Strategic Theology* (Ramsey, N.J.: Paulist Press, 1982).

4. On the role of philosophy, as well as theology, in Catholic social teaching, see E. De Jonghe, "Nature and Method of Catholic Social Doctrine," in David A. Boileau, ed., *Principles of Catholic Social Teaching* (Milwaukee, Wis.: Marquette University Press, 1994).

5. Ernst Troeltsh, *The Social Teachings of the Christian Churches,* vols. 1 and 2, trans. Olive Wyon (New York: Harper & Row, 1960).

6. Jean-Yves Calvez and Jacques Perrin, *The Church and Social Justice: The Social Teaching of the Popes from Leo XIII to Pius XII, 1878–1958,* trans. J. R. Kirwin (Chicago: Henry Regnery Co., 1961).

7. Roger Charles with Drostan Maclaren, *The Social Teaching of Vatican II: Its Origin and Development* (San Francisco: Ignatius Press, 1982).

8. Amintore Fanfani, *Catholicism, Protestantism, and Capitalism* (Notre Dame, Ind.: University of Notre Dame Press, 1984).

9. Heinrich Pesch, *Ethics and the National Economy*, trans. Rupert J. Ederer (Manila: Divine Word, 1988); and Franz H. Mueller, *The Church and the Social Question* (Washington, D.C.: American Enterprise Institute, 1984).

10. Donal Dorr, *Option for the Poor: A Hundred Years of Vatican Social Teaching* (Maryknoll, N.Y.: Orbis Books, 1983).

11. See Sean McDonagh, *To Care for the Earth: A Call to a New Theology* (Santa Fe, N.Mex.: Bear & Company, 1986, 1987); *The Greening of the Church* (Maryknoll, N.Y.: Orbis Books, 1990); and *Passion for the Earth* (Maryknoll, N.Y.: Orbis Books, 1994).

12. Ian Linden, *Back to Basics: Revisiting Catholic Social Teaching* (London: CIIR, 1994).

13. Marie-Dominique Chenu, *La 'doctrine social' de l'église comme idéologie* (Paris: Les éditions du Cerf, 1979).

14. For the seminal work, see Gustavo Gutiérrez, *A Theology of Liberation: History, Politics, and Salvation*, trans. and ed. Sr. Caridad Inda and John Eagleson (Maryknoll, N.Y.: Orbis Books, 1973). See also Clodovis Boff, *Theology and Praxis: Epistemological Foundations*, trans. Robert R. Barr (Maryknoll, N.Y.: Orbis Books, 1987).

15. For Freire's ideas, I am indebted to personal conversations with him. On Gaete, see his three articles, "Socialism and Communism: A Problem-Ridden Condemnation," "Social Catholicism and Marxism: An Impossible Dialogue," and "Christians and Marxism, From Pius XI to Paul VI," as translated and edited in *Latin Americans Discuss Marxism-Socialism* (Washington, D.C.: United States Catholic Conference), pp. 16–66.

16. Ricardo Antoncich, *Christians in the Face of Justice: A Latin American Reading of Catholic Social Teaching*, trans. Matthew J. O'Connell (Maryknoll, New York: Orbis Books, 1987).

17. See Pablo Richard, "Liberation Theology Today: Crisis or Challenge?" in *The Notebook* (publication of Catholic Movement for Intellectual and Cultural Affairs, Pax Romana), vol. 16, no. 2–3 (Summer-Fall 1992), pp. 16–20; and Leonardo Boff, *Ecology and Liberation: A New Paradigm*, trans. John Cumming (Maryknoll, N.Y.: Orbis Books, 1995).

18. Diego Irarázaval, *Inculturation: New Dawn of the Church in Latin America* (Maryknoll, N.Y.: Orbis Books, 2000).

19. Ivone Gebara, *Longing for Running Water: EcoFeminism and Liberation* (Minneapolis, Minn.: Fortress Press, 2000).

20. Elsa Tamez, ed., *Teólogos de la liberación hablan sobre la mujer* (San José, Costa Rica: DEI, 1986).

21. Philip S. Land, SJ, *Catholic Social Teaching: As I Have Lived, Loathed, and Loved It* (Chicago: Loyola University Press, 1994).

22. See Michael Novak, *Freedom with Justice: Catholic Social Thought and Liberal Institutions* (San Francisco: Harper & Row, 1984), and *The Catholic Ethic and the Spirit of Capitalism* (New York: Macmillan, 1993).

23. See David Hollenbach, SJ, *Claims in Conflict: Retrieving and Renewing the Catholic Human Rights Tradition* (New York: Paulist Press, 1979).

24. David O'Brien, "A Century of Catholic Social Teaching: Context and Comments," in John A. Coleman, SJ., ed., *One Hundred Years of Catholic Social Thought: Celebration and Challenge* (Maryknoll, N.Y.: Orbis Books, 1991).

25. John Coleman, "Introduction: A Tradition Celebrated, Reevaluated, and Applied" and "Neither Liberal nor Socialist," in Coleman, *One Hundred Years of Catholic Social Thought.*

26. Andrew Greeley, *No Bigger Than Necessary* (New York: Meridian, 1977).

27. Brian Hehir, "The Right and Competence of the Church in the American Case," in Coleman, *One Hundred Years of Catholic Social Thought.*

28. Charles E. Curran, *American Catholic Social Ethics: Twentieth Century Approaches* (Notre Dame, Ind.: University of Notre Dame Press, 1982).

29. Gregory Baum, *The Priority of Labor: A Commentary on Laborem Exercens, Encyclical Letter of Pope John Paul II* (New York: Paulist Press, 1982).

30. Mary Hobgood, *Catholic Social Teaching and Economic Theory: Paradigms in Conflict* (Philadelphia: Temple University Press, 1991).

31. Christine Gudorf, *Catholic Social Teaching on Liberation Themes* (Washington, D.C.: University Press of America, 1981).

32. Michael J. Himes and Kenneth R. Himes, OFM, *Fullness of Faith: The Public Significance of Theology* (New York: Paulist Press, 1993).

33. Michael J. Schuck, *That They Be One: The Social Teaching of the Papal Encyclicals 1740–1989* (Washington, D.C.: Georgetown University Press, 1991).

34. Paul Misner, *Social Catholicism in Europe: From the Onset of Industrialization to the First World War* (New York: Crossroad, 1991).

35. Marvin L. Krier Mich, *Catholic Social Teaching and Movements* (Mystic, Conn.: Twenty-Third Publications, 1998).

36. Thomas Bokenkotter, *Church and Revolution: Catholics in the Struggle for Democracy and Social Justice* (New York: Doubleday, 1998).

37. Peter Henriot et al, eds., *Catholic Social Teaching: Our Best Kept Secret* (Maryknoll, N.Y.: Orbis Books, 1992).

38. Maria Riley and Nancy Sylvester, *Trouble and Beauty: Women Encounter Catholic Social Teaching* (Washington, D.C.: Center of Concern, 1991).

39. Fred Kramer, SJ, *Doing FaithJustice: An Introduction to Catholic Social Thought* (New York: Paulist Press, 1991).

40. Judith Dwyer, ed., *The New Dictionary of Catholic Social Thought* (Collegeville, Minn.: The Liturgical Press, 1994).

41. Walter Burghardt, *Preaching the Just Word* (New Haven, Conn.: Yale University Press, 1996).

42. David Boileau, ed., *Principles of Catholic Social Teaching* (Milwaukee, Wis.: Marquette University Press, 1998).

43. Perry J. Roets, SJ, *Pillars of Catholic Social Teaching: A Brief Social Catechism* (Lanham, Md.: International Scholars Publications, 1999).

44. J. Brian Benestad, *The Pursuit of a Just Social Order: Policy Statements of the U.S. Catholic Bishops, 1966–1980* (Washington, D.C.: Ethics and Public Policy Center, 1982).

45. Thomas Masaro, *Living Justice: Catholic Social Teaching in Action* (Franklin, Wis.: Sheed & Ward, 2000)

46. Brennan R. Hill, *Christian Faith and the Environment: Making Vital Connections* (Maryknoll, N.Y.: Orbis Books, 1998).

47. Charles E. Curran, *Catholic Social Teaching 1891–Present: A Historical, Theological, and Ethical Analysis* (Washington, D.C.: Georgetown University Press, 2002).

48. See the five-volume collection edited by Claudia Carlin, IHM, *The Papal Encyclicals 1740–1878, 1878–1903, 1903–1939, 1939–1958, and 1958–1981* (n.l.: Pierian Press, 1990).

49. See Schuck, *That They Be One*, pp. x, 1–3; and Coleman, *One Hundred Years of Catholic Social Thought*, p. 3.

50. While my own use of this three-stage model even on the ecclesial side precedes Schuck's study by nearly twenty years, I nonetheless felt encouraged by discovering Schuck's work and learned much from its analysis, which was far richer than my own early work in this area. My initial exploratory statement of this three-stage model appeared in *The Present Crisis of Catholic Social Action: An Interpretive Framework* (Santiago, Chile: PARA, 1973).

51. Schuck, *That They Be One*, pp. 2, 3, 46. Schuck uses as a description for his third stage the phrase "high capitalism" (referring to the development of mechanistic technologies begun in the second half of the nineteenth century). He appears to have drawn on the work of Franz Mueller, who used the periodization of Werner Sombart. See Franz H. Mueller, *The Church and the Social Question* (Washington, D.C.: American Enterprise Institute for Public Policy Research), p. 33.

52. Schuck, *That They Be One*, p. 118.

53. Schuck, *That They Be One*, pp. x, 180, 192.

54. This context-response model, as employed in this correlation of stages of industrial capitalism and strategies of the Catholic Church, represents an adaptation of Toynbee's model for the process of civilizations. See Arnold Toynbee, *A Study of History* (New York: Weathervane Books, 1972), Chapter 13. Yet I do not embrace Toynbee's full and final theory of human culture. For a critique of Toynbee's theory, especially its religious syncretism and its neglect of subcultures, see Christopher Dawson, "Arnold Toynbee and the Study of History," in John J. Mulloy, ed., *Dynamics of World History: Christopher Dawson* (LaSalle, Ill.: Sherwood Sugden, 1978). The context-response model also carries an affinity with David Tracy's theological model of critical correlation, which is a revision of Paul Tillich's method,

though neither Tracy nor Tillich formally incorporated social analysis as a methodological step. See David Tracy, *Blessed Rage for Order: The New Pluralism in Theology* (New York: Seabury, 1975), pp. 32–34, 43–56.

55. Any strategy of evangelization inevitably, even if unconsciously, assumes a social interpretation of the context to be evangelized. Similarly, interpretation of the social context is inevitably grounded on ultimately foundational theological assumptions. In his apostolic exhortation *Evangelii nuntiandi* (8 December 1975), Pope Paul VI wrote, "This question of 'how to evangelize' is permanently relevant, because the methods of evangelizing vary according to the different circumstances of time, place and culture (and require) discovery and adaptation" (Washington, D.C.: United States Catholic Conference, n.d.), section 40. For an analysis of the correlation of models of social interpretation (as well as of psychological interpretation) with models of theology, see William W. Everett and T. J. Bachmeyer, *Disciplines in Transformation: A Guide to Theology and the Behavioral Sciences* (Washington, D.C.: University of America Press, 1979).

56. Again, my first study of the stages of Catholic social strategy was *The Present Crisis of Catholic Social Action* in 1973. In 1980 I published a brief summary of the model in Chapter 4 of a book co-authored with Peter Henriot, SJ, *Social Analysis: Linking Faith and Justice* (Maryknoll, N.Y.: Orbis Books, 1980). In this brief form the model has been widely diffused; the book has gone through two American editions, thirteen reprintings, and more than ten foreign translations. Later I prepared a more developed statement of the economic stage theory in no. 141 of *Concilium* as "Economic Crisis in the North Atlantic Nations," in Gregory Baum, ed., *Neo-Conservatism: Social and Religious Phenomenon* (New York: Seabury, 1981), pp. 1–7. Still later, a more detailed analysis of the dynamics of the third stage appeared in my essay "Transforming the World Economy: The Crisis of Progress and the Priority of Labor," in John W. Houck and Oliver F. Williams, eds., *Catholic Social Teaching and the U.S. Economy* (Washington, D.C.: University of America Press, 1984), pp. 285–315. But until this present study, the model has not been developed in as full a statement as I wished.

57. In the early theological work of Gustavo Gutiérrez I first found these shifts codified as types of pastoral strategy. Actually Gutiérrez sketched four types of pastoral strategy. The first two were (1) the strategies of "Christendom," drawing on Catholicism's Counter-Reformation stage, shaped by the juridical theology of the Jesuit theologian Robert Bellarmine, and tending toward a political Augustinianism; and (2) "Neo-Christendom," growing initially from the early explorations of liberal Catholicism by Lamennais and Lacordaire, eventually expressing itself in the theology of the Mystical Body and in the Christian Democratic philosophy of Jacques Maritain, and characterized by lay initiatives in the "temporal order." The last two strategies, which Gutiérrez called "maturity in faith" and "dialogue" (or later, a "prophetic pastoral strategy"), represented for him simply two stages of one process, namely, the trends that led up to and flowed from the "progressive" orientation of Vatican Council II. See Gustavo Gutiérrez, *Lineas Pastorales de la Iglesia en América Latina: Analisis Teológico* (Santiago de Chile: Instituto Catechistico Latinoamericano, 1970). Later I came across another similar stage-analysis of Catholicism's encounter with modernity, in which the first stage is described as one of "rejection," the second of "competition," and the third of "cooperation." These stages proposed by the British scholar William McSweeney corresponded at least chronologically to Gutiérrez's stages and to their recasting here. See William McSweeney, *Roman Catholicism: The Search for Relevance* (New York: St. Martin's Press, 1980).

58. On this consistent and coherent core, see Schuck, *That They Be One*, pp. 180–88. Schuck divides the encyclicals in a way that parallels the three stages of this analysis—pre-Leonine (meaning before Pope Leo XIII), Leonine (from Leo XIII through to Pius XII), and post-Leonine (beginning with John XXIII). For one central theological study of the impact of historical consciousness on Catholic thought, see Chapter 9, "The New Context: The Horizons of Historical Consciousness," in David Tracy, *The Achievement of Bernard Lonergan* (New York: Herder and Herder, 1979).

59. This was the orientation of my first exploration in *The Crisis of U.S. Catholic Social Action*.

60. I am indebted to William Ryan, SJ, founder of the Center of Concern in Washington, D.C., and a Harvard-trained economic historian, for urging me to study more carefully the evolution of modern industrial capitalism in correlation with the evolution of Catholic social teaching.

61. The notion of "ideal type," derived from the social theory of Max Weber, is used throughout this study but without intending the epistemological model on which Weber based the notion. Reacting against neo-Marxist reductionism and drawing on neo-Kantianism, Weber saw ideal types as heuristic instruments grounded only in the mind. By contrast, I use the term more in the Hegelian sense of "moment," that is, the attempt to articulate the historical essence of a developmental stage as grounded in mind and reality. For Weber's view on the epistemological status of his ideal types, see his *The Methodology of the Social Sciences*, trans. and ed. E. A. Shils and H. N. Finch (New York: Free Press, 1949), pp. 101–3. For Hegel's critique of a Kantian approach, see the "Preface" and "Introduction" of G. W. F. Hegel, *The Phenomenology of Mind*, trans. J. B. Baillie (New York: Harper & Row Torchbooks, 1967), esp. pp. 107–16, 140–45. Hegel's dialectical understanding of historical moments was, of course, the "inverted" source of the Marxist notion of historical modes of production. See the "Preface" of Karl Marx, *A Contribution to the Critique of Political Economy*, trans. S. W. Rzanskaya, ed. Maurice Dobb (Moscow: Progress Publishers, 1970), pp. 19–23.

62. Speaking of a general crisis of industrialization rather than of industrial capitalism may seem more typical of liberal or capitalist interpretations. By contrast, the socialist tradition has critiqued modern society from the viewpoint of capital and speaks of capitalism rather than of industrialism. Thus Marx's masterwork is titled *Capital*. It has been the opposite tendency of the liberal (or capitalist) tradition to focus on technology rather than capital. See, for example, John Kenneth Galbraith, *The New Industrial State*, 2d ed., rev. (New York: New American Library, Mentor, 1971); Jacques Ellul, *The Technological Society*, trans. John Wilkinson (New York: Random House, Vintage, 1964); and Daniel Bell, *The Coming of Post-Industrial Society: A Venture in Social Forecasting* (New York: Penguin, 1970). A full critique of modern industrial society would

require addressing the structures of both capital and technology, and across both ideologies.

63. See Schuck, *That They Be One*.

64. Joe Holland, *The Evolution of Modern Industrial Capitalist Society and the Birth of the Postmodern Electronic-Ecological Era* (Washington, D.C.: The Warwick Institute, 1999).

65. On the emergence of "scientific" racism, see my monograph, *The River of Life: The African-American Story, Part One* (Washington, D.C.: NOBC, 2001).

66. There are, of course, other interpretations of the relationship among economics, politics, and culture. Michael Novak, following Daniel Bell, argues that they constitute three separate systems. But he still sees a normative affinity of the liberal economy with the liberal polity and of both with the liberal culture. In the Introduction to his book *The Spirit of Democratic Capitalism* (New York: Simon and Schuster, 1982), Novak acknowledged that a correlative of the capitalist economy is the liberal culture. He proposed that "democratic capitalism" encompasses "three dynamic and converging systems functioning as one: a democratic polity, an economy based on markets and incentives, and a moral-cultural system which is pluralistic and, in the largest sense, liberal...political democracy is compatible in practice only with a market economy. In turn, both systems nourish and are best nourished by a pluralistic liberal culture" (p. 14).

In contrast to Novak's compartmentalized approach to the liberal culture in relation to the capitalist economy, Roberto Managbeira Unger, in his study *Knowledge and Politics* (New York: Macmillan, Free Press, 1975), argued for an organic understanding of liberalism. While Managbeira Unger's focus was on liberalism's psychological and political unity, he also pointed to its economic expression as capitalism (pp. 151–52).

Further, Daniel Bell, while rejecting an organic linkage of economic, political, and cultural life, and concerned that the liberal culture undermines capitalist economics, nonetheless acknowledged the genetic unity of capitalist economics and liberal culture within the "bourgeois civilization" (see *The Cultural Contradictions of Capitalism* [New York: Basic Books, 1978], esp, pp. xvi-xvii).

67. This definition is based on capitalism's own self-understanding as articulated in the 1776 foundational work of Adam Smith, *An Inquiry into the Nature and Causes of the Wealth of Nations*, ed. Edwin Canaan (New York: Modern Library, 1937), especially the section titled Book IV. Marx proposed a deeper cultural insight into the nature of capitalism, namely, the evolving reduction of "use value" into "exchange values," which he labeled the "fetishism of commodities." In his view even labor became a commodity subordinate to the accumulation of capital. See Karl Marx, *Capital*, vol. 1, *The Process of Capitalist Production*, ed. Frederick Engels, trans. Samuel Moore and Edward Aveling (New York: International Publishers, 1967), esp. pp. 35–46. Ferdinand Braudel added the distinction between "public markets," where exchange was law-abiding, transparent, and regulated by large social institutions according to public criteria, and "private markets," which he saw as based on the elimination of public controls and transparency. He associated capitalism with the expansion of "private markets" to the point where their form of exchange shapes the entire social system. See his *Afterthoughts on Material Civilization and Capitalism*, trans. Patricia M. Ranum (Baltimore: Johns Hopkins University Press, 1977), pp. 49ff.

68. In theory, Marxist socialism assigns priority to the working class, while the capitalist state as an extrinsic institution is eventually to be negated. But Marx's term for negation is the Hegelian notion of *aufheben*, which also means retrieved in a richer holism than which it negated. Under capitalism, Marx criticized the state as extrinsic because it formally isolated politics from civil society, leaving the economy as autonomous. This alienation of the liberal state was to be abolished under socialism by expanding politics to all of life. This theory would lay the ground for a more holistic understanding of politics but also for the temptation to totalitarianism. See Shlomo Avineri, *The Social and Political Thought of Karl Marx* (Cambridge, England: Cambridge University Press, 1968), pp. 17–22, 43–52, 202–20.

Since the theory calls for the working class to be guided by the socialist political party and in turn by the socialist state, the state becomes the strategic vehicle of all society. The resulting tendency of the modern socialist tradition has been to expand the state, not by integrating politics with the rest of life, but rather by displacing other mediating institutions, in effect reducing society to the state. For an early and powerful critique of this reductionist interpretation of politics, see Simone Weil, *The Need for Roots*, trans. Arthur Wills (Boston: Beacon Press, 1955), pp. 42ff.

69. As mentioned in a prior note, Michael Novak, in the Introduction to his *The Spirit of Democratic Capitalism*, acknowledged that a correlative of the capitalist economy is the liberal culture.

70. Simone Weil, whose thought influenced my perspective, took the position that the uprootedness inflicted upon the industrial proletariat by modern capitalism was expanded by modern socialism. In her classic text, *The Need for Roots*, she wrote: "Under the name of revolution, and often using identical slogans and subjects for propaganda, lie concealed two conceptions entirely opposed to each other. One consists in transforming society in such a way that the working class may be given roots in it; while the other consists in spreading to the whole of society the disease of uprootedness, which has been inflicted on the working class" (p. 48).

Speaking later of a more rooted society, she proposed that, "such a form of (re-rooted) social existence would be neither capitalist nor socialist. It would put an end to the proletarian condition, whereas what is called Socialism tends, in fact, to force everybody without distinction into that class" (pp. 77–78). Similarly in *Oppression and Liberty*, trans. Arthur Wills and John Petrie (Amherst: University of Massachusetts Press, 1973), she wrote: "Marxism is the highest spiritual expression of bourgeois society...Each formula of Marxist doctrine lays bare the characteristics of bourgeois society, but at the same time justifies them. By dint of developing a criticism of the capitalist system of economy, Marxism ended by providing the laws of this same economic system with broad foundations" (p. 131).

Weil's view of modern socialism as a deepening of modern capitalism retrieved a traditional conservative viewpoint, espoused also by the Catholic popes, that liberalism was the parent of socialism.

71. See section 12 of Pope John Paul II's 1981 encyclical letter *Laborem exercens*. An English translation and commentary can be found in Baum, *The Priority of Labor*. By John Paul's acknowledgment, and as Baum recognizes, the principle of the

priority of labor was originally articulated by Karl Marx, but, according to the pope, Marxism failed to be faithful to its own principle and instead substituted the principle of the priority of capital as controlled by the state.

72. See Thomas Berry, *The Dream of the Earth* (San Francisco: Sierra Club, 1958) with his constant insistence that the Earth is primary and the human derivative.

73. I am indebted to correspondence with Paul Misner for the phrase "tertiary research."

74. As such, the study flows from what Richard McKeon called a dialectical thought mode, and what Paul Ricoeur described as the first moment of hermeneutic. See Richard McKeon, *Freedom and History*, and Paul Ricoeur, *Interpretation Theory: Discourse and the Surplus of Meaning* (Fort Worth, Tex.: Texas Christian University Press, 1976), esp. chap. 4.

75. For an encyclopedic review of the Protestant tradition of social teaching during the modern industrial capitalist period, at least from a US perspective, see the fine study by Gary Dorien, *Soul in Society: The Making and Renewal of Social Christianity* (Minneapolis, Minn.: Fortress Press, 1995). For a broader perspective on Protestant social Christianity across the industrial and colonial world, see Julio de Santa Ana, ed., *Separation Without Hope? Essays on the Relation Between the Church and the Poor During the Industrial Revolution and the Western Colonial Expansion* (Maryknoll N.Y.: Orbis Books, 1978).

76. See Peter F. Drucker, *Post-Capitalist Society* (New York: HarperCollins Publishers, 1994).

Chapter 2

1. For an analysis of the distinct consequences of the distinct societal models of religious monopolies and religious pluralism, see David Martin, *A General Theory of Secularization* (New York: Harper & Row, 1978). According to Martin's theory, in religiously pluralistic societies societal opposition does not become strongly anticlerical, while in religiously monopolistic societies, like the Catholic Latin nations, societal opposition tends to become militantly secularist.

2. On the distinct experience of liberalism in Latin Catholic lands, see Michael Novak, *The Catholic Ethic and the Spirit of*

Democratic Capitalism (New York: Macmillan, 1993), pp. 99–100. Alexis de Tocqueville, in his study *The Old Regime and the French Revolution*, explained how isolated the French aristocracy had become, and how generally detested they were by the other social classes (see *The Old Regime and the French Revolution*, trans. Stuart Gilbert [Garden City, N.Y.: Doubleday, 1955], pp. 22–31).

3. The classical roots of this aristocratic vision are ancient and articulated in Book III of Plato's *Republic*. See *The Collected Dialogues of Plato, Including the Letters*, ed. Edith Hamilton and Huntington Cairns, trans. Lane Cooper et al. (Princeton, N.J.: Princeton University Press, 1961), pp. 575–845.

For a contemporary theological analysis of the "restoration theology" underlying this conservative strategy, in contrast to a more progressive theological orientation open to the contemporary world, see Walter Kasper, *Theology and Church*, trans. Margaret Kohl (New York: Crossroad, 1989), pp. 45–53. Kasper describes the restoration model of theology, which came to dominate this period, as one that sees modern autonomy as a defection or apostasy from classical Catholic theonomy. This same anti-modern orientation continued beyond this stage, he argues, in the work of Romano Guardini and Karl Adam. By contrast, a progressive theological model sees modern human autonomy as the realization of theonomy. For Kasper, the Catholic expression of this progressive orientation springs from the transcendental Thomism of Joseph Maréchal, as well as the later work of Karl Rahner and Johann Baptist Metz.

Another contemporary position, not discussed by Kasper, may be seen in the socially radical Latin American liberation theology (for example, the work of Gustavo Gutiérrez). It challenges the autonomy of the bourgeois individual from the wider community and sees most European theology as falsely universalizing the bourgeois experience of the middle class.

Yet another may be found in the emerging postmodern ecological theology (for example, the natural theology of Thomas Berry). It radically questions the modern autonomy of humanity from nature, as well as from the Divine and from the organic fabric human community. Still other distinct positions would include feminist, black, and Asian theologies. (See the references to Gutiérrez and Berry in the Introduction.)

4. See the following analysis of papal encyclicals for these periods.

5. On this see the subsequent discussion, particularly under the restoration popes and Pius IX. This was also the perspective of Jacques Maritain in his *Three Reformers: Luther, Descartes, Rousseau* (London: Sheed & Ward, 1928).

6. The term *bourgeoisie* is used initially here in its older sense of the literate urban classes of merchants, master artisans, and professionals, that is, the "middle class," which stood between the aristocracy and the peasantry, and not yet in the later sense of the capitalist business class.

7. On the relationship of the Reformation to print and the urban educated classes, see Steven Ozment, *Protestants: The Birth of a Revolution* (New York: Doubleday, 1992), pp. 19–20, 45–66. Without disparaging the authentically religious dimensions of the Reformation, Ozment claimed that the urban printers' guild "had an economic stake in fanning religious conflict by publishing Protestant propaganda" (19). He also noted that the religious revolution began in free imperial cities (19). Jaroslov Pelikan, in *The Idea of the University: A Reexamination* (New Haven, Conn.: Yale University Press, 1992), emphasized the centrality of the free university to the Reformation and to the subsequent development of Protestantism.

8. See J. Derek Holmes and Bernard W. Bickers, *A Short History of the Catholic Church* (New York: Paulist Press, 1984), 173–75.

9. See Holmes and Bickers, *Catholic Church*, pp. 174–75.

10. See Holmes and Bickers, *Catholic Church*, pp. 160–72.

11. For a historical review of the Enlightenment, see Peter Gay's two-volume study *The Enlightenment: An Interpretation*, vol. 1, *The Science of Freedom*, and vol. 2, *The Rise of Modern Paganism* (New York: W. W. Norton, 1966, 1969). See also Ernst Cassirer, *The Philosophy of the Enlightenment*, trans. Fritz C. A. Koelln and James P. Pettegrove (Princeton, N.J.: Princeton University Press, 1951).

12. See Holmes and Bickers, *Catholic Church*, pp. 173–210.

13. See E. E. Y. Hales, *Revolution and Papacy* 1769–1846 (Garden City, N.Y.: Doubleday & Company, 1960), pp. 67–90; J. Derek Holmes, *The Triumph of the Holy See: A Short History of the*

Papacy in the Nineteenth Century (London: Burns & Oates, 1978), pp. 15–38; François Houtart and André Rousseau, *The Church and Revolution: From the French Revolution of 1789 to the Paris Riots of 1968; from Cuba to Southern Africa; from Vietnam to Latin America*, trans. Violet Nevile (Marynoll, N.Y.: Orbis Books, 1971), pp. 27–54; Roger Aubert, Johannes Beckmann, Patrick J. Corish, and Rudolf Lill, *The Church Between Revolution and Restoration*, trans. Peter Becker (New York: Crossroad, 1981), pp. 1–49.

14. See Aubert et al., *Revolution and Restoration*, p. 11.

15. On the ancient roots of the Franco-papal alliance, see Judith Herrin, *The Formation of Christendom* (Princeton, N.J.: Princeton University Press, 1987), pp. 390–476. On the situation of Catholicism in France on the eve of the revolution, see Holmes, *The Triumph of the Holy See*, pp. 16–20; Aubert et al, *Revolution and Restoration*, pp. 3–18.

16. See Georges Lefebvre, *The Coming of the French Revolution*, trans. R. R. Palmer (New York: Vintage, 1957), Part II.

17. Eric Hobsbawm, *The Age of Revolution 1789–1848* (New York: New American Library, 1962), pp. 86–87.

18. See Holmes, *The Triumph of the Holy See.*

19. Hales, *Revolution and Papacy*, pp. 91–129.

20. Hales, *Revolution and Papacy*, pp. 139–54.

21. Owen Chadwick, *The Popes and the European Revolution* (Oxford: Clarendon Press, 1981), pp. 482–83.

22. Chadwick, *The Popes and the European Revolution*, pp. 492–504.

23. Chadwick, *The Popes and the European Revolution*, pp. 508–13, 535.

24. Henry Littlefield, *History of Europe 1500–1848* (New York: Barnes & Noble, 1959), pp. 135–46.

25. Hobsbawm, *Age of Revolution*, pp. 138–140.

26. Hobsbawm, *Age of Revolution*, p. 139.

27. Hobsbawm, *Age of Revolution*, p. 146; see also pp. 138–39. See also Littlefield, *History of Europe*, pp. 145–56.

28. Hobsbawm, *Age of Revolution*, pp. 137–62, esp. p. 148.

29. Hales, *Revolution and Papacy*, pp. 227–60.

30. On the institutional revival of Catholic Christianity in France, especially after the revolution of 1848, see Holmes, *The Triumph of the Holy See*, pp. 66–71, 114–19.

31. Aubert et al., *Revolution and Restoration*, pp. 90–91.

32. Aubert et al., *Revolution and Restoration*, p. 92.

33. Holmes, *The Triumph of the Holy See*, pp. 129–62.

34. See Holmes, *The Triumph of the Holy See*, pp. 61–64.

35. For this and the following section on Lamennais, see Holmes, *The Triumph of the Holy See*, pp. 71–77.

36. On Lammenais, see again Holmes, *The Triumph of the Holy See*, pp. 71–77, 90–98; and Alec Vidler, *Prophecy and Papacy: A Study of Lamennais, the Church, and the Revolution* (New York: Scribner, 1954).

37. Aubert et al., *Revolution and Restoration*, pp. 91–92.

38. On liberal Catholicism, see Holmes, *The Triumph of the Holy See*, pp. 74–77.

39. On liberal Catholicism, see again Holmes, *The Triumph of the Holy See*, pp. 74–77. On the religious strength of a majority oppressed by a minority of another religion, so obvious in the Irish and Polish cases, see Martin, *A General Theory of Secularization*.

40. On the development of Social Catholicism, see Holmes, *The Triumph of the Holy See*, pp. 108–26.

41. Aubert et al., *Revolution and Restoration*, pp. 85–86.

42. On Romanticism, particularly in Germany where it proved so influential for the next stage of Catholicism, see Aubert et al., *Revolution and Restoration*, pp. 216–27.

43. Eric O. Hanson, in *The Catholic Church in World Politics* (Princeton, N.J.: Princeton University Press, 1987) sees the instrumental dimension of politics as dealing with "political, economic, and military power." By contrast, he sees the expressive dimension as dealing with "the articulation of collective ideas, promotion of collective norms, and the representation of symbolic ideas" (p. 5).

44. See Hanson, *The Catholic Church in World Politics*.

45. On the papacy of Pius IX, see Holmes, *The Triumph of the Holy See*, pp. 101–60; Roger Aubert, *Le pontificat de Pie IX* (Paris: Bloud et Gay, 1964); Roger Aubert, Johannes Beckmann, Patrick

J. Cornish, and Rudolf Lill, *The Church in the Age of Liberalism*, trans. Peter Becker (New York: Crossroad, 1981); Alec R. Vidler, *The Church in an Age of Revolution: 1789 to the Present Day* (London: Penguin Books, 1961), pp. 146–56; E. E. Y. Hales, *Pio Nono: A Study in European Politics and Religion in the Nineteenth Century* (Garden City, N.Y.: Doubleday & Company, 1962); Anthony Rhodes, *The Power of Rome: The Vatican in the Age of Liberal Democracies, 1870–1922* (New York: Franklin Watts, 1983), pp. 9–66.

46. Holmes, *The Triumph of the Holy See*, p. 102.

47. Hales, *Pio Nono*, pp. 64–65.

48. Hales, *Pio Nono*, pp. 60–77.

49. Hales, *Pio Nono*, p. 64.

50. Hales, *Pio Nono*, pp. 74–75, 79–83.

51. Holmes, *The Triumph of the Holy See*, p. 104.

52. Hales, *Pio Nono*, pp. 81–93.

53. Holmes, *The Triumph of the Holy See*, p. 105.

54. Hales, *Pio Nono*, pp. 87–106.

55. Hales, *Pio Nono*, pp. 108–21.

56. Aubert et al., *The Church in the Age of Liberalism*, pp. 306–15.

57. On the wave of revolutions, see Hobsbawm, *Age of Revolution*, pp. 140, 154–62.

58. Michael Harrington, the late socialist leader in the United States, regularly commented that the historical strength of European socialism had been due to its campaign for voting rights for the working class, something that the European bourgeoisie was reluctant on its own to concede. (This is from personal conversations with Harrington.)

59. Holmes, *The Triumph of the Holy See*, pp. 111–26.

60. See Arturo Gaete, "*Socialismo y communismo: historia de una problemática condenación*," *Mensaje* (Jesuit monthly of Santiago, Chile), vol. 20, no. 200 (July 1971): pp. 290–302.

61. Holmes, *The Triumph of the Holy See*, pp. 113–26.

62. Hales, *Pio Nono*, pp. 176–90.

63. Hales, *Pio Nono*, pp. 190–264.

64. Holmes, *The Triumph of the Holy See*, pp. 134–35.

65. Holmes, *The Triumph of the Holy See*, pp. 134–37.

66. Holmes, *The Triumph of the Holy See*, pp. 135–53.

67. Holmes, *The Triumph of the Holy See*, pp. 138–43.

68. An English translation of the Syllabus of Errors can be found in Colman J. Barry, *The Modern Era: 1789 to the Present*, vol. 3 of *Readings in Church History* (New York: Newman Press, 1965), pp. 70–74. The encyclical is found in Claudia Carlin, IHM, *The Papal Encyclicals 1740–1878*, (n.l.: Pierian Press, 1990), pp. 381–86. On the Syllabus of Errors see Holmes, *The Triumph of the Holy See*, pp. 145–51; Hales, *Pio Nono*, pp. 266–304; Aubert et al., *Revolution and Restoration*, pp. 293–99.

69. The claim for strong Jesuit influence over Pio Nono at this time is made in Hales, *Revolution and Papacy*, p. 284.

70. On the following treatment of Pius IX and Vatican Council I, see Holmes, *The Triumph of the Holy See*, pp. 154–59; Hales, *Pio Nono*, pp. 306–27; and Aubert et al., *Revolution and Restoration*, pp. 312–30.

71. David I. Kertzer, *The Kidnapping of Edgardo Mortara* (New York: Alfred A. Knopf, 1997).

72. David I. Kertzer, *The Pope Against the Jews: The Vatican's Role in the Rise of Modern Anti-Semitism* (New York: Alfred A. Knopf, 2001).

73. On the fall of the Papal States and the aftermath, see Hales, *Pio Nono*, pp. 327–47.

74. Hales, *Pio Nono*, p. 347.

75. Rhodes, *The Power of Rome*, p. 33.

76. Hanson, *The Catholic Church in World Politics*, p. 340.

77. See Martin, *A General Theory of Secularization*, p. 107.

78. Hales, *Revolution and Papacy*, pp. 342–43.

Chapter 3

1. As already noted, reference to all encyclicals in this study, except for those after 1981, will be to the English translations found in Claudia Carlin, IHM, *The Papal Encyclicals*, 5 vols. (n.l.: Pierian Press, 1990). For the encyclicals before Pius VI, see *Papal Encyclicals*, vol. 1, pp. 5–165. *A quo primum* is found on pp. 41–44.

Traditionally only the first word of an encyclical's title is capitalized (unless it is a word that on its own is normally capitalized), since the title is actually a citation of the opening words of the document. When referring to particular citations within encyclicals, it is customary to give the paragraph number taken from the original Vatican texts. (The paragraphs are so numbered in the Cirlen volumes). So as not to overburden these chapters with excessive footnotes, all references to a given encyclical within a particular paragraph of this text will be placed at the end of the paragraph. Finally, if in a reference below only a paragraph is cited, then it refers to the last mentioned encyclical in the notes.

2. See Carlin, *Papal Encyclicals*, vol. 1, p. 3.

3. Par. 6.

4. Pars. 5, 6.

5. See Carlin, *Papal Encyclicals*, vol. 1, pp. 9–10.

6. See Carlin, *Papal Encyclicals*, vol. 1, pp. 11–14.

7. See Carlin, *Papal Encyclicals*, vol. 1, pp. 15–17.

8. See Carlin, *Papal Encyclicals*, vol. 1, pp. 19–22.

9. See Carlin, *Papal Encyclicals*, vol. 1, pp. 23–26, esp. pars. 10, 11, 15.

10. See Carlin, *Papal Encyclicals*, vol. 1, pp. 27–40, esp. pars. 5, 11. 16, 22.

11. See Carlin, *Papal Encyclicals*, vol. 1, pp. 41–44.

12. See Carlin, *Papal Encyclicals*, vol. 1, pp. 41–44.

13. See Carlin, *Papal Encyclicals*, vol. 1, pp. 51–73, esp. pars. 20, 29, 52.

14. See Carlin, *Papal Encyclicals*, vol. 1, pp. 75–103.

15. See Carlin, *Papal Encyclicals*, vol. 1, pp. 105–7. On the bull *Unigenitus*, see Hubert Jedin, ed., *History of the Church*, vol. 6 (New York: Crossroad, 1981), pp. 381ff.

16. See Carlin, *Papal Encyclicals*, vol. 1, pp. 113–19.

17. See Carlin, *Papal Encyclicals*, vol. 1, pp. 121–26.

18. See Carlin, *Papal Encyclicals*, vol. 1, pp. 127–28.

19. See Carlin, *Papal Encyclicals*, vol. 1, pp. 129–31, esp. par. 4.

20. See Carlin, *Papal Encyclicals*, vol. 1, p. 132–35. The citations are from par. 1.

21. Par. 2.

22. Par. 2.

23. Par. 2.

24. See Carlin, *Papal Encyclicals*, vol. 1, pp. 137–38.

25. See Carlin, *Papal Encyclicals*, vol. 1, pp. 141–42.

26. See Carlin, *Papal Encyclicals*, vol. 1, pp. 159–61, esp. pars. 1, 4.

27. Pars. 5, 6.

28. See Carlin, *Papal Encyclicals*, vol. 1, pp. 163–65, esp. pars. 2, 3, 5.

29. See Carlin, *Papal Encyclicals*, vol. 1, pp. 171–75.

30. Par. 7.

31. For the citations noted above, see Pars. 1, 8.

32. See Carlin, *Papal Encyclicals*, vol. 1, pp. 177–84.

33. See esp. pars. 2, 3, 27.

34. Par. 7.

35. Pars. 7, 13, 16.

36. On Jesus' role as a lay teacher, see John P. Meier, *A Marginal Jew* (Garden City, N.Y.: Doubleday, 1991), the chapter titled, "Jesus' Status as a Layman," pp. 345ff. On the originally egalitarian and even democratic character of the original Jesus movement, see Elizabeth Schüssler Fiorenza, "Discipleship of Equals: Ekklesial Democracy and Patriarchy in Biblical Perspective," in Eugene C. Bianci and Rosemary Radford Ruether, *A Democratic Catholic Church: The Reconstruction of Roman Catholicism* (New York: Crossroad, 1992), pp. 17–33.

37. See pars. 18, 32. He argued that the ancient right of metropolitan bishops to consecrate other bishops, as originally stated by the Council of Nicea, itself derived from the right of the Apostolic See, and that the century-old practice of metropolitan authority was now returning to its point of origin in the Apostolic See. Thus he wrote: "So today the Pope as a duty of his office appoints bishops for each of the churches, and no lawful consecration may take place in the entire Catholic Church without the order of the Apostolic See" (par. 18). He also wrote of the church as the "seamless garment of Christ" and again saw the new polity as causing schism. He spoke of "the bond of spiritual marriage which unites [the] churches."

He addressed cathedral canons in relationship to their bishops as forming "one clerical body as limbs which are united with their head, which the civil power is unable to destroy or overthrow."

38. Par. 32.

39. Carlin, *Papal Encyclicals*, vol. 1, pp. 189–93.

40. Pars. 6, 7.

41. Par. 8.

42. Pars. 14–19.

43. Par. 19.

44. Michael J. Schuck, *That They Be One: The Social Teaching of the Papal Encyclicals 1740–1989* (Washington, D.C.: Georgetown University Press, 1991), p. 9. The reference could have been to Jean-Jacques Rousseau's *Discourse on the Origin of Inequality Among Men* (1755), or perhaps to early French socialists like Gabriel Bonnot de Malby (1709–85), or to the unknown figure called Morelly, or even to the French revolutionary François Noël Babeuf (executed in 1797 and often considered the first communist martyr) and his "Conspiracy of the Equals." On the early history of modern European socialism, see Albert S. Lindemann, *A History of European Socialism* (New Haven, Conn.: Yale University Press, 1983), pp. 37–85.

45. Roger Aubert, Johannes Beckmann, Patrick Corish, and Rudolf Lill, *The Church Between Revolution and Restoration*, trans. Peter Becker (New York: Crossroad, 1981), pp. 95ff.

46. Aubert, et al., *Church Between Revolution and Restoration*, pp. 95ff.

47. See Carlin, *Papal Encyclicals*, vol. 1, pp. 199–203. This first Leo had established the doctrinal pre-eminence of the bishop of Rome amid the early trinitarian and christological controversies of the young imperial church and had personally confronted the barbarian invader, Attila the Hun. See J. Derek Holmes and Bernard Bickers, *A Short History of the Catholic Church* (New York: Paulist Press, 1983), pp. 37–39.

48. Par. 11.

49. Pars. 11–14.

50. Pars. 17–21.

51. Pars. 20–24.

52. See Carlin, *Papal Encyclicals*, vol. 1, pp. 205–8.

53. Pars. 1, 9.

54. See Carlin, *Papal Encyclicals*, vol. 1, pp. 209–15.

55. Reminiscent of the bishops of Catholicism's Roman rite, the priests of the Roman great mother-goddess (originally Cybelene of Anatolia) were castrated eunuchs who wore long gowns, jewelry, and headgear called *mitras* (mitres). Drawing on the myth of Attis, the priest of the goddess was called to be faithful to the great mother and to remain a boy forever. See M. Renee Salzman, "Magna Mater: Great Mother of the Roman Empire," in Carol Olson, ed., *The Book of the Goddess Past and Present* (New York: Crossroad, 1990), pp. 60–67.

56. Par. 15.

57. Pars. 18–19.

58. E. E. Y. Hales, *Revolution and Papacy 1769–1846*, pp. 265–67, 282–83.

59. See Carlin, *Papal Encyclicals*, vol. 1, pp. 221–24.

60. Pars. 1–3.

61. Pars. 3–5.

62. On the Carbonari, see Hales, *Revolution and Papacy*, p. 265.

63. Par. 6.

64. See par. 10.

65. Pars. 12–13. On the end of the restoration, see E. J. Hobsbawm, *The Age of Revolution 1789–1948* (New York: New American Library, 1962), pp. 137–62.

66. The book's full title was *Il trionfo della Santa Sede e della Chiesa controgli assalti dei Novatori*. It was translated into French and German and had a significant influence on the ultramontane movement. Regarding this book and the papacy of Gregory XVI, see J. Derek Holmes, *The Triumph of the Holy See: A Short History of the Papacy in the Nineteenth Century* (London: Burns & Oates, 1978), p. 1 (the title of Holmes's own book repeats Capellari's shortened title); Aubert et al., *Revolution and Restoration*, pp. 262–68; and Roger Aubert, Johannes Beckmann, Patrick J. Corish, and Rudolf Lill, *The Church in the Age of Liberalism*, trans. Peter Becker (New York: Crossroad, 1981), p. 3.

67. Gregory the Great (590–604) had consolidated the early temporal power of the papacy with "the Patrimony of Peter" (lands donated by wealthy Roman families in exchange for papal protection). He had taken advantage of a weakened Constantinople to develop a uniquely Western church and then fostered missionary outreach to territories of little interest to Constantinople (most famously by sending the monk Augustine to England). The older Gregory had also developed a papal alliance with Western monasticism, heightening preeminence for the Western church and papal authority over it (see Holmes and Bickers, *Catholic Church*, pp. 47–52).

68. Thus he wrote, "All Catholics whether priests or laymen are forbidden to pretend that slavery and the slave trade are lawful" (Holmes, *Triumph of the Holy See*, p. 83).

69. See Carlin, *Papal Encyclicals*, vol. 1, pp. 229–31.

70. Pars. 1, 4, 5, 8.

71. See Carlin, *Papal Encyclicals*, vol. 1, pp. 233–34.

72. Pars. 2–4.

73. See Carlin, *Papal Encyclicals*, vol. 1, pp. 233–41. On the pope's recent sufferings, see pars. 1–2.

74. Par. 19.

75. Par. 5.

76. Par. 19.

77. Pars. 9–17.

78. Par. 17.

79. Par. 10.

80. Par. 14.

81. Pars. 18–19.

82. Pars. 18–19.

83. Par. 4.

84. Pars. 22–24.

85. See Carlin, *Papal Encyclicals*, vol. 1, pp. 249–51.

86. Par. 6.

87. See Holmes, *The Triumph of the Holy See*, p. 90; Hobsbawm, *Age of Revolution*, p. 142.

88. See Carlin, *Papal Encyclicals*, vol. 1, pp. 243–47.

89. Pars. 2–4.

90. Pars. 7–11.

91. Par. 13.

92. See Carlin, *Papal Encyclicals*, vol. 1, pp. 253–57.

93. Par. 6.

94. See Carlin, *Papal Encyclicals*, vol. 1, pp. 259–61. The phrase *Catholic Action* has its roots in France at the beginning of the nineteenth century. According to Aubert, Lamennais "coined the term," although it was also used by an ex-Jesuit who in 1801 founded a body modeled on the Marian Congregation and described it as the "Central Office of Catholic Action" (see Aubert et al., *Revolution and Restoration*, pp. 227–28, 235).

95. On the emergence of these groups, see Aubert et al., *Revolution and Restoration*, pp. 189–239.

96. Par. 15.

97. As late as the 1987 World Synod of Bishops, meeting in Rome on the theme of the laity, the European Catholic bishops were still uneasy with the word *laity*, for it meant to them anticlerical secularizing forces. I cite this from the personal experience of being in Rome at the time and conversing there with bishops, Vatican staff, and journalists.

98. Aubert et al., *Revolution and Restoration*, p. 91.

99. According to Aubert, "Already in 1822 (Lamennais) had written…of the unhappy condition of the workers in the new liberal society." Aubert sees this as "the first landmark of Social Catholicism in France" (Aubert et al., *Revolution and Restoration*, p. 235 n. 17).

100. See the Preface by Cardinal Manning to Kathleen O'Meara, *Frederick Ozanam Professor at the Sorbonne: His Life and Works* (New York: Christian Press, 1911), p. xviii.

101. See Carlin, *Papal Encyclicals*, vol. 1, pp. 263–65.

102. See Carlin, *Papal Encyclicals*, vol. 1, pp. 267–71.

103. Pars. 4, 9.

104. Par. 1

105. Par. 4.

106. Par. 4

107. Par. 9.

108. See Carlin, *Papal Encyclicals*, vol. 1, pp. 277–84.

109. Pars. 1–7.

110. In commenting on this innovation, Schuck proposes: "There — no doubt through the hand of neo-Thomist Joseph Kleutigen — the pope anticipates the correlation of faith and reason found in the First Vatican Council's *Dei Filius* document and in the subsequent Leonine period encyclicals" (Schuck, *That They Be One*, p. 20). Thus, though the encyclicals prior to Leo XIII relied predominately on biblical-patristic resources and only the subsequent Leonine corpus turned to a neo-Thomist natural law orientation (a contrast that Schuck emphasizes), the influence of neo-Thomism actually began in seminal form with the first encyclical of Pius IX. For a summary of these contrasts, see Schuck, *That They Be One*, pp. 180–88.

111. Schuck writes, "Noting the distinction between mechanical and pastoral metaphors, Andrew Ettin relays how Voltaire despised the latter, once exclaiming, '*Ah! Le bon temp ce siècle de fer!*'…Pope Gregory, on the other hand, thought dimly of the grand implement of the new iron age, remarking: '*chemin de fer—chemin enfer*'" (Shuck, *That They Be One*, p. 40). Schuck draws here on Andrew Ettin, *Literature and the Pastoral* (New Haven, Conn.: Yale University Press, 1984), p. 35; and on Anthony Rhodes, *The Power of Rome in the Twentieth Century: The Vatican in the Age of Liberal Democracies: 1870–1922* (London: Sidgwick & Jackson, 1983), p. 53. He then adds: "The popes also decry atheistic and materialistic interpretations of the physical world inspired by Isaac Newton's laws of matter and motion. These 'naturalistic' understandings of the world are exemplified in Diederot's observation that 'the world is no longer a divine thing; it is a machine which has its wheels, its ropes, its pulleys, its springs, and its weights.' Voltaire (*Elèments de la philosophie de Newton*, *[1737]*) and Baron d'Holbach (*Système de la nature* [1770]—placed on the Index in 1775) popularize this worldview on the continent…The popes lament materialistic disregard for the human soul. In *Histoire naturelle de l'âme* [1745] and *L'homme-machine* (1747–48), Julien Offray de Lamettrie reduces the Christian notion of the soul to an operation of the brain (Schuck, *That They Be One*, p. 12). The citation of Diederot is from Emmet John Hughes, *The Church and the*

Liberal Society (Notre Dame, Ind.: University of Notre Dame Press, 1961), p. 62.

112. See, for example, Fritjof Capra, *The Turning Point: Science, Society, and the Rising Culture* (New York: Bantam, 1983); Carolyn Merchant, *The Death of Nature: Women, Ecology, and the Scientific Revolution* (New York: Harper & Row, 1980); Charlene Spretnak, *The Spiritual Dimension of Green Politics* (Santa Fe, N.Mex.: Bear, 1986); Gibson Winter, *Liberating Creation: Foundations of Religious Social Ethics* (New York: Crossroad, 1981).

113. Pars. 4–15.

114. Par. 16.

115. For the early development of the socialist movement, see Albert S. Lindemann, *A History of European Socialism* (New Haven, Conn.: Yale University Press, 1983), pp. 37–85.

116. Par. 17.

117. Pars. 19–33.

118. Pars. 29, 36.

119. An English translation may be found in Carlin, *Papal Encyclicals,* vol. 1, pp. 291–93.

120. Par. 4.

121. See Carlin, *Papal Encyclicals,* vol. 1, pp. 295–303.

122. Par. 3.

123. Par. 3.

124. On Antonelli's role, see Rhodes, *Power of Rome,* pp. 35–37.

125. Par. 6.

126. Michael Schuck, in another insightful observation, cites Bernard Murstein and Edward Shorter to describe this reported weakening of personal morals in a way that anticipates how the consumerist ideology of industrial capitalism would later and more powerfully attempt to undermine the moral character of the inner psyche of the self. It does this by appealing artistically to the rebellious erotic spirit of cultural modernism's expressive individualism, especially through advertising.

Bernard Murstein argued that "as sin became more socially acceptable during the age of reason and enlightenment, prostitution flourished." According to Edward Shorter, "A revolution in eroticism occurs between the middle of the eighteenth and the end of the nineteenth centuries. Illegitimacy rates soar due to 'heightened ego awareness [public education] and...weakened superego controls [social dislocations of market-place economy, such as absence of the father due to separation of home and workplace].'"

See also Schuck, *That They Be One*, p. 36 n. 32. Schuck cites Bernard Murstein, *Love, Sex, and Marriage Through the Ages* (New York: Springer, 1974); Edward Shorter, "Illegitimacy, Sexual Revolution, and Social Change in Modern Europe," in Theodore K. Rabb and Robert I. Rotberg, eds., *The Family in History* (New York: Harper & Row, 1971), pp. 48, 63; and Owen Chadwick, *The Secularization of the European Mind in the Nineteenth Century* (Cambridge: Cambridge University Press, 1975), p. 3. See also related sections on the development of advertising, cinema, and electronic media in Chapters 2 and 3 herein. This criticism resonates with a similar theme in Daniel Bell, *The Cultural Contradictions of Capitalism* (New York: Basic Books, 1978).

127. Pars. 14–15.

128. Par. 18.

129. Par. 25.

130. Par. 22.

131. Pars. 22, 33.

132. Pars. 26–28.

133. Pars. 29–35.

134. See Holmes, *The Triumph of the Holy See*, p. 130.

135. *Cum sancta mater ecclesia* (1859) and *Qui nuper* (1859), in Carlin, *Papal Encyclicals*, vol. 1, pp. 355–56, 357–58.

136. *Nullis certe verbis* (1860), in Carlin, *Papal Encyclicals*, vol. 1, pp. 359–61.

137. *Quanto conficiamur moerore* (1863), in Carlin, *Papal Encyclicals*, vol. 1, pp. 369–73.

138. See Carlin, *Papal Encyclicals*, vol. 1, pp. 381–86.

139. On this history leading up to the Syllabus, as well as its drafting and aftermath, see Aubert et al., *The Church in the Age of Liberalism*, pp. 293–99. See also Hales, *Pio Nono*, pp. 266–73.

140. Aubert et al., *The Church in the Age of Liberalism*, p. 296.

141. Hales cites the Latin original for the anathematized proposition 80: "Romanus pontifex potest ac debe cum progressu, cum liberalismos et cum recenti civilitate sese reconciliare et componere," in *Revolution and Papacy*, p. 370 n.3.

142. See Hales, *Revolution and Papacy*, pp. 272–73, 370 nn. 6, 7.

143. The official English translation is found in Pope Paul VI, *On Evangelization in the Modern World* (Washington, D.C.: United States Catholic Conference, 1976).

144. Pars. 1, 2.

145. Par. 3. In the encyclical quotation marks are found around this text, though no source is given for the quotation. Presumably the words are from a liberal author.

146. Par. 3.

147. For a critical summary of the Newtonian cosmology of a "world-machine," see Capra, *The Turning Point*, pp. 53–74.

148. Par. 4.

149. Par. 4.

150. Par. 4.

151. Par. 4.

152. Par. 5.

153. Par. 7.

154. Par. 8.

155. Par. 8.

156. Par. 8.

157. Par. 9.

158. Pars. 9–12.

159. See Carlin, *Papal Encyclicals*, vol. 1, pp. 389–91.

160. See Carlin, *Papal Encyclicals*, vol. 1, pp. 393–97.

161. Par. 10.

162. Par. 12.

163. See Carlin, *Papal Encyclicals*, vol. 1, pp. 399–402.

164. *Vix dum a nobis*, for which an English translation may be found in Carlin, *Papal Encyclicals*, vol. 1, pp. 435–38. The citation is from par. 7.

165. Par. 13.
166. See Carlin, *Papal Encyclicals*, vol. 1, pp. 403–5.
167. Par. 4.
168. Pars. 5–8.
169. See Carlin, *Papal Encyclicals*, vol. 1, pp. 407–8.
170. Par. 4.
171. See Holmes, *The Triumph of the Holy See*, p. 160.

Chapter 4

1. For a detailed analysis of the local, national, and global stages of modern industrial capitalism, see Joe Holland, *The Evolution of Modern Industrial Capitalism and the Birth of the Postmodern Electronic-Ecological Era* (Washington, D.C.: The Warwick Institute, 1999).

2. Again, Michael Schuck in his masterful study of the overall patterns of modern papal social teaching, *That They Be One: The Social Teaching of the Papal Encyclicals 1740–1989* (Washington, D.C.: Georgetown University Press, 1991), describes this whole period as "Leonine," with the prior period called "pre-Leonine" and the subsequent one "post-Leonine." While my own periodization was articulated twenty years before Schuck's study was published, I was happy to see another scholar confirm the three-stage pattern and also to offer a richer analysis than my own initial efforts. See especially p. x of Schuck's study.

3. For one rich study on the ethos of the rising bourgeoisie and its alienation from the aristocratic orientation of traditional Catholicism, see Bernard Groethuysen, *The Bourgeois: Catholicism and Capitalism in Eighteenth Century France*, trans. Mary Ilford (New York: Holt, Rinehart, and Winston, 1969).

4. See Jacques Maritain, *Integral Humanism: Temporal and Spiritual Problems of a New Christendom* (Notre Dame, Ind.: University of Notre Dame Press, 1968). For theological reflection on the contrast of these two paradigms, see Gustavo Gutiérrez, *A Theology of Liberation: History, Politics and Salvation*, trans. Caridad Inda and John Eagleson (Maryknoll, N.Y.: Orbis Books, 1973), pp. 53–62.

5. See the later analysis of the encyclicals of this stage.

6. On the societal-ecclesial history of this strategy and its context, see Roger Aubert et al., *The Church in a Secularized Society*, trans. Janet Sondheimer (New York: Paulist Press, 1978) and *The Church in the Industrial Age* (New York: Crossroad, 1981); Gabriel Adriáni et al., *The Church in the Modern Age* (New York: Crossroad, 1981); Richard L. Camp, *The Papal Ideology of Social Reform: A Study in Historical Development 1878–1967* (Leiden: E. J. Brill, 1969); Michael P. Fogarty, *Christian Democracy in Western Europe 1820–1953* (Notre Dame, Ind.: University of Notre Dame Press, 1957); Eric O. Hanson, *The Catholic Church in World Politics* (Princeton, N.J.: Princeton University Press, 1987); J. Derek Holmes, *The Triumph of the Holy See* (London: Burns & Oates, 1978), chaps. 6–8, and *The Papacy in the Modern World 1914–1978* (New York: Crossroad, 1981), chaps. 1–5; Paul Misner, *Social Catholicism in Europe: From the Onset of Industrialization to the First World War* (New York: Crossroad, 1991), chaps. 5–15; Gianfranco Poggi, *Catholic Action in Italy: The Sociology of a Sponsored Organization* (Stanford, Calif.: Stanford University Press, 1967); Anthony Rhodes, *The Power of Rome in the Twentieth Century: The Vatican in the Age of Liberal Democracies, 1870–1922* (New York: Franklin Watts, 1983), and *The Vatican in the Age of Dictators: 1922–1945* (New York: Holt, Rinehart, and Winston, 1973); William McSweeney, *Roman Catholicism: The Search for Relevance* (New York: St. Martin's Press, 1980); Jean-Guy Vaillancourt, *Papal Power: A Study of Vatican Control over Lay Catholic Elites* (Berkeley and Los Angeles: University of California Press, 1980); Lillian Parker Wallace, *Leo XIII and the Rise of Socialism* (Raleigh, N.C.: Duke University, 1966). Again, along with Schuck's work, I am especially indebted to the works of Misner, Wallace, Aubert, McSweeney, and Rhodes.

7. McSweeney's *Roman Catholicism* does an especially fine job of chronicling this climax, yet also the looming breakdown. See pp. 95–115.

8. See Claudia Carlin, IHM, ed., *The Papal Encyclicals*, 5 vols. (n.l.: Pierian Press, 1981). The publication of all the modern papal encyclicals in a single place represents an invaluable contribution to scholars of this tradition.

9. See McSweeney, *Roman Catholicism*. Note his subtitle: *The Search for Relevance*.

10. See Holmes, *The Triumph of the Holy See,* 160.

11. On Pius IX and socialism, see Arturo Gaete, "Socialism y communismo: historia de una problematíca condenactión," in *Mensaje* (Jesuit monthly of Santiago, Chile), vol. 20, no. 200 (July 1971), pp. 292–96.

12. The strategic importance given to the threat of socialism can be documented from the pages of the monthly journal of the Italian Jesuits, *Civiltà Cattolica,* founded in 1850 under the patronage of Pius IX. Between 1872 and 1874, shortly before Pecci's election as pope, the journal published twelve articles on socialism and communism and the factors favoring its growth. The twelve articles encompassed some two hundred pages. See Gaete, "Socialismo y communismo," 290–302. See also Wallace, *Leo XIII and the Rise of Socialism,* esp. pp. 75–76.

13. On Leo XIII identifying socialism as a distinct and primary enemy, see Gaete, "Socialismo y communismo," pp. 296–302; Wallace, *Leo XIII and the Rise of Socialism,* pp. 111–15.

14. Rhodes, *Power of Rome,* p. 69.

15. On the life and papacy of Leo XIII, see Aubert et al., *The Church in the Industrial Age,* esp. pp. 1–26; Holmes, *The Triumph of the Holy See,* 193–260; Misner, *Social Catholicism in Europe,* esp. pp. 204–325; Rhodes, *Power of Rome,* pp. 67–78; Camp, *The Papal Ideology of Social Reform,* pp. 10–12, 25–32, 47–56, 77–86, 111–16, 138–43; Wallace, *Leo XIII and the Rise of Socialism.*

16. Rhodes, *Power of Rome,* p. 70.

17. Aubert et al., *The Church in the Industrial Age,* pp. 10–25.

18. See the following section on Leo's encyclicals.

19. *Le Monde,* 31 May 1887, cited by Rhodes, *Power of Rome,* p. 178.

20. Rhodes notes this in *Power of Rome,* p. 72.

21. Wallace, *Leo XIII and the Rise of Socialism,* p. 12.

22. On this letter and its impact, see Wallace, *Leo XIII and the Rise of Socialism,* pp. 80–83.

23. See McSweeney, *Roman Catholicism,* pp. 73, 79–83.

24. On these parallel structures in the early Leonine period, see Aubert et al., *The Church in the Industrial Age,* pp. 209–45, and Adriáni, *The Church in the Modern Age,* pp. 378–457.

25. On Catholic Action, see Vaillancourt, *Papal Power*, and Poggi, *Catholic Action in Italy*.

26. On the evolution of Christian Democratic parties, see Fogarty, *Christian Democracy in Western Europe*, pp. 186–339.

27. See Misner, *Social Catholicism in Europe*, pp. 227–61.

28. This judgment is from my own observations. For one careful study of a contemporary Catholic institutional resistance in the United States to the endorsement of unions, which Leo so boldly proclaimed, see Patrick J. Sullivan, *U.S. Catholic Institutions and Labor Unions 1960–1980* (Latham, Md.: University Press of America, 1985).

29. See Aubert et al., *The Church in the Industrial Age*, pp. 208–9; and Fogarty, *Christian Democracy in Western Europe*, pp. 281–91. As is clear from the Fogarty summary, many family movements were in fact women's movements ancillary to men's workers' movements. At this time there really was no full and mature family movement commensurate with the movements for Thomism, Christian Democracy, and Social Catholicism.

30. Leo bemoaned these claims both in his encyclical on Christian marriage, *Arcanum* (see par. 13) and in his encyclical on socialism, *Quoad apostolici muneris* (pars. 8–9). See the discussion of these encyclicals in the next chapter.

31. Oskar Kohler, in Aubert et al., *The Church in the Industrial Age*, speaks of Leo's "World Plan" (see p. 3).

32. On the centrality of socialism for Leo's strategy, see Wallace, *Leo XIII and the Rise of Socialism*. On the other elements of his grand design, see the analysis of his encyclicals in the following section of this chapter.

33. Though led by Blanqui, the Paris Commune nonetheless came to be associated with Karl Marx, because his essay, *Civil War in France*, praised the event. For the history of socialism at the time, see Albert S. Lindemann, *A History of European Socialism* (New Haven, Conn.: Yale University Press, 1983), pp. 86–184. For a persuasive correlation of the socialist threat and Leo's strategy, see Wallace, *Leo XIII and the Rise of Socialism*.

34. See Wallace, *Leo XIII and the Rise of Socialism*, chaps. 2, 3, 7.

35. Karl Marx and Frederick Engels, *Selected Works* (New York: International Publishers, 1968), pp. 387–88.

36. Rhodes, *Power of Rome*, p. 88.

37. McSweeney, *Roman Catholicism*, p. 72.
38. Holmes, *The Triumph of the Holy See*, p. 183.
39. See the following reference.
40. For the encyclical itself, see the analysis in the next section. Leo's comment on *Aeterni patris* is reported in McSweeney, *Roman Catholicism*. McSweeney takes it from Pierre Thibault, *Savoir et pouvoir: Philosophie thomiste et politique cléricale au xixe siècle* (Laval, Quebec: Les Presses de l'Université Laval, 1972), pp. 101ff. See Gerald A. McCool, *Catholic Theology in the Nineteenth Century: The Quest for a Unitary Method* (New York: Crossroad, 1977), pp. 84–86, 134–38, 167; Lester R. Kurtz, *The Politics of Heresy: The Modernist Crisis in Roman Catholicism* (Berkeley and Los Angeles: University of California Press, 1986), pp. 15–16, 38–41; Misner, *Social Catholicism in Europe*, p. 128.
41. Regarding the revival of Thomism, see the following discussion herein, under Leo's encyclicals, of the text *Aeterni patris*. See also Thibault, *Savoir et pouvoir*; Gabriel Daly, OSA, *Transcendence and Immanence: A Study in Catholic Modernism and Integralism* (Oxford: Clarendon, 1980), pp. 7–25; McCool, *Catholic Theology in the Nineteenth Century*; Thomas F. O'Meara, OP, *Church and Culture: German Catholic Theology, 1860–1914* (Notre Dame, Ind.: University of Notre Dame Press, 1991), esp. pp. 33–50; and Harry W. Paul, *The Edge of Contingency: French Catholic Reaction to Scientific Change from Darwin to Duhem* (Gainesville, Fla.: University of Florida, 1979).
42. On this "reemergence of pluralism," see McCool, *Catholic Theology in the Nineteenth Century*, pp. 241–67.
43. See McCool, *Catholic Theology in the Nineteenth Century*, pp. 168–69; McSweeney, *Roman Catholicism*, pp. 70–71.
44. On the significant emphasis placed on social ethics by the neoscholastics, see O'Meara, *Church and Culture*, p. 42, 177–84. On the proposed middle ground between individualism and collectivism, as developed in the Christian democratic movement, see Fogarty, *Christian Democracy*, pp. 27–100.
45. McCool, *Catholic Theology in the Nineteenth Century*, p. 141.
46. McCool, *Catholic Theology in the Nineteenth Century*, pp. 177–83; Paul, *The Edge of Contingency*, pp. 179–94.

47. The underlying cosmological model is that of the ancient great chain of being, descending from a higher spiritual order to a lower material and ascending in return to the spiritual. On the chain of being, see Arthur Lovejoy, *The Great Chain of Being: The Study of the History of an Idea* (Cambridge, Mass.: Harvard University Press). On the hierarchical patriarchy of Aquinas, see Paul Sigmund, ed., *Thomas Aquinas on Politics and Ethics* (New York: W. W. Norton, 1988), pp. 37–38.

48. McSweeney, *Roman Catholicism*, p. 68. Again, McSweeney draws on Thibault, *Savoir et pouvoir.*

49. On the shift to an indirect, lay-oriented strategy, see McSweeney, *Roman Catholicism*, p. 68.

50. For the beginnings of Christian Democracy, see Hans Maier, *Revolution and Church: The Early History of Christian Democracy, 1789–1901*, trans. Emily M. Schossberger (Notre Dame, Ind.: University of Notre Dame, 1969).

51. On Leo's rapprochement with liberal democracy, see Wallace, *Leo XIII and the Rise of Socialism*, pp. 277–308; Rhodes, *Power of Rome*, pp. 67–178; Aubert et al., *The Church in the Industrial Age*, pp. 233–45.

52. On the first and second waves of Christian Democracy, see Misner, *Social Catholicism in Europe*, pp. 80–90, 227–87.

53. On the story of Leo, the Center Party, and Bismarck, see Rhodes, *Power of Rome*, pp. 77–97.

54. Rhodes, *Power of Rome*, pp. 77–97.

55. Rhodes, *Power of Rome*, pp. 77–97.

56. Rhodes, *Power of Rome*, p. 97.

57. Karl Otmar Von Aretin, *The Papacy and the Modern World*, trans. Roland Hill (London: Weidenfeld & Nicholson, 1970), pp. 113–14, as cited in McSweeney, *Roman Catholicism*, p. 53.

58. Misner, *Social Catholicism in Europe*, pp. 227–39.

59. An English translation of the encyclical may be found in Carlin, *Papal Encyclicals*, vol. 2, pp. 278–84.

60. Rhodes, *Power of Rome*, p. 116.

61. On Leo XIII's policy of *Ralliement*, promoted by his secretary of state Cardinal Rampolla, see Rhodes, *Power of Rome*, pp. 107–18.

62. On the failure of Leo's *Ralliement,* see Rhodes, *Power of Rome,* pp. 119–24.

63. On Leo's intransigence (whether due to his own wishes or rather to keep a balance between the two poles of the curial factions), see Rhodes, *Power of Rome,* pp. 98–106. See also Misner, *Social Catholicism in Europe,* pp. 240–61.

64. On Leo's relationship to Italy and the Roman Question, see Rhodes, *Power of Rome,* pp. 98–106.

65. On Leo and the American and Irish experiences, see Rhodes, *Power of Rome,* pp. 125–158.

66. On the experience of Catholic Action in Italy, as well as for a more general analysis of Catholic Action against the horizon of the Constantinean church's hierarchical segregation of clergy and laity, see Poggi, *Catholic Action in Italy.* On Leo's decision on how to interpret the name Christian Democracy, see his encyclical letter *Graves de communi re,* in Carlin, *Papal Encyclicals,* vol. 2., pp. 479–84.

67. See the analysis of Leo's political encyclicals in the following section.

68. For the history of Christian Democracy, see Fogarty, *Christian Democracy.*

69. Although there is now a wealth of studies on Social Catholicism, the finest is, I believe, Paul Misner's *Social Catholicism in Europe.* This splendid work is the most comprehensive investigation of this complex tradition up to World War I. I am especially in the author's debt for the analysis in this section. Misner describes Social Catholicism as "Catholic responses to economic modernization in particular, hence to the industrialization process and its consequences in the social classes" (p. 3). For more on the origins and development of Social Catholicism up to *Rerum novarum,* see also Jean Baptiste Durouselle, *Le débuts du catholicisme social en France (1822–1870)* (Paris: Presses universitaires de France, 1951); Alec R. Vidler, *A Century of Social Catholicism 1820–1920* (New York: Scribner, 1954); and Joseph N. Moody, ed., *Church and Society: Catholic Social and Political Thought and Movements, 1789–1950* (New York: Arts, 1953).

70. Henri Daniel-Rops, *The Church in an Age of Revolution 1789–1870*, trans. John Warrington (New York: E.P. Dutton & Co., 1965), p. 337.

71. See Misner, *Social Catholicism in Europe*, pp. 35–55. Later in North America a radical version of this agrarian-oriented romantic medievalism, drawing on the anti-statist anarchist tradition of the ancient peasant communes, would appear with the itinerant French teacher Peter Maurin, on whose ideas Dorothy Day drew to create the Catholic Worker movement. For Maurin's own free-verse communication of his ideas, see his collection of essays, *Easy Essays* (Chicago: Franciscan Herald, 1984). See also Mark H. Ellis, *Peter Maurin: Prophet in the Twentieth Century* (New York: Paulist Press, 1981); Anthony W. Novitsky, *The Ideological Development of Peter Maurin's Green Revolution*, Ph.D. dissertation, State University of New York at Buffalo, 1976; and Arthur Sheehan, *Peter Maurin: Gay Believer* (New York: Hanover House, 1959). Ellis criticizes Novitsky for seeing Maurin's ideological roots as simply reactionary and notes that he also drew on the progressive French-Catholic figures of Leon Harmel and Marc Sangnier (p. 175).

Interestingly, the ideas of Peter Maurin, who also drew on the Russian anarchist-ecologist Peter Kropotkin, sound surprisingly like radical voices in the contemporary Green movement. Indeed, Maurin even called for a "Green Revolution," in contrast to the "Red Revolution." His use of "green" was a reference to the work of Irish "scholars" (he was referring to Irish monks but deliberately avoided the term) who spread Irish monasticism across Europe during the "Dark Ages." Also influenced by Mounier, Maurin described himself as a "communitarian personalist."

72. In 1809 Adam Müller (1779–1829) wrote *Die Elemente der Staatskunst*, a romantic work appealing to the Middle Ages for a "revitalization of the estates and corporations of the *ancien regime*." Rooting his model in the family farm, he challenged Adam Smith and provided "the starting point for an on-going conservative Christian analysis of the new economy." See Misner, *Social Catholicism in Europe*, pp. 36–38; and also Paul Misner, "Adam Müller and Adam Smith: A Romantic-Catholic Response to Modern Economic Thought," in Joseph F. Gower,

ed., *Religion and Economic Ethics* (Lanham, Md.; University Press of America, 1990), pp. 175–98.

73. See Misner, *Social Catholicism in Europe*, pp. 22–34. On the rise of Germany to economic leadership, see William Otto Henderson, *The Rise of German Industrial Power, 1834–1914* (Berkeley and Los Angeles: University of California Press, 1975).

74. Misner, *Social Catholicism in Europe*, pp. 40–41.

75. Misner, *Social Catholicism in Europe*, p. 41; cited from Paul Droulers, *Catholicisme et mouvement ouvrier en France au xixe siècle: L'attitude de l'épiscopat*, in François Bédarida and Jean Maitron, eds., *Christianisme et Monde ouvrier* (Paris: les Editiones Ouvrieres, 1975), pp. 37–64.

76. Misner, *Social Catholicism in Europe*, pp. 50–51, 60–63.

77. Misner, *Social Catholicism in Europe*, p. 51.

78. Misner, *Social Catholicism in Europe*, pp. 63–67.

79. Misner, *Social Catholicism in Europe*, pp. 67–70.

80. Misner, *Social Catholicism in Europe*, pp. 70–72.

81. Misner, *Social Catholicism in Europe*, p. 73.

82. This shift is a central theme in Misner, *Social Catholicism in Europe*.

83. As David Martin has shown in his study of modernizing secularization, Catholic movements in religiously mixed societies adapted more easily to a liberal interest-group model and managed to preserve a dynamic institutional religious base, whereas in totally Catholic societies discordant interest groups, like the workers' movement, were early on forced outside the dominant system and as a result turned to anticlerical secularizing strategies. See David Martin, *A General Theory of Secularization* (New York: Harper & Row, 1978).

84. On these and Kolping, see Misner, *Social Catholicism in Europe*, pp. 46–48, 95–100.

85. On Kettler, see Misner, *Social Catholicism in Europe*, pp. 90–95, 126, 136–47.

86. Misner, *Social Catholicism in Europe*, p. 147. See also the discussion of Bismarck in this study's chapter on Stage II of industrial capitalism.

87. Misner, *Social Catholicism in Europe*, pp. 181–88.

88. Misner, *Social Catholicism in Europe*, p. 50.

89. See again, Holmes, *The Triumph of the Holy See*, pp. 71–77, 90–98; Alec Vidler, *Prophecy and Papacy: A Study of Lamennais, the Church and the Revolution* (New York: Scribner, 1954).

90. See Kathleen O'Meara, *Frederick Ozanam Professor at the Sorbonne: His Life and Works* (New York: Christian Press Association, 1911); Misner, *Social Catholicism in Europe*, pp. 58–60.

91. See Misner, *Social Catholicism in Europe*, pp. 45, 75. The late American socialist Michael Harrington always maintained that one of the reasons why socialism proved so much stronger in Europe than in the United States was that it had been the main movement campaigning for the right of workers to vote. This is from recollections of personal conversations.

92. See Misner, *Social Catholicism in Europe*, pp. 52–54. On Christian socialism generally, see John Cort, *Christian Socialism: An Informal History* (Maryknoll, N.Y.: Orbis Books, 1988).

93. Misner, *Social Catholicism in Europe*, pp. 84–86.

94. Misner, *Social Catholicism in Europe*, pp. 84–86.

95. Misner, *Social Catholicism in Europe*, pp. 158–62, 192. Again, Harmel would be a significant influence on Peter Maurin of the Catholic Worker movement in North America. See Ellis, *Peter Maurin*, p. 175 n. 11.

96. Misner, *Social Catholicism in Europe*, pp. 148–68.

97. Misner, *Social Catholicism in Europe*, pp. 175–81.

98. Misner, *Social Catholicism in Europe*, pp. 169–75.

99. Misner, *Social Catholicism in Europe*, pp. 175–81.

100. Misner, *Social Catholicism in Europe*, pp. 178–79.

101. Misner adds an important qualification to this "loss of the working class": "The Catholic Church did not 'lose' the whole of the working class to socialism nor the whole of the middle class to anticlerical liberalism. There were examples of solid Christian culture across the class strata that remained bulwarks of Catholic influence on society until at least the cultural revolution of the 1960s" (see *Social Catholicism in Europe*, p. 196).

102. Misner, *Social Catholicism in Europe*, pp. 190–97.

103. Rhodes, *Power of Rome*, p. 142.

104. Gibbon's own English translation of the Latin "Memorial," as well as the reflection he wrote on it for his biography, can be found in Aaron I. Abell, ed., *American Catholic Thought on Social Questions* (New York: Bobbs-Merrill, 1968), pp. 143–61.

105. Abell, *American Catholic Thought on Social Questions*, p. 144.

106. For this ongoing history, see the review of contemporary literature on Catholic social teaching in Chapter 1.

107. Misner, *Social Catholicism in Europe*, pp. 127–28.

108. Misner, *Social Catholicism in Europe*, pp. 189–212.

109. See Wallace, *Leo XIII and the Rise of Socialism*, pp. 254–67.

110. On the history of the writing, see Misner, *Social Catholicism in Europe*, pp. 204–5, 217; Wallace, *Leo XIII and the Rise of Socialism*, p. 268 n. 55.

111. The official English translation may be found in Carlin, *Papal Encyclicals*, vol. 2, pp. 241–57.

112. That the threat of socialism was the main reason for Leo's support of capitalist reform is the thesis of Lillian Wallace's study in papal diplomatic history, as her title implies, *Leo XIII and the Rise of Socialism*.

113. Misner, *Social Catholicism in Europe*, p. 5.

114. See the analysis of *Rerum novarum* in the next section.

115. See Misner, *Social Catholicism in Europe*, p. 217.

116. See Misner, *Social Catholicism in Europe*, pp. 220–21, 275, 286.

117. On its fortieth anniversary, Pius XI issued his 1931 social encyclical *Quadragesimo anno*; on its seventieth anniversary, John XXIII issued his 1961 encyclical *Mater et magistra*; on its eightieth anniversary, Paul VI issued a 1971 public letter (addressed to Cardinal Maurice Roy, president of both the Pontifical Council of the Laity and of the Pontifical Commission on Justice and Peace) entitled *Octagesima adveniens*; and on its ninetieth and one-hundredth anniversaries, John Paul II issued his 1981 social encyclical *Laborem exercens* and his 1991 social encyclical *Centesimus annus*. English translations of these anniversary documents, as well as of *Rerum novarum*, can be conveniently found in David O'Brien and

Thomas Shannon, eds., *Catholic Social Thought: The Documentary Heritage* (Maryknoll, N.Y.: Orbis Books, 1992).

118. See Aubert et al., *The Church in the Industrial Age*, pp. 331–34.

119. An English translation may be found in Carlin, *Papal Encyclicals*, vol. 2., pp. 479–86.

120. See Aubert et al., *The Church in the Industrial Age*, p. 24. Aubert cites, "A. Harnack, *Reden und Aufsätze II* (2nd ed., 1906), 267–93."

121. The entire rise of ultramontanism had, of course, been accompanied by increasing papal centralization and intervention across the entire church. Indeed, throughout the second half of the nineteenth century the rise of Thomism to a position of intellectual hegemony for both philosophy and theology had been as much the work of papal power as of scholarship and ideas. Again, for a history of the triumph of Thomism, including through intellectual repression, see McCool, *Catholic Theology in the Nineteenth Century*, esp. pp. 129–44; O'Meara, *Church and Culture*, pp. 29–50.

Chapter 5

1. For analysis of and commentaries on the Leonine encyclicals examined in this and the later chapter, see Michael Schuck, *That They May Be One: The Social Teachings of the Papal Encyclicals 1740–1989* (Washington, D.C.: Georgetown University Press, 1991); Paul Misner, *Social Catholicism in Europe: From the Onset of Industrialization to the First World War* (New York: Crossroad, 1991); Mary E. Hobgood, *Catholic Social Teaching and Economic Theory: Paradigms in Conflict* (Philadelphia: Temple University Press, 1991); Peter J. Henriot, Edward P. DeBerri, and Michael J. Schultheis, *Catholic Social Teaching: Our Best Kept Secret* (Maryknoll, N.Y.: Orbis Books, 1985); John Desrochers, *The Social Teaching of the Churches* (Bangalore: Desrochers, 1982); Donal Dorr, *Option for the Poor: A Hundred Years of Vatican Social Teaching* (Maryknoll, N.Y.: Orbis Books, 1983); Jean Yves Calvez and Jacques Perrin, *The Church and Social Justice: The Social Teaching of the Popes from Leo XIII to Pius XII (1878–1958)*, trans. J. R. Kirwin (Chicago: Henry Regnery Co, 1961); Franz H. Müller, *The Church and the Social Question* (Washington, D.C.: American

Enterprise Institute, 1984); Richardo Antoncich, *Christians in the Face of Justice: A Latin American Reading of Catholic Social Teaching*, trans. Matthew J. O'Connell (Maryknoll, N.Y.: Orbis Books, 1987); Marie-Domenique Chenu, *La doctrine sociale' de l'église comme idéologie* (Paris: Les éditions du Cerf, 1979); Christine Gudorf, *Catholic Social Teaching on Liberation Themes* (Washington, D.C.: University of America Press, 1981); Georges Jarlot, *Doctrine pontificale et histoire* (Rome: Gregorian University, 1964); Michael Novak, *Freedom with Justice: Catholic Social Thought and Liberal Institutions* (San Francisco: Harper & Row, 1984); and Richard L. Camp, *The Papal Ideology of Social Reform* (Leiden: E. J. Brille, 1969).

2. See the historical analysis of the preceding chapter.

3. Schuck, *That They Be One*, p. ix.

4. English versions of the two encyclicals and all other encyclicals by Leo XIII may be found in Claudia Carlin IHM, *The Papal Encyclicals 1878–1903* (n.l.: Pierian Press, 1981), pp. 5–16. Though not officially so numbered, this is the second volume of a five-volume set on the contemporary papal encyclicals from 1740 to 1981. I will, therefore, refer to this one as volume 2.

5. Pars. 2–3. As in earlier chapters, rather than encumber every sentence that refers to a distinct section in these encyclicals, I will frequently place all paragraph references in a single note at the end or toward the end of each paragraph of this text. Paragraph references will always refer to the last cited encyclical. Again, the traditional manner of referencing citations within a papal encyclical is to note the official paragraph number of the encyclical text. These paragraph numbers are listed in the Carlin collection.

6. Pars. 5–7.

7. Pars. 11–17.

8. Par. 12.

9. Pars. 16–17.

10. Par. 1.

11. An English translation may be found in Carlin, *Papal Encyclicals*, vol. 2., pp. 91–101.

12. Pars. 1–2.

13. For this older analysis, see the appropriate sections of the prior chapter.
14. Par. 24.
15. Pars. 1, 9, 21, 22.
16. Par. 10.
17. Pars. 12–16.
18. Pars. 17–20.
19. Par. 19.
20. Par. 20.
21. Par. 21.
22. Par. 4. An English translation of the entire encyclical may be found in Carlin, *Papal Encyclicals*, vol. 2, pp. 29–40.
23. Par. 17.
24. Pars. 5–7.
25. Pars. 17, 5–8.
26. Pars. 14, 24–27.
27. Pars. 13, 28–30.
28. Par. 21.
29. Par. 27.
30. Par. 29.
31. Par. 22.
32. Pars. 22–23.
33. Par. 23.
34. Par. 1.
35. Pars. 2–3.
36. Pars. 4–5.
37. Pars. 5–6.
38. Par. 6.
39. Par. 7.
40. Par. 8.
41. Par. 9
42. Par. 9
43. Pars. 9–10.
44. Par. 11.

45. An English translation of the text for *Aeterni patris* can be found in Carlin, *Papal Encyclicals*, vol. 2, pp. 17–27.

46. Par. 2.

47. Pars. 3–4.

48. Par. 4.

49. Par. 6. On Catholic theological uses of analogy, see David Burrell, *Analogy and Philosophical Language* (New Haven, Conn.: Yale University Press, 1975); and David Tracy, *The Analogical Imagination: Christian Theology and the Culture of Pluralism* (New York: Crossroad, 1981).

50. Par. 4.

51. Pars. 5, 7.

52. Pars. 8–9.

53. Pars. 10–23.

54. Par. 24.

55. Pars. 25–27.

56. Pars. 28–29.

57. An English translation may be found in Carlin, *Papal Encyclicals*, vol. 2., pp. 479–86.

58. See the English translation in Carlin, *Papal Encyclicals*, vol. 2, pp. 51–58.

59. Pars. 1–2. On the assassination of Alexander and its relation to Leo's strategy, see Lillian Parker Wallace, *Leo XIII and the Rise of Socialism* (Raleigh, N.C.: Duke University Press, 1966), pp. 114–15.

60. Pars. 4, 23.

61. Pars. 3–5.

62. Par. 6.

63. Par. 7.

64. Pars. 11–12.

65. Par. 4.

66. Pars. 11, 15, 18.

67. Pars. 11, 13, 25.

68. Pars. 25, 27.

69. See, for example, Leo's encyclical *Libertas* (1888), par. 2, in Carlin, *Papal Encyclicals*, vol. 2. p. 169. An English translation of *Immortale Dei* can be found in the same volume of Carlin, pp. 107–20.

70. Pars. 6–7, 36.

71. Pars. 10–11, 13.

72. Pars. 25, 32, 34.

73. Par. 44.

74. Par. 48.

75. The English translation may be found in Carlin, *Papal Encyclicals*, vol. 2, pp. 169–81.

76. Par. 15.

77. Par. 16.

78. Par. 17.

79. Pars. 7–17. On the Italian situation, see Wallace, *Leo XIII and the Rise of Socialism*, p. 226 n. 53.

80. Par. 2.

81. Pars. 18–22, 33.

82. Par. 41.

83. Par. 41.

84. Par. 44.

85. Pars. 42–44.

86. An English translation can be found in Carlin, *Papal Encyclicals*, vol. 2, pp. 211–24. See esp. par. 3.

87. Pars. 1–3.

88. As mentioned earlier, the zealot party had been more oriented toward populist lay mobilization on the cultural terrain, in order to defend the church against political attacks, while the politician party had been more oriented toward negotiations on the political terrain via concordats with the state's own elites. Thus Leo's growing orientation toward the laity may have reflected a certain frustration with his original strategy toward political leaders and perhaps the ascendancy of the zealots within his own Vatican coalition. Pars. 10–15.

On Catholic Action in Italy, see Gianfranco Poggi, *Catholic Action in Italy: The Sociology of a Sponsored Organization* (Stanford, Calif.: Stanford University Press, 1967).

On Catholic lay mobilization in general, see Jean-Guy Vaillancourt, *Papal Power: A Study of Vatican Control over Lay Elites* (Berkeley and Los Angeles: University of California, 1980.

89. Par. 16. The quotation is from Vatican I's constitution *Dei Filius.*

90. Par. 42.

91. Par. 42.

92. See *Quod apostolici muneris,* pars. 2, 9, in Carlin, *Papal Encyclicals,* vol. 2., pp. 12, 14–15.

93. Par. 2, in Carlin, *Papal Encyclicals,* vol. 2., p. 18.

94. Par. 16 in Carlin, *Papal Encyclicals,* vol. 2., p. 66.

95. Pars. 22–23 in Carlin, *Papal Encyclicals,* vol. 2., pp. 73.

96. Par. 22

97. Par. 23.

98. Par. 25.

99. Par. 34 in Carlin, *Papal Encyclicals,* p. 99, as well as par. 4 on p. 124. Paul Misner, in his magisterial study, points out how important the Third Order of Saint Francis became in the early phase of Social Catholicism (see Misner, *Social Catholicism in Europe,* pp. 237–38). While Misner's elaboration takes us beyond the encyclicals, it provides one fascinating example of the prophetic movements that were shaping the papal acceptance of Social Catholicism, as well as how threatening to ecclesial elites some of these movements eventually became. According to Misner, many of the pioneers of early Social Catholicism were Third Order Franciscans, particularly Leon Harnel. Following *Rerum novarum,* and presumably encouraged by it, a Franciscan provincial in Marseilles published an 1893 article urging that the Third Order should "treat capitalism as an enemy." In that same year, a congress of religious and lay Franciscans dramatically announced: "Whereas, if socialism has become the imminent threat to our society, it is capitalism, to wit, the unjust predominance of capital and the abuses that have resulted therefrom, that is the true cause of the present social disorder" (Misner, *Social Catholicism in Europe,* p. 238). These citations indicate that the

term *capitalism* was in use among church activists, yet was consistently avoided by Leo, even though he regularly identified countless other "isms," for example, naturalism, rationalism, materialism, idealism, socialism, communism, and nihilism. Eventually, Misner notes, in Rome's eyes the Third Order movement proved threatening, along with many other developments in the lay mobilization, and it was forced back by papal order to a "primarily religious role."

100. Par. 35.
101. Par. 35.
102. Par. 23.
103. Par. 13 in Carlin, *Papal Encyclicals*, vol. 2., p. 130.
104. Par. 13.
105. Par. 6 in Carlin, *Papal Encyclicals*, vol. 2., p. 198.
106. Par. 6.
107. Par. 8.
108. Par. 4. For the full text, see Carlin, *Papal Encyclicals*, vol. 2., pp. 207–10.
109. Par. 5.
110. Par. 17 in Carlin, *Papal Encyclicals*, vol. 2., p. 231.
111. Par. 9 in Carlin, *Papal Encyclicals*, vol. 2., p. 239.
112. Carlin, *Papal Encyclicals*, vol. 2., pp. 241–67.
113. Par. 1.
114. Par. 1.
115. Par. 2.
116. Par. 3.
117. Par. 4.
118. Par. 5.
119. Pars. 6–7.
120. Pars. 7–10.
121. Par. 14. See pars. 12–14 for his full discussion on family.
122. Par. 15.
123. Par. 16.
124. Par. 17.
125. Par. 18.

126. Par. 19.

127. Par. 19.

128. Par. 19.

129. Par. 20.

130. Par. 20.

131. Par. 20.

132. Par. 20.

133. Par. 22.

134. Par. 22. This section on the obligations of the rich is the longest numbered paragraph in the document, with the one on the mutual obligations of justice between capital and labor being the second longest.

135. Pars. 23–24.

136. Pars. 24–25.

137. Par. 26.

138. Par. 26.

139. Pars. 27–28.

140. Par. 29.

141. Par. 32.

142. Par. 32.

143. Pars. 33–34. Following Aristotle, Scholastic philosophy had distinguished distributive and commutative justice. Distributive justice serves the common good through the legal guidance of the distribution of resources according to a principle of proportionate equality. Thus, the state was to guarantee that the organic role of the working class, both in the workplace and in wages, be defended through legislation that protects its proportionate right as an authentic part of the social whole, and do this in the name of the common good. Later a new phrase would be introduced to guide reflection on justice for labor, namely, the concept of social justice, but this concept was not yet present in Leo's thought. See Johannes Messner, *Social Ethics: Natural Law in the Western World*, trans. J. H. Doherty (St. Louis: B. Herder Book, 1965), pp. 319–24.

144. Par. 35.

145. Par. 36.

146. Par. 37.

147. Par. 38.

148. Par. 39.

149. Pars. 40–42.

150. Pars. 43–45.

151. Pars. 46–47. For his concern about the Italian immigration to America, see his 1888 encyclical *Quam aerumnosa*, in Carlin, *Papal Encyclicals*, vol. 2., pp. 191–94.

152. Note that here Leo was reflecting the growing sense of a civil society apart from the state. Liberalism had, of course, defined civil society as separate and "private," in contrast to the traditionally "public" sphere of politics. Catholic social thought later did begin to accept the distinctive nature of this sphere of common life, and for it developed the institutional category of "social justice." See Messner, *Social Ethics*, pp. 323–24.

153. Par. 48.

154. Par. 49.

155. Par. 50.

156. Par. 51.

157. Par. 53.

158. Par. 54.

159. Pars. 54–55.

160. Pars. 57–64.

161. Again, the entire Leonine Corpus is included in Carlin, *The Papal Encyclicals 1878–1903*.

162. Carlin, *Papal Encyclicals*, pp. 92ff.

163. Carlin, *Papal Encyclicals*, pp. 361–69. See pars. 3, 6, 16, 17, 22.

164. Carlin, *Papal Encyclicals*, pp. 277ff.

165. Carlin, *Papal Encyclicals*, pp. 183ff.

166. Carlin, *Papal Encyclicals*, pp. 159ff.

167. Carlin, *Papal Encyclicals*, pp. 325ff.

168. Carlin, *Papal Encyclicals*, pp. 409ff., par. 2.

169. Carlin, *Papal Encyclicals*, pp. 451ff., pars. 2, 10.

170. Carlin, *Papal Encyclicals*, pp. 499ff., pars. 11, 20.

171. Carlin, *Papal Encyclicals*, pp. 471ff., par. 1.

172. Carlin, *Papal Encyclicals*, pp. 388ff.

173. Carlin, *Papal Encyclicals*, pp. 157–58, par. 3.

174. Carlin, *Papal Encyclicals*, pp. 479ff., pars. 6–10.

175. Pars. 1–2.

176. Pars. 3–4.

177. Pars. 4–10.

178. Pars. 11–19.

179. Pars. 21–26.

180. On the later development of Catholic Action in Italy, see Poggi, *Catholic Action in Italy*; for a wider analysis of the modern papacy and its controlled lay mobilization, see Vaillancourt, *Papal Power.*

181. Par. 27.

Chapter 6

1. On the history of Pius X's pontificate, see Roger Aubert et al., *The Church in the Industrial Age*, trans. Margit Resch (New York: Crossroad, 1981), pp. 381ff.; Anthony Rhodes, *The Power of Rome in the Twentieth Century: The Vatican in the Age of Liberal Democracies, 1870–1922* (New York: Franklin Watts, 1983), pp. 179–222; J. Derek Holmes, *The Triumph of the Holy See: A Short History of the Papacy in the Nineteenth Century* (London: Burns & Oates, 1978), pp. 261–85; William McSweeney, *Roman Catholicism: The Search for Relevance* (New York: St. Martin's Press, 1980), pp. 80–86; Gabriel Daly, OSA, *Transcendence and Immanence: A Study in Catholic Modernism and Integralism* (Oxford: Clarendon Press, 1980); and Lester R. Kurtz, *The Politics of Heresy: The Modernist Crisis in Roman Catholicism* (Berkeley and Los Angeles: University of California, 1986).

2. Rhodes, *Power of Rome*, pp. 217–20, 222.

3. Rhodes, *Power of Rome*, p. 220

4. Rhodes, *Power of Rome*, pp. 221.

5. On modernism, see Daly, *Transcendence and Immanence*; Kurtz, *The Politics of Heresy*; Holmes, *The Triumph of the Holy See*, pp. 261–85; and Thomas Franklin O'Meara, *Church and Culture: German Catholic Theology, 1860–1914*

(Notre Dame, Ind.: University of Notre Dame Press, 1991), pp. 165–86.

6. Holmes, *The Triumph of the Holy See*, p. 281; Kurtz, *The Politics of Heresy*, pp. 164–65.

7. Paul Misner, *Social Catholicism in Europe: From the Onset of Industrialization to the First World War* (New York: Crossroad, 1991), pp. 306–15.

8. On the Sodalitium Pianum, see Holmes, *The Triumph of the Holy See*, pp. 275–85; Kurtz, *The Politics of Heresy*, pp. 160–65. Knowledge of the details of this secret spy group became public with the dossier organized by Emile Poulat (see *Intégrisme et catholicisme: Un réseau secret international antimoderniste: La "Sapinière," 1909–1921* [Tournai: Casterman, 1969]; idem, *Catholicisme, démocratie et socialisme: Le mouvement catholique et Mgr Benigni* [Tournai: Casterman, 1977]).

9. See the subsequent chapter in which the encyclical itself is analyzed.

10. On the pontificate of Benedict XV and interaction of his papacy with the societal context, see J. Derek Holmes, *The Papacy in the Modern World, 1914–1978* (New York: Crossroad, 1981), pp. 1–31; Rhodes, *Power of Rome*, pp. 223–48; and Gabriel Adriáni et al., *The Church in the Modern Age*, trans. Anselm Biggs (New York: Crossroad, 1981), pp. 21–23, 35–47.

11. Holmes, *The Triumph of the Holy See*, pp. 283–85.

12. On the pope's role in relation to the war and its aftermath, see Rhodes, *Power of Rome*, pp. 223–48; Adriáni et al., *The Church in the Modern Age*, pp. 35–47; and Holmes, *The Papacy in the Modern World*, pp. 1–31.

13. Regarding Benedict XV's support for victims of war, as well as the near bankruptcy of the Vatican and the subsequent turn to American support, see Rhodes, *Power of Rome*, pp. 223–48; and Holmes, *The Papacy in the Modern World*, pp. 1–31.

14. See Rhodes, *Power of Rome*, pp. 223–48; and Holmes, *The Papacy in the Modern World*, pp. 1–31.

15. On the political orientation of the Vatican during this period, see Aubert et al., *Church in the Industrial Age*, pp. 491–92.

16. Holmes, *The Papacy in the Modern World*, pp. 17–18.

17. Holmes, *The Papacy in the Modern World*, pp. 21–26.

18. On Pius XI's great fear of communism, see Anthony Rhodes, *The Vatican in the Age of Dictators: 1922–1945* (New York: Holt, Rinehart, and Winston, 1973), pp. 18–19.

19. On Achille Ratti, Pius XI, as well as on the ecclesial and societal history of his papacy, see Rhodes, *The Vatican in the Age of Dictators*, pp. 17–218; Holmes, *The Papacy in the Modern World*, pp. 77–118; Adriáni et al., *The Church in the Modern Age*, pp. 23–28, 39–58. For his program and motto, see his inaugural encyclical, *Ubi arcano Dei consilio* (1922), esp. par. 49. This encyclical and the others mentioned here are discussed in the next chapter.

20. See Eric Hobsbawm, *The Age of Extremes: A History of the World, 1914–1991* (New York: Random House, 1994), especially the chapter titled "The Age of Total War," pp. 21–53.

21. On totalitarianism, see Hannah Arendt, *The Origins of Totalitarianism* (New York: World Publishing, 1971); Carl J. Friedrich and Zbigniew K. Brzezinski, *Totalitarianism, Dictatorship, and Autocracy* (New York: Praeger, 1968).

22. For an early analysis of these new conditions by a key thinker in the German Catholic tradition of "solidarism," see Heinrich Pesch, *Ethics and the National Economy*, trans. Rupert J. Ederer (Manila: Divine Word Publications, 1988). The German original was published in 1918. Pesch was a teacher of Oswald Nell von Brünning, reportedly the principal drafter of Pius XI's historic social encyclical *Quadragesimo anno*.

23. See the discussion of these encyclicals in the next chapter.

24. On fascism and the papacy in Italy and on the papal condemnation of Nazism, see Holmes, *The Papacy in the Modern World*, pp. 33–76, 93–94.

25. For more on Pius XI's anti-Nazi encyclical, see the analysis of that document in the next chapter. Regarding his attitude and strategy toward fascism, see Rhodes, *The Vatican in the Age of Dictators*, including his whole review of Pius XI's papacy, especially pp. 24–35, 211–17; and Holmes, *The Papacy in the Modern World*, 92–93, for his comment about the pope's appraisal of the "weakness" of democracy.

26. Holmes, *The Papacy in the Modern World*, pp. 39–64, 101–7; Rhodes, *The Vatican in the Age of Dictators*, pp. 14–15, 31–32, 173–78.

27. See Rhodes, *The Vatican in the Age of Dictators*, pp. 117–23. On fascism as providing a strategic opening, see pp. 26–31.

28. On the fascist attacks in both Italy and Germany on Catholic Action, see Holmes, *The Papacy in the Modern World*, pp. 57–75, 107–17. On the hostility of the German bishops to Hitler, and alternately the support of the Italian bishops for Mussolini, see pp. 101–3, 68–70.

29. Holmes, *The Papacy in the Modern World*, p. 70.

30. See the analysis of *Quadragesimo anno* in the next chapter. On Pius XI's rejection of a Catholic-socialist coalition, see Holmes, *The Papacy in the Modern World*, pp. 38–39, 49–50.

31. On Pacelli's role in the papacy of Pius XI, see Rhodes, *The Vatican in the Age of Dictators*, pp. 175–83, 199–201, 203–4.

32. See Rhodes, *The Vatican in the Age of Dictators*, p. 213.

33. See Peter C. Kent, "A Tale of Two Popes: Pius XI, Pius XII, and the Rome Berlin Axis," *Journal of Contemporary History* 23 (1988), 589–608. I am indebted to an article by Frank J. Coppa for pointing this out (see the next note).

34. See the fine article by Frank J. Coppa, "The Hidden Encyclical of Pius XI Against Racism and Anti-Semitism Uncovered – Once Again," *The Catholic Historical Review*, vol. 84, no. 1 (January 1998). Coppa summarizes two recent books on the subject: Georges Passelecq and Bernard Suchechy, *L'Encyclicque Cacheé de Pie XI: Une occasion manquée de L'Eglise face à l'antisémitisme* (Paris: Editions La Découverte, 1995); and Robert A. Hecht, *An Unordinary Man: A Life of Father John LaFarge, S.J.* (Lanham, Md.: The Scarecrow Press, 1996).

35. On the Lateran Agreements between Italy and the Vatican, see Rhodes, *The Vatican in the Age of Dictators*, pp. 37–52; and Holmes, *The Papacy in the Modern World*, pp. 52–55. The $92.1 million figure, based on 1929 dollars, is taken from James Gollin, *Worldly Goods: The Wealth and Power of the American Catholic Church, the Vatican, and the Men Who Control the Money* (New York: Random House, 1972), p. 438.

36. Because of a Vatican policy of secrecy, accurate information about Vatican finances is difficult to obtain and often impossible.

Nonetheless several studies have reported what seem to be the basic outlines of the Vatican's role as a modern capitalist actor. Nino Lo Bello, *The Vatican Empire* (New York: Simon and Schuster, 1968), while accurately narrating the institution changes, proposes the most dramatic interpretation of the Vatican's subsequent wealth—suggesting that by the 1960s its portfolio was in excess of $5.6 billion (p. 135). Agreeing with the institutional history but offering a more conservative estimate of approximately $500 million is Gollin's study, *Worldly Goods,* p. 472.

37. On the theological debate over whether "the church," in contrast to its members, can be described as in need of reform and even at times as sinful, see Bradford E. Hitze, "Ecclesial Repentance and the Demands of Dialogue," *Theological Studies* 61 (2000), pp. 207–38.

38. On the pontificate of Pius XII, see Rhodes, *The Vatican in the Age of Dictators,* pp. 219–336; Holmes, *The Papacy in the Modern World,* pp. 119–200; Adriáni et al., *The Church in the Modern Age,* pp. 29–34, 77–96, 156–58, 198–209; and Carlo Falconi, *The Silence of Pius XII,* trans. Bernard Wall (Boston: Little, Brown and Company, 1970). For an insightful study of how the entire Leonine strategy survived until (and finally begins to break down during) the pontificate of Pius XII, see McSweeney, *Roman Catholicism,* indeed the entire work, but especially p. 87, where McSweeney describes Pius XII as "the last of the emperor-popes." McSweeney also refers to Pius XII's death as "the end of the Old Catholicism" (p. 86). Throughout this study McSweeney regularly uses the phrase "Leonine strategy" to encompass the popes from Leo XIII to Pius XII.

39. On the reemergence of these modernizing and left-leaning forces, see McSweeney, *Roman Catholicism,* esp. pp. 86–91.

40. The quotation is cited in Holmes, *The Papacy in the Modern World,* p. 158. See also Holmes's wider comments, pp. 152–68, as well as the following notes.

41. Rhodes, *The Vatican in the Age of Dictators,* p. 341. An alternative view, though not informed by the same scholarly resources as Rhodes employs, may be found in Falconi, *The Silence of Pius XII.*

42. John Cornwell, *Hitler's Pope: The Secret History of Pius XII* (New York: Viking, 1999). The critique of Cornwall's text as

representing poor scholarship and sensationalist journalism is from a personal interview with Gerald Fogarty, professor of history at the University of Virginia. For favorable views of the role of Pius XII during World War II, see Margherita Marchione, *Yours Is a Precious Witness: Memoirs of Jews and Catholics in Wartime Italy* (New York: Paulist Press, 1997); idem, *Pope Pius XII: Architect for Peace* (New York: Paulist Press, 2000); and Pierre Blet, *Pius XII and the Second World War: According to the Archives of the Vatican* (New York: Paulist Press, 1999).

43. The statement is cited in Rhodes, *The Vatican in the Age of Dictators*, p. 258. On Pius XII's diplomatic style, see Holmes, *The Papacy in the Modern World*, pp. 133–39.

44. See Rhodes, *The Vatican in the Age of Dictators*, p. 258.

45. See Holmes, *The Papacy in the Modern World*, p. 38. Montini's comment is cited in Rhodes, *The Vatican in the Age of Dictators*, p. 238.

46. For the initial German bishops' antipathy for Hitler and the initial enthusiasm of the Italian bishops for Mussolini, as well as papal pressure on the Germans and the later apprehension of the papacy, see Rhodes, *The Vatican in the Age of Dictators*, pp. 23–78, 161–322.

47. On the issue of the Jews, see Rhodes, *The Vatican in the Age of Dictators*, pp. 337–52. On the meeting with the German cardinals, see pp. 226–30. The quote from Pius XII is on p. 228.

48. Holmes notes ties from resistance days between militant Catholics and militant socialists (see *The Papacy in the Modern World*, p. 171).

49. On the Vatican's initial assumptions that the Americans were incompetent, that Germany would successfully invade England, and that the Allies would be defeated, thus leaving the Catholic Church to contend with Hitler for many years to come, see Rhodes, *The Vatican in the Age of Dictators*, 248–50, 265.

50. Cited in Rhodes, *The Vatican in the Age of Dictators*, p. 268.

51. Rhodes, *The Vatican in the Age of Dictators*, p. 267.

52. Rhodes, *The Vatican in the Age of Dictators*, p. 264.

53. Rhodes, *The Vatican in the Age of Dictators*, pp. 271–74.

54. Rhodes, *The Vatican in the Age of Dictators*, p. 267.

55. On Taylor's former position with United States Steel, see George Q. Flynn, *Roosevelt and Romanism: Catholics and American History, 1937–1945* (Westport, Conn.: Greenwood Press, 1976), p. 98.

56. See Thomas T. McAvoy, CSC, *The Americanist Heresy in Roman Catholicism, 1895–1900* (Notre Dame, Ind.: University of Notre Dame Press, 1963).

57. See Gerald P. Fogarty, *The Vatican and the American Hierarchy from 1870 to 1965* (Wilmington, Del.: Michael Glazier, 1985), pp. 332–45; also Holmes, *The Papacy in the Modern World*, pp. 171–74.

58. On the Vatican's diplomatic turn to the Americans and on the growth of the Vatican-American alliance in the postwar years, see Fogarty, *The Vatican and the American Hierarchy from 1870 to 1965*, pp. 246–345.

59. For Pius XII's alliance with the Americans yet reservations about American culture, as well as his support for a new international community, for world peace, and for a global struggle against poverty, see Holmes, *The Papacy in the Modern World*, pp. 180–84. For a more recent analysis of the birth of a new "world church," see Walbert Bühlmann, *The Coming of the Third Church: An Analysis of the Present and Future of the Church*, trans. Ralph Woodhall (Maryknoll, N.Y.: Orbis Books, 1977).

60. On Pius XII's internationalization of the College of Cardinals while protecting Italian control over the Vatican curia, see Holmes, *The Papacy in the Modern World*, pp. 187–88.

61. For background on the influence that Maritain had on Monsignor Giovanni Battista Montini, a key adviser to Pope Pius XII and unofficial chaplain of the Italian Christian democratic movement, also later to become Pope Paul VI, see the extensive biography by Peter Hebblethwaite, *Paul VI: The First Modern Pope* (New York: Paulist Press, 1993), pp. 67–294.

62. Jacques Maritain, *Integral Humanism: Temporal and Spiritual Problems of a New Christendom*, trans. Joseph W. Evans (Notre Dame, Ind.: University of Notre Dame Press, 1973).

63. Maritain continued the pre-Leonine social analysis, which saw modernity as passing through three stages of successive

degradation, namely the Reformation, the Enlightenment, and the French Revolution. See his work, *Three Reformers: Luther, Descartes, Rousseau* (London: Sheed and Ward, 1928).

64. Jacques Maritain, *The Peasant of Garonne: An Old Layman Questions Himself About the Present Time*, trans. Michael Cuddihy and Elizabeth Hughes (New York: Holt, Rinehart, and Winston, 1968).

Chapter 7

1. For the English translations of the encyclicals of Pius X, see Claudia Carlin, IHM, ed., *The Papal Encyclicals 1903–1939*, vol. 3 (n.l.: Pierian Press, 1981), pp. 5–138.

2. Carlin, *Papal Encyclicals*, vol. 3, pp. 5–10.

3. Par. 14.

4. Par. 14.

5. Carlin, *Papal Encyclicals*, vol. 3, pp. 11–18, with the citation from par. 22.

6. Carlin, *Papal Encyclicals*, vol. 3, pp. 19–28.

7. Par. 17.

8. Par. 26.

9. Par. 29.

10. Carlin, *Papal Encyclicals*, vol. 3, pp. 29–35.

11. Carlin, *Papal Encyclicals*, vol. 3, pp. 37–44.

12. Pars. 4–6.

13. Par. 6.

14. Pars. 7–8.

15. Pars. 15–16.

16. Pars. 18–20.

17. Pars. 23–26.

18. Carlin, *Papal Encyclicals*, vol. 3, pp. 45–51, with the citation from par. 3.

19. Carlin, *Papal Encyclicals*, vol. 3, pp. 71–98. The author of *Pascendi* was reportedly Joseph Lemius, OMI, procurator general of the Oblates of Mary Immaculate. See Gabriel Daly, OSA, *Transcendence and Immanence: A Study in Catholic Modernism and Integralism* (Oxford: Clarendon Press, 1980),

p. 179. On Lemius's interpretation of modernism, see Daly, *Transcendence and Immancence*, pp. 180–89, 232–34.

20. Par. 1.

21. Pars. 1–4. Lemius argued that modernism was a single theory, though disguised as countless unconnected fragments. In Daly's judgment, however, this conspiratorial unity was more a creation of Lemius's mind than an actual reality (see Daly, *Transcendence and Immanence*, p. 180).

22. Par. 4.

23. Par. 5.

24. Pars. 6–39.

25. Daly, *Transcendence and Immanence*, p. 150.

26. Par. 26.

27. The classical clerical-lay paradigm, based on the metaphor of hierarchical organicism, was an ecclesial counterpart to the classical aristocratic-peasant paradigm. The clerical state, a legal innovation of the Constantinean church, represents a legal overlay on the sacrament of ordination. Ordained leaders may be found in the Book of Acts and in the epistles of Paul, but these leaders were lay. The Christian clerical state began as a privilege extended to the ordained by the Roman imperial state and expanded to a greater role in medieval Christendom. (This distinction between the clerical state and the sacrament of ordination is confirmed by the fact that a priest may be "laicized" but remains a priest.)

These historical facts were surely not lost on the many lay leaders of the modernist movement. As Kurtz points out, the short-lived modernist publication *Il Rinnovamento*, founded by Baron Friedrich von Hügel and Antonio Fogazzaro, had three lay co-editors (Antonio Aiace Alfieri, Alessandro Casati, and Tommaso Gallarati Scotti) and proposed a vision of a "lay reform movement." This may have been threatening to what Kurtz calls "the burgeoning clerical bureaucracy of the Vatican." See Lester R. Kurtz, *The Politics of Heresy: The Modernist Crisis in Roman Catholicism* (Berkeley and Los Angeles: University of California Press, 1986), pp. 13, 29.

For more on the modern papacy's attempt to mobilize yet simultaneously to contain and to restrain the laity, see Gianfranco Poggi, *Catholic Action in Italy: The Sociology of a Sponsored*

Organization (Stanford, Calif.: Stanford University Press, 1967); and Jean-Guy Vaillancourt, *Papal Power: A Study of Vatican Control over Lay Catholic Elites* (Berkeley and Los Angeles: University of California Press, 1980). For an intriguing exploration of the connection between the crisis of late modern hypermasculine science and its roots in a medieval clerical theocracy, see the study by the distinguished historian of technology David F. Noble, *A World Without Women: The Clerical Christian Culture of Western Science* (New York: Alfred A. Knopf, 1992).

28. Par. 28.

29. Par. 38. On Leo XIII and the condemnation of "Americanism," see Thomas McAvoy, CSC, *The Americanist Heresy in Roman Catholicism, 1895–1900* (Notre Dame, Ind.: University of Notre Dame Press, 1963), published earlier as *The Great Crisis in American Catholic History, 1895–1900* (Chicago: Henry Regnery Company, 1957).

30. Pars. 40–43.

31. Pars. 44–56.

32. Carlin, *Papal Encyclicals*, vol. 3, pp. 99–113. The length of this encyclical—fourteen pages, in contrast to other encyclicals typically running between three and nine pages, except for the lengthier ones on modernism (twenty-five pages) and Charles Borromeo (twelve pages)—suggests it was of great strategic importance. That possibility is strengthened by its position as next in line after the one on modernism and right before the one on Charles Borromeo, the great Counter-Reformation pastoral reformer.

33. Carlin, *Papal Encyclicals*, vol. 3, pp. 115–26.

34. Carlin, *Papal Encyclicals*, vol. 3, pp. 127–30.

35. Par. 1. Carlin, *Papal Encyclicals*, vol. 3, pp. 131–33.

36. Par. 6.

37. Carlin, *Papal Encyclicals*, vol. 3, pp. 135–38.

38. See *Il fermo proposito*, par. 26, in Carlin, *Papal Encyclicals*, vol. 3, p. 44.

39. Carlin, *Papal Encyclicals*, vol. 3, pp. 143–51. For the references, see pars. 3–4.

40. On the causes and problems, see pars. 5–18.

41. Par. 25.

42. Par. 23.
43. Pars. 21–26.
44. Pars. 27–33.
45. Carlin, *Papal Encyclicals*, vol. 3, pp. 153–59.
46. Carlin, *Papal Encyclicals*, vol. 3, pp.161–62.
47. Carlin, *Papal Encyclicals*, vol. 3, pp. 163–67.
48. Carlin, *Papal Encyclicals*, vol. 3, pp.169–70.
49. Carlin, *Papal Encyclicals*, vol. 3, pp. 171–75.
50. Par. 17.
51. For the document on Saint Jerome (see par. 18 on "critical methods" and par. 44 on the "Christian family"), see Carlin, *Papal Encyclicals*, vol. 3, p. 194.
52. Carlin, *Papal Encyclicals*, vol. 3, pp. 195–201.
53. Carlin, *Papal Encyclicals*, vol. 3, pp. 203–5.
54. Carlin, *Papal Encyclicals*, vol. 3, pp. 207–11, 217–20.
55. Carlin, *Papal Encyclicals*, vol. 3, pp. 213–16.
56. For Pius XI's blaming Christian employers for the spread of communism among the workers, see *Divini redemptoris* (1937) in Carlin, *Papal Encyclicals*, vol. 3, p. 547 (par. 50).
57. Carlin, *Papal Encyclicals*, vol. 3, pp. 225–39. See especially pars. 7–18, 49.
58. Pars. 19–31.
59. Par. 28.
60. Pars. 32–55.
61. Carlin, *Papal Encyclicals*, pp. 241–48. The preceding quotations are from par. 1.
62. Pars. 2–3.
63. Pars. 4–10
64. Pars. 12–34.
65. Carlin, *Papal Encyclicals*, pp. 249–57.
66. Pars. 1–14.
67. Pars. 14–16.
68. Par. 20.
69. Par. 27.

70. Carlin, *Papal Encyclicals*, vol. 3, pp. 241–69.

71. Carlin, *Papal Encyclicals*, vol. 3, pp. 271–79. The quotation is from par. 1

72. Pars. 1, 2, 24.

73. Carlin, *Papal Encyclicals*, vol. 3, pp. 281–343.

74. Carlin, *Papal Encyclicals*, vol. 3, pp. 353–72, esp. pars. 11–17, 31–36, 49, 60, 68, 79.

75. For the encyclical on marriage, see Carlin, *Papal Encyclicals*, vol. 3, pp. 391–414. For this and the following paragraph, see especially pars. 1, 22–24, 26–29, 45, and 50–78. For the encyclical on Augustine, see Carlin, *Papal Encyclicals*, vol. 3, pp. 373–90.

76. Par. 74.

77. Pars. 44–92.

78. Par. 23.

79. Carlin, *Papal Encyclicals*, vol. 3, pp. 415–43.

80. Par. 3.

81. Par. 10.

82. Pars. 11, 14.

83. Pars. 17–24.

84. Pars. 25–28.

85. Pars. 29–30.

86. Par. 30.

87. Pars. 31–35.

88. Par. 38.

89. Pars. 39–40.

90. Pars. 41–43.

91. Pars. 44–50.

92. Pars. 52–57.

93. Par. 58.

94. Pars. 59–60.

95. Par. 61.

96. Pars. 63, 74.

97. Par. 78.

98. Pars. 79–80.
99. Pars. 81–87.
100. Pars. 88–96.
101. Par. 101.
102. Pars. 102–3.
103. Pars. 105–6.
104. Par. 107.
105. Par. 108.
106. Par. 109.
107. Par. 110.
108. Par. 112.
109. Par. 113.
110. Par. 116.
111. Par. 118. The discussion of socialism encompasses pars. 111–23.
112. Pars. 118–20.
113. Pars. 121–22.
114. Pars. 123–26.
115. Pars. 127–31.
116. Par. 132.
117. Par. 132.
118. Par. 133–35.
119. Par. 136.
120. Pars. 137–47.
121. Carlin, *Papal Encyclicals*, vol. 3, pp. 445–58, esp. pars. 26, 44, 62.
122. Carlin, *Papal Encyclicals*, vol. 3, pp. 459–523.
123. Carlin, *Papal Encyclicals*, vol. 3, pp. 525–35, esp. pars. 4–8, 43.
124. Carlin, *Papal Encyclicals*, vol. 3, pp. 537–54, pars. 1–3.
125. Pars. 4, 9–16.
126. Par. 22
127. Par. 38.
128. Par. 50.
129. Par. 58.

130. Carlin, *Papal Encyclicals*, vol. 3, pp. 255–66.

131. Claudia Carlin, IHM, *The Papal Encyclicals 1939–1958*, vol. 4 (n.l.: Pierian Press, 1990). The entire volume includes solely Pius XII's texts.

132. Carlin, *Papal Encyclicals*, vol. 4, pp. 5–22, esp. pars. 1–11.

133. Pars. 28–33.

134. Pars. 34–77.

135. Par. 78.

136. Pars. 36–51.

137. Pars. 58–77.

138. Pars. 84–87.

139. Pars. 87–90.

140. Par. 89.

141. Pars. 90–91.

142. Par. 92.

143. Pars. 95–108.

144. Par. 110.

145. Carlin, *Papal Encyclicals*, vol. 4, pp. 23–30.

146. For the encyclical on Portugal, see Carlin, *Papal Encyclicals*, vol. 4, pp. 31–36.

147. Carlin, *Papal Encyclicals*, vol. 4, pp. 37–63.

148. On the prior juridical or institutional model of the church, see Avery Dulles, *Models of the Church* (Garden City, N.Y.: Doubleday, 1974), esp. chapter 2. For Dulles's treatment of the mystical model, see chap. 3.

149. See Emile Mersch, *The Theology of the Mystical Body* (St. Louis: Herder, 1958). See also Dulles, *Models of the Church*, chap. 3, esp. pp. 47–48. J. Derek Holmes claims that the German J. M. Sailer (1751–1832), influenced for a time by Schelling's romanticism, was the first modern Catholic theological figure to revive the Pauline notion of the church as Christ's body. (See J. Derek Holmes, *The Triumph of the Holy See: A Short History of the Papacy in the Nineteenth Century* [London: Burnes & Oates, 1978], p. 164.) For more on Sailer, see Thomas Franklin O'Meara, OP, *Romantic Idealism and Roman Catholicism: Schelling and the Theologians* (Notre Dame, Ind.: University of Notre Dame Press, 1982), pp. 40–47.

150. Pars. 1–16.
151. Pars. 44, 57, 98.
152. Pars. 57–63.
153. Pars. 64–66.
154. Par. 105.
155. See, for example, pars. 3, 18, 66, 73, 92, 98, 105, 109.
156. Carlin, *Papal Encyclicals*, vol. 4, pp. 65–79.
157. Carlin, *Papal Encyclicals*, vol. 4, pp. 81–88.
158. Carlin, *Papal Encyclicals*, vol. 4, pp. 89–90.
159. Carlin, *Papal Encyclicals*, vol. 4, pp. 91–103.
160. Carlin, *Papal Encyclicals*, vol. 4, pp. 105–7.
161. Carlin, *Papal Encyclicals*, vol. 4, pp. 109–10.
162. Carlin, *Papal Encyclicals*, vol. 4, pp. 111–18.
163. Carlin, *Papal Encyclicals*, vol. 4, pp. 119–54.
164. Esp. pars. 5, 14, 20, 103–8, 119–28, 178, 194.
165. Pars. 12–14.
166. Pars. 5, 16, 39–45, 66–69, 83–84, 116.
167. Carlin, *Papal Encyclicals*, vol. 4, pp. 155–56, esp. pars. 3, 6, 8.
168. Carlin, *Papal Encyclicals*, vol. 4, pp. 157–65.
169. Carlin, *Papal Encyclicals*, vol. 4, pp. 167–69, esp. pars. 2–3.
170. Carlin, *Papal Encyclicals*, vol. 4, pp. 171–73.
171. Par. 5.
172. Par. 9.
173. Carlin, *Papal Encyclicals*, vol. 4, pp. 175–84.
174. Carlin, *Papal Encyclicals*, vol. 4, pp. 185–87.
175. Carlin, *Papal Encyclicals*, vol. 4, pp. 189–202.
176. Pars. 2–3, 5–6, 17–18, 23, 30–40.
177. The social justice section includes pars. 49–54.
178. Par. 52.
179. Pars. 52–53.
180. Pars. 56–60.
181. Pars. 56, 58.
182. Par. 70.

183. For example, par. 71.

184. Carlin, *Papal Encyclicals*, vol. 4, pp. 203–378.

185. Carlin, *Papal Encyclicals*, vol. 4, pp. 239–53, esp. pars. 15, 19, 24, 32, 45, 55, 57.

186. Carlin, *Papal Encyclicals*, vol. 4, pp. 291–313, esp. pars. 44, 129, 172–74.

187. Carlin, *Papal Encyclicals*, vol. 4, pp. 347–65.

188. Pars. 1–2, 4, 17, 23, 40–42, 117–19, 154–57.

189. Pars. 17–18, 25, 32, 63.

190. Pars. 10, 71–73, 80–114, 139–40, 139–40.

191. On the negative image of Pius XII, which surfaced only after his death and yet very quickly, see J. Derek Holmes, *The Papacy in the Modern World, 1914–1978* (New York: Crossroad, 1981), pp. 199–200.

Conclusion

1. For more on the notion of root metaphors, see Joe Holland, "Linking Social Analysis and Theological Reflection: The Place of Root Metaphors in Social and Religious Experience," in *Tracing the Spirit: Communities, Social Action, and Theological Reflection*, ed. James E. Hug (New York: Paulist Press; Washington, D.C.: The Woodstock Theological Center, 1983), pp. 170–91; and idem, *The Global-Local Postmodern Electronic-Ecological Era: Religious Myth, Sexual Symbol, and Technological Design* (Washington, D.C.: The Warwick Institute, 1992).

2. See Joe Holland, "The Next Stage of Catholic Social Teaching," *Convergence* (Barcelona) 7 (July 1997), pp. 23–31; and idem, "Pax Romana in the New Electronic Planetary Civilization: The Poor, Ecology, and Prophetic Spirituality," *Convergence* (Barcelona) 11 (July 2000), pp. 44–47.

3. On the successive historical-societal roles of speech, handwriting, mechanical printing, and now electronics, see Joe Holland, *The Global-Local Postmodern Electronic-Ecological Era: Religious Myth, Sexual Symbol, and Technological Design*.

4. See David C. Korten, *When Corporations Rule the World* (West Hartford, Conn.: Kumarian Press; San Francisco: Berrett-Koehler Publishers, 1996).

5. On academic deconstructionism as the subjective side of late modern global capitalism, see the rich study of Fredrick Jameson, *Postmodernism, or, the Cultural Logic of Late Capitalism* (Durham, N.C.: Duke University Press, 1991). By *postmodernism* Jameson means deconstructionism. On the origins of deconstructive postmodernism as a poetic movement in Lima, Peru, and on its subsequent evolution and spread, see Perry Anderson, *The Origins of Postmodernity* (London: New Left Books, 1998).

6. See Bruce B. Lawrence, *Defenders of God: The Fundamentalist Revolt Against the Modern Age* (Columbia, S.C.: University of South Carolina Press, 1995).

7. For a helpful summary of the scientific revision of modern economic theory already under way, see Robert Costanza et al., *An Introduction to Ecological Economics* (Boca Raton, Fla.: International Society for Ecological Economics, 1997).

8. On the new ecological paradigm for cosmology, see Thomas Berry, *The Great Work: Our Way into the Future* (New York: Bell Tower, 1999); Thomas Berry and Brian Swimme, *The Universe Story: From the Primordial Flaring Forth to the Ecozoic Era—A Celebration of the Unfolding of the Cosmos* (San Francisco: Harper-Collins, 1992); Fritjof Capra, *The Turning Point: Science, Society, and the Rising Culture* (New York: Bantam, 1983); and idem, *The Web of Life: A New Scientific Understanding of Living Systems* (New York: Doubleday, 1996). On the Catholic theological side, see Drew Christiansen, SJ, and Walter Grazer, *"And God Saw That It Was Good"—Catholic Theology and the Environment* (Washington, D.C.: United States Catholic Conference, 1996). For another Catholic but ecumenically inclusive perspective, see Brennan R. Hill, *Christian Faith and the Environment: Making Vital Connections* (Maryknoll, N.Y.: Orbis Books, 1998). For a mainline Protestant perspective, see Larry L. Rasmussen, *Earth Community, Earth Ethics* (Maryknoll, N.Y.: Orbis Books, 1997). For an eco-feminist perspective, see Charlene Spretnak, *States of Grace: The Recovery of Meaning in the Postmodern Age* (New York: HarperCollins Publishers, 1993); and Sallie McFague, *Metaphorical Theology: Models of God in Religious Language* (Philadelphia: Fortress Press, 1993).

9. I am indebted to William Ryan, SJ, an economist and founder of the Center of Concern, for this insight. For a helpful summary of the scientific revision of modern economic theory already under way, see Costanza et al., *An Introduction to Ecological Economics*.

10. See, for example, Ian G. Barbour, *When Science Meets Religion: Enemies, Strangers, or Partners* (New York: HarperSanFrancisco, 2000).

11. See Enrique Dussel, *The Invention of the Americas: Eclipse of "the Other" and the Myth of Modernity*, trans. Michael D. Barber (New York: Continuum, 1995).

12. See Joe Holland, *Humanity's African Roots: Remembering the Ancestors' Wisdom* (Washington, D.C.: National Office for Black Catholics, 2001).

Index